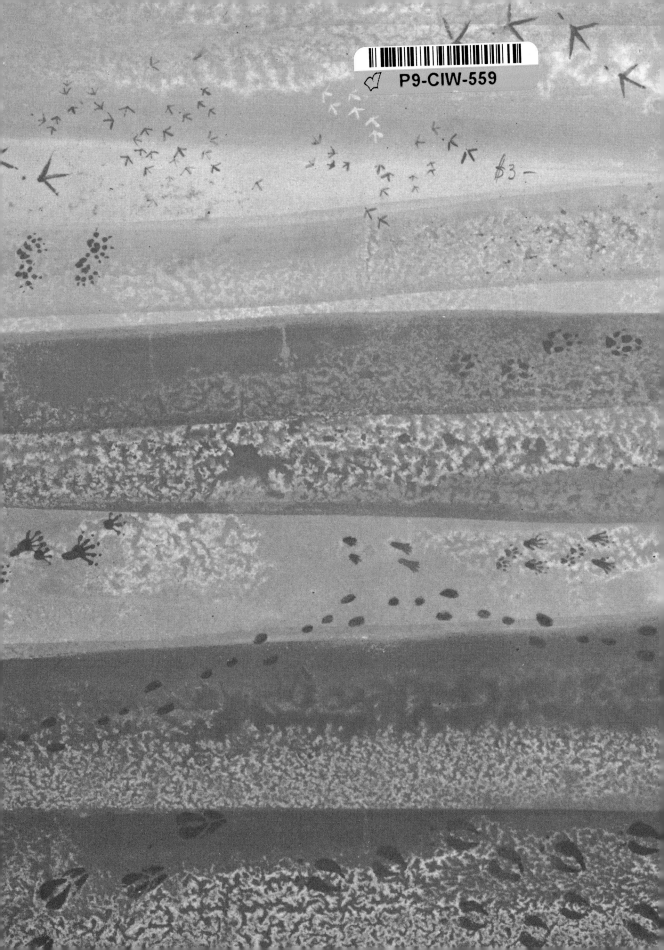

ANIMALS YOU WILL
NEVER FORGET

ANIMALS
YOU
WILL NEVER
FORGET

From Reader's Digest

The Reader's Digest Association, Inc., Pleasantville, New York
The Reader's Digest Association Ltd., Montreal, Canada

INTRODUCTION

From its earliest days Reader's Digest has published some of the most outstanding animal stories ever written. ANIMALS YOU WILL NEVER FORGET is a collection of 72 of these stories — all of them true — about beloved pets or wild animals that have assumed a special significance in the lives of the authors.

There are humorous stories, stories of high adventure and stories that will warm your heart. You will meet a horse that is a ham, a coquette of a hen, a fish that likes to dance, a cat that is a dandy. You will travel far and wide: to the Antarctic with a team of huskies, to Burma with a herd of elephants, to a tiger-infested jungle in Singapore. You will be moved by the lesson a small boy learns from a mouse, by the special bond between a girl and a falcon, by the two horses who make their peace after the death of their young mistress.

After reading this book you will understand why Walt Whitman wrote:

"I think I could live with animals, they are
    so placid and self-contained....
Not one is dissatisfied, not one is demented
    with the mania of owning things,
Not one kneels to another, nor to his kind
    that lived thousands of years ago,
Not one is respectable or unhappy over the
    whole earth."

CONTENTS

Blind Fair Ellen

by ALBERT PAYSON TERHUNE

SUNNYBANK FAIR ELLEN was a strange little golden collie, a dog that never saw a glimmer of light. She was born blind—as are all dogs—and she remained blind throughout more than a decade of such gay happiness as falls to the lot of few collies or humans. When the other pups of the litter opened their eyes, Fair Ellen's lids remained tight shut. A week or so later they opened. But expert vets found there were dead optic nerves behind. There seemed to be but one merciful thing to do. I loaded my pistol to put her out of her misery. It was my wife who intervened, reminding me that Fair Ellen had no "misery" to be put out of—that she was the gladdest and liveliest member of the litter.

When the six-week-old family of pups were turned loose in the huge "puppy yard," they began at once to explore this immense territory of theirs. At almost every fifth step Fair Ellen's hobbyhorse gallop would bring her into sharp contact with the food dish, the fence wires or some other obstacle which her four brothers avoided with ease. Always she would pick herself up after such a collision, with tail wagging and fat golden body wriggling as if at some rare joke. Not once did she whimper or fail to greet each mishap merrily.

Then I noticed that never did she collide with the same obstacle a second time. Coming close to food dish or the like, she would make a careful detour. In less than a week she had learned the location of every obstacle, big or small, in the yard. She could traverse the whole space at a gallop—without once colliding with anything. It was not a spectacular stunt, perhaps. But to me it seemed—and still seems—a minor miracle.

It was the same, presently, when I took her out of the puppy yard for a walk with me. Into tree trunks and into building corners and posts and benches and shrubbery clumps the poor little dog bungled, but never into one a second time. Bit by bit I enlarged our daily rambles. I was teaching her the lay of the whole forty-acre place. And never did a pupil learn faster. Within a few weeks Ellen could gallop all over the lawns and the orchard and the oak groves and could even canter along close to the many-angled kennel yards and stable buildings without a single collision. She had some nameless sense. I don't know what it was; but by reason of it I often saw her stop

dead short not six inches from a wall or a solid fence toward which she had been galloping at express-train speed.

It was on one of these educational rambles of ours that her fast-running feet carried her into the lake up to her neck. With a gay bark she began to swim. Most dogs, on their first immersion in lake or river, swim high and awkwardly, but Ellen took to water with perfect ease, as to a familiar element. She swam out for perhaps a hundred feet. Then she hesitated. I called her by name. She turned and swam back to shore, to my feet, steering her sightless course wholly by memory of my single call. Thereafter her daily swim was one of Ellen's chief joys.

I noted something else in my hours of unobserved watching. That yardful of collie pups was one of the roughest and most bumptious of all the hundreds of litters I have bred and raised; their play was strenuous almost to the point of mayhem. Yet when Fair Ellen joined in their romps, as always she did when she was in the yard with them, they were absurdly gentle, awkwardly gentle; very evidently they were seeking not to hurt her.

Ellen invented queer little games which she played, for the most part, all alone. One of these was to listen for the winnowing of homecoming pigeons' wings. The birds might be flying so high as to make this winnowing inaudible to human ears, but Ellen would hear. Always she would set off in pursuit, running at full speed directly under the pigeons, swerving and circling when they swerved and circled, guided wholly by that miraculous hearing of hers—the same sense of ear which told her from exactly what direction a thunderstorm was coming, long before we could hear thunder.

A veterinarian told me there was no reason to think Fair Ellen's blindness would be carried on in any puppies she might have. He was right. She had several litters of pups during her twelve years, and every pup had perfect sight and perfect health in every way. I sat up with her all night when her first puppies were born. There were nine of them. She did not seem to have the remotest idea what or whose they were. The night was bitterly cold. Ellen for once in her life was jumpy, with taut nerves. For many hours I had a man-sized job keeping her quiet and keeping the nine babies from dying of chill. At last, long after sunrise, Ellen began groping about her with her nose, snuggling the puppies close to her furry, warm underbody and making soft, crooning noises at them. Then I knew that my task had ended; that her abnormally keen ears had caught Mother Nature's all-instructive whisper. Thereafter she was an ideal little mother.

As the years crawled on, Ellen's jollity and utter joy in life did not abate. Gradually her muzzle began to whiten. Gradually the sharp teeth dulled from long contact with gnawed bones. Her daily gallops grew shorter, but the spirit of puppylike fun continued to flare.

One afternoon Ellen and I went for one of our daily rambles—the length of which was cut down nowadays by reason of her increasing age. She was in dashing high spirits and danced all around me. We had a jolly hour loafing about the lawns together. Then, comfortably tired, she trotted into her yard and lay down for her usual late afternoon nap. When I passed by her yard an hour later she was still lying stretched out there in the shade. But for the first time in twelve years the sound of my step failed to bring her eagerly to her feet to greet me. This was so unusual that I went into the yard and bent down to see what was amiss.

Quietly, without pain, still happy, she had died in her sleep.

The Day
I Met Midnight

IT WAS MY FIRST day on the ranch in California's San Fernando Valley. I was twenty that spring of 1912, and I was going to learn to be a cowboy. In my brand-new outfit—blue jeans, boots, bandanna and cheap Stetson—I felt self-conscious and a bit nervous. Sitting on the top rail of the corral, I watched the loops snake out among the milling horses, as one by one the men roped their mounts and led them outside to saddle up. A white mustang in the bunch caught my eye. He was a beauty—lovely head and neck, trim legs, deep chest and good quarters. Just my kind of horse, I thought—strong and speedy. I wondered whose he was.

The straw boss's voice interrupted my thoughts. "Can you ride, kid?" George, a lanky six-footer in a high-crowned hat that made him seem even taller, had looked me over skeptically the day before when he hired me, on a trial basis, at thirty dollars a month and found. Now he grinned in my direction reassuringly.

"Yes, some," I said. I was careful not to make any claims. Back home on our farm in Wisconsin my father had taught us boys what he knew about handling horses. Dad

made us break them to ride without a saddle —he said they became gentler that way. So I thought I knew horses a little. But these men were professional wranglers. Also, one of them had tipped me off the night before. "These fellows take you for a tenderfoot, kid," he said. "They'll put you on a horse that will try to throw you."

George's voice was casual. "Anything there you like, kid?"

I pointed to the white mustang. *"He's* a lot of horse," I said.

"Yeah." George's arm moved. The mustang whirled like a flash, but too late. The noose settled over his head, and he came in snorting. George tied a piece of quarter-inch rope around his neck and handed the other end to me. "We call him Midnight," George said. "When you get the mud off him, take him down to the shed and I'll fix you up with saddle and bridle and a rope."

I led Midnight outside and tied him to the rail, then got a brush. I was doing pretty well at cleaning him when my brush touched his left hock. His kick was so quick that only reflex action saved me. I stepped away and looked at his head. He was looking me

14

right in the eye, and I knew he was not afraid. You can read a horse's character from his head. Midnight had small ears and the broad forehead and wide-spaced eyes that indicate intelligence. But more than anything else there was a quality of spirit that looked out at me. With a head like that I didn't think he could be vicious. But he was an outlaw horse; he was at war against men.

"That's good enough," George said. He was sitting his horse with his rope in hand, the noose open.

I walked to Midnight's head and untied him. It was then I noticed that not a single man was mounted except George; they were all busy about their gear. They were waiting to see whether I would lead or ride the horse to the shed. I put a half hitch on Midnight's nose, and before he realized it I was on his back. We went away from there in standing leaps, and suddenly the men were all in the saddle with George in the lead. Their yells were enough to scare any horse, but I managed to keep Midnight's head up, and the ride ended at the shed. I quickly slipped off his back. I wanted no more until I had a saddle on him.

I stepped to his head to remove the torturing half hitch, and as I touched it he reared, struck me in the chest and left shoulder with his front hooves and knocked me spinning in the dust. He came after me screaming, his teeth bared, but I kept rolling until I was under the shed's loading platform.

Then I saw the reason for George's open loop. He had that horse roped and drawn up to his saddle before I got my first full breath. He watched while I brushed off the dust. "You all right?" he asked.

"Yeh," I said. "Nice roping."

"Would you rather have another horse today and top this one off sometime when you feel better?"

I was mad to my toes. "No. If I could ride that black-hearted so-and-so bareback, I can ride him all day. Show me a saddle and bridle. We're gonna get acquainted."

George turned to one of the cowboys. "Shorty, dig out some gear and we'll get Slim and Midnight on the way to getting acquainted."

Well! Now it was "Slim"—not just "Kid." Shorty stepped down from his horse and passed me with a grin. I tried to grin back. He returned with a good double-rigged saddle and bridle. Midnight objected throughout the entire proceedings, but with George holding his head and Shorty helping, we got it done.

"Want me to hold him while you get set?" George asked.

My left shoulder and arm felt nearly normal. I looked at Midnight. "I don't think so," I said. "Maybe I can make him think it isn't important if I just step into the saddle." George gave me an honest grin and turned Midnight loose.

Quietly, with the reins in my left hand, I took hold of the left cheek strap of his bridle, put my right hand on the saddle horn, pulled him toward me, and as he started to turn I went into the saddle. Strangely enough, Midnight didn't seem to think it was important.

Then the foreman gave us orders for the day. We were to comb a certain area and bring in everything, particularly every longhorn we found. The boss had an offer from a motion-picture firm for all the longhorns he could furnish. There weren't many, he knew, perhaps a carload, but he wanted them off the place.

So we went to work. Midnight fought his head continually, but he was surefooted and quick. We had brought quite a few cattle down the coulees when suddenly I saw sticking up from the brush the longest pair of

horns I had ever seen. As we closed in, the steer made a fast break up a knoll. Now, a longhorn can run like a deer, and my respect for Midnight went up several notches when he turned that steer and kept him going through the live oaks and the grease-wood beyond.

But suddenly the steer raised up and leaped over something. We were going too fast to stop: either hit the obstacle or jump. I gave Midnight my heels and lifted the reins. That beautiful, obstinate son of Satan chose that moment to fight the bit and blundered straight into a patch of cactus that the steer had jumped over. By the time I got Midnight stopped on an open sandy spot my right knee felt as though it were on fire from the cactus spines in it. I had a notion I had ruined my horse. Luckily, I was wearing buckskin gloves and could pick the spines out of my knee; they work deeper if you move around. Then I got out of the saddle. Midnight was a mess from his nose to his heels. I knew from the pain in my leg what he must be suffering, but he stood there perfectly still, looking at me with a question in his eyes that brought a lump to my throat.

Just then, Joe, the foreman, rode up. He looked Midnight over carefully. "We can't get them out without tying him down," he said. "And if we do that they'll just work into him deeper until they kill him. You'd better take your saddle off, Slim." He drew his revolver.

"No, Joe, wait," I said. "I got him into this. I want to get him out if I can. Just stand by and let me try."

The foreman hesitated. "OK," he said, finally. "But stay out of line with his head, because the first mean move he makes I'm going to put a bullet in him."

I reached out to Midnight's nose and picked off two strong spines driven in just above and between his nostrils. He flinched and looked startled, but made no move to retaliate. By the time I got his face and neck clean, his ears had come forward. On down I worked and he never moved a muscle, though his coat was turning gray with sweat. Joe sat his horse quietly, and now and then I heard a gentle cussword. Down to Midnight's front hooves, back on his sides and belly, down his hind legs, and he stood like a statue. I even took a large piece of cactus out of his tail. As I finished each section, I took off my gloves and ran my hands over him to make sure that I had gotten all the spines. Finally I stepped around to Midnight's head and looked at Joe. He took a deep breath and put away his gun.

"I'm obliged to you," I said and meant it.

"It's the damnedest thing I ever saw," said Joe. He looked at his watch, then off to where the men were moving the cattle into the corrals. "It's time for dinner. Let's go in."

As we rode in he gave me something of Midnight's history. He had been a stallion in a herd of wild horses, and he had never stopped fighting. This morning, Joe said, was the first time he'd seen Midnight use his front hooves and teeth on a man, though. "I expect it was that half hitch you had on his nose that made him so mad."

"I reckon that was it," I replied. "He just doesn't like men."

"No, he don't like men, and if you'd had the same treatment that he's had since he first met men, you wouldn't like them either."

We watered our horses and led them under a covered tie rack where they would be in the shade. "No need to tie 'em," Joe said. "They'll stand."

Joe went in to dinner, while I went to the bunkhouse to get out a cactus spine that had broken off under my trousers. When I entered the cook shack, I was greeted with a chorus of remarks about my riding and given instructions about the various parts of a saddle and bridle, with explicit directions as to the purpose of the reins. Nothing was said about cactus. But Krimpy, the ranch-house joker, remarked, "If you're gonna follow a steer that close in the brush, ride the steer and give your horse a rest." They were kidding in a way that let me know I was accepted.

After dinner someone produced a bat, ball and gloves and we started up a game of ball. I was taking a lead off third base and was pleading with Krimpy, who was at bat, to bring me home, when everyone stopped and stared at me. Suspecting a trick, I clapped my foot back on third—and received a push in the back that knocked me off the base. I turned, and there was Midnight, standing quietly looking at me. He had walked out from the cool shade of the horse rack, trailing his reins.

I said, very gently, "Midnight, what are you doing here?"

He came forward two steps and, putting his head against my chest, began to move it up and down slowly. My hands came up and found the velvety spots behind his ears. I was aware of the cowboys gathering around and soft oaths of wonderment. Midnight had taken out his spite on most of them, and they could not believe their eyes. George's chuckle broke the quiet. "Well, Slim, it sure looks like you and Midnight got acquainted."

"Yeah," was all I could say. The lump was back in my throat again.

Joe broke it up with, "Let's go, men." Then, as they turned away, he dropped a final word. "I don't want to see any of you dabbing a rope on Midnight. He's Slim's horse from now on."

I reckon he's still my horse in whatever pasture of Paradise he roams, for he gave me the love of his wild heart as none of the many horses I've known ever could. I am an old man now, and those days are far gone. But the memory of Midnight is still as bright as the day he put his head against my chest to thank me and to say that he was sorry and wanted to be friends.

18

A Deer Comes
to Breakfast

by IRVING PETITE

I HAD SEEN a lot of deer, sometimes five in a single day, on our farm in the Cascade Range southeast of Seattle. But not until one came to live with me—from infancy to young buckhood—did I realize how ignorant I was of many of their most appealing habits and peculiarities.

My enlightenment began one June night. I was lying in bed, just dozing off to sleep, when, amid the peaceful jangling of the cowbells, I heard a skittering and a Lilliputian sneeze under the window. Then came a cry, like that of a large cat mewing—or was it a human infant? In all my years of ranching and roaming the mountains I'd never heard any animal sound like it. I slipped outside and by lantern light discovered, backed against the house, a fawn. He was a nervous bundle of legs and speckled hide, focused in two large jet eyes below huge ears spread as if for flight. Knee-high to a daisy stem and weighing no more than three or four pounds, he was of the small variety called blacktail deer and obviously quite newly born.

My dog, Bozo, and three small cats regarded him sympathetically. He seemed to have no instinctive fear of them, or of me. But he wasn't, then or ever, willing to allow himself to be handled.

"What ails you?" I asked, reaching out my hand. He flicked his wing-size ears, sniffed my wrist and licked it with his enormously long tongue. Then he made that strange mewling sound again, and whatever he said, it was in earnest. After talking with him awhile I went back to bed, thinking he would scamper into the woods when his mother called. But an hour later he was still there, mewling softly. So I moved a mattress out onto the back patio to keep him company. He hopped onto my bed, stilted and tilted on the blankets and finally fell into a heap against my back, legs all scrambled like a newborn colt's, and slept.

With first light I opened an eye to find him gnawing at my hair. Perhaps, I decided, his mother had been run over by a car, or perhaps she'd had triplets and this was the odd fawn. In any case, he seemed to be with me to stay. As I rose and walked to the back door, he trotted around me in small circles, huge ears and dainty tail up, tap-tap-tapping on his shiny little hooves, excited but

19

with no real fright. He stopped to lick Bozo's fur, which greatly embarrassed the dog, who skulked quietly away. I had raised dozens of kids and calves, but none had the same kind of sophistication, of pride, as this new-born fawn. Later his name came easily: We called him Man because he was what every man should be—independent yet loyal, free yet responsible.

Wondering what to feed him that first morning, I put the cat food out. Man sniffed it; then in went his delicate muzzle along with the cats' noses and, possibly for the first time in his young life, he ate. Damp, fishy, canned cat food! Thereafter, for nearly two years, it was ever thus: a startling—and amazing—time, as Man continued to do what seemed highly unnatural to me but what obviously came naturally to him.

After the cat food he took milk from a bottle, but he was impatient with the pro-cess—reinforcing my theory that he had never had a "natural" meal. In three days he was shouldering the cats from their pan of milk, and the bottle was discarded. Be-sides quantities of wet and dry cat and dog food, Man soon showed a relish for berries of all kinds. Like any infant, too, he tried dirt, sand and coal dust. He loved new taste sensations, natural or manufactured, and never seemed to suffer an ache in any of his four stomachs. Tobacco, candy wrappers, bananas (he preferred the skins), book-bindings, raw bacon and cooking oil were as desirable to him as apple-tree leaves or thistle blooms or cabbage roses.

One summer day when my brother's fam-ily and I were swimming in the creek, Man lay down in the shade of sword ferns near our pile of towels, to enjoy our company from that elegant distance which he always kept. Suddenly, poised for a dive, my nephew yelled: "Look at the deer. He's frothing!" I bolted for Man, who sat sedate but was

indeed frothing daintily at the lips. I was relieved when I discovered that the bath soap, a new bar, was gone from where we had put it atop the towels. And Man's usu-ally chlorophyllin breath had a new but familiar scent—Lux.

As usual, Man seemed gratified at our amazement. For from the first he was given to prankster tendencies. When he was about five months old, one of his favorite games developed around a low front-room window, which I frequently left open. He would leap in through it, skitter across a rug noisily—then quietly turn and leap out again with-out making a sound. If, taking for granted that he was still in the house, I happened to close the window, he would come to the front door and lick the knob, making it rattle until I opened it. He would "grin" at my confusion at finding him outside. At other times, when locked out, Man would stand on the steps and "ngonk" or "onk" (his in-fant voice was changing) with piteous urgency until I let him in.

When Man was young, Bozo and my brother's dog, a Dalmatian, ganged up to chase him. But by the time he was six weeks old he could outdistance them and would lead them off into the creek canyon. There he took to the water, which he loved, to hide his scent, and while they yippered along an old trail he would sneak back by another route. They would return much later, tongues dragging, to find him dozing in the flower bed.

One evening a lumberman making a de-livery brought along his nearsighted boxer. Man came closer and closer, stepping with exaggeratedly stiff legs until the boxer spotted him. Then he took off in short leaps, taunting the unwary dog, and the chase was on! Down the canyon they went, dis-appearing into the gathering twilight. By the time the lumber was unloaded it was dark, and the lumberman had called until he was hoarse. When the boxer finally returned, he had to be hoisted into the truck cab, for he could scarcely crawl! Then, as the truck drove out, I felt a moist muzzle in my palm. Even in the dark I could tell that Man was "laughing."

Man never learned to fear guns. Once my brother, seeing him follow some hunters through our place, joined the tail end of the procession. Soon he found Man standing in the midst of three hunters and their grade-school-age sons—"giving them quite a lecture on wildlife." Another time, Man came running to the front door and rattled the knob. Only a moment after I let him in, I was called to the door again by a knock. There, mud-spattered and shaking all over, stood a hunter. "I'm lost," he panted. "And, weird as it may sound, I was following a deer in the forest and he led me out!" Then

he looked past me, mouth agape. Man was stretched out on the davenport!

Man loved to ride in the car with me, although he could never quite decide whether he preferred the back seat or the front. Only once did he stay put for any length of time. It was during hunting season, and he stood at the back window and amazed several carloads of hunters by nodding his spike horns at them solemnly as they passed.

After too many close calls in hunting season—and because he liked people so much—I took Man on his last automobile ride: to Woodland Park Zoo, in Seattle. I go to see him often, and he always recognizes the sound of my motor when I drive up to the yard that he shares with two other blacktail deer. He lifts his head and comes to the fence, muzzle twitching in anticipation of an apple, a cigarette, a banana peel. . . . "Ngonk!" he says.

The Duck
That Took Milwaukee
by Storm

by GORDON GASKILL

Toward the close of April 1945, when World War II was drawing to its end in blood and fury, there began in Milwaukee, Wisconsin, one of the most fantastic episodes of modern Americana—a mixture of heart and hoopla, ludicrous but tender, wacky but wonderful. It centered on a simple drama as old as the coming of spring, and the heroine was a mallard duck, a few pounds of anonymous brown feathers.

Normally a mallard is among the wariest, shyest of earth's creatures. Yet for some unfathomable reason this duck chose to nest in the roaring heart of downtown Milwaukee. The place she picked was one of the pilings that protected a bridge carrying the city's main street, Wisconsin Avenue, across the foul, greasy Milwaukee River. A bare four steps away, some eighty-seven thousand people and clanging streetcars crossed the bridge every day; the bridge itself roared open from time to time to let ships through. In this unlikely spot, she made a shallow bowl in the rotting top of the upended white-oak log, lined it with down plucked from her breast and settled in to lay eggs.

A city electrician named Ray Clemens was among the first to notice the mallard. Clemens telephoned the Milwaukee *Journal's* nature editor, the late Gordon MacQuarrie, who was highly skeptical. "I'm telling you it's a *duck!*" Clemens said, nettled. "A mallard duck with three eggs already." MacQuarrie sent a photographer to Wisconsin Avenue to see. For the next five weeks, Gertie the Great, as the *Journal* immediately named her, shared headlines with the war. So many people flocked to see her that they often blocked bridge traffic. Radio, photographs and newsreels extended her audience to millions more. Abroad, military newspapers and radio networks kept almost daily track of her.

But Gertie needed help. Where the Milwaukee River crosses the heart of the city, it becomes a travesty of a river—polluted and dark, bound tightly between concrete walls and oil-soaked timbers, with no greenery, no natural place where a hungry duck might forage. Just across the river, below the other end of the bridge, a little mud had collected around some debris, and Gertie got into the habit of flying to this mud patch to peck out what she could find.

23

Soon the crowds began dropping food there: corn, bread, cookies, lettuce leaves. Gertie seemed to respond to this thoughtfulness and on April 28 produced news that echoed in press and radio: GERTIE LAYS FOURTH EGG. She went on laying until at last she had nine. (Three later disappeared.)

On May 2 there was a crisis: For the first time since Gertie had nested on the piling, the bridge had to be opened to let two ships pass. Larger crowds than ever came to watch. The bridge tenders, working as gently as they could, set the great lift machinery going to raise the two cantilevers; the two ships eased by as unobtrusively as possible, and Gertie didn't bat an eye. On May 4 it was announced that marine contractors were supposed to start work on a $1040-piling-replacement job near Gertie's nest. City authorities decided to put it off, saying, "It might bother her."

The next day press and radio flashed the word: GERTIE STARTS INCUBATING. As motherhood neared, Gertie began to get all kinds of presents, sent to the shanty of the bridge tenders, who became her unofficial guardians. Hundreds sent her cards.

Then a shadow appeared. Lawrence Hautz, state president of the Izaak Walton (conservation) League, told a reporter, "This whole thing is headed for tragedy. What's going to happen when those ducklings are hatched? If they try to swim, that river is so full of oil their little wings will mat and they'll sink." When this sobering thought was published, the mayor read it, frowning; so did the city commissioners. Presently the city public-works department announced that no oil would mat the wings of the ducklings. When the hatching date drew near, it would start up its great pumps and send two and a half million gallons of clean lake water every hour into the Milwaukee River to flush away the oil.

On May 8—VE Day—Milwaukee celebrated the end of the war with Germany. The following Sunday, May 13, was Mother's Day. Gimbels department store, situated at the end of the bridge, had decorated one window as "Gertie's Window" with stuffed ducks and ducklings. By now Gertie was an established Milwaukee institution. Streetcar motormen often stopped their cars in mid-bridge, dashed out to peer over the railing, then came back to shout to their passengers, "Gertie's OK!" Schoolteachers took their classes to watch her. The humane society stationed a guard, and the Boy Scouts organized a Gertie patrol to protect her.

Tension mounted as the hatching day neared. Hautz, still uneasy, acquired two long-handled dip nets, a huge roll of absorbent cotton and five pounds of cornmeal. He placed these in the bridge tenders' shanty with a sign: FOR EMERGENCY USE FOR GERTIE ONLY—plus his name and all possible telephone numbers, asking that he be called at any hour of day or night if something went wrong. On May 29 the city's pumps began forcing lake water down the Milwaukee River. The superintendent of bridges ordered rowboats in readiness.

May 30, the predicted hatching day, was also Memorial Day, and Milwaukee celebrated it with fervor. A great parade was routed down Wisconsin Avenue. As it neared the bridge, the crowds whispered in unison a great "S-s-sshhhhhh!" The bands instantly stopped their music; the marching thousands almost tiptoed across the bridge.

At 5:30 that afternoon the news was flashed: GERTIE'S FIRST DUCKLING BORN. The newspapers named it Black Bill. Thousands rushed to the bridge. In the next twenty-four hours one egg after another hatched out. By the evening of May 31 Gertie had five ducklings. That night one of the worst storms in years struck Milwau-

24

kee, bringing high winds and rain. Shortly after midnight Hautz's phone rang. It was bridge tender Alex Rehorst: "Things are in a terrible mess down here. The damned little ducks keep falling out of the nest into the river. And Gertie's gone!"

"Dip out all the ducklings you can and take them into your shanty," Hautz said. "I'll be right there." Within a few minutes he was rocketing down Lincoln Memorial Drive to the bridge, where he found the night tenders had managed to collect four of the ducklings. "There's still one egg left in the nest, not hatched," one tender said.

"Get it!" Hautz said. He was almost certain the cold rain had destroyed any life in the exposed egg. Still. . . . He examined it closely and found a quarter-inch hole. Every embryonic duckling has a hard "egg tooth" on its bill, with which it cuts its way out of the egg. When Hautz saw the tiny bill inside still moving feebly, he decided to try to peel the shell away from the egg membrane and save the duckling. It had to be done with exquisite care, for often the duckling's yellow "life sac" (on which it lives for the first few hours of life) is attached inside to the membrane. If the sac is ruptured, the duckling dies.

Hautz set to work. Absorbed, dripping with perspiration, he barely noticed people now crowding into the shanty. A late news flash had alerted the city to the drama. At last he peeled off the final bit of shell; the membrane and life sac were still intact. The duckling seemed dead, but very gently Hautz fluffed up the tiny feathers, sifted them with cornmeal flour to dry them and then placed the duckling inside his hat, which he had filled with absorbent cotton. This he set on a chair near the open stove door. Soon the duckling began to move, and before long it could be put in the cardboard box with the other four. Carefully he fed them, dipping their beaks in milk and crumbled-up yolk of a hard-boiled egg.

Not until about 3 a.m. did Hautz have time to worry about Gertie. Taking one of his long-handled nets, he climbed into a rowboat and shoved off, with the bridge tenders at the oars. They spotted her half a block away, gently herded her downriver to the mud patch where she usually fed and there caught her in a net. Gertie was soon reunited with her five ducklings in the warm shanty. By 5 a.m. Hautz was exhausted but still not satisfied. Gertie and her brood had to have a better home. His eyes fell on "Gertie's Window" in Gimbels store. Just the thing! He dialed the store manager, who snapped wide-awake when Hautz asked, "How would you like to have the *real* Gertie in your window, with all her family?"

Hautz listed what he wanted: clean sand on the floor, plenty of fresh water, infrared lamps for heating, a humidifier, a thermometer, no drafts and an attendant to make sure the temperature was always between 70 and 72 degrees. By 6:30 a.m. the window was alive with workmen; by 9:30 queues were forming to see Gertie and family. So great were the crowds that a barricade had to be erected.

But mallards are made for freedom. On June 3, Gertie and her family were taken to Juneau Park lagoon on the outskirts of the city. The five ducklings were released first, but huddled together on the grass, not knowing what to do. Then Gertie was freed —and made an eager flight straight toward the lagoon, until she recollected that she was a mother. She came back, put herself at the head of her family and with great dignity led them into the water. They swam off briskly, followed by telephoto camera lenses and binoculars, and cheers.

A Study of Feline Character

Condensed from My Summer in a Garden

by CHARLES DUDLEY WARNER

FROM THE MOMENT Calvin came to live with us, appearing out of the great unknown, he assumed a recognized position in the family, for his individuality made itself felt at once. He was large, powerful and as graceful as a young leopard. When he stood up to open a door—he opened all the doors with old-fashioned latches—he was portentously tall. His soft, fine coat was a shade of quiet Maltese; from his throat downward, underneath, he wore the whitest, most delicate ermine. His finely formed head showed his aristocratic character: the ears small and cleanly cut, a tinge of pink in the nostrils, his face handsome and the expression exceedingly intelligent. And no person was ever more fastidiously neat.

It is difficult to convey a just idea of his gaiety in connection with his dignity, which his name expressed. He had times of utter playfulness, delighting in a ball of yarn or pursuing his tail with hilarity. Mice amused him, but he considered them too small game to be taken seriously. I have seen him play for an hour with a mouse, and then let him go with royal condescension.

He did not care for children and he disliked cats, evidently regarding them as feline and treacherous. Occasionally when a night concert was heard in the shrubbery, Calvin would ask to have the door opened; you would hear a rush and a "psstzt," the concert would explode and Calvin would quietly come in and resume his seat on the hearth. There was no trace of anger in his manner, but he wouldn't have any of that about the house.

He had extraordinary persistency in getting his own rights. His diet was one point. He knew as well as anyone what was in the house and would refuse beef if turkey was to be had. Yet he would eat bread if he saw me eating it and thought he was not being imposed upon.

The intelligence of Calvin was phenomenal. He could do almost anything but speak, and sometimes in his face you would see a pathetic longing to do that. He could help himself in many things. There was a furnace register in a certain room, where he used to go when he wished to be alone, that he always opened when he desired more heat;

27

but he never shut it, anymore than he shut the door after himself.

His fondness for nature was most noticeable. He could content himself for hours at a low window, looking into the ravine and at the great trees, noting the smallest stir there; he delighted, above all things, to accompany me walking about the garden, hearing the birds, getting the smell of the fresh earth and rejoicing in the sunshine. He followed me and gamboled like a dog, rolling over on the turf in joy. When it stormed he sat at the window, keenly watching the rain or the snow; a winter tempest delighted him.

I hesitate to speak of his capacity for affection, for I know from his own reserve that he would not care to have it much talked about. We understood each other perfectly: When I spoke his name and snapped my fingers he came to me; when I returned home at night he was pretty sure to be waiting for me near the gate, and would rise and saunter along the walk, as if his being there were accidental, so shy was he of showing feeling. He had the faculty of making us glad to get home—his constancy was so attractive.

He never forgot his dignity. If he asked to have the door opened and was eager to go out, he went deliberately. I can see him now, standing on the sill, looking about at the sky as if wondering whether it was worthwhile to take an umbrella, until he was near having his tail shut in.

He liked companionship, but he wouldn't be fussed over or sit in anyone's lap. Often he would sit looking at me, and then, moved by a delicate affection, come and pull at my coat and sleeve until he could touch my face with his nose, and then go away contented. He would come to my study in the morning and sit quietly on the table for hours, watching the pen run over the paper, then go to sleep among the papers.

28

When the mistress was absent from home, and at no other time, Calvin would come in the morning to the head of the bed, look into my face, follow me about when I rose and in many purring ways show his fondness, just as if he were plainly saying, "I know that she has gone away, but I am here."

Calvin's life was natural and unforced. He ate when he was hungry, slept when he was sleepy, strolled about the garden, lay on the green grass and luxuriated in all the sweet influences of summer. You could never accuse him of idleness, yet he knew the secret of repose. He had good habits and a contented mind. I can see him now walk in at the study door, sit down by my chair, bring his tail artistically about his feet and look up at me with unspeakable happiness in his handsome face. The vulgar mewing and yowling of the cat species was beneath him; he sometimes uttered a sort of articulate and well-bred ejaculation when he wished to call attention to some want of his, but he never went whining about. He had a mighty power of purr to express his measureless content with congenial society, a musical organ with stops of varied power and expression.

Calvin's departure was as quiet as his advent was mysterious. No illness ever had more dignity and sweetness and resignation in it. It came on gradually, in a kind of listlessness and want of appetite. Whatever pain he suffered he bore in silence. He sat or lay day after day almost motionless; his favorite place was on the brightest spot of a Smyrna rug, where the sunlight fell. If we went to him and exhibited our interest in his condition, he always purred in recognition of our sympathy, and looked up with an expression that said, "I understand, old fellow, but it's no use."

One sunny morning he rose from his rug, went into the conservatory (he was very thin then) and walked around it deliberately, looking at all the plants he knew. Then he went to the bay window in the dining room and stood a long time looking out upon the field, now brown and sere, and toward the garden, where perhaps the happiest hours of his life had been spent. It was a last look. He turned and walked away, laid himself down upon the bright spot in the rug and quietly died.

We buried him under the twin hawthorn trees in a spot where he was fond of lying and listening to the hum of summer insects and the twitter of birds.

MY FRIENDS
THE HUSKIES

Condensed from the book

by ROBERT DOVERS

My Friends the Huskies

THE SEALER *Tottan* stood against the sea ice off Port Martin, the French base on Adélie Coast, Antarctica, waiting to relieve the scientists who had passed the year there. So far the only contact with these men had been by radio, but now we saw black dots coming out over the featureless frozen sea— a sledge pulled by a team of huskies. Of all on board I was naturally the most interested, for these dogs were to be my charges. I had been posted as Australian observer with this French Antarctic Expedition of 1952, which was to spend a year on the polar ice charting the coast, recording meteorological observations and studying the penguins. Even now, at the ship's side, there was a group of Adélie penguins, the funny, inquisitive little folk, about fourteen inches tall, that are found all along the thousands of miles of Antarctica's coastline.

When the sledge reached the ship, a steel pin was driven into the ice to moor it and two bearded men in travel-stained windproofs clambered aboard. The dogs flopped down on the ice and, with tongues hanging out, looked about in lazy interest. I was not greatly impressed with them at this stage. Although most of them were big dogs, they seemed a rather nondescript lot.

The penguins lost no time in waddling up to examine the new arrivals. Apart from pricking their ears and watching intently, the huskies showed no signs of excitement as the birds approached. The leading penguin was a yard away when it happened. The huskies suddenly sprang, there was a mass of snapping and snarling dogs, a pitiful, strangled squawk, and all that was left of the little black-and-white creature was an ugly red stain on the snow and a few bedraggled feathers. It had occurred so quickly that no one could have saved the bird.

But did this slaughter send the other penguins scuttling to safety? Not a bit of it. They continued to advance, no longer friendly, but with flippers outspread, neck feathers fluffed up in anger and uttering shrill sounds of rage. The huskies flattened

31

down against the snow and waited. Only the intervention of a sailor, who took the penguins, one by one, by the scruff of their necks and threw them into the nearby water, saved them from being massacred.

This was my introduction to the huskies. Later Georges Schwartz, who had been looking after them for the past year, showed me all the camp's dogs—twenty-odd in three teams, each group chained to a long line.

The first team, comprising mainly three-year-olds and thus at its best age for work, was lead by Bjorn, a powerful but not over-intelligent dog. He bullied the other huskies unmercifully, particularly his second-in-command, Fram. If the driver threw a morsel of meat to one of the others, Bjorn would drop on the dog like a thunderbolt, so that all of them were terrified to touch anything while he was looking on. As for patting one of the other dogs, it was quite out of the question—Bjorn would move in, fangs bared and a deep, growling rumble like a lion's issuing from his formidable jaws. No amount of beating will ever break a leader of this habit; he will brook no interference in his rights over his team.

The second team, six young dogs all about a year old, was presided over by Boss, a grizzled warrior of eight years. There was something indomitable about Boss that took your heart immediately. On a sledge trip, having once been set off in the right direction, he needed no further commands. The cut of the sledge runners behind was straight without the slightest deviation. But at eight he was long past his prime and was beginning to fail from sheer age. His gallant spirit spurred him on, but the blood no longer coursed so freely to warm him in bitter cold, and the once tireless muscles had stiffened. The last team was the one which had met us at the boat. It was composed of old dogs and was led by Pickles, a great,

handsome husky with the same characteristics as Bjorn. He was most fanatically attached to Judy, the bitch of the team.

The next feeding day—the dogs were not fed every day—I watched and helped as I could while Schwartz took a sledge down to the dump of frozen seal carcasses, loaded on a complete carcass and dragged it back to the first dog line. The moment the dogs scented this meat they began to howl like wolves. As we hacked the seal into four-pound lumps, their excitement rose to a crescendo and fights broke out all over the dog lines. Then, as each husky was thrown a chunk, he dragged it to the farthest limit of his chain to protect it, and fell on it ravenously, tearing great mouthfuls loose and gulping them down, pausing only to bare his fangs momentarily at his neighbors. Watching them feed dispelled any idea that these were normal, friendly dogs, such as we know in civilization.

I chose Bjorn's team for my first try at driving the huskies. The job involved was simple. The seals killed during the voyage had been tossed ashore where the ship had berthed, and I now had to haul them on the sledge, two carcasses at a time, to the food dump near the dog lines, a distance of some five hundred yards. When I appeared with the harnesses, pandemonium broke out—every husky leaped to the end of his chain clamoring to be taken. Going out with a sledge was not considered work, and each dog hoped his team would be chosen. Every husky, that is, except one. Fram, lieutenant of Bjorn's team, was so incurably lazy that he resented interrupting his slumbers even for a jaunt with a sledge.

The first precaution was always to tie the sledge to something solid before harnessing any dog. Otherwise, while I was getting the last dogs from the lines, I would hear an excited howling, and sledge and huskies would whip past at a gallop for a joyous, unattended tour of the bay ice.

I harnessed Bjorn first—the leader always claims this right—and then the beautiful, intelligent and gentle bitch, Ifaut. The bitch was always the nucleus about which our teams were built, the relationship of leader and bitch being a near man-and-wife arrangement. Bjorn never showed the least interest in any other female, nor Ifaut in any dog but Bjorn. Fram was then harnessed, and never wasted any time before falling on his stomach and licking Bjorn's lips as a token of submission; but this Bjorn always reinforced with a few heavy growls and a snap or two just to be sure that Fram realized his place. Fram would wait until the next dog was brought up. This was usually Maru, a great, shambling, friendly husky who was to be only too well-known to us later as the Terror of the Penguins. Fram would immediately attack him. Bjorn, excited by the noise, would then attack Fram. When this was over, Maru would be found at the end of his trace gazing at the distant penguins with hungry eyes. Finally, the other dogs could be harnessed up, though Bjorn found it necessary, as do all husky leaders, to subjugate each one in turn.

That first day, I succeeded in harnessing the team with no more than the ordinary number of fights, but it seemed to me that I would never get the snapping and snarling beasts straightened out. Finally I was able to loose the tie rope and call out, *"Ee, ee, les chiens!"* And as I clung grimly to the steering handles, away we went like the wind, the dogs wild with excitement and for the moment quite uncontrollable. The commands were simple: *"Ee, ee!"* for "go"; *"Heely!"* for "right"; *"Yuck!"* for "left"; and *"Whoa!"* for "stop." To emphasize them, I was supplied with a twenty-foot

rawhide whip, which none but a circus performer could possibly use. My efforts with this infernal weapon often resulted in my wrapping the thong about my own neck—no doubt a source of amusement for the dogs.

This time they headed gleefully for one group of penguins after another, and I suppose I must have covered most of the bay. Finally, with much blasphemy and screaming of *"Yuck!"* I managed to steer the team toward the carcass dump. Since there was a twenty-foot ice cliff just beyond it, with freezing water beneath, I could not help wondering how I would stop them. I need not have worried; a food dump was much too interesting to be passed by and, without any command from me, the team pulled up against it and began squabbling over the nearest carcass. Bjorn, the leader, immediately fell upon Fram, not because Fram had done anything, but just as a matter of principle. After Fram had taken his beating like a good lieutenant, he and Bjorn fell upon the other huskies. Ifaut, the gentle lady, avoided all this male squabbling and profited from the diversion by steadily gulping down seal meat.

With two seal carcasses strapped on the sledge, I began the return trip. I had just reached the level snow at the top of the slope and was breathing a sigh of relief, when the dogs took charge, whisked the sledge out of my hands and bounded off toward camp in high glee. There is nothing more humiliating for a would-be dog driver than to be seen running after his team, some hundred yards behind, panting and desperately croaking, "Whoa!" while the huskies bound gaily ahead. I finally found the silly beasts with the sledge jammed against a pile of ice, lying down in their harness, with their great tongues lolling out in happy smiles. They were, no doubt, very pleased with their efforts in breaking in their new guardian. I could almost hear Bjorn remarking to Fram,

33

"Of course, he's young and inexperienced, but with a little more training we may be able to do something with him."

We gradually took over the duties of the men we were relieving and prepared to settle in for our year at Port Martin. The *Tottan,* which had taken three of our new party fifty miles west to Pointe Géologie so that they could study the emperor penguins, now returned to take the old party of scientists home. But before the ship could berth —it was held offshore by rough weather—a disaster occurred which changed all our plans.

At 3 a.m. I was awakened by the night-duty man rushing through the sleeping quarters crying, *"Incendie!"* Although my French was not then very good, I had no trouble deciding what he meant. Slipping on a pair of trousers and a jersey, I seized a fire extinguisher and hurried down the passageway. It was hopeless. One entire room was an inferno, and the fifty-mile blizzard blowing outside was fanning it beyond control. The main hut was engulfed as we watched. And in less than half an hour Port Martin had virtually ceased to exist as an Antarctic base. We saved only the scientific records, the weasels (our 2½-ton Caterpillar tractors), the dogs, a small emergency hut, a few supply dumps, instrument shelters and odds and ends of personal belongings.

Everyone huddled into the tiny emergency hut to escape the cold, and after some radio discussion with the *Tottan*—fortunately our radio sets were in the weasels and thus untouched—the decision was taken to abandon the base and return to France immediately. When the ship was able to berth, we loaded the dogs aboard, with such gear as we could salvage in a few hours, and sailed for Pointe Géologie to pick up the three men there. With the main base gone, we assumed that Pointe Géologie would also be abandoned.

But Mario Marret, who had charge of that outpost, felt that since the place teemed with seals it would be possible to survive despite the loss of Port Martin. He decided to stay on for the full year, and when he offered me a post, I accepted.

The *Tottan* did not stay long; the season was well advanced, and she had to leave before the sea froze over. It took only four hours to land our few remaining supplies. Then the seven of us—Marret, Prévost, Rivolier, Duhamel, Vincent, Lépineux and I— watched the ship steam away, leaving us to our own devices for the coming year. We felt very small indeed in the frozen vastness of the Antarctic.

The base at Pointe Géologie consisted of only one small hut and three polar tents, but it afforded one of the finest views in the world. Our camp was on an island surrounded by a stretch of unbroken ice. Beyond was a bay studded with icebergs of fantastic shapes, the water showing indigo blue under the light of the midnight sun. A huge glacier jutted out from shore, its crevasses glowing with emerald green, its white snow-field tinged with pink. Save for a few rocky outcrops, everything else was perpetual ice. A two-hundred-foot ice cliff marked the coastline; behind it the undulating and featureless ice plateau extended in blank, unchanging whiteness to the Pole. This deep ice mantle shrouds the whole Antarctic continent, which is larger than North America; its thickness is generally believed to be between ten thousand and twelve thousand feet. The surface is polished smooth by the ever-present wind, for Adélie Coast is the windiest place in the world.

The blizzards, sweeping down from the Antarctic plateau accompanied by far-below-zero temperatures, are experiences to be remembered with a shudder. When the wind beats up above the seventy-mile-an-hour mark and visibility is reduced to a yard, then one considers it a blizzard. Anything else is merely drifting snow. Marret, who had spent a previous year there, saw snow falling vertically only once; at all other times it was sheeting by horizontally. To know the blizzard is to know Adélie Coast; everything else becomes insignificant. Such were the conditions in which my friends the huskies worked willingly and happily.

The first problem with the dogs was to secure them so they would not destroy the penguins. It sounds easy enough to chain a dog so that he cannot escape, but the ingenuity of the whole seven of us was severely taxed for the rest of the year without our ever achieving absolute certainty that no husky could get loose. The new dog lines took a day to complete, and I was quite sure they would hold. The base was a half-inch wire cable anchored at each end to steel pickets drilled into solid rock. The individual chains were knotted on the cable at intervals, and each dog was fastened to his chain with a heavy clip.

But the huskies had been on the new lines only a day when Maru slipped his collar and made for an Adélie penguin rookery just behind the camp. I followed in hot pursuit with a whip. There was already a trail of dead penguins through the rookery, and at the head of it Maru was killing with savage speed, not to eat but from sheer blood lust. He was horribly efficient—one quick sideways bite and a penguin lay quivering. He would barely release one bird before closing his jaws on another.

When he saw me, Maru began to play hide-and-seek in the rookery, pausing every few seconds to seize a penguin by the throat. He could easily have escaped the cuts of my whip by taking to flight; but he merely quickened his pace enough to keep just

ahead of me. When I finally recaptured him, one hundred fifty Adélie penguins lay dead as the result of a few minutes' work. Maru thus achieved the first rating as a public enemy but, alas, he was to be joined by many others before the year was out.

In harness Maru was reasonably satisfactory. He had no great enthusiasm for pulling, but he minded his own business and was always so interested in the passing penguins that he never gave trouble. Watching penguins, he was a caricature of Walt Disney's big bad wolf looking at the fat little pigs. His eyes would follow the birds' every move, his great tongue rolling in an ecstasy of anticipation, his eyes alight with dreamy reminiscence. Strangely enough, despite his record as a penguin killer, he became a great favorite of Prévost, the biologist.

Since Bjorn's team, of which Maru was a member, was the best we had, we used it most frequently for camp chores. Although Bjorn had made himself undisputed king of all the other huskies, he was sadly lacking in intellectual capacity. His only interest in life was pulling a sledge, and from the moment he was put in harness until he was taken out, he pulled. Though he tried his utmost to understand what was wanted, mental problems, such as what to do on the command "left," were often too much for him. When the command to turn one way or the other was given, the rest of the team would usually veer off in the correct direction; seeing their leader heading in the opposite one, they would swing around and follow him. At this I would scream with rage, and Bjorn would realize that he was not doing what was required. He would stop to consider the problem, only to be bumped by Fram, his lieutenant, swinging in behind. This gave him an opportunity to save face as he fell on Fram and beat him up for heading wrong. Fram then turned on the other dogs and gave them a small beating by way of passing on the reproof. Ifaut, the intelligent and beautiful bitch, would be standing at the end of her trace apart from the others, facing in the required direction all the time, throwing a glance of contempt at her blundering menfolk. On seeing her, a wave of understanding would dawn on Bjorn; finally realizing what direction he should take, he would bound off, throwing a sideways nip at Fram in passing, as if to say, "Now follow me, and don't get me into trouble again."

In that early period, a half-grown puppy named Roald became rather my pet. Being too young to work, he was tied at the end of the dog lines with a six-month-old bitch, Yacka, and they became devoted playmates. Later, we allowed Roald to run loose. The other dogs regarded his carefree liberty as unfair favoritism and took great pleasure in nipping him whenever he came within reach. There would be a scuffle, some startled yelps, and Roald would streak for our hut, his tail between his legs, while the aggressor yawned complacently. It was a severe shock for Roald when his little playmate, Yacka, first became strangely beautiful to the other dogs. The grizzled old warrior Boss, who never wasted such an opportunity, lost no time in breaking his chain and joining Yacka. Roald, seeing her and Boss apparently playing together, raced over to join in the fun. He bounded round and round the two, barking and prancing, but to his annoyance neither Boss nor Yacka took the least notice of him. Feeling peeved, he gave Boss a nip on the back leg.

Perhaps it would be kindest to draw a veil over what followed. Boss turned round with a look of stunned astonishment and fell on Roald like a flash of lightning. Yacka too, vexed by the interference, joined Boss in the attack. Pieces of Roald flew in all directions, and he barely saved himself, by

fleetness of foot, from complete destruction. He spent several days under the hut afterward, trying to understand what change had come over his little friend Yacka. After all, he had only wanted to play.

As the weeks slipped by and the sun at midday became lower in the sky, bringing even colder temperatures with its retreat northward, we began to expand our little hut. Originally 12 by 18 feet, it was tight against snow and wind, and its coal-burning stove was a pulsing heart of warmth-giving life amid the frozen wastes. But as seven of us lived, cooked and worked in the building, the only privacy was in sleep, and even that was apt to be violated by the foot of the man in the bunk above. So, by tearing down one wall and using packing cases for building material, we finally achieved two rooms, a porch and a garage, all securely tied down with wire cables.

Packing cases also came in handy when puppies were due to arrive. The first expectant mother was Judy, the bitch of Pickles' team. I fixed her a maternity hospital just behind the hut by lining and curtaining a packing case with coal sacks, and putting rocks over it to hold it down in the wind. When I brought her in from the dog lines, Judy, an old husky who had been through this before, headed straight for her new quarters and after a brief inspection crawled inside and made herself comfortable.

It was blowing a minor blizzard when the pups found their way into the world. There were three of them to begin with, but Judy soon reduced the number by eating one. Several hours later a second pup was found frozen stiff just outside the kennel. Now, however, Judy began to take care of the third. She tucked him between her back legs, curled her tail around him, pushed her head against him to keep him warm. In that little niche of warm fur and flesh he was safely protected from the 50-below-zero cold.

For the grown huskies, this sort of weather was normal, of course. When the wind rose and the drift snow began to sheet past, they just curled up, backs to the wind, with their paws tucked about their sensitive nose tips, and went comfortably to sleep. After a few hours in a blizzard not a dog could be seen; all would be buried and would remain so until the weather improved. You could always tell when a blizzard was over: The huskies would emerge and start shaking the ice from their fur. Ice was a problem for the dogs in a blizzard. If they remained snowed in too long their fur froze to the ice beneath, so that they could release themselves only by losing some, hair. The more experienced huskies, aware of this danger, got up and shook themselves every three hours or so. For the others, we toured the dog lines regularly, giving all a gentle kick to be sure they did not become iced in.

Paton, Judy's surviving pup, thrived in the warmth and overfeeding of his mother's care. And being the sole pup in the camp, he was soon outrageously spoiled. As a result, he became little more than a round distended stomach propped up on four inadequate legs. Fortunately, Ifaut provided competition for him in a few weeks by producing four beautiful pups. She proved to be an ideal mother, making her kennel a warm haven for the little bundles of fur nestled against her stomach.

Boss, the grizzled old leader and victor of a thousand bloody battles, had to fight yet another, this time with Astro, a large white wolflike dog, the most serious threat to his leadership in the team. Wise in the ways of the pack, Boss knew he could not afford even the semblance of defeat, or the whole team would fall on him together.

Boss's strength was failing now, however, and his teeth were bad from years of chewing rock-hard frozen seal meat. He had only one of the big fang teeth in usable condition, and it is with lightning slashes of the fangs that a husky does most damage. Boss had to bite at an extraordinary angle to get results. And so the old veteran fought less and less now and to a great extent held his position as leader by pure bluff.

Normally, battles between dogs are a mere test of brute strength and savagery. The Astro-Boss battle was different. Astro was heavier and taller than Boss and at his prime, a year and a half old. He was strength and savagery personified. Against him was the old champion, lighter and smaller and minus half his teeth, but past master of every slash and parry of the game. Brute force versus science. Astro, the challenger, with nothing to lose and everything to gain. Boss, desperate, his leadership at stake.

It started over a piece of frozen seal meat lying near Boss. Astro sneaked toward it to steal it, and Boss, seeing him, growled deeply. Astro growled back and continued to advance. Boss leaped at him with one of his usual furious, bluffing rushes. But instead of recoiling as he should have done, Astro struck back, slashing down across Boss's shoulder, drawing blood.

A less experienced dog would have tried to pull free and thus had his shoulder laid open. But Boss yielded with the blow, falling heavily to the ground on his back. Astro instantly shifted his grip to Boss's throat. These holding tactics are always the weakness of young dogs, for in the thick fur of the husky they do little damage. The more experienced husky concentrates on swift, punishing slashes that tear through fur and flesh alike. Boss slowly moved his head across one of Astro's forefeet and seized the other just on the ankle joint where the flesh is thin. Then, with a quick levering of his head against Astro's free leg, he sent the big white husky flying through the air. Before Astro could recover, Boss jumped astride and with swift, raking bites attacked his tender underside. Astro snarled and snapped at Boss's grizzled forehead. One of Boss's ears, already torn and tattered, was laid open, and both huskies were now bleeding freely.

Astro shifted his grip to Boss's foreleg, and as his powerful jaws closed I could hear the bones crunch. Boss was badly hurt and rolled away to ease the pressure, still raking Astro with swift, slashing bites. As Astro once more went for Boss's throat, the two huskies met in midair. Astro reeled back, then came leaping in again with his head low. This was the move Boss had been waiting for. Incredibly swiftly, he swung his body aside, and as the snarling head of the big white husky came level with his shoulder, struck down across the muzzle. His fang tooth cut into Astro's nose and ripped up toward his eyes. It was the end of the fight.

There was no use putting Boss back in the lines for a while now; he would just get involved in another fight. So, putting his wounded leg in a plaster cast, we installed the old warrior in a private kennel behind our hut, as we had done with the expectant mothers, Judy and Ifaut. Temporarily, Boss seemed delighted with his new quarters. Soon, however, he took stock of his companions. His eyes lighted on Judy and her little pup. He seemed puzzled. Then he saw Ifaut. He thought for a few minutes. Then he must have realized what this was—a maternity ward! Jumping to his feet, Boss began to howl indignantly. Nothing so humiliating had ever happened to him before!

In early March, when winter began in earnest and the sea started to freeze up, the first emperor penguins arrived. We were glad to see them, for we were enduring the rigors of Pointe Géologie mainly to study these birds. A reasonable man might well ask to study them under more clement conditions, but the emperor penguin is not a reasonable bird. It practically never sets foot on land. It lives and feeds in the ocean and spends the summer on pack ice. And in the Antarctic winter it sites its rookeries on the frozen-over sea and raises its young under the cruelest conditions in the world.

There were soon to be twelve thousand of them on the sea ice just off Pointe Géologie, and Prévost, our biologist, would be the first man to observe them through an entire breeding season. The emperor is the largest of penguins. He stands three feet six inches high and can weigh up to eighty-five pounds. His severe coloring of black back and white front is relieved by a gorget of gold on either side of the throat. Several startled emperors were soon wandering about the rookery with large red identification numbers painted on their backs—markings so ludicrously out of place in our isolated surroundings as to seem indecent.

By the end of March, courting couples were everywhere. In mid-May the emperors' eggs were laid. At this stage the males were fat with accumulated blubber, the females extremely thin. The female lays only one large egg and immediately passes it over to the male, leaving him to guard it while she goes away to sea to feed. Probably she says to her husband, "Would you mind Junior for a few minutes while I get something to eat?" Then she disappears to the north, and he does not see her again until the end of July. Although we investigated the sea ice by weasel, we were never able to come to the end of it; but we estimated that open water, which the female had to reach to feed, must have been a hundred miles away.

Unable to leave the rookery on account

of his charge, the male waits the better part of three months, living on his stored-up blubber. Toward the end he grows very thin and sometimes uses up his reserves of blubber before the egg hatches. Thus from time to time we would see a male, complete with egg—which he carries on the upper side of his feet and covers with his stomach by leaning forward—shuffling his way northward from the rookery in search of food.

From the moment it hatches until it reaches maturity and can fend for itself, the chick faces a grim struggle for survival. There is an enormous mortality. But when one considers the truly frightful midwinter in the Antarctic—intense cold, high winds and the nearest source of food, the open sea, scores of miles away at best—the wonder is that any of the chicks survive.

Another public enemy was soon marked down, along with Maru, as a three-star penguin killer. This was Helen, the black bitch on Boss's team, and we learned to keep the closest kind of watch on her. Helen was one of our most remarkable huskies, but so small that she seemed quite out of place in a team of sledge dogs. I was at first shocked to find this poor little female among them when she seemed so much more suited to life as a pet in a suburban home. But her small body was a mass of steel sinew that was completely tireless. Even at the end of a hard journey when all the other huskies were content to drop in their tracks from fatigue, Helen would still be on her feet, snapping at this dog or that, trying to stir up trouble. She was never so happy as when blood and fur were flying, and she was so startlingly savage that no dog dared put fangs to her, even amid the excitement of a general brawl.

And now Helen began to show signs of needing a lodging in our packing-case maternity ward. She objected strongly to being removed from her team. Unlike Judy and Ifaut, she treated her new kennel with contempt, preferring to sleep outside in the snow. And what made it difficult for me was that she objected vocally, making her loudest protests at night, when she sustained particularly piercing howls for eight hours without a break. But her howling finally stopped —at 4 a.m. one night during a blizzard. I struggled into my windproofs, pulled on fur boots and gloves and went out to investigate. I found Helen nosing six newborn pups in a puzzled manner, but making no attempt to protect them. All were outside the kennel. I installed Helen in the kennel and then pushed the newborn pups into the softness of her stomach. With her back to the opening and the pups underneath her legs, all seemed to be well, so I returned to my warm bed.

About four hours later, when I made a further inspection, I found six little bodies lying outside the kennel frozen as hard as rocks and Helen happily asleep. I decided to put her back in her team at once. She left the kennel without a backward glance at her dead puppies. The trouble with Helen seemed to be that she had no softer side. Perhaps this had started at the time of her first litter two years before when, because of a shortage of dogs, she had had to be taken on a sledging journey with her pups almost due. She had pulled her way with the team until the last moment, then produced the pups on the ice. The new puppies had frozen to death at once, and Helen was harnessed up and went on pulling. A husky's life is not altogether an easy one.

A new drama was soon being enacted in the dog lines. It began when Helen was mated with Astro. Old Boss, whose whole authority rested on his ancient prestige, felt the situation keenly. There was dejected shame in his attitude. His young and high-spirited team seemed delighted with this unpunished transgression. It could have passed had not the young Labrador cross, Pomme, sensing Boss's dejection, begun a series of tentative attacks. Finding Boss's defense half-hearted, he swung in on him in full battle. Waking from his mood of helplessness, Boss returned the offensive, and a real fight began. The other members of the team were beside themselves with excitement.

Backward and forward rolled the two combatants. Boss was swift and sure, slashing and cutting, each quick movement drawing blood; Pomme was blundering and heavy, but tireless in the flush of his youth. Though Boss was undoubtedly winning on points, he was unable to hurt the big Labrador cross seriously through his matted fur. And every now and then Pomme, for all his ungainliness a very powerful dog, was able to sink his fangs into Boss. What was worst for Boss was that he was physically incapable of a long fight. He needed a swift, decisive battle to win, and every minute the combat continued, his hope of victory diminished. In the breaks he stood gasping, with blood dripping from his wounds. Then, as soon as he recovered his breath, he would launch his tired old body against Pomme once more.

It was in such a breathing space that the tragedy occurred. The concerted leaping of all the excited dogs against their chains broke out a pin at one end of the center trace, and the whole team of blood-mad huskies closed in on the two fighters. I caught just a glimpse of Boss's expression as the eight powerful young huskies fell on him while I raced across to try to stop the inevitable. I had only an inkling of what must follow, but Boss knew.

He sank down, belly to the ground, to protect his soft underside, and with his lips drawn back over his broken teeth prepared to defend himself. Then he was hidden by a mass of snarling and snapping huskies, each determined to repay the old leader for past beatings. They had no fear of him now. It was the end of Boss. Had I left him there a few minutes longer they would certainly have killed him. Perhaps it would have been as well that way, because what I succeeded in pulling clear of the cruel fangs was no longer Boss but a poor tattered remnant in spirit and body of the grand old husky we had all known so well.

As seven of us were now living on stores meant for three, Marret decided to search the burnt-out base of Port Martin for further supplies. The plan was to go there in the one weasel we had, dig out and start the three weasels abandoned there, and use the four machines to tow back sledges filled with whatever food and equipment we could find which had escaped the fire. Because we were short of gas for the journey, we would have to go the shortest possible way, which was over the frozen sea. The snout of a glacier which projected far out from the coast lay across this route and presented a continuous wall of ice cliffs two hundred feet high. But by making daily scouting trips with the dogs, Vincent and I finally discovered a passage through which we could get to Port Martin.

There was now nothing to delay our departure—except the date, June 21, which is traditionally celebrated in the Antarctic as midwinter day. Our hut seemed hardly the setting for the party of the year, but we festooned it with the red pennants used as trail markers, masked the bare wood ceiling by hanging a white tent lining from the rafters and concealed the bunks with a roll of green canvas. Dipping recklessly into our stores, Lépineux and Rivolier, our best cooks, produced a fitting meal; and each of us dug deep into his poor supply of clothing to produce his gayest and cleanest garments for the occasion.

It was warm and merry in the hut, though the wind and snow whistled past outside. As we sat down to the groaning table, the seven gayest men in that sector of the Antarctic were determined to do justice to the wine and fine food—the four of us who were facing the long and hazardous weasel trip being perhaps the most determined. In the center of the table stood our greatest treasure—our sole bottle of champagne. Amid the mounting festivity there was a moment of shocked silence as Marret accidentally spilled his one allotted glass. But he carried it off. "Anyone can have champagne to drink," he remarked. "True luxury is having champagne to waste."

Then someone suggested that the small puppies be brought in to share our festivities. Soon they were squabbling under the table, stuffed with food and having a wonderful time. A little later a wandering emperor penguin was invited inside. He stood solemnly at the end of the table and viewed the proceedings with a disapproving eye. To cheer him up, we offered him a spoonful of brandy and two vitamin C pills. The effect was startling. The previously dignified and no doubt teetotaling bird began to behave in a manner that made his condition unmistakable. A fighting drunk if ever I saw one. With raucous cries he chased the pups about the floor, and when all pups were hiding, trembling with fear, he turned his aggression on the men. Regretfully, we were obliged to show our new friend the door.

Six hours later, Marret, Duhamel, Vincent and I set off for Port Martin in the weasel. The journey, which took upward of a month, proved to be as difficult as we had feared. As we traveled over the sea ice,

always conscious that the water was only a yard below us, we frequently came to open leads which we had to bridge with timbers. Once the head of a seal popped up in our headlights from the apparently solid ice just ahead. This led us to the somber reflection that where a seal can come up a weasel can go down.

At Port Martin, we chipped out and salvaged from the ice two of the abandoned weasels. Even our invincibly competent mechanic, Roger Vincent, was not equal to starting the third. Despite almost constant blizzard we also unearthed gasoline, food and gear from the buried supply dumps. When we somehow got back over the same peril-strewn route—with *three* weasels now, each dragging a well-filled sledge—it was incredibly good to have the frigid journey behind us. And as we drifted off to sleep in the warm bunks of our hut (we had forgotten what temperatures above freezing felt like), the howling of the dogs sounded like music.

The salvaged supplies transformed the whole future of our group. We now had ample food for the rest of the year and, in fact, everything we needed to make us a normal expedition. The weasels were particularly useful for long-range explorations. But I could never feel for them what I did for the unpredictable, warm-blooded dogs. Since Boss's defeat and demoralization, his team had had no leader. We had to find a dog to take over the team, but the question was, which? A leader should not only be intelligent; he should also possess the fighting ability to control his team by fear. The two qualities do not necessarily go together.

But one rather significant thing had happened recently. Fram, the lazy lieutenant in Bjorn's team, had broken his chain and made a bloody tour of the dog lines, in which he had attacked and beaten every husky in the lines save one, his own leader Bjorn, with whom he still lived in a state of cringing fear. This showed his ability as a fighter, and there was little doubt about his intelligence—if a marked skill at avoiding work could be classed as such. Every one of us had had experience with Fram's sly cunning, when driving Bjorn's team. Every trace would be taut, but the sledge would not be advancing as it should. If a finger was hooked over Fram's trace he could be pulled back a yard before he realized his laziness had been detected. He could travel for miles with just enough strain on his trace to give the impression he was pulling. So it seemed just possible that Fram was smart enough to be the new leader we needed.

Physically, he was a magnificent specimen: a big husky of about a hundred pounds, with a deep chest and heavy thighs mounted on short, sturdy legs. His forehead was broad, his eyes sharp and inquisitive. He was, of all our dogs, the most typical of the popular conception of a husky. For want of a better candidate, Fram got his chance.

Before his first journey as leader, we put Fram in harness at the sledge alone, then brought over the members of his team, one by one, for mutual introduction. This was accomplished much more speedily than we had anticipated, and comparatively painlessly. A brief scrimmage ensued as each husky was attacked and beaten; then he formally acknowledged his new leader by fawning and licking Fram's jaws. Astro, the big white husky, offered no resistance at all. He saw in Fram a much tougher proposition than he could hope to handle, so immediately acknowledged Fram's leadership in the approved fashion and elected himself as Fram's lieutenant. Fram also wasted no time in claiming another perquisite of his new office—the attentions of the bitch, Helen.

As we traveled, I took stock of the team

and felt confident that it would be a good one. Each day, Fram emerged more and more as a distinct individual. With his team he was stern authority, bullying, punishing and meeting the least infringement of his rule with swift attack. With me he displayed a tremendous dignity that was unassailable by a mere man; one could get so close to Fram but no closer. "You have your place in the team, and I have mine," his attitude said quite clearly. "There is no reason to attempt familiarity."

Moreover, he had an amiable obstinacy of purpose that I found impossible to combat. The behavior of the team when we went seal hunting was a case in point. I had long established the conduct of the teams about a seal carcass while the driver was skinning the beast. Severe discipline was always necessary then, for the sight and smell of fresh blood titillated the dogs' ravenous appetites to a point of frenzy, and unless the driver kept them under control, there would be a sudden stampede. So, when the team arrived about fifty yards from the seal, they would be halted, while I went ahead on foot to shoot the quarry. When the blubber was stripped off, I would call up the huskies. They would drag up the sledge, then sit round in a half circle, tongues hanging out, watching each slash of the knife avidly. From time to time I would throw each husky, in turn, a chunk of meat.

Fram did not agree with this procedure. He considered that there was no point in waiting for my call; the gunshot was sufficient advice that there was now no chance of frightening the seal. So, as soon as the shot rang out, he brought the sledge up. His gang of young toughs, encouraged by this, came rushing in with jaws agape. I was prepared to withstand boarders when suddenly Fram turned about and gave a few quick snaps. In a moment the team was sitting in the usual half circle facing Fram, who had planted himself, facing them, between the dogs and the seal.

I offered the big dog a chunk of seal meat by way of reward. He spurned it, leaving it untouched where it had fallen. He then got up and made a close inspection of the seal. Selecting a choice piece, he tore it off and gulped it down, watching my reactions as he did so. At the same time, the other huskies had all been eyeing the first morsel that I had thrown to Fram. It became too much for them, and there was a concerted rush. Fram's lazy insolence dropped away, and he sprang into action. Immediately the team recoiled into a half circle with Fram watching over them, growling. I then tried to give each husky a piece of seal, as was my usual custom. Fram objected strongly, falling on each dog as the meat was thrown to him, so that the meat lay where it had fallen, with the dog cringing on his belly.

This was a bit thick! The time had come for me to assert my waning authority. Fram was telling me I could not feed his team without his approval. So I took the whip off the sledge and advanced on Fram. As the whip fell, the dog in front of Fram took advantage of the diversion to edge toward his piece of meat. But even as the whip cut Fram, a deep-throated growl from him stopped the other dog, who whined in submission and remained still. Fram was determined not to surrender his opinion, so for the rest of the day he accepted beating after beating, but still exercised his authority over the team. Not one of those dogs ate a morsel. In the end I had to confess I was beaten. And this was the thin edge of a very long wedge. Fram won point after point in a similar manner. I was gradually made to feel that I was a very minor piece of equipment of the sledge; all I had to do was to leave the management up to him.

One of our main undertakings for the year was a journey westward to map and survey the coast. Four of us were to go—Marret, Vincent, Rivolier and myself—and as the project would take almost two months, we planned it with much thought. We packed only the most concentrated rations and for transport decided to take two weasels and eleven dogs. We exercised great care in the selection of the dogs. The time had long passed when all the huskies looked alike to us; now we knew each one as a distinct personality. In fact, we probably knew the characters of the huskies better than we knew each other's. We finally chose Fram's team and elements of Bjorn's. The plan was that a strong team of eight dogs headed by Fram would pull a loaded sledge, while three reserve dogs would be attached to a weasel sledge and run free of load so they would always be fresh. Fram's team consisted of Astro, Helen, Roald, Maru, Pomme, Seismo and Wild. Bjorn and two younger huskies, Milk and Tiki, made the reserve.

On November 5, Marret, Vincent and Rivolier clambered into the weasels, and the procession moved off. The lead weasel, towing a heavily laden barge, was followed by the second machine towing an even more heavily laden barge and a sledge carrying a ton of gas. The three reserve dogs were attached to this gas sledge, and I brought up the rear with Fram's team, pulling their own loaded sledge. Down the slope from the hut the convoy moved, out over the sea ice and across the frozen bay toward the polar sun. The roaring of the weasel motors broke the cold Antarctic silence, and now and then as the dogs settled down to pulling, one of them whimpered. The sledge runners made a soft swishing, and, walking alongside, I pulled on my gloves and parka hood, for the wind chilled bare flesh to the bone.

The long journey was filled with trying difficulties for the weasels. In the zone of crevasses, which we struck on the second day out, they sometimes broke through deceptively solid-looking snow bridges and were barely saved from plummeting to the lethal depths below. Frequently they shed their tracks and sometimes slipped and fell over on their sides and had to be jacked upright again. And before a quarter of the journey was done we had smashed a mainspring and used our only spare to replace it.

Accidents were not limited to the machines. Once when we were ten miles inland from the coast Seismo had a shock that he no doubt remembered for a long time. We were crossing a zone of blue ice when we encountered a strip of snow. If Seismo had asked the other dogs or me, he would have been informed that this was a thin snow bridge over a crevasse. As it was, all the other dogs leaped the danger, landing on the firm ice on the other side. Seismo jumped only halfway, the snow dissolved under his feet and he went hurtling into the abyss. Standing on the sledge, I shot safely across, catching a momentary glimpse of Seismo dangling ten feet down in his harness, much too startled even to yelp. The next second he came shooting out of the crevasse like a jack-in-the-box as the onward movement of the other dogs dragged him back to safety. Before he could collect his wits, he was back in his place in the team, pulling and wearing a most puzzled expression.

Never was Bjorn's lack of intelligence more clearly demonstrated than on this journey. He was chained to a weasel sledge carrying a ton of gas. The general idea was that he could run alongside it or, if he wished, he could jump aboard and ride. But poor Bjorn had been brought up as a well-trained husky. The first lesson he had ever been taught was that the job of a husky when attached to a sledge is to pull. So, when he found himself attached to that sledge weighing a ton, he pulled as hard as he could, nonstop. Somewhere in the fuzzy recesses of his brain he had come to associate the whir of the weasel starter with the command to mush. So each time he heard the starter he would jump down from the sledge, put his back into it and pull. In those hundred weary miles poor Bjorn never realized it was the weasel and not he that dragged that massive load. And this despite the fact that alongside him were Milk and Tiki, sitting on the weasel sledge with pleased smiles on their faces!

It was on this trip that the battle for kingship of the huskies took place. For months we had been expecting it. Until recently Bjorn had been secure in his position of king dog, the undisputed master in battle of every dog in the lines. But Fram, since his promotion to team leader, had demonstrated that he too could handle any other dog. The final combat was inevitable, for there must always be a king dog.

It was difficult to estimate who would win. If Bjorn had forced the issue when Fram first became a leader, there would have been no doubt about the outcome. The long years that Fram had spent in submission to him would have won the day for Bjorn. But Bjorn was uncertain and hesitated. In hesitating, he gave Fram confidence, while the wily Fram avoided battle and undermined Bjorn's bullying self-assurance. Thus it was two months before the heavyweight championship was settled.

We did not see the fight when it occurred, and afterward we could only deduce what had happened. Fram, as was customary, was roaming free, and Astro, his big white lieutenant, had broken loose and was with him. The two of them, prowling about, had evidently found themselves on an ice shelf ten feet above the sleeping and unprepared Bjorn. The first intimation Bjorn had of battle must have been when two hundred pounds of husky in two snarling lumps dropped out of the heavens above him.

We pictured Bjorn suddenly awakened to find the most decisive battle of his life already in progress, not against one husky but against two who, through past training, moved as though directed by one mind. Perhaps, if it had started with preliminary skirmishes, Bjorn might yet have won, for he was enormously powerful and almost impervious to punishment. But the battle was half lost to him before he knew it had commenced.

Bjorn probably attempted to concentrate on Astro, trying with a swift attack to put the lesser enemy out of action first. But Fram must have been too cunning for that, pressing the attack until Bjorn lay exhausted and whimpering on the ground. Thus Fram won the husky kingship of our polar world.

On our return trip, Pomme distinguished himself at one overnight camp by eating my fifteen-foot sealskin whip. I came out of the tent in the morning to find him at the final stage of this repast. He had managed most of his fifteen-foot meal, and he stood there with a dreamy expression in his eyes, masticating gently, with the butt of the whip still hanging sadly out of his mouth. Otherwise, the return was almost without event. Fram proved to be at his very best in the broken terrain that we encountered. He continually looked back, so that, when the sledge lurched on a dangerous ice slope, without a word from his driver he would bring his team to one side to save it from slipping to disaster. When running along narrow snow cornices, with a drop of a hundred feet on either side, there was no need to shout directions to him; before I could decide what should be done, Fram would take the necessary action and avert the danger. More and more on that trip, I realized that the fewer orders I gave Fram, the less trouble we had.

When we got back to the hut, there was a touching reunion between Bjorn and Ifaut, separated by the journey. It was like husband and wife coming together after a long absence. Bjorn showed her his half-healed wounds, and she licked them sympathetically, baring her teeth at Fram, who was chained nearby. After a few days near Ifaut, Bjorn recovered most of his old spirit.

All that remained for us now was to fill in the little time left until the arrival of the *Tottan*. We had come through our year on the ice unscathed. But over the dog lines was the shadow of death: The directors of the expedition in Paris had radioed us that arrangements could not be made to bring them back to France. All must be shot.

There are no rewards for the husky. All his adult life he lives on a chain, in the open, racked by the wind and snow and bitter cold. He suffers the stern discipline of the driver and the even sterner discipline of his leader. He is fed meat frozen so hard that an ax can hardly cut it. Water he never knows: He slakes his thirst with dry, cold snow. His only relief from boredom is battle with other huskies. Every day he works, his team is expected to pull a heavily laden sledge from twenty to thirty miles, and when he is no longer capable, there is no leisured old age —only execution. Thus the average husky's lot is not a happy one. But ours, owing to circumstance, were not even to live out their normal span. We found this hard to accept, for we had become extremely fond of our dogs despite their savagery.

We often speculated as to whether they would turn on a badly injured driver if he were on his own—a question, fortunately, that was never resolved. I do not think they

45

would, since from puppyhood they have been taught that the one unforgivable sin is to bite a man. During the whole year with this group I was bitten only once, by mistake. I was leading another dog across Fram when he leaped, but misjudged his stroke. Immediately he cowered back, struck by the enormity of his crime. Any one of us could wade into a snarling, seething mass of huskies, all engaged in a desperate free-for-all, and cuff the blood-mad brutes without risk of being bitten.

It was sad, now, to walk past our canine comrades, each of whom followed our progress with trusting and friendly eyes, and to think that soon we must be their executioners. To say that we were not looking forward to this massacre would be a masterpiece of understatement. Yet each man volunteered to do away with his own favorite husky. Each of us wanted to be sure that the dog would know nothing. The thought of taking old Boss on his last walk was a melancholy one. As for Fram . . .

Then one day Marret shouted from the wireless set, "Our dogs are saved!" A message had just come through from Paris saying that satisfactory arrangements had been made for taking the huskies to France, and that all dogs, including even the useless veterans like Boss, were to go back.

Seven days after Christmas the high crow's nest of the *Tottan* appeared over the horizon. The motor launch was an interminably long time in being lowered and in covering the few miles to shore. After a year that seemed to have passed away almost unnoticed, this last hour was endless.

Without regret we closed the door of the hut for the last time, then trooped down to the landing. The huskies were driven to the water's edge, their traces were cut, and one by one they were lowered, still in harness, into the waiting launch. A little later I stood on the *Tottan*'s afterdeck looking back. In the far distance I could see the bright light of the midnight sun showing reddish on the polar plateau. Then that too was gone, and our horizon was the boundless sea.

I took leave of my fellow adventurers sadly—men and dogs—at the ship's side in Australia. When I gave a final pat to Fram, who left a gap in my life no other dog will ever fill, it was like saying farewell for the last time to an old and dear friend. Fram and his team were soon pulling a sledge at Chamonix; most of the others were scattered in the Alps. Boss, who had known the full gamut of a husky's life, who had been born among the Eskimos in Greenland, served as a team member, fought his way to leadership and finally had been deposed after years of unremitting service, who in the normal way of things would have been eased to a well-earned rest with a bullet in his skull, found a closing chapter to his years so just that I hesitate to record it, for fear of being accused of romancing.

Each morning, inside the wall surrounding a certain gracious home not far from Paris, a servant would approach a spacious kennel with a bowl of chocolate. A grizzled, scarred old dog would emerge from the kennel to receive it. He would then be taken to the center of the garden, to a tree where he would lie most of the day, warming his old bones under a friendly sun, interrupted only at midday when a bowl of soup would be brought to him. Accustomed to such attentions, he would not even get to his feet; he would merely lean his head over the bowl and lap up the soup while lying on his side. Yes, Boss lazed out his last years in the sunshine near Paris, visited frequently by his human friends and idolized by the lady who volunteered to provide a home for him. No one who knew the grand old husky could dispute his claim.

Achilles, the Amusing Tortoise

by WALLACE STEGNER

I HAVE NEVER been able to explain to others my peculiar affection for Achilles—people do not usually think of reptiles as desirable pets. A desert tortoise, half gentle buffoon, half philosopher and wholly harmless, he lived a ruminative, affectionate life.

Achilles was a clean pet; neither germ nor flea could find sanctuary on his tough rind; he could be flushed off with the garden hose and kept as aseptic as an operating room. He was completely indestructible. He wandered into the street, yes; but when he heard the thunder of approaching doom he played that he was a traffic button, and if anything ran over him he shrugged it off. Once he was flipped like a tiddlywink into the gutter by a truck, but after the earth stopped shaking he just poked his head out and began clawing himself up onto the curb. In the house he fitted neatly under radiators, where he stayed out of sight. He never came begging to the table. He did not need to be put outside at regular intervals. In all the time he lived with me, I never had to slide out of bed and feel for slippers on the cold floor because Achilles hadn't been taken care of; he took care of himself. And from November until February he stayed in a closet out of sight and contemplated his soul. Whenever I opened the closet door, there he was, and I had a comfortable feeling.

A tortoise is an interested but not inquisitive house guest. He will walk solemnly around the borders of the rug admiring the colors under his nose, elbowing himself along with admirable deliberation. If you put a book in his path he will hiss and pull in his neck and wait to see if the book wants to start anything. If it doesn't, he will climb over it and resume his walk. He will not go around it. He will not go around anything. If the obstacle is too high to crawl over, he will fall asleep comfortably in front of it.

There are advantages in being cold-blooded. You or I would fly into a temper and kick the book out of the way. Not Achilles. Where our hot blood makes us run ourselves to death in a few years and makes our earthly span a wailing and gnashing of teeth, the tortoise takes things philosophically, and his life expectancy is something over a century. Insoluble problems put him to sleep. Bad weather puts him to sleep. Anything unpleasant puts him to sleep. Conversely, anything pleasant brings him the pure and undiluted joy that only the innocent

47

and very wise can know. In his waking months, from February to November, Achilles lived the life of Riley, and enjoyed every minute of it.

About the end of February, he would begin to thump and rattle around in the closet. When I opened the door he rowed himself out, moving ponderously as an alderman. After the long hibernation his leathery skin hung in folds, but was he bothered by his clownish appearance? Not he. Posturing and prancing, he did push-ups from the floor with sensuous delight. When I picked him up to scratch his neck or tickle him under the arms, he squirmed and wriggled with delight, and on his face appeared an expression that could only be called a leer.

His principal joy in the spring was food. He ate grass like a horse, tearing off beakfuls with a sidewise swinging motion, lifting his wrinkled neck and chewing with his eyes full of placid peace. In an afternoon he could mow ten square feet of grass. He drank water like a fussy hen, dipping his

nose and lifting his neck to let the water run down, leering meanwhile at onlookers. He loved raw peas, cabbage and string beans, which he ate with regular chopping strokes as if his jaws worked on springs. Three bites to a string bean, no more, no less. Strawberries put him in a frenzy of bliss. I cherish the memory of Achilles munching strawberries, with the juice running down his rhythmic jaws, his whole face beatific.

For three years we lived, two bachelors, in perfect harmony. And then my landlady, visiting one day at a friend's house, discovered another tortoise—a city gigolo whose shell was painted blue and gold, with a gilt border. She borrowed him, thinking Achilles would enjoy a little company, and brought him home. She knew not what she did. When she set the stranger on the rug in front of Achilles, the atmosphere was electric. My tortoise, a mousy friar beside this court gallant, hissed like a steam cock and ducked. So did the gilded one. Then both lay like two concrete pillboxes, immobile and suspicious. We watched and waited. After a while the visitor's head came out again; he uncurled his tail, did a push-up and stood on tiptoe hissing. Achilles hissed back. I wanted Achilles to annihilate the gigolo. I had seen him bounce trucks off his back. He was not going to be taken over by any town tortoise with painted toenails.

The visiting tortoise weaved sideward and back, still hissing. I looked at Achilles and was surprised to see that his face was anything but belligerent. He wore the same coy leer that he wore when I tickled him. Then, stepping high, the gilded one waltzed around Achilles, watching him all the time. Achilles rotated to watch the dance. His beaked face smiled. The truth struck both my landlady and me at the same time. Achilles, the philosophic bachelor, was a *lady* tortoise—and there was no doubt in the world that she was in love. My landlady, her mouth open and her face getting red, gave me the kind of a look that hangs on the air for ten minutes afterward. Then she hurriedly picked up the painted tortoise and fled.

Achilles was pitiful. For hours after the charmer had gone she wandered around the rug hissing questioningly. She was no longer philosopher: She was lorn female, and acted it. She could not sleep before this problem. She explored under the radiators, under the sofa. Then, returning to the middle of the rug where the miracle had happened, she lay down waiting for it to happen again. I took her out and staked her on the lawn, but she wouldn't eat. When I went out two hours later, the broken string lay on the lawn, but Achilles had disappeared. Whether she ever found her gallant I do not know. Somewhere, perhaps, she did. *Omnia vincit amor.*

The Four-Legged Curate of Williamstown

by HELEN HUSTED

WHEN THE Reverend Dr. A. Grant Noble accepted the double job of rector of St. John's Parish, Williamstown, Massachusetts, and chaplain of Williams College, he knew he would have a curate to help him, but he didn't know there would be an assistant curate too. And he particularly didn't know his assistant curate would be living under his kitchen porch. But that's what happened. The assistant was not shaped in the conventional mold; quite otherwise—"he" turned out to be a Shetland pony named Queenie.

Queenie had a confirmed weakness for men and cigarettes. She would roll her black eyes under her mop of wild mane, sidle up to a total stranger and with her long lips filch his cigarettes from his pocket before he knew what she was up to. Queenie was a gift horse but there was nothing wrong with her mouth! With it she could untie knots, eat ropes and straps, slide bolts, lift latches, manipulate gates. She was a present from a friend. Arriving unexpectedly with just a phone-call warning, she had been put in a little room beneath the kitchen porch. This was to be her home; or at least the place where she took her meals, for Queenie didn't like to stay home nights. The rector found this out many times, the most memorable of which was Easter Eve. He had a full day ahead, starting with a 7:30 a.m. service. He had looked forward to a good night's sleep. But at half past two the phone rang, and a voice said, "State trooper calling. Do you own a gray horse?"

"Why, no," answered the sleepy rector. Then remembering, "Why, yes. That is, we've got a pony for the children under the back porch."

"Well, someone has been trying to break in the back door of the Adams farm near South Williamstown," stated the trooper. "They couldn't see anything but a stray horse loose in the vegetable garden. Eating plenty. Can't catch it. Adams is awful mad. Could be it's your horse?"

Dr. Noble dressed hastily. Sure enough,

50

the room under the kitchen porch was empty. The stout tie rope had been chewed through. When the police car drew up, the rector piled in. He felt angry, yet outdid himself to be polite. The eight miles passed agreeably. The irate Adams, somewhat mollified by the arrival of the rector, was openly amused by his cheerful, frantic efforts to retrieve the pony. Adams reckoned he'd drive the family in to church in the morning to see how the rector looked by daylight.

During the long drive back at five miles an hour, with Queenie trotting docilely behind, the rector and the trooper talked. The rector listened to some knotty local problems, found out about trouble spots in the

county, discussed how he might help. This was just the first of many nocturnal talks Queenie arranged.

It was not long before Queenie also made her contribution to the work of the Sunday school. It happened this way. One morning the phone rang: "Mr. Noble, this is Mary Fox next door. I put my baby out in his carriage for a sunbath an hour ago. When I went out to get him, there was your pony licking him and she wouldn't let me come near the carriage. Your pony is wonderful, but when she won't let me near my own baby, things have gone too far."

The rector hurried over and led home the would-be nursemaid. But from then on Queenie was a favorite of all the children. She let them ride on her back at Sunday-school picnics. She pulled them on their sleds in winter. She drew them in her basket cart in the Memorial Day parade.

One night Queenie made campus history. Freshmen were being initiated at a secret fraternity meeting. All was mystery and solemnity until Queenie busted in. She'd seen the sacred mysteries, so there was nothing to do but make her a member too. Around midnight the rectory phone rang. A voice said, "Sir, your pony came to our initiation. Sorry we couldn't get her home before. Shall we bring her now?"

"No," said the rector. "I'll come over."

That night the rector got to know the fraternity boys without his collar on. After that they got the habit of dropping in to swap stories and make sure Queenie hadn't forgotten how to give the grip.

Then Queenie paid a call on the president of Williams College. The hospitable Dr. and Mrs. James Phinney Baxter III were happy when they heard footsteps on the front porch and a ring at the doorbell. Dr. Baxter hurried to throw open the door. A horse walked in! She stepped over to the table and helped herself to some of the presidential cigarettes. Pretty soon the rectory phone rang. A voice said, "Good evening, Mr. Baxter calling." "How do you do, sir," said Dr. Noble. "So kind of you to call." "Not at all," said President Baxter. "I hoped you might be able to drop over. Your Pegasus is in my parlor." That was how the president and the new rector became close friends.

It wasn't long before Queenie had introduced the rector to many people he might not otherwise have met. Women waking up at night to the sound of horse's hooves would think, "No, that's not the milk wagon. It's poor Dr. Noble bringing his pony home. He'll be tired tomorrow. I'll drop by to give him a hand—and to hear what that beast's been up to."

Queenie once attended a meeting of the Women's Auxiliary. The ladies were having coffee in the rectory living room after a meeting. Suddenly screams from the back of the house rent the air. The rector rushed for the kitchen, thinking the new hired girl had met with an accident. There by the stove stood Queenie, and on the table stood the maid. Queenie had broken out again, climbed the kitchen steps and opened the back door. There was no pushing her back down the steps. So with the best grace he could muster, the rector led the pony through the house and on the way introduced her to all the ladies.

Owing to Queenie's activities, parish calls were going fine. But lack of sleep was getting the rector down, and he winced at the sound of the telephone at night. So, after ten months of active service, the assistant curate was reluctantly retired to a distant farm. Queenie had had one of the shortest terms of service of any curate. But her work was done. As the rector put it, "She had broken down more barriers than the ones under the kitchen porch."

Amends to
the Camel

by RODNEY GILBERT

For MANY YEARS now I have never looked a camel in the eye without feeling under obligation to expiate in public print a crime that I once perpetrated when I said, as everyone else seems to have said before me, that the camel was an ill-tempered, evil-smelling, stupid anachronism. Recently I came upon an even more abusive attack upon the beast's character.

A big proportion of all that has been written about camels has been about the Arabian camel, the tall, one-humped beast. My particular friend is the two-humped, long-haired, short-legged Bactrian camel, bred and used throughout Mongolia, northern Tibet and Central Asia generally. No Occidental with any common sense ever gets into a situation where familiarity with the Bactrian camel is possible. I, however, used to enjoy notoriety in the Far East for getting into just the situations sensible persons kept out of. In the fall of 1918 I was commissioned to advance into western China and Turkestan, to explain World War I and victory to certain Muhammadan potentates. At the town of Ningsia my camel expert deserted me, and it became my duty to groom and feed my two querulously talkative ani-mals. I started off into the uninhabited Ala-Shan and the dreary desert beyond, sometimes leading my beasts, sometimes riding them, pitching my tent each morning in a gale with the thermometer 30 degrees below zero, collecting dry dung for my fire by the light of the morning star, cooking mutton stew and tea, packing and unpacking the patient but obviously lonely and bewildered camels.

Then I fell in with a string of a thousand camels and eighty men going my way and my troubles were over; but for the rest of the winter I kept on learning more and more about camels. I learned that the greatest obstacle to sympathetic understanding with the camel is his nose rope, made fast to a wooden pin through his nostrils. A heavy-handed person can give this rope a jerk that is extremely painful. The result is that when anyone approaches a camel with outstretched hand, he throws his head as high as he can, edges clumsily away and screams his protest. If you can take the leading rope without exciting any such demonstration, you may be sure you have won the camel's confidence. It requires infinite patience, but once your mount does have such confidence, he regards you as a friend and will even lower his head and gurgle affectionately as a hint that he would enjoy having his ears scratched.

Orientals almost never pet domestic animals. The camel driver takes excellent care of his beasts, but he has no desire for their affection and therefore does not get it. Consequently, the attentions that my two beasts bestowed on me never failed to astonish the men of the wilderness. If we met other caravans and camped with them, the strangers would invariably be told of my trick camels. I would be asked to walk off and call them, have them put their heads down to be scratched, talk to them and have them reply with unearthly squeaks, stroll about so that they would follow and frisk around me like a couple of puppies.

One was a female, and if I did not send her about her business, she would follow me into the heart of the camp, stand behind me and make little chirping noises above my head; and then, if I stood still, she would put her muzzle on my shoulder, close her eyes in contentment and drool green saliva down the front of my sheepskin coat. This was the final act in my performance, which never failed to elicit exclamations.

Once for six weeks I was separated from my two devoted beasts. When finally I entered the compound where they had been kept for me by a Chinese friend, they were on the farther side, eating from a pile of hay. They heard the squeak of the hinge, looked to see who had entered and then, with shrill cries of delight, came charging for me at a terrific pace. My Chinese friend was terrified and bolted. They brought up in front of me almost on their haunches, raising their heads high above mine, and spat their rank-smelling cuds into the air. It was a physically unpleasant yet gratifying demonstration, and brought me much ad-

vertising among the whole colony of animal dealers, who could not believe that a camel had any affection for anyone.

That camels can be not only affectionate but solicitous for a rider's welfare I learned on another occasion. Near the Tibetan frontier I had contracted flu, and although the attack did not last more than five days, I continued to have a fever for some time afterward. Deciding to work it off, I set out for the town of Dangar on the back of my young female camel. We had not done a mile before I was thoroughly tired and had developed a backache so severe that it was actually nauseating. I squirmed about, trying all sorts of positions, and my mount looked around frequently to see what was the matter. Finally, when I had fallen forward over the hump, she stopped and took a good look at me, made some sort of remark in her throat and very carefully sank to the ground.

It was as plain a suggestion to get off and rest as a human being could have made, and I took it. Now, being young, this animal was often foolish. She usually refused to kneel at all. When I wanted to mount her I always tried to have someone hold her head until I was firmly seated, because otherwise she would be up with a leap, and many a time she left me sprawling on the ground. On this occasion, however, she not only knelt but stayed down, inspecting me once in a while with her big, birdlike eyes. When I came to get painfully on again she turned her head and watched me, waiting until I was securely in my place, and then very slowly got up in the three successive upheavals customary with a camel under a heavy pack.

If she had done so with any speed I should not have had the strength to hold on. My young lady, however, managed the business as if she were a balancer with a bucket of water on her back which she was not to

spill. We went through this performance not once but a dozen times that day. I have told this story often, and have never failed to contrast it with the behavior of the noble horse, because a horse will always take advantage of a rider he thinks has anything the matter with him.

One of the most attractive features of camels is their conversational ability. They comment on everything that goes on around them, and they make a wider variety of noises than any other domesticated beast. They grumble when they are loaded and scream when they think they are about to suffer indignity. But, when you come to understand their language, you discover that they can ask very politely for their food, thank you when you have attended to their wants, express pleasure at seeing you and almost inquire into the state of your health.

I hope I have established that the camel has unsuspected charms. But one must sample them while muscles are resilient and circulation still so vigorous that one can freeze solid by night and thaw out by day for weeks on end. In other words, intimacy with the camel in the deserts of Asia must be a prerogative of youth. To those who enjoy mummifying desert heat and paralyzing desert cold, I recommend the much-abused camel as a gentle, loyal and affectionate friend.

The Exploits of Alice

by BRUCE HUTTON

ONE DAY IN 1912, when bullock teams were used for much of the rural hauling in Australia, a wagon piled high with heavy bales of wool bogged down while crossing a railroad track near Tenterfield, New South Wales. An express was due any minute. In a freight yard nearby, a sixty-six-year-old Indian elephant named Alice was unloading circus wagons from a string of flatcars. Attracted by the shouts of the bullock driver, Alice eyed the straining animals and then, without a word of command, lumbered over, braced her mighty forehead against the immobilized dray and effortlessly heaved it across the track. Moments later the express roared through. On another occasion, when a wheat wagon sank in sand near Berrigan, New South Wales, Alice stepped in after fourteen powerful horses had struggled in vain for half an hour. She pushed the wagon onto solid ground in thirty seconds. A weighbridge showed that she had eased thirty-three thousand pounds out of the unwilling sand.

Alice was the most remarkable animal I have ever known. But it was not only for her intelligence and her might that two generations of Australian circusgoers fondly remember her. Equally fascinating was her playful side. At the end of one of our per-formances in Melbourne, a shy little girl was holding behind her back a floral tribute which she was to present to one of the performers. Alice sidled up to her noiselessly, snatched the bouquet and put it to good use as a flyswatter.

Another day, when the Big Top had been erected in a West Australian park, Alice ambled over to watch two small boys on a seesaw. One of them vacated his seat; the other stayed put. Whereupon Alice placed one ponderous foot on the empty end of the board and bore it to the ground. Experimentally releasing the pressure, she watched the boy descend, then again gently depressed her end. For some minutes she continued this game, apparently enjoying it thoroughly, until she was recalled to her chores.

Wirths' Circus, one of the two oldest and largest in Australia, purchased Alice in 1899 from a circus in India. She was then fifty-three years old. She had had an elementary amount of ring training, and was reputed to have had some timber-working experience in Burma. She was not inordinately large: She weighed 8624 pounds and stood about eight feet six inches high. Even at fifty-three, she was still in her prime. The Wirths knew they had procured an unusual pachyderm; they just didn't know how unusual.

57

It was in 1902, after three years of "visual training" working alongside Gunny Sah, the chief loading elephant, that Alice took over as queen of the herd. Gunny Sah died, and it became Alice's job to head up the dangerous business of moving cages of wild animals up and down inclined skids between the ground and flatcars, of placing the cages so as to conserve every inch of space, of pushing or hauling the weighty circus wagons. This was steady work, for the railroad gauges in Australia's six states varied, and a circus was compelled to switch trains a number of times in making a circuit of the continent.

What made Alice unusual even among elephants was the way she used initiative to cope with emergencies. Once the front wheels of a heavily laden wagon that she was pushing ran off the edge of a flatcar. Half the vehicle hung perilously in midair. *Without direction,* Alice stepped to the ground and, with her trunk, lifted and jockeyed the wagon back to its proper position. I often saw Alice move a five-ton truck, laden with tents and other gear, from a flatcar to a platform alongside without guidance. First she lifted the front end diagonally onto the platform. Then she calmly trundled to the rear and repeated the performance. Quicker than a mobile crane could have done it, she had that lorry off the train and ready to be driven away.

Alice was not only unexcelled at her job—she knew it, too. And despite her amiable nature, she occasionally revealed a flash of professional jealousy. Once, at Port Fairy, Victoria, she had stopped work for breakfast when she heard the second loading elephant being ordered about by Charlie West, the circus's transport boss. She raced to the scene, butted her understudy away and did the job herself. Charlie claimed that Alice understood everything he said. During

lulls in her work she would regularly sidle up to him for a quiet "chat." Often when he was talking to somebody else, Alice would interrupt with her strange "prattling." "Shut up," West would say, "I'm not talking to you!" Alice would shut up and, what's more, wait until she was spoken to.

Alice's presence of mind saved the life of Eileen Wirth a number of years ago. Another elephant had knocked Eileen to the ground and would have trampled her to death had not Alice rushed over and butted the murderous elephant away. There was also the classic episode of about 1914, in Sydney, still recalled by circus folk. During the Grand Parade in the Big Top a tiny tot leaped out of the audience and raced into the path of the oncoming elephants. While women screamed, and others looked on horrified, Alice calmly lifted the child high in the air with her trunk and delivered her back into the outstretched arms of her anxious parents.

Birds and small animals seemed to arouse Alice's maternal instinct. Among the oddly assorted creatures she sheltered at various times were a lovebird, a cat, a three-legged steer and a flock of geese. None of these animals had any qualms about their safety while near their gargantuan protector; they seemingly reveled in the privilege.

Keeping Alice tethered was a major problem because of her love of mischief. No matter how the men schemed to confine her she frequently managed to undo her chains, as well as those of her closest friend, Doll. On a New Zealand tour she once loosened her own and Doll's shackles, and the ungainly pair shambled into a nearby brickyard. There they upset pile after pile of bricks and did considerable damage. The brickyard proprietor called his lawyer, and both rushed to the circus. When they got there, they demanded to inspect the elephant line. Alice and Doll were in their accustomed places, as innocent-looking as the rest.

In 1946, on Alice's hundredth birthday (the normal life-span of Indian elephants ranges from forty-five to sixty years), we staged a special party at an evening performance in Melbourne. It was decided that Alice must cut her own birthday cake and that Jessie, another member of the herd, would toast her in champagne. Fred Schafer, then in charge of the elephants, trained Alice for her task of pulling the cork by having her practice on a bottle with a carrot in the neck. The party was a spectacular success. When Alice was led to the five-foot-high cake to cut it with a large knife, she was extremely nervous. But she did the job as she had been taught, and also drew the cork from the champagne bottle without mishap.

In November 1953, when Wirths' was about to leave Melbourne for a New Zealand tour, it became evident that old age was getting the better of Alice. She was then one hundred and seven and had been with our circus for fifty-four years. So she was left behind for a rest at the Melbourne Zoo. Despite every care from the zoo, Alice fretted so much at being absent from her old friends that she became ill, and when the circus came back, she was in a pitiable condition.

I have often watched the return of animals to the circus after an illness, and the welcome accorded them by their comrades is a joy to behold. With Alice, it was a particularly moving experience. A trailer truck was sent to the zoo to collect her, and even before the other elephants could see her they picked up her scent and began trumpeting their welcome. Back in the herd, Alice immediately responded by fondly caressing the others with her trunk. Her listlessness fell away as if by magic; a sprightliness returned to her step. Alice never worked or performed again, however. The spirit was more than willing, but the failing body could not respond. For three years, until April 1956, Alice traveled as "guest of honor" with the circus. But during this period she lost more than half a ton in weight and had to be coaxed from place to place.

On the last day of the 1956 Easter season in Sydney, Alice ate her hay as usual. But at 6 p.m., when the circus was packing up to leave, she swayed on her feet while being coaxed to step into her truck. Plainly the effort was beyond her. Doll was brought alongside to help maintain her balance, but to no avail. Soon afterward, with legs crossed and looking as though her bones had turned to jelly, Alice collapsed completely. One of the country's ablest veterinarians was called, and a rapid inspection sufficed to tell him that the feeble old lady would never be able to rise again. He recommended that she be put out of her misery. With the Wirths' sorrowful concurrence, and as hardened circus men stood nearby weeping unashamedly, Alice was shot through the center of the forehead.

Alice's passing was reported in newspapers all across Australia. Hundreds of letters and telegrams of sympathy reached the circus. We had lost not only our most extraordinary but our most lovable performer.

The Company We Keep

by JOHN and JEAN GEORGE

EARLY ONE MORNING we were called to a Poughkeepsie, New York, police station near our home to claim our Canada goose and mallard duck.

The desk sergeant read us a memorandum: "Picked up at 3 a.m. walking down the middle of College Avenue making loud squawks and quacks." Then he added, seriously, "Looks like a clear-cut case of vagrancy and disturbing the peace."

"Not guilty," said John, equally serious. "They were just calling their mother."

"And where was their mother?"

"He was home in bed," John explained.

"HE! What do you mean *he?*"

"I mean that I am a mother goose!" John stated with some pride. "Nothing in this world would convince that gosling that I am not. You see, I helped her out of her eggshell. I was the first moving thing she saw, and to a hatching bird that is always 'mother.' Animal behaviorists call this 'imprinting.' Somewhere in her little mind is an impression of me, and she thinks she looks like that impression. She doesn't know she's a goose and wouldn't recognize a goose if she saw one. Her idea of a goose is me. The duck, on the other hand, thinks he is a goose; the goose was the first thing he responded to on hatching.

"Last night something awakened the gosling, and she needed to know whether to be frightened or to go back to sleep. So she went out to look for me, calling as she went. The duck went with her because he thinks that she is his mother, and since she was calling he thought he ought to call too."

"Well, now," said the officer, "I don't know of any law that states that a gosling can't look for its mother. Case dismissed."

John and the officer went out to get the accused. John called. The gosling cocked her head and came running. John got into the car, and the gosling followed and sat down beside him. The duck followed the gosling and sat down contentedly beside her. Order had been reestablished in the birds' mysterious world.

To become a mother goose gives one insight into the life of the gosling that cannot be gained by a thousand trips into the wilderness to study geese. We need such insight because we write and illustrate books about wild birds and mammals, so every time we start another animal biography we bring the principal characters into our home. This may seem a hectic way to get the animal point of view, but it is rewarding.

Jean learned what it would be like to see in the dark through the eyes of a guest in

61

our home—a fox named Fulva. Every night in the inky blackness of the yard, Jean and Fulva played with a tennis ball. It was a one-sided game. Jean could not see Fulva, much less the ball. A wet nose would touch her hand, and a ball would be pressed there. Jean would throw it. There would be only the sound of the ball bouncing on the earth. Soon the wet nose would touch her again, and the ball would be in her hand.

"To look and look and see only blackness," Jean recalls, "and to be aware that your fellow player sees not only you, but the ball, the insects and the stirring leaves makes you feel terribly limited."

Fulva, denned in our fireplace by day, became active, according to the inner timing of a fox, in the evenings. She would steal on absolutely silent feet about the house looking for Jean and, when she found her, would honor her with a fox's greeting of affection. First she would biff her with her delicate paws, hoping that Jean would biff back, like a healthy fox pup. After a few exchanges she would press her nose into Jean's hair and, using her sharp fox teeth, rake out all the bobby pins, combs or ribbons. We think that to Fulva they were brambles and burrs, intolerable objects from a fox's point of view. This ceremony over, she would tug at

Jean's skirt and lead her into the yard so they could play.

Fulva never got her sexes mixed as the goose did, and said as much by biting all men—including John—and playing with all women. John was unhappy in his role as enemy of a fox and did not cheer up until spring, when Falco, the male sparrow hawk, fell in love with him.

The hawk courted John according to the rules of the bird world. Having staked off the kitchen, where his nest box was nailed above the door, he defended his home against all intruders, particularly against Jean. If she came near the door Falco would divebomb her with outstretched talons. Consequently John became cook, and the strange couple had the kitchen to themselves. While the hamburgers sizzled, Falco went through his courtship dance, fanning his wings, bowing, bobbing his head and emitting soft throaty sounds. John would wave his hands in response and talk to him. Falco, thrilled by these attentions, would sail around the kitchen flashing his wings and calling. This went on for a month. Then a pet crow arrived in our house and Falco abandoned John and flew off into the wilderness.

The crow was named "New York" by our young son, Craig, because he was "as noisy as New York City." The pet grew and prospered like his namesake and all but ran the house. In the morning he flew in the window, perched on Jean's head and announced the day. Then he would help himself to any food that we didn't throw ourselves on to protect. He considered the children's toys his natural inheritance. One day Twig, our daughter, came crying to us saying she wasn't going to play with that crow any more—he had taken the pieces of her puzzle and hidden them in the apple tree.

In the autumn New York walked the children to the school-bus stop. It would have been easier for him to fly, but a crow is a highly social bird and motivated by what the gang is doing. The only gang he knew walked. So he walked—down the road in front of Twig and Craig, strutting and tossing pebbles in the air. Occasionally he startled a neighbor with a gravelly "hello," the only word he mastered. When the school bus picked up the children he would fly home and report a job well done to Jean, who was by then busy at the dishpan. If he attempted to help with this chore she would gather him up—feathers, feet and squawk—and put him out the door. Then she would count the silver.

Later that autumn the wild crows discovered New York, and would awaken the neighborhood at five o'clock, cawing at him. One November morning he flew off with them and never came back.

All our wild guests are free to come and go, and by picking their own moments of departure they have, we feel, a better chance of survival. They usually leave in the spring or fall—times when intense biological drives eclipse their memories of man, or guide them in spite of their poor training.

We acquire our guests while they are quite young, when they become devoted to whoever is caring for them. After they can eat on their own, and are tame and fearless, we generally permit them to go free, hoping that they are attached to us and will stay around the yard and house. The most valuable animals are those that visit the woods and permit us to follow them to see what they do in a natural environment. We have followed raccoons on fishing trips (the big ones get away from them, too). We have swum underwater with mink—they are not all blood and fury, they play with pretty stones at the bottom of the streams.

Some animals we just can't get rid of. We released a raccoon in the woods five times, only to come home and find him in the sugar can or happily peeling wallpaper off the walls. We were growing desperate, when one February night a female raccoon dropped by and we never saw the young fellow again.

We have learned to work with the nature of the animals. Once a raccoon made off with our car keys and carried them up in a sixty-foot tree. John started to put on his climbing spurs, but then remembered that an outstanding characteristic of raccoons is that they like to carry food and trinkets to water and swish them around in it. So Jean put the dishpan outdoors on a table and started splashing the water. Down the tree loped the bandit with the keys in his teeth. He bounced onto the table and dunked them in the water. Since that day we have saved a great deal of effort by splashing in dishwater when a raccoon—of which we have had seventeen—trundled off with something we needed.

We have been many things to many animals, but to all raccoons we have been simply benefactors. Almost any raccoon that gets a taste of civilization seems to feel that man was created for one thing—to indulge raccoons in the material comforts of life. A bed, for instance. We came home late one night to find three of our masked pets with their heads on our pillows, the covers bunched up over them, blissfully sleeping amid the ruins of crackers and prunes.

More raccoons went into the cage for unruly guests than any other animal. There were days when they were caged continuously, especially during the period in which we had Meph, a fully equipped skunk, living with us. The raccoons would tease Meph until he raised his tail to spray—and then would utterly frustrate him by grabbing his tail and pulling it down. This we considered cause to lock them up.

We have been able to tame most of the animals and birds we have had. The others we handle by capitalizing on their wildness. We had a weasel that would chase John every evening in the hope of biting him. By running fast, John could lead the weasel where he pleased. Once a motorist saw them sprinting around the yard and called out cheerfully, "That's the tamest weasel I've ever seen. He follows you like a dog!"

Animals have found desirable retreats in our home for mysterious reasons. A little screech owl would wait patiently on the turntable of an old windup Victrola for someone to give it a crank and turn it on, sending him spinning. We still don't know what kind of owl joy this brought to him, but he stayed with us for a year persisting in this pleasure. One bird we kept for only a short time was a turkey vulture. We turned him free because we were about to lose two very good human friends. They insisted that he depressed them sitting on the open door staring at them.

One does not live closely with animals without understanding some of the laws and motivations of the wild. One of the most interesting laws we have observed is the finality of the departure of the young from their parents. One October afternoon the fox goes under the fence as if called by an irresistible force, and we know she will not be back. The owl circles the lawn, climbs high into a tree, swirls his head and looks fiercely at the horizon. He flies along the path his eyes picked, in a determined, steady flight, and we know he is gone.

Encumbered by a human point of view, we look upon these departures with some sadness. There will be no visits home. This is it. But we know, too, that these departures are the seeds of the future—that the wilderness will again burst with young, come another spring.

The Dog
That Bit People

Probably no one man should have as many dogs in his life as I have had, but there was more pleasure than distress in them for me except in the case of an Airedale named Muggs. He gave me more trouble than all the other fifty-five put together.

He really wasn't my dog, as a matter of fact: I came home from a vacation one summer to find that my brother Roy had bought him while I was away. A big, burly, choleric dog, he always acted as if he thought I wasn't one of the family. There was a slight advantage in being one of the family, for he didn't bite the family as often as he bit strangers. We used to take turns feeding him to keep on his good side, but that didn't always work.

In the years that we had him he bit everybody but Mother, and he made a pass at her once but missed. Angered one day because Muggs refused to chase rats in the pantry, Mother slapped him and he slashed at her, but didn't make it. He was sorry immediately, Mother said. He was always sorry, she said, after he bit someone, but we could not understand how she figured this out. He didn't act sorry.

Mother used to send a box of candy every Christmas to the people the Airedale bit. The list finally contained forty or more names. Nobody could understand why we didn't get rid of the dog. I think that one or two people tried to poison Muggs—he acted poisoned once in a while—and old Major Moberly fired at him once with his service revolver near the Seneca Hotel on East Broad Street—but Muggs lived to be almost eleven years old and even when he could hardly get around he bit a congressman who had called to see my father on business.

My mother had never liked the congressman—she said the signs of his horoscope showed he couldn't be trusted—but she sent him a box of candy that Christmas. He sent it right back, probably because he suspected it was trick candy. Mother persuaded herself it was all for the best even though Father lost an important business connection because of it.

"I wouldn't be associated with such a man," Mother said. "Muggs could read him like a book."

Muggs never bit anyone more than once at a time. Mother always mentioned that as an argument in his favor; she said he had a quick temper but that he didn't hold a

65

grudge. She was forever defending him. I think she liked him because he wasn't well. "He's not strong," she would say, pityingly, but that was inaccurate; he may not have been well but he was terribly strong.

One time Mother went to call on a woman mental healer who lectured on the subject of "Harmonious Vibrations." She wanted to find out if it was possible to get harmonious vibrations into a dog.

"He's a large, tan-colored Airedale," Mother explained.

The woman said that she had never treated a dog, but she advised my mother to hold the thought that he did not bite and would not bite. Mother was holding the thought the very next morning when Muggs got the iceman, but she blamed that on the iceman. "If you didn't think he would bite you, he wouldn't," Mother told him.

He stomped out of the house in a terrible jangle of vibrations.

One morning when Muggs bit me slightly, more or less in passing, I reached down and grabbed his short, stumpy tail and hoisted him into the air. It was a foolhardy thing to do. As long as I held the dog off the floor by his tail he couldn't get at me, but he twisted and jerked so, snarling all the time, that I realized I couldn't hold him that way very long. I carried him to the kitchen and flung him onto the floor and shut the door on him just as he crashed against it. But I forgot about the back stairs. Muggs went up the back stairs and down the front stairs and had me cornered in the living room. I managed to get up onto the mantelpiece above the fireplace, but it gave way and came down with a tremendous crash, throwing a large marble clock, several vases and myself heavily to the floor.

Muggs was so alarmed by the racket that when I picked myself up he had disappeared. We could not find him anywhere, although we whistled and shouted, until old Mrs. Detweiler called after dinner that night. Muggs had bitten her once, in the leg, and she came into the living room only after we assured her that Muggs had run away. She had just seated herself when, with a great growling and scratching of claws, Muggs emerged from under a davenport where he had been quietly hiding all the time, and bit her again. Mother examined the bite and put arnica on it and told Mrs. Detweiler that it was only a bruise. "He just bumped you," she said. But Mrs. Detweiler left the house in a nasty state of mind.

Lots of people reported our Airedale to the police, but my father held a municipal office at the time and was on friendly terms with the force. The cops suggested that it might be a good idea to tie the dog up, but Mother said that it mortified him to be tied up and that he wouldn't eat.

In his last year Muggs used to spend practically all his time outdoors. He didn't like to stay in the house for some reason or other—perhaps it held too many unpleasant memories for him. Anyway, it was hard to get him to come in, and as a result the garbageman, the iceman and the laundryman would not come near the house. We had to haul the garbage to the corner, take the laundry out and bring it back, and meet the iceman a block from home.

After this had gone on for some time we hit on an ingenious arrangement for getting the dog in the house so that we could lock him up while the gas meter was read, and so on. Muggs was afraid of only one thing, an electric storm. Thunder and lightning frightened him out of his senses (I think he thought a storm had broken the day the mantlepiece fell). He would rush into the house and hide under a bed or in a clothes closet. So we fixed up a thunder machine out of a long, narrow piece of sheet iron with a wooden handle on one end. Mother would shake this vigorously when she wanted to get Muggs into the house. It made an excellent imitation of thunder, but I suppose it was the most roundabout system for running a household ever devised. It took a lot out of Mother.

A few months before Muggs died, he got to "seeing things." He would rise slowly from the floor, growling low, and stalk, stiff-legged and menacing, toward nothing at all. Sometimes the Thing would be just a little to the right or left of a visitor. Once a Fuller Brush salesman got hysterics. Muggs came wandering into the room like Hamlet following his father's ghost. His eyes were fixed on a spot just to the left of the Fuller Brush man, who stood it until Muggs was about three slow, creeping paces from him. Then he shouted. Muggs wavered on past him into the hallway, grumbling to himself, but Mother had to throw a pan of cold water on the Fuller man before he would stop shouting.

Muggs died quite suddenly one night. Mother wanted to bury him in the family lot under a marble stone with some such inscription as "Flights of angels sing thee to thy rest," but we persuaded her it was against the law. In the end we just put up a smooth board above his grave along a lonely road. On the board I wrote, with an indelible pencil, "Cave Canem." Mother was quite pleased with the simple classic dignity of the old Latin epitaph.

The White Lady

Condensed from the book

by LEONARD DUBKIN

ONE JUNE EVENING, while idly exploring a clump of trees in a weed-grown Chicago lot, I made an exciting discovery. Under one of the trees was a huge dome-shaped structure. All sorts of vines had twined around the lower branches, forming an almost impenetrable mass of foliage that curved upward from the ground like an igloo, to a height of eighteen or twenty feet. It was the kind of thing one might find in a tropical forest, but here in the city, with a factory nearby and with cars whizzing past, it was strange indeed. Inside, this unusual grotto was even stranger. It was musky-smelling and dimly lit, like a room with the shades drawn. And hanging head downward everywhere from the leafy, sloping roof were clusters of sleeping bats—more than two hundred of them, I estimated.

That summer and fall I often returned to watch this bat colony. My entrance into the grotto, through the inconspicuous opening I had made, always excited the bats at first. But if I remained quiet they soon ignored me. About seven in the evening they would start to stretch and squeak. Soon they were whirling around the tree trunk in a mass of wings. Then, as if at a signal, the whole flock, leaving their young behind, would swarm out of the foot-and-a-half opening

at the top like a puff of smoke. For a couple of hours the air overhead would be filled with bats hunting insects. Then they would disappear, not to return until dawn. The homecoming at dawn was a bedlam of squeaking, darting figures; it was usually an hour before all the mothers had identified their young and were again hanging with them from the roof, composed for sleep.

In mid-October that year the bats all left for some unknown place of hibernation. But early next May the first of them came back. A week later all seemed to have returned. They were restless and excitable—the young were being born. On May 28 I found a bat hanging from a limb head upward instead of the usual downward position. She was clutching the vegetation above with her thumbs (located on the wingtips) and her feet clawed the air. She made no sound, but her lips were bared and her teeth moved as if she were gritting them. Suddenly she bent her feet up under her body so that the tail membrane which was stretched between them curled under her like a pocket. Soon a tiny, mouselike creature, its wings crumpled around its head, emerged and lay motionless in the pocket. The mother licked it, turning it over and over, until it emitted a barely audible squeak. It twisted

about in its cradle, brought one wing down to its side, then the other, and began crawling shakily upward toward its mother's stomach. The mother bit through the umbilical cord, picked the baby up by the back of the neck—exactly like a cat picking up her kitten—and placed it near one of her breasts. While it was suckling, the placenta emerged, then the mother grasped the roof with her feet, and, hanging head downward now, wrapped one wing around her baby. The whole thing had taken just four minutes.

So engrossed was I in the birth that I had hardly noticed that this baby bat was completely white. But now I realized that I had watched the birth of an albino bat—a creature very seldom found. This summer, instead of observing the colony as a group, I would be able to distinguish this one bat from the others and watch its individual development. When the baby white bat was only a day old, it was already hanging beside its mother. Among the others it was as conspicuous as a bright star in a dark sky. That same day I edged forward in the grotto and closed my hand around it. Then, with the mother and a few other bats flying frenziedly around my head, I sat down to examine my rare discovery. Her eyes were still closed, and she wobbled as she crawled across my palm, her folded wings trailing like silken garments at her sides. She sniffed as she went, and when she came to the end of my little finger she clamped her feet on it, swung herself over the edge and hung motionless. "White lady," I whispered, "you are a rare thing." From that moment she was always the white lady to me.

Just then there was a flutter of dark wings under my hand; in a flash the baby bat was snatched away by her mother. The action was so instantaneous that it appeared she had plucked off her baby in full flight. Yet there had been no pull on my finger. The mother had swiftly spread her tail membrane as the baby let go of my finger and grasped her fur, and off they sailed together. Now, with the white lady to guide me, I discovered that the bats had a strongly developed, proprietary sense of position on the roof. Each day the white lady and her mother hung in a particular spot, part of a compact cluster of twenty-six bats, each with its own place in the group. And if a bat hung itself up in any group but its own, the others all turned on it and squeaked menacingly.

Until she was five days old the white lady clung to her mother when she flew abroad at night. But after the fifth day, when the white lady's eyes opened, she was left in the grotto—possibly because she could now hide from danger. The first few nights the white lady hung for an hour or so after her mother left. Soon, however, she began to spend her time with one or two other young bats—scrambling about among the vines, chasing or being chased with playful biting and squeaking. Later, I often saw her among a group of forty or more, all squeaking, biting, crawling over and under each other.

I began taking the white lady home with me in a cigar box with air holes in the top. Transferred to the canary cage I had fixed up with screen wire around it, she would at first crawl about on the bottom, sniffing at the screen, then climb up on a perch and hang downward for about half an hour. She did not sleep, and her eyes followed my every movement. Later she would embark on an exploratory tour, sniffing and trying to squeeze through every slight opening. Often I'd find the cage empty in the morning, although she was almost full grown now and there seemed no opening large enough. It was sometimes a problem to find her—especially if she was hanging on white kitchen curtains, or from a white wall fixture.

I always took the white lady back to the

grotto in the morning on my way to work. As soon as the box was open she would sniff the air, then utter a faint, nearly inaudible squeak. Instantly the mother would leave her perch, swoop down and snatch up her daughter in one of those instantaneous pickups which always left me feeling I had witnessed magic. When she was twenty-three days old the white lady flew for the first time. I had intended to take her home with me that evening, but when I reached to pick her up she launched herself out into the grotto, her white wings flashing around and around the trunk. While I watched—for almost two hours—she launched herself again and again, trying her new-found skill. Twice her wings brushed against my face, as though to be sure I was paying attention, like a child who cries, "Look at me, look what I can do." I did not take her with me that evening—not on this, her first night of flight.

The next evening I came to the grotto before the adults had gone out. There, whirling around with the rest, was the white lady. I knew that now, for the first time, she would be going out to hunt with the others. So I went outside to await their exit. There was the usual black, smokelike eruption as the bats left the grotto. Gradually the mass resolved into myriad pairs of beating wings, and soon above me I saw the white lady. She was zooming, diving and zigzagging as skillfully as the others, even though this was her first time aloft on her own wings!

This was not surprising, though. These wings, which were evolved by primordial bats, are still the most efficient on earth, bird wings included. The only control a bird has over its wing feathers is the ability to turn them slightly and to spread groups of them more or less. A bird's wing in flight is almost as rigid as that of an airplane with its ailerons. But the wing of a bat is skin spread along its arm and between its fingers. As easily as a man can bend his fingers a bat can flap the whole wing or any part of it, can change lift, pitch or angle of any part.

Tonight I kept my eyes on the white lady. She was graceful, airy, insubstantial. As the sun sank, the whiteness of her body changed to rosy pink, and from her wings there flashed, as she tilted them, a shaft of orange light reflected from the sun. Then suddenly the air was empty, as though a magician had waved his wand. From that day on I went to the grotto every evening. If the bats were outside when I walked across the field, the white lady would welcome me by diving toward me and flashing her wings near my face as she skimmed by. (None of the other bats ever took such liberties.)

One evening as I was examining a disabled grasshopper on the palm of my open hand, there was a sudden blur of white wings and the grasshopper disappeared. The white lady had taken it from my hand, just as her mother had snatched her from me when she was a baby. I found another insect—a brown beetle—and placed it on my palm. Almost immediately the white lady swooped like a dive bomber; the beetle, too, was gone. I fed her four more insects in this manner, the last one a tiny ladybird beetle. In the darkness I could not see the insect as it crawled over my hand, but, from twenty feet above, the white lady swooped down and snatched it without touching my hand.

One evening I went to the grotto early, caught the white lady in a net and released her at home to photograph her. I had adjusted the camera and was waiting for her to come within range when, to my horror, she flew directly toward the revolving blades of an electric fan I had neglected to turn off. Powerless to do anything, I stood there, convinced that she was flying to her death. But she was not even touched by the blades. She flew into the fan and came out the other

71

side as easily as a child jumping rope. Flying to her death, indeed—she had known exactly what she was doing! After that first dash into the fan, she did it again and again, apparently glorying in her ability to fly through the whirling blades. I was tempted to try an experiment: I turned the fan from its low speed—800 revolutions per minute —to a higher speed—1200. She dashed toward it as before, but this time she did not go through. She zoomed up over the top.

Much as I had watched the bats, I had never before recognized any manifestations of "radar" which enables bats to fly in darkness and to avoid obstacles. Later I found that two Harvard professors (Robert Galambos and Donald Redfield Griffin) had proved that bats in flight broadcast sounds inaudible to the human ear, and guide themselves by the echoes returned. When a bat's mouth was stopped up it bumped repeatedly into wires strung across the room. The same thing happened when its ears were plugged and it could not receive the reflected signals. But whether its eyes were open or sealed shut made no appreciable difference.

This chance experiment with the fan emboldened me to try another that same evening. I decided to see if the white lady could find her way back to the grotto—five miles from our home. With some misgivings I opened the window and watched the white flash as she darted away. But the next morning I found her hanging from her usual place on the grotto roof. How much farther could I take her? One evening toward the end of August I decided to try another experiment. I waited until the bats were circling the tree trunk just before leaving, then caught the white lady in my net and drove fifteen miles through crowded traffic to Jackson Park on the South Side, where I released her. As I watched her fly off I was filled with remorse: She was headed in the wrong direction. In a minute or two she would be over the lake, where she would probably fly until she became exhausted. What a fool I was to have taken her so far. Nonetheless, I decided to return to the grotto and wait, all night if necessary, to see if—through some miracle—she might return. When I arrived there by the quickest possible route, I found the white lady out hunting insects, none the worse for her experience.

Toward the end of September I had to drive to Milwaukee and I took the white lady along. Just as I started back I released her and then I drove directly to the grotto. There she was in her usual place. She had flown ninety miles over unfamiliar territory in less than two and a half hours.

From this time on, through the early fall, the bats became more and more lethargic. They slept more soundly, and many did not leave the grotto at night but continued hanging from the roof in deep sleep. One day about the middle of October I found the grotto deserted.

The next spring, on the first Sunday in May, with the warmth-laden breeze blowing a hint of the summer to come, I drove out to see if the bats had returned. But as I approached the place my heart sank. Where there had been a field with a little clump of trees, there was only a muddy plain. Where the grotto had been, there now stood a steam shovel, its great open jaws resting on the earth. Now I would never know what happened to the white lady.

But at least I had learned that bats are playful and friendly, not the malicious, spiteful little animals most people believe. And I had seen the birth of the white lady, watched her grow and witnessed her first flight. It was as though I alone had been present at the production of a work of art, watching it grow from an insignificant beginning to a thing of beauty.

A Bird
Who Made Good

Condensed from the book

by ELSWYTH THANE

AT FIRST HE didn't even have a name. He was as unwelcome as that. For weeks after I had run out into a driving rain to rescue the little ball of wet feathers making feeble, foot-high flops across our Vermont lawn, he was known simply as "the bird." He was going to be a nuisance, and we didn't want to bother with him. He was sure to mess up the house, and in the fall we couldn't possibly take him to our New York apartment. When the weather cleared, if he lived that long, he'd just have to look after himself outdoors.

Meanwhile we were stuck with him, and we particularly resented the time it took to feed him. His bread, soaked in milk, and hard-boiled egg yolk had to be pushed down his throat with forceps, and his orange juice had to be poured in with a medicine dropper. If he wasn't fed often enough, or if he woke in the morning before we did, he yelled till somebody came. His voice was high, sweet, tireless—and it carried well.

We got awfully sick of him, and he went right on living and loving it. He wasn't afraid of us, he liked his food and his bed (a cracker box lined with Kleenex), and he liked being in a warm house away from the rain. He was to the manor born, and nothing could upset his dignity.

The wide yellow gapes at the sides of his bill became less noticeable, the frowsy bits of baby down were gradually replaced by feathers, and the two horns of fluff on his head developed into a crest. Resignedly— since we might as well do it right—we read up on his kind, having deduced by the pattern of his brown feathers, his stout beak and scruffy crest, and by the presence of a male purple finch in our cherry hedge, that that was his kind. Luckily, purple finches are largely vegetarians and thrive on the same kind of food that canaries eat. If he had required insects we might not have raised him at all. He soon learned to pick at canary seeds for himself, and to drink water from a glass ashtray.

He enjoyed everything that went on, especially teatime around the fire, for he loved people. He "listened" attentively to the conversation from a nearby chair back or lampshade, definitely one of the party. And he loved to ride on people's shoulders, or to sit in the window and watch for visitors. Even though noisy car motors frightened him at first, it wasn't long until he'd fly to the window every time he heard a car coming up the road. He loved music on the radio, too, and he even loved the typewriter.

The first time he heard its intermittent clatter he was somewhat startled. For about an hour he peered from his perch on a branch in the window. (These branches, designed to keep him off the furniture, had been installed at various strategic points all over the house.) When he finally decided the machine wasn't coming after him, he flew down onto the table and queried, "Che-wee?" The typewriter went right on making a noise, so during its next pause he flew to the ribbon box, experimentally. But when I struck a key he hopped back to the table. When the carriage was still again he lighted on the lever that turned the roller. I struck a key. He stayed. I hit another and he couldn't take it. But he learned. Soon he could ride the typewriter carriage, his toes wrapped tight, his expression grim and determined, with the same kind of fearful joy some people get out of a roller coaster. When I wrote letters with a pen, he chased the point as it traveled across the paper, trying to catch it in his beak. All this was inconvenient for me, of course, but if there was anything in it for him, who was I to complain?

Oh, yes, he had won. All the way along, he had won. His name was Che-Wee, and he recognized the sound of it and would fly from the next room—sometimes—if called.

Perhaps it was his self-possession that finally broke us down. He never fluttered, never panicked at an unexpected movement. He would always step up obligingly on any forefinger that gently nudged his tummy. He never regarded himself as a stranger. We were his family, and this was his home.

Or perhaps it was his curiosity that got us. Anybody busy doing something was irresistible to him. Tying a parcel or a shoe-

lace, snipping a paragraph from a newspaper, sewing—it was all a game invented for his entertainment. Even driving a nail didn't scare him. A hammer job sometimes meant that a fresh branch was being tacked up. He would rush to sit on it while the hammer was still hitting the tacks.

He knew what he wanted, too. We noticed if he took something from our fingers—such as a raspberry—which was too big for one bite, he'd carry it to his ashtray and finish it there. So we experimented and discovered that he preferred the seeds, which we had kept sprinkled in some gravel on the windowsill, in a dish instead. Loose food was for wild birds; he had had advantages, he knew how to behave! So we bought him more ashtrays.

Where he would sleep after he outgrew his baby bed was something he solved for himself, too. After trying various possibilities, he chose a clothes hook in a big closet, where he could lean against the comforting wall, one foot cuddled into his feathers and his head tucked under his wing. The closet was warm and we closed the door on him each evening and let him have it.

He asked for a bath long before we thought he was old enough to know about such things. As soon as he dispensed with the medicine dropper and learned to drink by himself, he began to make bath motions, throwing drops of water over himself. Astonished, I set out a small dish of water, and he hopped to its edge at once with an it's-about-time expression, and plopped in and began to splash with his wings, his crest sticking straight up. Che-Wee's crest was like a dog's tail, it meant everything—but laughter much more than anger. He roared with laughter in that first bath, as he did ever after when he bathed.

Unlike a dog, Che-Wee seemed to enjoy being laughed at. It even seemed sometimes that he clowned deliberately. One evening he played for some time with a dead leaf, tossing it over his head and flourishing it like a signal flag, while a roomful of people applauded and giggled. The next day he found the dead leaf where he had left it, and—this was good for a laugh last night— he went into the act again, like the little ham he was, though there was no one but me to be entertained.

Flower-fixing time was a lark for him. When I laid an armload of blossoms on the table, he was pecking at them in no time— wherever a drop of sweet could be found. No vase arrangement, however inspired it might be, lasted long.

He wasn't making the mess of the house we had expected, though. Seed eaters are clean and odorless, and the spots he left were small and dry and usually brushed off

with little damage. And although I hadn't set out to housebreak him, I gradually realized that my natural reaction to brush him off and scold if he made spots had its effect. More than once he flew away from my shoulder or hand—just in time. Then I really went at it, so that by the age of eighteen months he was pretty well shoulder-desk-and-manuscript-broken.

He seemed to know, and even anticipate, the family's daily routine. He was always on hand before breakfast to see the oranges cut and get his vitamins. He supervised the dishwashing from a towel rack over the sink. When meal preparations began, he perched on the back of a chair even before the table was laid, alert for snacks.

He had a sense of responsibility for us, too. If somebody lay down for a doze he perched on the sofa or even on the sleeper's shoulder, very still, often with one foot tucked under him in his own most relaxed state—but without closing his eyes, as though he mounted guard. And when you roused he met your gaze companionably.

As that summer ended we realized it was impossible to turn Che-Wee out. So we said we'd put him in the birdhouse at the Zoological Park when we went to New York for the winter.

But by then I had begun to weaken; it seemed like putting a child into an orphan asylum. The master of the house said with noticeable resignation that he supposed we could get an exhibition cage, and I could keep him in the apartment.

Some people questioned our right to keep a "wild" bird in the house. But I haven't much doubt that it would have been kinder to chloroform Che-Wee than to leave him to make his own way in the bird world. Besides, he showed no knowledge of missing the society of his peers.

For example, there was the time he encountered his first bird—one of a nestful of baby field sparrows we found. I brought the strongest and noisiest into the house and held it out to Che-Wee. He watched its approach nervously, and then flew away into the next room and stayed there. Really, the thing had *feathers!* Surely he wasn't required to make friends with objects like that? So it would seem that Che-Wee had forgotten he was a bird. He thought he was people!

One dim little instinct did linger and I confess it made my heart ache. He collected things to build a nest with. Bits of stick and straw were carried around, rather aimlessly, then lost track of. Thread or string was busily gathered up, loop on expert loop across his bill, till the last dragging end was clear of his feet—and then there was a puzzled sort of pause—let's see, now, what was I going to do with this?—oh, well—and the treasure was abandoned.

Che-Wee's affectionate, humorous and unconsciously pathetic presence about the house caught us all by the heart. His dignity, his insouciance, his busy flights, his inquiring late arrivals into a conversation, with a what-are-we-talking-about-now effect—above all, his touching confidence in our wisdom and good intentions—there was no possible answer to him but a foolish devotion on our part which was way beyond his size.

The Farm Horse
That Became
a Champion

by PHILIP B. KUNHARDT

IF YOU HAD BEEN one of the thirteen thousand spectators at the National Horse Show in New York's Madison Square Garden on November 7, 1959, you would have experienced an unexpectedly moving moment. In the middle of the evening the arena was cleared, the lights were dimmed and the band struck up a triumphal march. All eyes followed a spotlight toward the entrance gate at the west end of the ring. There a big gray horse—obviously not a Thoroughbred—appeared, preceded by five small children. As a blond young man and his wife led the horse to the center of the huge arena, the audience rose and began clapping. In a moment the applause was deafening. The young couple and their children beamed and bowed their thanks, the horse stomped his feet and the thunderous clapping went on and on.

The horse was Snow Man, and he was being declared the Professional Horsemen's Association champion in open jumping—one of the highest honors the horse-show

world has to bestow. That he and his owners, the handsome de Leyer family, were being so wildly cheered was enough to make even the coldest cynic believe in fairy tales. For, less than four years before, Snow Man had been on his way to the slaughterhouse, a tired farm horse that nobody seemed to want or care about. Fortunately, somebody did care—and this is the story of that caring.

One wintry Monday in February 1956, twenty-eight-year-old Harry de Leyer set out from his small riding stable at St. James, Long Island, for the weekly horse auction in New Holland, Pennsylvania. Harry, who had been brought up on a farm in the Netherlands, had always loved horses. In 1950 he married his childhood sweetheart, Joanna Vermeltfoort, and came to the United States. With only a smattering of English and $160 in capital, Harry and Joanna first tried tobacco farming in North Carolina, then worked on a horse farm in Pennsylvania. Soon the two young Dutch immigrants had a few horses of their own, and within five

77

years Harry was offered the job of riding master at the Knox School for Girls on Long Island. Now the father of three children, he was interested, of course, in doing anything he could to build security for his family.

When Harry headed for the Pennsylvania horse auction that February day, he was aiming to add to his stable for the uses of the school. He arrived late, however; most of the horses had been sold. Wandering outside, he saw several sorry-looking animals being loaded into a butcher's van. These were the "killers"—worn-out workhorses that nobody wanted, except the meat dealer. The sight made Harry sad. He felt pity for any horse, however useless, that could not live out his last years in a green pasture. Suddenly Harry spotted a big gray gelding plodding up the ramp. The horse was chunky, but lighter than the others, and there was a spirited pitch to his ears, a brightness in his eyes. Unaccountably, on instinct alone, de Leyer called to the loader to bring the horse back down.

"You crazy?" said the meat dealer. "He's just an old farm horse."

Probably, Harry thought. The animal's ribs showed, his coat was matted with dirt and manure, there were sores on his legs. Still, there was something about him. . . .

"How much do you want for him?" de Leyer asked.

That's how it all started. Harry de Leyer redeemed an old plug for eighty dollars. The whole de Leyer family was out to greet the horse next day. Down the ramp of the van he came, stumbling over his big feet. He looked slowly about, blinking in the bright winter sun. Then, ankle-deep in snow, covered with shaggy white hair, he stood as still as a statue. One of the children said, "He looks like a snow man." Hence—his name.

They all set about turning Snow Man into a horse again. First they clipped him lightly, and then they washed him—three times. In a while the horseshoer came. Finally, cleaned and curried and shod, Snow Man was ready for his first training session as a riding horse. Harry laid a dozen thick wooden poles on the ground, spacing them a few feet apart. To walk across the network of poles a horse had to lift his feet high and space his steps. When Snow Man tried it, poles flew every which way, and he stumbled and wove.

But Snow Man learned fast. By spring he was carrying the novice riders at Knox, and some of the girls even began asking for him in preference to the better-looking horses.

When school closed that summer, Harry de Leyer made what might have been the biggest mistake of his life: He sold Snow Man to a neighborhood doctor for double his money, with the understanding that the doctor would not sell Snow Man, except back to him. After all, Harry told himself, he *was* in the horse business. Now Snow Man began showing a side that hadn't previously come to light. He insisted on jumping the doctor's fences, no matter how high they were raised, and coming back to the de Leyer home—cross-country over fields and lawns, through backyards and gardens. Irate citizens called the police. The doctor was glad to let de Leyer have Snow Man back.

The feeling was mutual. For in some strange way de Leyer had come to believe that he and Snow Man shared a common destiny. Solemnly he promised himself never again to part with the horse.

Seeing that Snow Man liked to jump, de Leyer began giving him special schooling as a jumper. With kindness and hard work, he helped Snow Man over tougher and tougher obstacles. Finally, in the spring of 1958, he decided to put the big gray to his first real test—at the Sands Point Horse Show on Long Island, where he would compete with some of the top open jumpers in the land.

Incredibly, out on the Sands Point jump course Snow Man seemed able to do no wrong. Again and again spectators held their breath, expecting the ungainly-looking animal to come crashing down on the bars—but he never did. By nightfall of the second day of the three-day show he had achieved the seemingly impossible: He was tied for the lead in the Open Jumper Division with the great old campaigner Andante.

Then, with success so close, on his final jump of the day Snow Man landed with his feet too close together, and a back hoof slashed his right foreleg. By tomorrow it would be swollen and stiff. But de Leyer was not a man to give up easily. He cut a section out of a tire tube, slipped it over Snow Man's injured leg like a sock, tied up the bottom and filled the top with ice. All night long he kept the improvised sock full

79

of fresh ice, told Snow Man over and over how they would win next day. When morning came, the leg was neither stiff nor swollen. And on the final round Snow Man beat the mighty Andante!

Harry de Leyer now saw that he had a potential champion—possibly even a national champion. But giving Snow Man a chance to prove it meant hitting the horse-show circuit in earnest, vanning to a new show each weekend, putting up big entry fees, riding his heart out—a long, tiring summer and autumn that could end in little reward. After talking it over, Harry and Joanna decided that Snow Man deserved a try, and so to Connecticut they went. Then, the summer and early fall became one happy rush toward more and more championships. And finally it was time for the biggest show of all—the National at Madison Square Garden.

The National Horse Show lasts eight days. Horses that lack either consistency or stamina are weeded out long before the final night. After seven days Snow Man was tied in the Open Jumper Division with a chestnut mare, First Chance. For their jump-off on the eighth day the course was long and intricate. It wove around the Garden oval in four overlapping loops; it included quick turns and changes of direction—combinations which call for perfect timing and coördination. First Chance went first. Whether it was the tenseness of the moment, the wear and tear from so many days of jumping or the difficulties of the course, no one can be

sure. At any rate, First Chance "knocked" several barriers.

Now it was up to Snow Man to run a cleaner course. Slowly he headed for the first jump. De Leyer nudged him with his knees, and the big gray exploded over it. Now up and over Snow Man went, and up and over again. Over the brush jump, over the chicken coop, the hog's-back, the bull's-eye, the striped panel. There were a few touches, but far fewer than First Chance had made. Finally he approached the last jump. Harry de Leyer sat up in the saddle and threw the reins across the horse's neck. He was showing, for everyone to see, that it was not he who was responsible for this great performance, that it was the horse. Snow Man rumbled up to that final jump, and he thrust and he sailed and it was done! An old and unpedigreed farm horse had won it all—the National Horse Show Open Jumper Championship, the Professional Horsemen's Association Trophy and the American Horse Shows Association High Score Award. He was declared "Horse of the Year" in open jumping.

Then, the following year, Snow Man was "Horse of the Year" once more. And if you had been one of the vast crowd that filled Madison Square Garden that November evening to watch the de Leyer family and their big gray receive the ovation, you, too, would have stood . . . and clapped . . . and perhaps even cried—for the victory of a horse and a man who cared.

The Bear That Came for Supper

by ROBERT FRANKLIN LESLIE

I MET BOSCO in the remote wilderness near Mount Robson in western Canada. At the end of a long day of backpacking I had made a lean-to in a clearing beside a stream and was preparing to catch supper. Then I looked up—and there he was: an enormous boar black bear, slowly circling the clearing within thirty yards. He wasn't Bosco to me yet, and I viewed his presence with trepidation. My provisions were vulnerable if he was in a piratical mood, since I was unarmed. However, I decided to go about my fishing. The bear came along.

I have lived with wild creatures for thirty years, respecting their first fear—fast movements—and now I let him see the reason and the beginning in every slow, deliberate move I made. Soon he was sitting on his haunches less than five feet away, intensely interested in my activity. When I landed a fourteen-inch Loch Levin, I tossed it to him. He gulped it without bothering to chew. And when I flipped out the fly again he moved closer, planted his well-upholstered fanny on the turf beside my boot, and leaned half his five hundred pounds against my right leg!

I plied the gray hackle along the riffles and got another strike. Before reeling in, I eased over a yard, convinced the bear would grab fish, line, rod—and maybe me. But he didn't. His patience and dignity were regal as he sat rocking back and forth, watching carefully. When I released the trout from the hook, he bawled a long-drawn-out "Maw!" I held the wriggling fish high by the lower lip, stepped over to my "guest" and shakily dropped the prize into his cavernous red mouth. When drizzly darkness set in, I was still fishing for that bear, fascinated as much by his gentle manners as by his insatiable capacity. I began to think of him in a friendly way as Big Bosco, and I didn't mind when he followed me back to camp.

After supper I built up the fire, sat on the sleeping bag under the lean-to and lighted my pipe. All this time Bosco had sat just outside the heat perimeter of the fire, but the moment I was comfortably settled he walked over and sat down beside me. Overlooking the stench of wet fur, I rather enjoyed his warmth as we sat on the sleeping bag under the shelter. I listened to the rain thumping on the tarp in time with the steady, powerful *cur-rump, cur-rump* of the heartbeat beneath his thick coat. When smoke

81

blew our way, he snorted and sneezed, and I imitated most of his body movements, even the sneezing and snorting, swaying my head in every direction, sniffing the air as he did.

Then Bosco began licking my hands. Guessing what he wanted, I got him a handful of salt. Bosco enthusiastically nailed my hand to the ground with eight four-inch claws—claws capable of peeling the bark from a full-grown cedar, claws that could carry his five-hundred-odd pounds at full gallop to the top of the tallest tree in the forest, claws that could rip a man's body like a band saw. Finally the last grain of salt was gone and again we sat together. I wondered if this could be for real. I recalled Sam Ottley, trail foreman on the King's River in the Sierra Nevada, whom I had seen sharing tent and rations with a bear; but Sam's creature was old and toothless, no longer able to live off the country. This monster was the finest prime specimen I had ever seen.

Bosco stood up on all fours, burped a

long, fishy belch and stepped out into the rainy blackness. But he soon was back—with a message. He sat down near the sleeping bag and attempted to scratch that area of his rump just above his tail; he couldn't reach it. Again and again he nudged me and growled savagely at the itch. Finally I got the message and laid a light hand on his back. He flattened out to occupy the total seven feet of the lean-to as I began to scratch through the dense, oily hair. Then the full significance of his visit hit me. Just above his stubby tail several gorged ticks were dangerously embedded in swollen flesh. Little by little I proved that the flashlight would not burn, so he allowed me to focus it on his body. When I twisted out the first parasite, I thought I was in for a mauling. His roar shook the forest. But I determined to finish the job. Each time I removed a tick I showed it to him for a sniff before dropping it on the fire, and by the last one he was affably licking my hand.

A cold, sniffing nose awakened me several times during the night as the bear came and went. He left the sleeping bag wetter and muddier each time he crawled around over me, but he never put his full weight down when he touched any part of my body. The next day I set off again, over a ridge, down through a chilly river, up the next crest, through thickets of birch and alder and down a wide, north-running river canyon. To my surprise, Bosco followed like a faithful dog, digging grubs or bulbs when I stopped to rest. That evening I fished for Bosco's supper.

As the days passed and I hiked north, I used a system of trout, salt and scratch rewards to teach the bear to respond to the call, "Bosco!" Despite his perpetual devotion to food, he never lagged far behind. One evening he walked over to the log where I was enjoying my pipe, and began to dig at my boots. When I stood up he led me straight to a dead, hollow bee tree at which he clawed vigorously but unsuccessfully. Returning to camp, I covered my head with mosquito netting, tied shirt, pants and glove openings and got the hatchet. I built a smoke fire near the base of the tree and hacked away until the hollow shell crashed to earth, split wide open and exposed the hive's total summer production. For my understanding and efforts I received three stinging welts. Bosco ate twenty pounds of honeycomb, beebread and hundreds of bees. He snored most of that night at the foot of the sleeping bag.

At campsites Bosco never tolerated long periods of relaxation and reflection; and true to my form where animals are concerned, I babied his every whim. When he wanted his back scratched, I scratched; when he wanted a fish dinner, I fished; when he wanted to romp and roll with me in a meadow, I romped and rolled—and still wear scars to prove that he played games consummately out of my league. During one particularly rough session, I tackled his right front leg, bowling him over on his back. As I sat there on his belly regaining wind, he retaliated with a left hook that not only opened a two-inch gash down the front of my chin but spun me across the meadow. When I woke up, Bosco was licking my wound. His shame and remorse were inconsolable. He sat with his ears back and bawled like a whipped pup when I was able to put my arm around his neck and repeat all the soft, ursine vocabulary that he had taught me.

After that experience I let Bosco roll me around when he had to play, but I never raised another finger toward originality. If he got too rough, I played dead. Invariably he would turn me over, lick my face gently and whine.

There were times when he spent his excess energy racing around in hundred-yard circles, building up speed to gallop to the top of the tallest fir. When he returned to camp immediately afterward, I could detect absolutely no increase above his normal breathing rate. He panted only when we walked for long periods in full sun and he got thirsty.

It is not my intention either to attribute character traits to the bear which he could not possess or to exaggerate those he had. I simply studied him for what he was and saw him manifest only the normal qualities of his species, which were formidable enough without exaggeration. Other than calling him Bosco, I never attempted human training with him; conversely, I did everything possible to train myself to become a brother bear. Like all sensitive mammals, Bosco had his full complement of moods. When serious, he was dead earnest; when exuberant, a volcano. Being a bear, he was by nature

uninhibited; so I never expressed even a shade of the word "no." The feeling we developed for each other was spontaneous, genuine, brotherly bear affection. When it occurred to him to waddle over my way on his hind legs, grab me up in a smothering bear hug and express an overflowing emotion with a face licking, I went along with it for two reasons: First, I was crazy about that varmint; second, I nourished a healthy respect for what one swat from the ambidextrous giant could accomplish.

Although he was undisputed monarch of all his domain, I think Bosco considered me his mental equal in most respects. It was not long before he taught me to expand communication through a language of the eyes. How a bear can look you in the eye! Terrifying at first, it grows into the most satisfactory medium of all. Bosco and I would sit by the campfire, honestly and intimately studying each other's thoughts. Once in a while he would reach some sort of conclusion and hang a heavy paw on my shoulder. And I would do the same. It must have made an odd picture, but many times as I looked into those big, yellowish-brown eyes, I felt an awed humility as if the Deity Himself were about to effect a revelation through this, another of His children.

Although his size and strength made Bosco almost invulnerable to attack by other animals, he had his own collection of phobias. Thunder and lightning made him cringe and whine. When whisky jacks flew into camp looking for food, he fled in terror, the cacophonic birds power-diving and pecking him out of sight.

Bosco's phenomenal sense of smell amazed me. Trudging along behind me, he would suddenly stop, sniff the air and make a beeline for a big, succulent mushroom two hundred yards away; to a flat rock across the river under which chipmunks had warehoused their winter seed supply; to a berry patch two ridges over.

One afternoon when we were crossing a heath where dwarf willows grew in scattered hedgelike clumps, Bosco suddenly reared up and let out a "Maw!" I could detect no reason for alarm, but Bosco stood erect and forbade me to move. He advanced, began to snarl—and pandemonium broke out. Every clump of willows sprouted an upright bear! Black bear, brown bear, cinnamon bear and one champagne (all subdivisions of the same species). But these were young bears, two-year-olds, and no match for Bosco. He charged his closest contestant with the fury of a Sherman tank, and before the two-year-old could pick himself up he dispatched a second bear and tore into a thicket to dislodge a third. At the end of the circuit my gladiator friend remembered me and scoured back, unscathed and still champion.

That night we sat longer than usual by the campfire. Bosco nudged, pawed, talked at great length and looked me long in the eye before allowing me to retire. In my ignorance I assumed it was a rehash of that afternoon's battle. He was gone for most of the night.

Along toward next midafternoon I sensed something wrong. Bosco did not forage, but clung to my heels. I was looking over a streamside campsite when the big bear about-faced and broke into a headlong, swinging lope up the hill we had just descended. I did not call to him as he went over the crest full steam without once looking back. That evening I cooked supper with one eye on the hillside, then lay awake for hours waiting for the familiar nudge. By morning I was desolated; I knew I should never again see big brother Bosco. He left behind a relationship I shall treasure.

RASCAL

Condensed from the book

by STERLING NORTH

I WAS ELEVEN YEARS OLD that summer of 1918, and lived alone with my father in our big ten-room house. He was an absent-minded, scholarly man whose real-estate business frequently took him away on trips, and since my brother, Herschel, was fighting in France and my two grown sisters lived elsewhere, I was often left to myself. But I did not lack for companionship.

My numerous pets included several cats and four yearling skunks (until a slight accident occurred and a delegation of neighbors urged me to give them up); Wowser, my huge, affectionate, perpetually hungry Saint Bernard; and Edgar Allan Poe, the crow, who lived in the belfry of the Methodist Church next door, and shouted, "What fun! What fun!," the only phrase he knew, as dignified parishioners came to church services, weddings and funerals. But my newest friend and most constant companion was Rascal, my pet raccoon.

I had raised him from a kit, and now he ate at the table with Dad and me, occupying my old high chair and drinking warm milk from a bowl. He reached the milk by stand-ing in the chair and placing his hands on the edge of the tray. His table manners were excellent—much better than those of most children—and he chirred and trilled his satisfaction with the arrangement. Rascal slept with me, too, and at night his comforting furry presence made me feel less lonesome when my father was away.

He went fishing with me and explored the Wisconsin woods around Brailsford Junction, where we lived. He fitted nicely into the basket on my bicycle and soon became a cycling maniac, standing on the wire mesh with his feet apart, his hands gripping the front edge of the basket. As we tore down the hills his tail plumed out behind, and the natural black goggles around his bright eyes made him look like Barney Oldfield coming down the stretch. He was a demon for speed, and I took him everywhere.

One day I was in the living room, sanding the ribs of the eighteen-foot canoe I was building while Rascal scampered over the unfinished craft. Up our street curved a racy Stutz Bearcat; it parked in front of our house, and out stepped my beautiful married sister, Theodora. She had driven down from Minnesota for a visit, bringing with her one of her maids.

"Theo, Theo!" I shouted happily as I ran out to embrace her.

"Hello, sonny boy—my, you're all covered with sawdust."

"Well, you see, Theo, I'm building a canoe."

"That's nice, but where is it?"

"I keep it in the living room," I said, dropping my eyes.

I could not explain that back in the winter, when I started the project, it had been too cold to work in the barn. I loved this sister, but I was slightly in awe of her. She had been kind to me after Mother died four years earlier, but she was a martinet concerning deportment, dress, housekeeping and much besides. Theo gave the living room one sweeping glance and raised her hands in horror. "Merciful heavens! I've never seen such a mess in my life."

"I sweep up the sawdust and shavings every evening."

"Yes, I can see them, right there in the fireplace."

"Daddy and I do a good job of batching it," I said.

"Batching it! That's just the trouble," Theo said severely. "Now, Sterling, I've brought along Jennie to clean this house from top to bottom. I'll cook some decent food. We'll hire a full-time housekeeper, and we'll get that canoe out of the living room this minute."

"Can't you just leave us alone?" I said mournfully. I told Theo we were living exactly the way we wanted to live, and then I added defiantly, "Anyhow, you're not my mother."

"Oh, sonny boy," she said, suddenly contrite and fighting back the tears. She came around the end of the canoe and kissed me tenderly on the cheek.

Theo had not seen Rascal until this moment. He had been lying low, watching and listening shrewdly. He may not have been a perfect judge of character, but he reacted with surprising sensitivity to various modulations of voice. He knew when he was being praised or scolded, and when people were feeling affectionate or angry. He didn't altogether trust this auburn-haired stranger, although his eyes strayed often to her shining hair. His virtual invisibility was due to the fact that he was lying on a large jaguar-skin rug, which blended with his stripings. When Rascal rose from that skin, like the disembodied spirit of the Amazonian jaguar, it startled Theo nearly out of her wits.

"What in the world is *that?*"

"That's Rascal, my good little raccoon."

"You mean it lives in the house?"

"Only part of the time."

"Does it bite?"

"Not unless you slap him or scold him."

"You get that thing right out of here, Sterling."

"Well, all right," I agreed reluctantly, knowing that Rascal could open the screen door and let himself back in anytime he pleased.

"Now help Jennie with the luggage," Theo ordered, "and put it in the downstairs bedroom."

I didn't dare tell her that I was sleeping in that room and that Rascal slept there, too. Giving Theo the downstairs bedroom didn't worry *me*. She always took this big room with its adjoining bath. She said none of the other beds was fit to sleep in. But my difficulty would come in trying to explain the arrangement to Rascal. Raccoons have definite patterns in their minds, and Rascal had decisively chosen the same bed that Theo wanted. He also preferred a room with a bath. Each evening I left a few inches of water in the washbasin so that Rascal could get a drink at any time during the night, or perhaps wash a cricket before he ate it. How was I to reveal to this small creature of habit that he was being evicted?

As a kit, Rascal had lived in a hole in our red oak tree, and I saw him only when I took him out to feed him warm milk. Wowser, my exceptionally responsible watchdog, was his guardian. He slept under the oak tree at night, and remained there almost constantly by day, always protectively alert, though his 170 pounds of muscled grace appeared somnolent and his great relaxed jaws always drooled a little. (Pat Delaney, a saloonkeeper who lived up the street, said Saint Bernards drool for the best possible reason. He explained that in the Alps these noble dogs set forth every winter day, with little kegs of brandy strapped beneath their chins, to rescue wayfarers lost in the snowdrifts. Generations of carrying the brandy, of which they have never tasted so much as a drop, have made them drool continuously. The trait has now become hereditary, Pat said.)

One afternoon Rascal appeared at the door of his hole, gave a quavering trill, then emerged tail first and backed down the tree cautiously in the manner of a little bear. Wowser was very much disturbed and yelped a few questions, looking up to see how I felt about this new problem. I told him not to worry, just to wait and watch.

Rascal started immediately for my shallow, cement bait pond, which was always alive with minnows. Without hesitation he waded in and methodically felt over the bottom with his sensitive prehensile fingers, causing shiners and chubs to dash frantically for safety. This was his first fishing expedition, yet he knew precisely the tech-

nique used by all raccoons for catching minnows. Presently Rascal's clever little black hands seized a four-inch shiner. Then the washing ceremony began. Although the minnow was perfectly clean, Rascal sloshed it back and forth for several minutes before retiring to enjoy his meal.

All raccoons are fascinated by shining objects, and when Rascal began to spend his days outside his nest, I gave him three bright new pennies. He felt them carefully, smelled them, tasted them, then with the happiness of a miser hid them in a dark corner with such other treasures as glass marbles, a brass doorknob and my broken Ingersoll watch. Poe-the-Crow was perched on the porch rail, teasing the cats but keeping just beyond their reach. This raucous old bird, who cawed and cussed in crow language, was arching his wings and strutting like a poolroom bully as Rascal pushed open the screen and trundled into the sunlight, carrying a penny that shone like newly minted gold.

Poe and Rascal had taken an instant dislike to each other when first they met. Crows know that raccoons steal birds' eggs and sometimes eat fledglings. In addition, Poe was jealous. He had seen me petting and pampering my small raccoon. But Rascal was large enough now to pull a few tail feathers during their noisy squabbles, and Poe, who was no fool, was taking few chances. The penny, however, was so tempting that the crow threw caution to the winds and made a dive for it. (Crows, too, are insatiably attracted to glittering trinkets, and in addition are inveterate thieves.)

Rascal was carrying the coin in his mouth and, when Poe swooped, his beak closed not only on the penny but on half a dozen of Rascal's coarse, strong whiskers. Attempting a fast getaway, he found himself attached to the raccoon, who with a high scream of fury began fighting for his property and his life. A furious tangle of feathers and fur ensued as Rascal and Poe wrestled and struggled. I arrived to untangle them, and both were angry with me. Rascal nipped me slightly for the first time, and Poe made several ungracious comments.

The penny, meanwhile, had rolled from the porch into the grass below, where the crow promptly spotted it, seized it once again, and by devious routes made for the Methodist belfry, where he presumably stored his loot.

Rascal's actions were not guided solely by instinct. He was perfectly capable of learning by experience, as I discovered when I first took him to my secret fishing place on the river. There was a sandbar there with a deep and quiet hole below it. I left my bicycle in the willows and began assembling my jointed pole and reel, running my silk line through the tip, and so on. Rascal needed no such elaborate preparations. Working his way along the sandbar, examining every inch of the shallows, he soon encountered a large crayfish, an armored monster of which he had no previous knowledge. Had he been informed by his mother, he would have grasped it just behind the claws, thus avoiding any danger from those waving sawtooth pincers. But having no one to teach him, he was pinched several times before he crushed the head with his needlesharp teeth, washed his prey and gobbled up the delectable tail.

Once pinched, twice shy. The very next time that Rascal caught a crayfish he handled it with the professional skill of an old and wise raccoon.

On the way home I bought a bottle of strawberry pop. Without so much as a by-your-leave, Rascal put one of his little hands into the bottle, licked off his fingers and began begging. I waited until I had finished all but the last half inch of the bottle, then poured a few drops into Rascal's open and eager mouth. To my amazement he grasped the neck of the bottle, rolled over on his back and, using both hands and both feet, held it in perfect position while he drained the last sweet drops. Strawberry was his favorite flavor from then on. He never did learn to like lemon sour.

At the table one morning, after breakfast-for-three had become part of our daily ritual, I gave Rascal a lump of sugar. He felt it, sniffed it and then began his usual washing ceremony, swishing it back and forth through his bowl of milk. In a few moments, of course, it melted entirely, to Rascal's utter bafflement. He felt all over the bottom of the bowl to see if he had dropped it, then turned over his right hand to assure himself it was empty, then examined his left hand in the same manner. Finally, he looked at me and trilled a shrill question: Who had stolen his sugar? I gave him a second lump, which he examined minutely. He started to wash it, but hesitated. A shrewd look came into his bright black eyes and, instead of washing away a second treat, he took it directly to his mouth and munched it with complete satisfaction. Never again did Rascal wash a lump of sugar.

Another lesson he learned swiftly was how to open the back screen door. I purposely had not repaired the faulty catch, because all my cats liked to open the door and walk in. Watching them, Rascal saw that the trick was to hook your claws into the screen and pull. Several nights later I was startled and delighted to hear his trill from the pillow beside me, then to feel his little hands working all over my face. My raccoon baby had climbed from his hole, opened the back screen door and found his way to my bed, which he decided was softer

and more comfortable than his own. Since he was clean as any cat and instinctively housebroken, from that night on we became constant bedfellows.

During the first few hours of Theo's visit, Rascal caused no trouble. Indeed, after she forced me to eject him from the house, he spent the rest of the day sleeping in the oak tree. But that night when the moon rose, he evidently backed down his tree, padded to the screen door, opened it with ease and went confidently to our bedroom and crawled in with Theo.

My father and I, sleeping upstairs, were awakened by a bloodcurdling yell. We rushed downstairs to find Theo standing on a chair, treed by a complacent little raccoon who sat on the floor below blinking up at this crazy human being who was screeching like a fire siren.

"He always sleeps in this bed," I explained to her. "He's harmless and perfectly clean."

"You take that horrid little animal out this minute," Theo ordered. "And hook the screen door so it can't possibly get back in."

"Well, okay," I said, "but you're sleeping in Rascal's bed. And he has just as many rights around here as you have."

"Don't be impertinent," Theo said, reassuming her dignity.

Three days later an incident occurred that was even more upsetting for Theo. Recently married, she treasured her engagement ring, a square-cut diamond of perhaps one carat, mounted in white gold. She had misplaced this ring on several occasions. Once we dug up eighty-five feet of sewer, only to find that she had transferred it to another purse.

True to form, she again lost her ring. She thought she had left it on the wide rim of the lavatory when she went to bed, and that it had either fallen into the drain or had been stolen. No one in Brailsford Junction ever locked his door. Not within memory had there been a robbery. We ransacked the house, hunted through the grass and the flower beds, and then made plans for again digging up the sewer. Finally, a farfetched possibility struck me. Just before dawn that morning I had heard Rascal and Poe having a terrible fight on the back porch. Before I could shake the sleep from my eyes, the cawing and screaming subsided and I had drowsed off again.

Feeling as keen as a Scotland Yard detective, I began to weave a theory. On this fourth night of Theo's visit I had not hooked the screen door. Rascal apparently had slipped into the house, reached the downstairs bedroom and wisely chosen not to create another scene. He had decided, however, to have a drink of fresh water, had climbed to the windowsill and then to the washbasin, and found it empty. But, joy of joys, there on the rim was the prettiest object he had ever seen in his life, a big diamond ring gleaming with blue-white radiance in the predawn light.

If my theory was sound, Rascal had picked up the ring and taken it to the back porch, where Poe-the-Crow had spotted the treasure. This would explain the crow-raccoon fight that had awakened me.

Quite probably the black thief had won again—at least in the matter of flying away with the loot. I had to ask permission of the Reverend Mr. Hooton before starting my climb to the seventy-five-foot-high belfry. The dark shaft was filled with cobwebs, and some of the cleats were loose, making me fear I might fall. But there could be no turning back. At long last I reached the airy little room at the top, with its widely spaced shutters furnishing a view of the town. I stood for a few moments regarding the world below me.

Remembering my mission, I began to search the dusty belfry. Behind a pile of discarded hymnals, which some dedicated idiot had lugged to this unlikely storage place, I found the ragged circle of twigs and leaves and black feathers that Poe-the-Crow called home. As some people keep their money in their mattress, Poe had made his bed even more uncomfortable with a pile of shining junk that overran the nest and spilled across the floor. Here were glassies and steelies and one real agate marble, all of which he had stolen during our marble games. Here was my football whistle, snatched while he hovered just over the line of scrimmage shouting, "What fun! What fun!" Here were scraps of sheet copper, a second key to our Oldsmobile and, wonder of wonders, Theo's diamond ring.

Poe dropped in now, and this time he didn't say, "What fun!" Instead he cawed and swore at me as though *I* were the thief and *he* the honest householder. I put several of these stolen articles into my pocket; my best marbles, the second key to our car, my football whistle and Theo's ring. But I left many of the shining trinkets, knowing that Poe couldn't tell sheet copper from a diamond ring. The crow's raucous criticism followed me all the way down that shaft and out into the sunlight.

Theo was so pleased at my recovery of her ring that she did not insist on the removal of my canoe from the living room. And she postponed the decision concerning a full-time housekeeper. She merely fed us delightful meals and left the house shining clean, with fresh curtains at the windows. Then with a good-bye kiss and a wave of her hand, she was off again.

The heavy fighting around Soissons, France, in July 1918 shocked Brailsford Junction. As the casualty lists grew and personal tragedy came to one home after another, we seemed much nearer to the trenches and shell-shattered wheat fields of France. There was a flurry of patriotism among the town's children, the girls knitting khaki wristlets, the boys competing to see who could collect the most peach pits, used in making charcoal for gas masks.

I had a war garden, in which Rascal assisted me, trundling along behind while I hoed, and helping me to pick peas from a late planting. All the peas he picked, however, he kept for himself, opening each pod as though it were a small clam and avidly shelling the green pearls into his mouth. He had little relish for the wax beans that were coming on by the bushel; so, while I picked beans, he often took a comfortable siesta under the rhubarb leaves.

One serious mistake I made was to give Rascal his first taste of sweet corn. When I twisted off a plump ear, stripped back the husk and handed it to him, he went slightly berserk. No food he had ever tasted compared with this juicy new delicacy. He ate most of the ear, then in a frenzy scrambled up another stalk, bore it to the ground and wrested off a fresh ear, which he guzzled greedily. It was still only half-eaten when he left it to climb yet a third stalk. He was drunk on the nectar and ambrosia called sweet corn. I thought his binge was amusing. But when I told my father about it, he looked serious and said, "I'm afraid you're in for trouble, Sterling."

I certainly was. That night, and on subsequent nights, Rascal disappeared for hours at a time, and he began sleeping soundly through most of the day. Angry voices were to be heard on our street each morning as one neighbor after another found his sweet-corn patch mauled by some fiendish night raider.

It was Cy Jenkins, the lumber dealer, who discovered raccoon tracks in the dust between his corn rows. After he spread the news, a delegation arrived one evening to sit in a circle around my unfinished canoe, voicing their complaints while Rascal huddled in my lap for protection.

"I seen that varmint's tracks right in my garden," Jenkins said triumphantly.

One neighbor after another echoed his indignation, and threats came whizzing around us like the buzz of angry hornets.

"Next moonlight night I'll shoot him!" "I'll set a trap, so help me!" "Skunks, woodchucks, coons! What next?"

"Now, just a moment," my father said quietly. (Among other civic responsibilities, he served as justice of the peace, and knew from long experience how to handle a group of angry people.)

Easygoing Mike Conway was willing to listen. "What do you suggest?" he asked.

"If Sterling buys a collar and a leash for his raccoon . . ."

"Not enough," Cy Jenkins growled.

"And builds him a cage . . ." my father added.

Rascal began to whimper, and I looked anxiously from face to face. Mrs. Walter Dabbett was the first to show any sympathy. Then someone laughed, and the tension suddenly eased.

"Well, it's settled then," my father said. "Sterling, why don't you bring some glasses and a pitcher of cold grape juice?"

The drink cooled everyone off, but as soon as the neighbors were gone I turned angrily on my father. "You can put criminals in jail, but not my good little raccoon. How would you like to be led around on a leash?"

"Now, Sterling," my father said soothingly. "It's better than having Rascal shot."

"Well, all right. But I think Rascal and I will run away and live together in a cabin in the woods."

My father pondered this a moment, then said, "How would you like to take a two-week trip, all the way to Lake Superior? Bring Rascal along."

"Do you really mean it?'"

"Of course I mean it. You can ask the Conway boys to feed Wowser and take care of your garden."

A reprieve! I snatched Rascal from the rug and started dancing around crazily. I asked, "When can we start, Daddy?"

"Why, tomorrow, I suppose," he said. "I'll just put a sign on the office door."

In his real-estate business, my father speculated largely in farm properties. He mortgaged each farm he acquired, used the money to buy another farm, then repeated the process. This reckless pyramiding of paper profits brought him close to disaster in every farm recession. But it paid off well in 1918, which was a boom year for farms, and he often put a sign on the door announcing that he was "Gone for the Day" or longer.

We started out in the Oldsmobile early the next morning, turning northward as we ascended the Rock River Valley. There were no superhighways in those days scorning the countryside with ribbons of unfeeling concrete, and the friendly little roads we followed were often unpaved and wandered everywhere. They clung to ancient game and Indian trails, skirted orchards where one might reach out to pluck an early apple, wound through valleys where we came so close to flower gardens and pastures of clover that we could smell all the good country smells, from new-mown hay to ripening corn.

The time sped quickly. At home my father was usually immersed in endless research for a novel about the Fox and Winnebago Indians. Somehow the book never got written, but his fund of tribal lore, as he pointed out this Indian trail or that, was always fascinating to me.

We had packed some sandwiches, hard-boiled eggs, fresh peaches, a dozen doughnuts. There was no reason to bring any special food for Rascal. He ate almost anything, just as though he were a person—which he definitely believed he was. We bought a tin pail of fresh cold milk at a farmhouse and feasted beside a bridge over a rushing stream. When Rascal had eaten, he curled up on the back seat and there slept happily all the afternoon.

By nightfall the farm odors and fragrances of southern Wisconsin had blended with the spicy aroma of northern firs and the scent of pine needles lying four inches thick on the forest floor. We stopped on a point that extended into a small clear lake, unpacked the duffel we needed and arranged our camp. We had Navy hammocks, and that first night we strung them between pine trees and the spare-tire rack of the Oldsmobile, and prepared to sleep beneath the canopy of the sky.

My father said he would show me how to climb aboard the hammock. Firmly grasping the dowel pin, he eased himself onto the tipsy bed. But before he could cover himself with a blanket the hammock flipped upside down. He landed unhurt on the padding of pine needles. I laughed myself breathless, and Rascal hurried over to see why my father was lying on the ground. "I'll bet it's easy," I said. I made a running dive, landed squarely in the hammock, held it for a minute and then did a somersault.

Now my father was laughing as hard as I, and Rascal was scampering around as though he understood the joke. Then, just at the appropriate moment, something else began to laugh—maniacal, spine-chilling laughter from far across the lake. "Holy Moses! What's that?" I asked.

"A loon," my father said. "He's laughing at *us*. He thinks we're crazy trying to sleep in hammocks."

I was suddenly completely happy, in love with the loony world and with my father and Rascal. I didn't care where I slept, or how many times I tipped out of my hammock.

We made our permanent camp south of Lake Superior on the Brule River, the finest trout stream in Wisconsin. It was characteristic of my parent that he had not told me the real reason for this trip. He had been asked to testify as an expert witness in a case being tried in Superior. Our camp was some twenty miles from the courtroom, so each day the court was in session my father would leave shortly after breakfast, taking his packet of notes and documents, and would return during the afternoon.

He was tranquil concerning my safety. He knew I could scarcely get lost if I stayed on the river or one of its branches, and that Rascal and I could swim if we fell into one of the deeper pools. Several recent showers lessened the danger of forest fires, and we had seen no sign of bears.

Two weeks of absolute freedom! I lost all sense of time. I had no watch and could only guess at the hour. I forgot what day it was. No school or church bells rang to remind us of passing time. Each day blended into the next and could only be remembered as the day we saw the porcupine or the day we found Lost Lake. We explored, fished and swam. It seemed scarcely possible that two weeks could fly past so swiftly. But one afternoon my father returned to tell me that the court case had been settled and that the following day would be our last on the Brule. For the first time since we had come to the north woods, I lay awake that evening, listening to the soughing of the wind high in the pines, realizing sadly that we must return to civilization.

The next morning Dad borrowed a canoe and took us downriver through one excellent trout pool after another. Rascal stood at the prow, peering ahead as might an animated figurehead, sniffing the breeze and occasionally turning to give us brief instructions. As always, he loved speed and a sense of danger, chirring with the most satisfaction when we were running white water.

We saw our first bears that day, and at last in a beautiful pool I caught a fine brown trout, one of the largest I would ever catch in a lifetime of fishing. By the scales in my tackle box he weighed just over four pounds.

When we got home, Edgar Allan Poe swooped down from the Methodist belfry shouting, "What fun! What fun!" Wowser, who had thought he was totally deserted, leaped to put his paws on my shoulders, knocked me flat on my back in the grass, then lovingly washed my face with his big tongue. Rascal and the crow were soon fighting over something, and Wowser stopped licking me long enough to put an end to the squabble.

It was a wonderful homecoming.

Sweet corn was no longer an issue, being dry in the husk. But I had promised to leash and cage my pet, and I could no longer postpone doing it. Money for a collar and for chicken wire was a problem. I had earned and saved enough to buy one Liberty bond, but my supply of ready cash was low. Not one of the boys I knew was granted an allowance or would even think of asking his father for a loan. I felt fortunate to be permitted to keep the money I earned from mowing lawns and selling my garden produce.

I took four precious quarters from my earthenware crock, put Rascal in the basket of my bicycle and pedaled sadly downtown. We stopped at Shadwick's Harness and Leather Emporium, which smelled delightfully of tanned leather, saddle soap and harness oil. Garth Shadwick, like his father before him, was a craftsman in leather, whose skill was known as far away as the state capital. He made handsome luggage, custom-fitted riding boots and engraved bookbindings. But most of his trade was in harnesses; and harness-making was a profession threatened by the automobile.

At the moment, Mr. Shadwick had a jeweler's glass in his right eye and was engraving initials on a silver nameplate. I waited patiently until he took the glass from his eye and looked up from his work.

"Well, Sterling?"

"We don't want to bother you, Mr. Shadwick, but. . . ."

"Boys and coons don't bother me," the harness-maker said.

He returned to his engraving for several minutes, then tossed it aside and exploded, "It's these goldanged automobiles, smelly, noisy, dirty things, scaring horses right off the road. Ruin a man's business. Well, son, speak up. What is it you want?"

"I want a collar for Rascal," I said, fighting the stinging moisture in my eyes, "and a braided leash to match. And they're making me build a cage to lock him up."

"Goldanged buzzards," the harness-maker said. "Cage for a little coon like that? Going after boys and coons now, are they? You want his name engraved on a silver plate on the collar?"

"I haven't got much money," I said hesitantly. "But that would be wonderful. His name is Rascal."

With swift precision, Shadwick went to work on a strong, light collar of pliable, golden-brown calfskin about an inch wide. He used his smallest awl to make the holes, and his smallest needle and lightest waxed thread. Then he brought out a tiny silver buckle from his safe and sewed it to the collar with almost invisible stitches. Finally he put his glass to his eye and on the nameplate inscribed "Rascal" in a fine Spencerian script. It was the sort of work he would have done if asked to make a harness for a fairy coach.

"That's the most beautiful raccoon collar I ever saw," I said.

"It's the *only* raccoon collar you ever saw," Shadwick chuckled gruffly, "and the only one I ever made. Better try it for size."

I wasn't certain Rascal would like to have the collar put around his neck, but I couldn't hurt Mr. Shadwick's feelings. I let the little raccoon feel it and smell it first. He liked the shining buckle and nameplate and the texture of the leather. Finally I slipped it around his neck, and to my surprise he didn't struggle. Instead he sat up on his square little bottom and felt the collar as a woman fingers her pearls. Mr. Shadwick brought a large mirror, and Rascal, who had never before seen his own image, became greatly excited. What other raccoon was being fitted for a collar this morning? He bumped his nose trying to get through the mirror. Then, talking and trilling, he raced around behind the glass to meet the other raccoon. Back he came, completely mystified. Finally he gave it up and merely sat and viewed himself, chirring happily.

The braiding of the leash took a little longer, and was done with the same elaboration and dexterity. When it was finished it was as slim as the tip of my steel fishing rod. At one end was fastened a silver harness ring; at the other, a snap to be attached to the collar.

I knew I didn't have money to pay for such an outfit. So I put my four quarters on the workbench and said it was a down payment. I would bring him something every week for the next six months.

The harness-maker gazed off through the window, his mind going back perhaps to his own boyhood, when there weren't any goldanged automobiles to ruin the finest profession in the world. "Why, son," he said, "I'd be cheating you if I took more than twenty-five cents for that leash and collar. Now get along with your little coon. I've got work to do."

I might have put off building Rascal's cage, but he developed a craving for a new nocturnal delight, the grapes hanging in purple clusters in nearby arbors, so I went down to the lumberyard and ordered chicken wire and two-by-fours. I had watched Rascal closely to discover which part of the backyard he enjoyed most. There could be no doubt about his preference; it was an area, some twelve feet square, extending from the base of the oak tree, below his hole, to the side of the barn. This included a smooth expanse of grass and clover and my bait pond with its water and constant supply of minnows.

Just as I had let him become slowly acquainted with his collar, I now invited his help in constructing the cage. I laid out a square, dug holes for the posts and sank a six-inch trench along each side for pegging down the bottom edge of the chicken wire. Rascal enjoyed it all, reached into each excavation and crawled back and forth through the tunnels in the rolls of wire. I used an old screen door for the entrance, but during the several days I spent building the cage I was careful not to close this exit. Never for a single moment did Rascal feel penned in.

But it seemed a wicked thing to take a wild raccoon from the woods and imprison him. Would Rascal yearn for his lost freedom? He *must* have more space, I thought, and more shelter. I had a small inspiration. I drew a circle on the part of the barn that formed the fourth wall of the cage, then cut a neat opening into a long-disused stall on the other side. Rascal loved holes of all sizes. While I put fresh straw in the stall and enclosed it with chicken wire, my raccoon spent most of his time going in and out of this pleasant little door. His home was becoming more attractive every day.

He still didn't understand, however, and every time the neighbors asked when I would lock him up, I would say, "Maybe tomorrow." But finally the cage was finished, and I could delay no longer.

I took Rascal to the enclosure and sat for

a long time talking to him and petting him while he ate his evening meal. Then, steeling myself to the dreadful deed, I stepped from the cage and hooked the door behind me. Rascal didn't understand what had happened. He came over to the door and asked me politely to open it and let him out. Then it suddenly struck him that he was trapped, caged, imprisoned. He ran swiftly around the square of wire, then into the barn through the hole I had cut, and all over the stall, then back again, frantic now.

I went into the house to get away from his voice, but it came to me through the open windows—pleading, terrified—asking for me, telling me that he loved me and had always trusted me. After a while I couldn't stand it any longer and I went out and opened his door. He clung to me and cried and talked about it, asking that unanswerable question.

So I took him to bed with me and we fell into a fitful sleep, touching each other again and again throughout the night for reassurance. Soon afterward I moved Wowser's doghouse to a spot just outside Rascal's door. Well aware of his new responsibility, Wowser lay there faithfully, his huge muzzle and deep, compassionate eyes turned toward the small prisoner. Rascal, reaching out, could pat Wowser's nose, and the Saint Bernard invariably licked the little paw. It was a relief to see such companionship, especially when, with the first school bells in October, I was gone most of the day.

The beginning of this school year was particularly memorable because I was entering junior high school and because two of my teachers were greatly gifted. Miss Stafford made English a delight. And Miss Whalen loved biology and loved teaching it.

Pretty, delicate, with lights in her hair and eyes, Miss Whalen captured our atten-

tion on the first day of school by asking each of us to bring one of our pets to biology class on various days. Bud Babcock was to bring his terrier; others were to bring goldfish, a parrot and a tame squirrel. Rascal and I had the honor of receiving the first such invitation.

On the appointed morning, I brushed and combed him until his dark guard hairs shone and his gray underfur was as soft as lamb's wool. I used silver polish on his nameplate and saddlesoap on his collar and leash. I wanted him to make a good impression.

Fortunately, biology was our first class, so we didn't have long to wait. Rascal's behavior was excellent. Clean, well-groomed, alert and polite, he sat on Miss Whalen's desk as though he had spent most of his life addressing biology classes. He gently examined her glass paperweight, which, when shaken, produced a snowstorm over a toy village.

"As you can see," Miss Whalen began, "raccoons are curious." Then she wrote on the blackboard: "Raccoon—an Indian word meaning 'he who scratches.' "

Slammy Stillman, the town bully and my sworn enemy, raised his hand. "Does he scratch because he has fleas?" This produced laughter, and Miss Whalen rapped lightly for order.

"I think," she said, "the Indians meant that raccoons scratch and dig for turtle eggs and other food along the shore. Sometimes they even dig for earthworms."

Slammy scowled and slumped in his seat.

"He looks like a little bear," Bud Babcock said.

"You're right, Bud," Miss Whalen agreed. "He is a cousin of the bear and is sometimes called a 'wash bear' because he washes all of his food."

She brought out a shallow enameled laboratory pan, which contained not only water but, to my surprise, a crayfish. This she put before Rascal on her desk. "Now let's see what the raccoon will do."

Rascal, like the little ham he always was, looked around the class and off through the windows while running his hands with a kneading motion all over the shallow pan. He knew exactly where the crayfish was, but he was showing off. Suddenly his body stiffened for a pounce, and two seconds later he had his prey fast in his grip and was washing it blissfully in anticipation of the forthcoming feast.

By this time the class was as happy as Rascal, and almost everyone clapped. Then Miss Whalen asked me if I would tell of my experiences with my raccoon, and I stood before the class, petting Rascal as I talked. I think we had the attention of everybody but Slammy, particularly when Rascal climbed onto my shoulder and started playing with my ear. I told them all the things we did together; how gentle he was; how he loved music on our Victrola and would sit dreamy-eyed listening to his favorite song, "There's a Long, Long Trail A-Winding."

"I even sleep with him sometimes," I confessed. "He's a wonderful pet."

Everyone wanted to touch him after that. So, one by one, my classmates came up and petted him. Slammy was the last in line and he slouched up, shifty-eyed and sneering. Just as he reached the raccoon, he snapped a rubber band in Rascal's face.

Very rarely had I heard Rascal emit his scream of rage. But this was pure fury—a fight-to-the-death cry—and in a split second Rascal sank his teeth deep into Slammy's fat hand.

Slammy yelled until you could have heard him in the assembly hall. He danced around shaking his hand and screaming, "Mad coon! Mad coon! You gotta shoot him now."

Miss Whalen's voice was cold and severe.

"Slammy Stillman, everyone in this room saw what you did. If you think this is a mad raccoon, then you need no other punishment than wondering if indeed you do have a case of rabies."

She gave him some iodine for his hand, then dismissed the class but asked me to stay. I didn't know what she would decree, but it proved almost as severe a punishment as she had given Slammy. She said, "I'm sorry, but under the circumstances you will have to cage your raccoon for the next fourteen days. If he should show signs of rabies, we would still have time to get Pasteur treatments for Slammy."

"But he isn't mad. You saw what happened," I cried.

"I certainly did. But we can't afford to take a chance." She was silent for a moment. Then she went on thoughtfully, "Rascal is a wonderful pet. Thank you for bringing him to class today."

For the next two weeks Rascal and I were jailmates for as many hours a day as I could join him. On the fourteenth day, when he had shown no sign of sickness, I opened the door and we frisked out into the autumn world. Slammy, unfortunately, would not die of rabies.

Spanish influenza, which had swept across Europe and the eastern states, hit Brailsford Junction late in October, killing more of our citizens than the war had. The schools were closed, and people scurried along the half-deserted streets wearing eerie-looking masks of white gauze. At least one person in four was dangerously ill, and twice that number were less seriously affected.

Mine was a milder case. But on this occasion my father seemed concerned. He bundled me in several sweaters and blankets and helped me into the car. I begged to take Rascal with me, and he consented. Then we drove slowly through the increasingly leafless countryside toward the old North homestead, now operated by my father's brother Fred, his gentle wife Lillian and their sons.

Aunt Lillie came out to greet us, wiping her hands on her apron. "Oh my, it's Willard and Sterling! Sterling, are you sick?"

"Just a touch of influenza," my father said. "I thought perhaps. . . . "

"Why, of course, Willard. He needs my care. We'll put him up in the bedroom next to ours, off the parlor. It won't be a bit of trouble. Come in for a cup of coffee."

Under her tender care I was soon up again; and as I grew stronger I helped with minor chores such as gathering eggs, feeding the calves and swilling the pigs. Rascal liked the lambs, the big workhorses and most of the other animals. But he never did learn to love pigs. Their squealing, slurping, struggling method of eating would send him up a nearby apple tree, which he would refuse to leave until the pigs had cleaned their troughs.

False Armistice Day and my twelfth birthday fell on the same date. Aunt Lillie answered three long rings on the party line, which meant a general message for all phones. It was during second breakfast, after milking, and we were all at the table. Even before she hung up the receiver she was saying, "Oh, how wonderful! Oh, thank our Heavenly Father. It's over, it's really all over. They've stopped all that terrible killing in France."

I couldn't have asked for a better birthday present (even if everyone *had* forgotten it was my birthday). Herschel would return from France, and we could go fishing together. With a rush I was jubilantly happy. I picked up my raccoon and danced him around and around.

That afternoon my father drove out to take me home. Aunt Lillie had cooked a very special feast of roast turkey with hickory-nut dressing. Suddenly she put her hand to her mouth in consternation. "Why, Sterling," she said, "it's your twelfth birthday, and not one of us remembered. I didn't even bake a cake." So everybody sang "Happy Birthday" anyway, and my father reached into his pocket and brought forth his watch with its chain finely braided from my mother's chestnut hair. For several generations that old watch had passed from father to son. Now he passed it on to me.

On the morning of November 11, the real Armistice was signed, and a sudden silence fell over the trenches of Europe. In Brailsford Junction, the celebration began early. The decorated fire engines, automobiles and horse-drawn conveyances crowded the streets in a noisy, happy parade. I interwove the spokes of my bicycle wheels with red, white and blue crepe-paper ribbons. With Rascal in the basket, I pedaled through the throng, ringing my bell as a small contribution to the joyous pandemonium of fire whistles and church bells.

But by afternoon my elation had subsided and I returned home to begin oiling my muskrat traps for the season ahead. As usual Rascal was interested in what I was doing. But when he came to sniff and feel the traps, a terrible thought slowed my fingers. Putting my traps aside, I opened a catalogue from a St. Louis fur buyer. There on the first page was a handsome raccoon, his paw caught in a powerful trap. How could anyone mutilate the sensitive, questing hands of an animal like Rascal? I picked up my raccoon and hugged him in a passion of remorse.

I burned my fur catalogues in the furnace and hung my traps in the loft of the barn, never to use them again. Men had stopped killing other men in France that day; and on that day I signed a permanent peace treaty with the animals and the birds.

The first flurry of snow came early in

December, whirling a few flakes into Rascal's hollow in the tree. I fashioned a metal hood over the entrance and lined the hole with some old blankets and an outgrown sweater of mine so that he would have a snug winter nest.

Raccoons don't actually hibernate, but they do sleep for many days at a time, emerging only occasionally for a meal. Every morning before I left for school, I would go into the cage and reach into the hole. It was a great satisfaction to feel Rascal's warm, furry body breathing slowly and rhythmically. Now and then he would awake sufficiently to poke his drowsy-eyed face out of the hole and look at me. I always rewarded him with a handful of pecans.

My financial problems increased as we approached Christmas. In previous autumns, by trapping muskrats, I had earned as much as seventy-five dollars for the purchase of gifts. But since signing my peace treaty, I had fallen back on shoveling sidewalks and selling *The Saturday Evening Post* door to door. The silver accumulated very slowly.

Then one Saturday, after a discouraging tour of the stores, I stopped at the post office to find two letters that relieved my mind in a number of ways. One was from Herschel, the first since the Armistice. The other was from my beloved sister Jessica, still taking postgraduate work at the University of Chicago.

Herschel had survived the war and influenza. However, he had been ordered to march to the Rhine to help establish a bridgehead near Coblenz and he would not be demobilized for six months at the earliest. He asked us not to send Christmas gifts, and said he would bring his presents with him when he came home.

Jessica's letters were always a joy. Flashes of temper were to be expected, but these were outweighed by her gaiety and good humor. She was coming home for Christmas, she said, and she enclosed a ten-dollar check, to help me with my Christmas shopping.

That eased my financial crisis so that I could turn to the pleasant tasks of buying a Christmas tree and decorating the house. My father paid little attention to such matters, and furthermore he was again away on business. Almost immediately I realized that my raccoon presented a new and difficult problem. How could we have both Rascal and a Christmas tree in the living room? (All of my favorite pets shared Christmas with us.) I could well imagine the damage he might do to the fragile glass balls and figurines. And yet we must have both. The answer to this dilemma struck me as a real inspiration.

There was a large semicircular bay extending from the living room, with six windows that overlooked the garden. This was where we always mounted our tree. I bought and decorated a thick spruce, which tapered gracefully to the star at its tip, and nearly filled the bay with its fragrant greenery. Then I made careful measurements of the bay and hastened to my workbench in the barn. In less than an hour I had finished my job.

When my father returned from his trip, I led him happily into the living room and pointed to my handiwork. There, safe behind a frame of chicken wire, as though it might try to escape to its native forest, was the decorated tree, every bauble secure from my raccoon.

"My word," my father said mildly. "What are you building, Sterling, another cage for Rascal?"

"You're warm," I said. "It's so that Rascal can't climb the tree and spoil all the ornaments."

"Well," my father said hesitantly, "at least it's unusual."

"Do you think Jessica will hit the ceiling?"

"She might," my father said. "You never can tell what Jessica might do."

Soon after, Jessica arrived on the one-train-a-day from Chicago, an old ten-wheeler usually pulling a baggage car, a passenger coach and sometimes a freight car and a caboose. The conductor helped her down the steps, and my father and I took her suitcase and her many packages. She was wearing a wide-brimmed velvet hat that looked very fashionable, a new coat with a fur collar and high-laced shoes that came to the hem of her dress. She had recently sold some poems and a short story and seemed quite affluent.

She kissed us, then held me off and looked at me critically. "You've outgrown your mackinaw, Sterling. And you'll catch your death of cold not wearing a cap."

"He never wears a cap," my father explained. And obviously I was clean and my hair was combed, so Jessica wasn't altogether disapproving.

We went homeward through the iron-cold air and bright sunlight, up Fulton Street, past all the stores, laughing and chattering and asking a hundred questions in the manner of most families gathering for Christmas. But as we entered the living room, I wasn't sure whether Jessica wanted to laugh or cry. I had done my best in decorating the house. I had put a wreath above the fireplace, hung holly from archways and chandeliers, even laced Christmas ribbons through the ribs of my canoe frame, which was supposed to hold our cargo of gifts. But suddenly I saw it through my sister's eyes—dust on the furniture, an unfinished boat, chicken wire.

"You simply *can't* go on living like this!" she said. "You simply *must* hire a full-time housekeeper."

"But, Jessica, I worked so hard on the tree and the cage to keep Rascal out."

Then she was laughing and hugging me in the crazy, spontaneous, affectionate way she had. But not to lose her advantage she quickly added, "At least we can take the canoe to the barn."

"It's cold as blazes out there," I explained. "I have to put the canvas on first."

"Well, put on the canvas, and we'll still have time to clean this room for Christmas."

"You don't understand," I said. "I spent all my money to build Rascal's cage, and then all the other money I could scrape together to buy presents. I haven't any left for canvas, and it will cost about fifteen dollars, I think."

Jessica looked at my father severely, then sighed, realizing we were both quite hopeless and greatly in need of her care. "Well, at least I can cook you some decent meals and clean up this house."

"You sound just like Theo," I protested.

"We're happy," my father said. "At least, we're as happy as we can be since your mother died."

"Don't be sentimental," Jessica said fiercely, wiping tears from her own eyes. "You just wait until I get an apron on. And, another thing, you're going to have a housekeeper whether you like it or not."

On Christmas Eve we wrapped our gifts in secrecy, then arranged them in the canoe: father's in the prow, Jessica's in the stern and mine amidships. After an early dinner we brought in the animals, Rascal first, to allow him time to wake up for the festivities; then Wowser and, finally, selected cats. Jessica immediately fell in love with my raccoon. And when she saw how he struggled to reach through the wire to touch the Christmas-tree baubles, she forgave me for building the barricade.

We always gave the animals their presents first, for, like children, they found it difficult to wait. Each cat received a catnip mouse; Wowser, who was confined to a bath towel on the hearth because of his drooling, got a new collar; and for Rascal there were candies and pecans. Then the family packages were handed out: a fur muff for Jessica; a beaver cap for my father; shoe ice skates, a rare item in our region, for me.

My father's presents to us displayed unexpected forethought. The summer before, we had picked up several rough and encrusted agates on the shores of Lake Superior. The best ones he had sent to a gemcutting firm in Chicago. Beautifully cut and polished, they were ringed like Rascal's tail from golden brown to deep maroon. There were three each for Jessica and me and, to my surprise, one for Rascal, who was delighted and quickly stored it in the corner where he kept his pennies.

One more large package still lay amidships. "To Sterling, from Jessica." Removing the wrappings I found an unbelievable gift —enough heavy, white canvas to cover my entire canoe. I was near to tears, but Jessica saved the day. "Now," she said, "we can get this canoe out of the living room."

On winter weekends I often skated all day, playing hockey for hours and cutting simple figures on the ice. It is the nearest thing to flying I know. When Rascal was awake, I taught him to be a living coonskin hat. He would take a firm grip on my hair, brace his hind paws on the collar of my mackinaw and enjoy the wildest rides he had ever experienced as we glided forward and back over Culton's Pond.

I also completed my canoe, stretching the heavy canvas over the ribs, varnishing the inside and enameling the outside with a bright green paint. By March, when the first signs of spring began to appear, the canoe was ready for launching.

Except for this, however, there was little to be happy about. Theo and Jessica had finally won their point. We were acquiring a full-time housekeeper whether we wanted one or not. Mrs. Quinn was said to be qualified in every respect: middle-aged, ugly, cranky-clean and no nonsense. She examined our house minutely, ran her finger over the furniture for dust and demanded my bedroom for herself. She also delivered an ultimatum: "No pets in the house!"

It was sadly apparent that my father would be no match for our new housekeeper, so I dreamed up several stratagems to outwit her. But deep in my heart I knew that nothing could save Rascal. Quite apart from her orders, he ran the constant peril of being shot. One night recently he had got out of his cage and raided the henhouse of a particularly irascible neighbor. The aggrieved victim had his shotgun loaded should it happen again.

Moreover, now that he had grown to young adulthood, Rascal was not entirely happy as a pet. One moonlit night I heard hair-raising screams of rage. Grabbing a flashlight, I went out to find Rascal and another male raccoon trying to get at each other through the chicken wire. I chased the intruder away and put iodine on Rascal's scratches. But on another evening I heard very different sounds—the tremolo crooning of an amorous female raccoon trying to reach Rascal for more romantic reasons. I began to realize that it was selfish of me to keep him from his natural life out in the woods.

One warm and pleasant Saturday, just before Mrs. Quinn was due to arrive, I made my decision. I can remember every detail of that day, hour by hour. Rascal and I had slept together, and we ate together at the dining-room table. He was not behaving well. He walked directly across the tablecloth to the sugar bowl, lifted the lid and helped himself. Thirteen pounds of raccoon is quite a centerpiece. But knowing in my heart what I was plotting, I couldn't scold or slap him.

I told my father that we would be away all afternoon and evening on a long canoe ride. I think he knew what I was planning. He looked at us quite sympathetically.

Taking jelly sandwiches, strawberry pop and more than a pound of pecans, I led Rascal to where my canoe was waiting on Saunders Creek. Soon we reached Rock River, and I turned upstream toward Lake Koshkonong. Rascal fell asleep during the hours that I labored against the current. Then he awoke toward sunset as we reached the quiet mirror of the lake itself, heading toward the dark, wild promontory named Koshkonong Point.

It was an evening of full moon, much like the one when I had found my little friend and carried him home in my cap, a helpless creature to whom I had fed warm milk through a wheat straw. Now he was capable in many ways, able to catch all the food he needed, able to climb, swim and almost talk.

We entered the mouth of Koshkonong Creek and paddled upstream into the depths of a wilderness. I took off Rascal's collar and his leash. Then we sat together in the canoe, listening to the night sounds.

It came at last, the sound I was waiting for: the crooning of a female raccoon. Rascal became excited, and soon he answered with a deeper crooning of his own. The female was now approaching along the edge of the stream, trilling a plaintive call, infinitely tender and questing. Rascal raced to the prow of the canoe, straining to see through the moonlight and shadow, sniffing the air and asking questions.

"Do as you please, my little raccoon. It's your life," I told him.

He hesitated for one full minute, turned once to look back at me, then took the plunge and swam to the shore. He had chosen to join that entrancing female somewhere in the shadows. I caught only one glimpse of them in a moonlight glade before they disappeared to begin their new life.

I left the pecans on a stump near the waterline, hoping Rascal would find them. Then I paddled swiftly and desperately away.

Last Escape

by FRED GIPSON

ALONG IN THE MIDDLE of the afternoon Grandpa Branch's horse showed up at the corral, stripped of everything but the bridle. The sight scared me sick. What had happened to Grandpa Branch? Dragged to death in the brush, maybe? I ran to saddle up and go look for his remains.

Just then Grandpa Branch walked in, stooped under the weight of the saddle he packed. "Rope me out a fresh horse," he shouted. "Fetch me another saddle girth and that new hard-twist rope I brung from town yesterday. Then go turn loose that catch dog. And hurry up!"

I wanted mighty bad to know what had happened, but it was no time to pester Grandpa with questions. He was setting his saddle on a big sorrel when I came up with the blue-ticked hound we used for catching wild hogs and varmints out of the brush. I couldn't wait any longer. "What's up, Grandpa?" I asked.

Grandpa yanked his black hat down tighter over his head. "That confounded old outlaw steer! He got away again!"

Less than a mile downriver Grandpa had ridden up on the old scalawag longhorn steer that every ranch hand on the Nueces River had been trying to catch or shoot for years. Grandpa had roped him, but when the steer ran against Grandpa's rope the saddle girth had parted, leaving Grandpa to ride his saddle off over his horse's ears. Of course, he had to release the rope. You couldn't hold a runaway steer without a horse under your saddle.

"But with a dog to locate him," Grandpa said, "and that rope drag to slow him up a bit, we'll catch that old *ladino*. We'll show that Pelly bunch whether I'm too old for cow work!"

The Pellys, who owned the next ranch, had been good friends of Grandpa's till one of the younger men hit Grandpa up to sign him on as foreman. He said that a man seventy-five years old had no business trying to work cattle. That sure had rankled Grandpa. After that episode he hadn't much use for the Pellys.

Now Grandpa swung up into his saddle and led off at a gallop. I followed, the catch dog Rattler loping along behind. I rode with mounting excitement. I was fifteen, and I never before had helped to run an outlaw steer. I'd heard old-timers tell about running brush-wild longhorns in the old days, and it sure had sounded exciting. But the wild longhorns were gone now—sold off or shot to help get rid of fever ticks and to make room for better cattle. The only one left alive that

105

anybody knew about was just this one old steer. He was big and had long, curved horns that spread more than five feet from tip to tip.

"Them horns ain't ornaments, neither," Jim Doughty of the Running W outfit had stated with conviction. Once Jim had crowded the old scalawag into the blind end of a draw and got a horse gored to death under him. Mexican *vaqueros* (cowboys) wouldn't run him anymore, he had hurt so many horses and men.

At a little clearing, Grandpa got off his horse and called to Rattler. He bent over, pointing to the sharp-pointed hoof marks in the sand. "Sic him, Rattler," he urged. "Go git him, boy!"

Rattler sniffed the tracks a time or two and then lined out. His trail voice rang through the mesquite, pretty as a bell. Grandpa mounted his horse, his black eyes snapping with excitement. "Now, git fixed to do some tall riding, boy!"

Rattler ran the trail slowly at first, but soon Grandpa and I were following his ringing voice at a steady trot. I could feel my pulse hammering in my ears. Up ahead was a big, tangled thicket of white brush and tornillo. Suddenly Rattler's voice lifted high with excitement. There was a violent crashing inside the thicket, and out the other side burst the scalawag steer. Right behind him went Rattler, baying at the top of his voice, with Grandpa hard on his heels, ripping holes in the brush where there weren't any. My horse carried me headlong into the gap Grandpa had made. The brush whipped me in the face, blinding me, and for a few scared seconds I shut my eyes. Then a dead branch slammed against my ribs, jarring me to my senses. You don't run wild cattle in the brush with your eyes shut—unless you want to get your brains knocked out.

The old steer kept traveling from thicket to thicket, mile after mile. He jumped barbwire fences that Grandpa and I had to kick down to get our horses over. He swam the river twice. He would have lost me and Grandpa half a dozen times if it hadn't been for Rattler. I was ready to call off the chase anytime after the first mile. But there was no quitting for Grandpa Branch. So I fought the brush and stayed with him.

Just at sundown Rattler brought the steer to bay, backed up against a clump of live-oak saplings. As we rode in sight, the old outlaw bellowed his defiance, an earsplitting blare that made the air quiver. My scalp shifted under my hat. With a sudden lunge the old steer charged Grandpa. His winded horse barely leaped aside in time. At the same instant, Grandpa whipped a wide loop down and out, in a peculiar backhand cast that was as true as it had been fifty years before—right around those widespread horns. Grandpa gave the rope a yank to take up the slack and made his dally around the saddle horn, all in one swift motion.

What happened next came so fast I never quite realized how it was. I saw the steer hit the end of the rope, then Grandpa's horse rocked sideways to his knees, with Grandpa yelling and trying to pull him back on his feet. But he was still half down when the steer charged again. Without thinking I spurred in and reached down with my loop and picked up both heels of that charging steer. I wheeled in such a short circle that my offside boot toe scraped dirt, and I hauled that fighting longhorn off Grandpa just before those lunging horns could rip into him. I couldn't have pulled that trick again in a thousand tries.

Grandpa's horse came to his feet at last and between us we stretched the old longhorn out on the ground—the outlaw that had evaded capture for fifteen years. The last of the wild ones! We left him lying on his side

with feet tied together around the base of a live-oak sapling. In the morning we would bring out a gentle bull and neck the wild one to him.

"It'll take a bull a day or two to drag him in," Grandpa said. "But he'll do it, I know he will. And when he does, I want to have Irv Pelly on hand."

Next morning I was up while the coyotes were still singing for daylight. Grandpa was in the kitchen ahead of me, having his usual "Mexican breakfast" of black coffee and cigarettes. In the yellow lamplight I could see his fierce old eyebrows pulled together in a worried frown.

"Boy," he said, "I been thinking. Far as I know, that old outlaw is the last wild longhorn out of the bunch Cabeza de Vaca and them other old Spanish boys let get away from them here in the brush." He glared at me. "Do you know," he said to me, "that it was around four hundred years ago? Them old cattle has lived here in the brush all that time, fighting panther and bear and wolf."

"Yes, sir," I said. "I read all about it in a book."

"You read about it in a book!" he flared. "Boy, I worked them cattle. I trailed them from the Rio Grande to the Injun reservation in Montana. I seen them build towns like Dodge City and Abilene. They made a cow country out of Texas and fed this entire nation when there was no other meat to be had!"

He broke off and stared at the red-checked tablecloth. "And now they're all gone. And all the good men and good horses that worked them. Nothing left but bone dust and recollections."

I had never seen Grandpa worked up like this before. He got up suddenly. "Well, dang it!" he said. "I'm gonna do it. I'm gonna go turn that old longhorn loose and let him live out his time in the brush. Where he belongs!"

I just couldn't believe what I was hearing. "But, Grandpa!" I protested. "What about Irv Pelly?"

"Irv Pelly!" Grandpa roared. "That blowhard won't ever git close enough to that old steer to even touch him with a rope!"

I could see it was time for me to hush. I went out and saddled our horses. When we rode into the clearing, the old outlaw was lying in the same position we had left him —mighty still, it seemed to me. Grandpa loped ahead and was staring down at the old longhorn when I rode up. "We killed him!" he said hoarsely. There was a note of hurt in his voice, and his face was gray. "But I don't understand it!" he complained. "That old steer's been run harder and longer than we run him yesterday. And we never broke him up none when we roped him."

"I guess he was just too wild to stand capture, Grandpa," I said. "I've read where some wild things just sort of will themselves to die when they're caught."

"You reckon that's what he done?" Grandpa said in an awed voice. A light leaped into his eyes and he straightened in his saddle. "That's it," he said. "He done it a-purpose! One way or another, he was bound to give us the slip." His voice lowered. "Looks like he's escaped for good this time."

The Obstreperous Owls of Hammel

by CARL C. ANDERSEN

ONE SUMMER EVENING some twenty years ago the members of the Town Council of Hammel, Denmark, were on their way home from a meeting. It was dark under the trees bordering the churchyard, and the town fathers, led by their venerable and portly mayor, Herr Marius Trust, were walking slowly. Suddenly there was a whirring in the air. The elders' hats were torn from their heads; unseen claws ripped into their faces. It was all over in a few seconds. When the dazed councilmen gathered under the nearest street lamp they looked at each other in horror and amazement. They were tattered, bloody scarecrows.

"Gentlemen," said Mayor Trust shakily, "we know that ghosts do not exist. But something in the graveyard there . . ." His voice broke off for a moment. "What will people think? How will we explain our condition?" The worthies pondered gloomily. "They will think," continued the mayor, "that we were drunk and fought with each other." It was finally decided that each would swear his family to silence and stay out of sight for a few days.

This was only the beginning, however. The town's bookbinder—a mild old gentleman whose shop was not far from the churchyard—was savagely attacked a few nights later by the invisible horror. On subsequent evenings there were several other victims of the clawing Thing.

The explanation of the mystery, when it came, was startling. Two men crossing the churchyard on a moonlit night saw their assailants: Not ghosts but three large owls swooped down on them in a power dive. The men had no chance to defend themselves before the birds had clawed and ripped and were gone.

The whole town was shocked. Like the storks of Ribe, the owls of Hammel were a time-honored institution. They hunted in the nearby forest of Frijsenborg, but they lived in such harmony with their human neighbors that no one suspected them of the attacks.

But now the war was quickly stepped up. The owls attacked one and all, with no respect for rank or propriety. Small owls got through the louvers of the church's bell tower and assaulted the sexton as he rang the Angelus, while their big relatives whizzed menacingly around outside the steeple.

School Inspector Foenns insisted that owls are harmless; but he was soon convert-

109

ed. As he was leaving the home of the Reverend Mr. Traerup after a church board meeting, a team of power-diving birds singled him out from his colleagues and left him a ragged, bleeding wreck. "It was as though they had decided to teach him a lesson," said Sexton Pedersen.

Even the marshal did not escape. Chief police authority of the district, he had been outspoken in his disdain for the people of Hammel who had allowed themselves to be panicked by owls. He would tolerate no hysteria, he had warned, and any attempt to molest the birds would be punished. But the owls showed no appreciation for his protection; a squadron of three ambushed him one evening.

Mayor Trust now demanded action. The Town Council agreed. A petition was sent to the Ministry of Agriculture requesting enactment of a special law permitting the citizens to shoot belligerent owls.

The Honorable Herr Soenderup, Minister of Agriculture at the time, found himself in a difficult position. The Danes take their wildlife seriously, and any breach of the conservation laws is a grave offense. After an exhaustive study of all the reports, the minister himself framed the reply to the Hammel petition: Under no circumstances could Hammel use firearms against the birds. The citizens could, however, plug

110

with cement the owls' nest holes in the trees around the churchyard. That was as far as the minister would go. He suggested that it might be wiser, however, to discover the cause of the birds' belligerence and attempt to remove it.

Mayor Trust made an exhaustive investigation which turned up some interesting facts. The people who had been assaulted in daylight agreed that every attacking squadron was led by an unusually large owl of rusty coloring. When he heard this, Niels Christiansen, huntsman and chicken farmer, came forward with important testimony. He had, some years ago, found a pair of owlets on a hunting trip. He had taken them home and caged them. They were fond of each other and huddled together by the hour. One morning the female owl lay dead at the bottom of the cage. Her mate, who had grown to huge size and had an unusually rusty coloring, was unapproachable in his grief. Usually friendly, the owl showed such terrible rage that Herr Christiansen didn't dare go near him. A few days later he was gone, having smashed out of the cage.

The huntsman's report sparked the memories of teachers and pupils at the high school across the road from the churchyard. One day when the children were on the playground an automobile had come along the road at a fast clip. An owl flew in front of the car and there was a crash of breaking glass as the windshield shattered. A female owl lay dead next to the horrified driver. At that moment a huge rust-colored bird emerged from an elm nearby and dived down to see what had happened. He made several vicious passes at the automobile and then withdrew to his tree.

The loss of his two mates had obviously turned Old Rusty into an embittered foe of the human race. And somehow he was able to enlist his usually peaceful fellow birds in a war of revenge.

The Town Council marshaled a group of young men to try to catch Old Rusty and his most aggressive lieutenants. Equipped with steel helmets, their faces protected with gas masks, and carrying nets, they climbed before dawn into the trees where the most active owls perched during daylight hours. A large crowd gathered around to watch the battle.

And a battle it was. One owl was snared in a net. Then Old Rusty's defense forces went into action. From their nests in trees all over the churchyard, owls took purposefully to the air. Forming in squadrons of threes and fours, they came down in whistling dives on their would-be captors. In less than half an hour it was all over; the forces of law and order withdrew from the field.

There was only one more possibility. One night when the owls had gone off on a hunting foray to the forest, a group of townsfolk plugged their nests with cement. The stratagem worked; the next morning the owls were gone. Hammel, though saddened by the affair, was relieved at its outcome. Minister Soenderup in Copenhagen expressed the gratitude of the Ministry of Agriculture that the matter of the owls had finally been resolved without violence.

But this was not quite the end. As the next winter drew near, the owls began to come back. The Danish winter is severe and the owls seem to like company in time of stress. Even Old Rusty returned to the big elm in the churchyard. And with him was a new mate. Perhaps this was why there were no further attacks. Old Rusty and Mrs. Rusty disappeared four years ago; but owls remain a symbol of Hammel, and the ones that continue to live there are tractable, as they had been for so many years.

I Learned About Cows from Her

by ROBERT ORMOND CASE

ON A SUNNY Saturday afternoon in Portland, Oregon (population almost 375,000), I was driving my daughter to her weekly swimming lesson. As we came to a heavily traveled boulevard we saw an unusual cavalcade approaching: a gaunt, wild-eyed milch cow trailed by numerous cars, and boys on bicycles and on foot.

"That poor cow!" I said indignantly. "Those ignorant city people are frightening her out of her wits."

At that time my daughter, aged nine, believed that Papa was equal to any crisis—a notion she later outgrew. "What are you going to do?" she asked.

"See that short piece of rope dangling from her neck?" I said. "After I leave you at the YWCA I'll go back and catch her and hold her for her owner, who's probably trying to find her."

Having milked cows as a boy, worked with beef cattle and written half a million words of Western fiction devoted largely to milling herds, thundering six-guns and men who bleed freely, I knew—so I thought—all about cows.

Later I learned that this particular cow had come at least seven miles, most of it at a gallop, and en route had knocked down two pedestrians and a street cleaner. She had treed a newspaper boy and tossed a dog over a hedge. She had crossed the baseball field at Grant High School, scattering the players and (to the delight of the spectators) flattening the umpire in passing. In brief, desolation lay behind her. The mob was not following her with sadistic intent but solely to see what she would do next.

I left my daughter at the Y, circled back and found the cow standing on the grassy edge of a side street, breathing heavily. The crowd surrounded her—at a respectful distance. I parked my car, pitying their ignorance. All this fuss and feathers about a well-meaning much-put-upon cow! I walked up to her in what the spectators assumed to be a fearless manner. She watched me narrowly as I approached, turning her head to view me

112

with one bulging eye, then the other. At thirty feet from her I had my first qualm, at twenty a serious doubt. At ten feet I halted and the truth dawned. Here was a cow foreign to my experience. Pushed to hysteria and completely off her bovine rocker, she was ready to charge anything that moved.

I turned and ran. But, like those comedians in the silent films, I seemed to make no progress. The cow's head caught me behind the knees; one horn was on each side and I grasped them. I found myself sitting on her head, not too uncomfortable but considerably puzzled about what to do next. Something must be done, obviously. I was being carried across the street like a batter-

ing ram. Dead ahead was the menacing brick wall of a warehouse.

In the middle of the street the cow surprised me by sliding to a halt. I stepped off, as from a bus. The spectators applauded. The cow headed up the street. Hard by was a small nursery and greenhouse whose sign invited: COME IN. The cow did so. Two fat men, father and son—father about 240 pounds, son 280—were seated on the greenhouse steps enjoying the sunshine. Suddenly the fat boy said, "Paw! There's a cow in the middle of our tulip bed!"

"Damned if there ain't!" the father agreed.

At that instant the cow charged. The father jumped up and ran into the green-

house. The fat boy was too slow; the cow knocked him down, stepped on the largest adjacent area—his stomach—and followed the father into the greenhouse. Paw dived under a bench in the potting room. The cow hooked savagely at the bench, turned and charged out, leaving ruin behind her. The fat boy had just come to his feet when the cow leaped out, knocked him down and again stepped on his stomach. Much annoyed, he seized the cow's foreleg, dragged her down and hung on. The spectators now filled the entire garden. Our man of destiny —me, the late expert on cows—was in the front rank, still eager to be of help. The fat boy was bellowing: What to do now? Sit on her head, I told him. The fat boy did so. Now get a rope, Paw.

Paw got a rope. Tie it around her horns, I directed. Wrap the other end around that tree. Paw did so. The fat boy got up and limped to the tree to help Paw haul in the line. The cow came up like a wounded cougar, once more charged the fat boy, knocked him down, again stepped on his stomach. The boy, now excessively annoyed, managed to snub her head against the tree.

A policeman who had just come up surveyed the scene with astonished interest. "What's going on here? What the Samm Hill —a *cow*?"

"What does it look like, a sea lion?" asked the fat boy bitterly.

"What d'you want me to do?"

"Shoot her!"

"Very well," said the officer, reaching for his revolver.

"Hold it!" Paw protested. "What'll we do with a dead cow?"

The officer holstered his gun. "Make up your minds, please."

My voice spoke from the safety of the crowd. But it no longer had the ring of authority. "Call the Humane Society."

They called the Humane Society. A truck came and let down a ramp, and attendants approached the cow. I expected new ruin to explode, but nothing happened. It may be that in the cow's dim, addled brain the rope about her horns spelled security. Perhaps she merely thought—but who knows what a cow thinks? Not I. In any event she went meekly up the ramp and into the truck. Later my daughter asked me about the poor cow. My reply was truthful but brief. "They caught her and the Humane Society took her. No dear, I didn't catch her, a fat boy did . . . How did the swimming go?"

The sagacious owner did not appear to claim the cow. After TB and other standard tests—including psychiatric help, no doubt —they gave her to an orphanage. I understand the little ones there loved her.

Since I was a former newspaperman, my pals on the Portland papers had a field day. Their Sunday headlines were pitiless: WRITER OF WESTERN STORIES STAGES IMPROMPTU RODEO . . . AUTHOR'S DILEMMA—BETWEEN HORNS OF . . . And so on. There was one minor sop for my damaged ego. To one of my interviewers, a grammarian of note, puns were anathema. I sent him away revolted and near tears. Nevertheless his feature story gamely ended: "Author Case was asked if he was badly frightened by the adventure. 'Oh, no,' replied Bob cheerfully. 'I'll have to admit, though, that I was a little bit cowed.' "

Doc Pete's Friend Charlie

by KEITH MUNRO

THE DAY Doc Pete killed Charlie was a black day for Winchester and all the Ontario countryside for miles around. To Doc Pete it was a great personal tragedy—he destroyed Charlie with his own hands, and I watched him do it.

Charlie was the prettiest, highsteppingest Standardbred you ever saw. He was black with a shimmer of bronze; an artist's model of a horse: arched neck, small head, patrician nose with nostrils like black velvet. When Charlie came stepping down the village street we kids would say, "Here comes Doc Pete," even before we could see who was driving. Then Charlie would whirl past, knees rising high at every stride, and Doc Pete would wave to us and call, "Hiya, Sports!"

That was the high point of the day for us, for we kids felt, more than did grownups, the bond that existed between Charlie, the stylish Standardbred, and Peter McLaughlin, the six-foot, broad-shouldered country doctor with the high forehead and the huge Roman nose.

The bond betwixt horse and man went back to Charlie's birth. He was a sickly colt, hardly able to stand on his trembly pins. Doc Bean, the veterinary, said he probably wouldn't live; but Doc Pete, looking at that splendid head, sensed the surging spirit in the frail body. He took the colt under his personal care, nursed him to health and named him for his favorite character— Bonnie Prince Charlie. The horse sure was princely and proud enough.

One of my early memories of Charlie is vivid and rather horrible—a half-grown, leggy colt caught in a barbed-wire fence, thrashing, tearing his flesh and screaming. I lived nearby and ran over when I heard him. Jed Todd, the hired man, was already there, but he couldn't control Charlie, let alone get him loose. Then Doc Pete arrived on a dead run and as soon as he spoke to Charlie and patted him, the frantic colt relaxed. He stood trembling, his blood spurting, while Doc Pete took the wire cutters and freed him.

When Doc Bean looked at Charlie's legs and said it might be best to destroy him, Doc Pete gave him one of the blackest looks I ever saw. He didn't say a word, just went to work on those poor torn legs. Charlie let him. He stood there snorting and trembling until Doc Pete got him bandaged and the bleeding stopped. But every time Doc tried to leave, Charlie would whinny him back.

Doc Pete's patients were treated in the barn that night and Doc stayed there with the black colt until dawn. Charlie was crippled for weeks, but Doc Pete kept massaging his legs until the day came when Charlie could again raise those knees high as he ran about the pasture.

The breaking in proved that Charlie was Doc Pete's horse and nobody else's. The hired man tried to harness him and it was quite a battle until Doc arrived. He rubbed Charlie's neck and nose and talked to him as the shafts were lowered over his flanks. Then Doc Pete got into the sleigh, took the reins and drove Charlie off just as though they'd been doing it for years—and as they were going to be doing for years to come.

Charlie's spirit wasn't the runaway spirit you see in so many horses; he never ran away with Doc Pete in all the miles they traveled together. He did dump him in the ditch a few times, though. Country doctors must get their rest as they can, so when Doc Pete finished setting a leg or ushering a new citizen into the world, he'd climb into the seat, tie the reins to the dashboard and say, "Home, Charlie." Then he'd go to sleep. But in winter the holes in the roads often got pretty deep, and more than once Charlie bounced Doc Pete right out into the snow. After a quarter mile or so, he'd realize that Doc Pete wasn't with him anymore. Doc Pete told me he could hear him coming back, whinnying loudly as though to say, "Doc Pete, where are you?" When he found him he'd stand and nicker as Doc Pete rearranged the buffalo robes and climbed back into the sleigh.

If Charlie found himself on a strange road he'd look back anxiously as though to say, "Do you know where you're going?" And Doc Pete would tell him, "We're just taking a shortcut to Dan McGregor's." Sometimes Doc Pete would hand me the reins and let me drive—I still remember the thrill the first time he did it, though it was many years ago.

It was fun to go to the barn at night when Doc Pete harnessed Charlie. As soon as he opened the stable door and Charlie saw him with the lantern, the horse would whinny. I remember one night Doc Pete answered, "We're going down to Jack Stuart's in the Melvin Settlement." Charlie whinnied again and Doc Pete said, "Yes, she is. I hope we get there in time." He was having me on, of course, but just the same, I asked him what Charlie was saying. He laughed and said that when he'd told Charlie where they were going Charlie had come back with, "Don't tell me Mrs. Stuart's having another baby so soon." I knew then that Doc Pete was kidding. But as I look back on it now, I'm not so sure.

Doc was inordinately proud of Charlie and he had good reason to be. There was the night the horse brought Doc Pete through the flood. Spring rain was melting the snow, and as they crossed the Nation River at Cass Bridge, Doc Pete saw that the water was rising. "Hurry up, old boy," he said to Charlie. "We've got to get back before the water runs over the road." They hurried, but when they returned to the bridge, men with lanterns stopped them. Ab McIntosh said, "Doc Pete, you'll have to stop with us tonight. The water's over the road. You can't make it."

But Doc Pete said he had to go through. On the other side of the river a young woman was due to have her first baby and he was worried about her and how scared she'd be. "Why, there's not more than three feet of water," he said, and drove on into the darkness.

Doc Pete knew it was Charlie's show. All Doc did was talk to him and for once Charlie was too busy to talk back. He had all he could do to keep his feet on the slippery gravel that was already washing out in spots. He moved deliberately, bracing himself against the swirling current and the chunks of ice that came charging at him out of the blackness. One huge piece almost upset the buggy but Doc Pete—who couldn't swim a stroke—leaned far out over the water, as though he were sailing a dinghy in a high wind, and righted it. When at last they came up out of the flood to other men with lanterns, one of them said accusingly, "Doc Pete, why did you do such a damfool thing?" Doc Pete got out, felt Charlie's legs, and when he found only a few minor cuts from the sharp ice, he straightened up and said, "Herman, you know this is the season when all my babies are born. Besides, I knew Charlie would get me through."

When cars grew common Doc Pete bought one—more to take the burden off Charlie's aging shoulders than for his own comfort, for he really hated cars. He couldn't talk to a car, except in cusswords. The car made Charlie a gentleman of leisure in summer, which he spent in pasture. Finally Doc Pete, thinking to lighten Charlie's burden in winter too, bought a young horse to help.

Doc Pete served the people of that Canadian countryside for fifty-five years. Charlie didn't last that long. I'll never forget his death. It was a hot, oppressive August day. Late in the afternoon a violent thunderstorm cleared the air, and back in the pasture Charlie and the new horse, glad to be cool again, got to running. They came thundering out into the lane, Charlie far out in front. No whippersnapper was going to beat him. Rounding a bend without slackening pace, he was suddenly confronted by a closed gate.

He tried to jump it. Charlie was no jumper; besides, he wasn't so young anymore. His front feet hit the top and down he came.

We half expected to see him jump to his feet with his familiar whinny. He struggled hard but couldn't seem to lift his head. I ran to Doc Pete's office, crying, "Charlie's hurt himself! He can't get up!"

Doc Pete hurried out. Charlie was moaning and his muzzle was white with froth. Doc Pete felt his body and legs, then as though he dreaded to find out for sure, he ran his hands along that proud, arching neck. He stood up and we kids waited. "His neck is broken," he finally managed, without looking at anybody.

One of us ran to get Jim Cooper, the barber. He came over with his deer rifle. But he couldn't bring himself to shoot Charlie. Doc Pete went into his office and came out with a big bottle of chloroform. He poured a lot of it on a wad of cotton. He bent down and I heard him say, "Good-bye, Charlie, old boy." He held the cotton to Charlie's nostrils and kept adding more chloroform until Charlie's convulsive breathing grew less and less.

By that time quite a few people had gathered. I saw my mother dabbing at her eyes with her apron, and she wasn't the only one who was crying. At last, Doc Pete stood up and threw that chloroform bottle as far as he could. Then he said, "We'll bury him right here where he fell."

We dug the hole wide and deep. Then Doc Pete left—said someone wanted him in the office. But we knew he couldn't stand to be around when lumps of earth began drumming on Charlie's body.

The Falcon and I

by JEAN GEORGE

I WAS ALONE in the attic. My children were off to school. The sweep of my broom was checked by an object behind the trunk: the old wooden box that held my girlhood diaries. Amused, I lifted a blue-leather one from the lot and opened it. I don't remember cleaning the rest of the attic. For the words I read startled me with intimations that were not there when I had written: "I spoke to my beloved falcon tonight, and I said to him: 'If there is a way to balance our wings on the sky we shall go that way together.' "

At thirteen I had had no other thought than that I adored the bird my twin brothers had given me. But these many years later those words crystallized my relationship with the falcon. We *had* balanced our wings together, for I had turned the wild, noble bird into a disciplined hunter precisely during the period when I myself was being groomed for womanhood. And there in the attic I began to understand for the first time the subtle ways in which the falcon and I grew up together, learning through passionate rebellion and quiet acceptance that freedom begins only when necessary restrictions are buried in habit.

I first saw the young sparrow hawk in the bottom of a bushel basket in our kitchen.

He flopped on his back and, eyes flashing, threatened me with his open talons. He looked ferocious—until a wisp of the natal down he was shedding landed comically on the end of his hooked beak. "He's wonderful!" I exclaimed, as my hand circled his steely-blue body. He cried "killie" in rage, and I winced as he dug his needle talons into my hand. Weeping and laughing, I pried the talons out of my flesh and pressed the hot, woodsy-smelling creature against my cheek. "You are only four weeks old and have a lot to learn," I whispered with great sadness, for only that morning my own nestlinghood had come to an end. My mother had finished telling me the facts of life.

My brothers, three years my senior and already knowledgeable falconers with hawks of their own, were both amused and pleased with the meeting of girl and bird. "The sparrow hawk is a noble bird," said my brother John. "It is one of the smallest of the true falcons, or noble birds of prey."

"And the training," my brother Frank added solemnly, "must begin immediately. Feed the falcon nothing—and I mean nothing—unless he takes it from your hand. Use this whistle"—he gave three notes—"then let him eat."

I was left alone with the young and the

119

noble. I tried to make the bird sit on my hand. He bit a finger. I stroked him. He flew at my face. There and then I named him Bad Boy.

All afternoon I tried to win him with succulent grasshoppers. He looked at them and screamed in hunger, but he would not take them from my hand. I cried. Then came a constricting fear: The little falcon would die of starvation right before my eyes! In desperation I threw him a grasshopper. Bad Boy stared in anger; then a yellow foot shot out and snagged the morsel. The bird wolfed. Certain that he would be won by my generosity, I reached out to take him. But he snapped at me and ran under the radiator. From there he fought my hand with such ferocity that it bled. John and Frank found me there, crying, and brought the gladiator out with gauntlets. Then I confessed what I had done.

"Now you musn't feed him anything until tomorrow. When he is hungry enough he *will* eat from your hand."

That night I resolved in my diary to "do it right—it will be less heartbreaking in the long run." The wisdom to "do it right" had stemmed from an earlier experience—when I'd spent a dollar and declared I hadn't. Supporting one untruth with another had become so agonizingly complicated that when I finally told the truth it was so simple I was startled. Alone there in the attic I saw that I had transferred that experience to the bird: It *was* easier—in the long run—to follow the rules.

I turned a page of the diary. It reported that I got up at 5 a.m. Bad Boy was still in his temporary home, the bushel basket. When he saw me he again bristled for a fight, bill open and talons exposed. But when I whistled the call that was to mean, "Come, food," and held out a grasshopper, his feathers relaxed and he nibbled tentatively at the grasshopper—then began to eat! I slipped my finger under his feet and lifted him out of the basket. Trembling, I fed him two, three, four grasshoppers. When he was done he was still perched on my hand. Quickly I apologized to the bird for the training. I remember explaining that it would get worse before it got better. "It is being done so that when you fly free you will know what you are doing," I wrote in my diary. Reading the words now, I was not sure whether they were addressed to the falcon or to myself. One day, noting that Bad Boy's wings had filled out to their full span, my brothers said: "It is time to put leg straps on him—falconers call them jesses—for now that he can fly you must have control of him."

On the kitchen table we cut the jesses, two slender strips of soft deer hide. An ingenious falconer's knot held the straps to the legs. Frank deftly put the jesses on Bad Boy, and I flipped him to my wrist, holding the straps. Bad Boy tried to fly, fell forward, tried to fly again and sat still. We snapped a leash to the jesses by a swivel designed to keep the leash from twisting or binding the bird. Then we took him out to the perch waiting for him and tied the leash to a circle of wire at the base of the pole. He hopped to his perch, bobbed his head, blinked his eyes and immediately tried to fly away. Apparently surprised when he was pulled back, he flopped and screamed at the end of the cord. Then presently he flew back to his perch and sat there quietly.

That night my first social-dancing lesson began. Over our loud protest, the neighborhood mothers had hired an instructor to teach their boys and girls. The frightened group gathered in our living room, and as my first partner put his arm self-consciously around my waist I suddenly remembered that I had not checked Bad Boy—he might be tangled in his new leash. I ran! When I returned I could hear the teacher droning on and on, "Step-together-step." I can still see that roomful of young adolescents—step-together-step, step-together-step. A boy breaks away to see if he can jump and touch the chandelier—step-together-step. A girl gets the giggles and has to get a drink of water—step-together-step. And next morning, when I forced Bad Boy to come halfway across the yard for food, the words passed my lips: "Step-together-step." The reluctant bird circled on his perch and "killied" for fifteen minutes—but in the end he, too, accepted the strange new rules.

Every summer our family vacationed in my father's old home in the Pennsylvania mountains. There, in the enormous mid-Victorian house we shared with cousins, aunts and uncles, I was trained in the female arts—cooking, sewing, housekeeping. And there Bad Boy became a falcon—a hunter. A few weeks after our arrival, my brothers informed me that Bad Boy was trained well enough to fly free, which meant I should take his leash off when I whistled him to my hand. "Don't feed him for a day," Frank told me. "Then try him out."

From the beginning there was something "off" about that day. Mother was upset with me because I had come down the rainspout instead of the steps. She thought I was too big for such displays—"undignified" she called it, using the word I resented so terribly. Added to that was my apprehension about flying the falcon free. If I lost that bird, my uncertain world would collapse. For I was truly happy, it seemed to me, only when I was with him. To console the hungry Bad Boy, I kept him company that afternoon, reading under the maple tree near his perch. But he kept begging me for food, and when I could stand it no longer I caught several crickets and fed them to him. He flapped his wings ecstatically.

The next morning I dared not confess to my brothers what I had done, so we prepared for the flight. John unsnapped the leash. I stood at the end of the long yard with the lure—a wooden block on a string, covered with feathers to look like a bird, on which food was tied. I whistled and waved the lure. The falcon sped down the yard, missed the lure and headed for the open sky. For the moment I was left breathless by his mastery of the air. His wings folded, spread, clipped the winds. He rode them higher and higher—and then he was gone.

John, Frank and I spelled each other all day in search. Night came. The perch under the maple tree was still vacant. I cried all night. At dawn I heard the familiar "killie, killie, killie." I dashed down the steps and there, on his perch, I found Bad Boy—lifting his wings and turning as if the leash were still snapped to the jesses! I fought down the impulse to run to him. I moved forward with great restraint. When I was two feet away, he jumped to my shoulder and pecked my chin—hard. He was *hungry*. When he was safely leashed I took the .22 rifle and brought down a house sparrow near the barn. On the run I went back to the falcon and unsnapped his leash. I walked to the end of the yard and, holding out the sparrow, whistled. He dropped onto his wings, swooped over the grass and hit my hand with a blow—exactly the way a trained falcon should. Needless to say, my brothers were awakened early that morning.

Bird and I sailed on smoothly from that day. He needed only to hear me whistle and he was on my shoulder or the lure. Even when I returned to school, with the blooming of the goldenrod, Bad Boy accepted my absence with no backsliding in his discipline.

But there was backsliding in *my* training. Mother came to my room with a package one night while I was getting ready for bed. She looked at me as woman to woman, and a knowing warmth softened her face. "You are developing nicely," she said and, to underline the alarming truth, opened the package—a girdle, silk stockings and a brassiere! I wanted to run, hide, drop dead—anything to escape—and after she left I buried them resentfully at the bottom of the bureau drawer like a guilty secret. In the following months several occasions arose when I should have worn them, and didn't. But Mother said nothing more than that my brothers seemed to be able to wear neckties now without grumbling.

One day I came home late from school to find my brothers on the back steps amid a clutter of tools, leather and patterns. "We're going to hood Bad Boy," Frank explained.

"Oh, no!" I protested. "It's cruel. He won't be able to see."

"Well, you're too busy to keep him in training. He's getting wild, breaking his tail feathers pulling at the leash. A hood will keep him quiet."

The completed hood was handsome, decorated with a topknot of chicken feathers and with a clever drawstring that could be easily tightened or loosened. I would not go with them to hood my bird, but I watched from the back porch. Confident that he would not tolerate this abuse, I waited for him to fly into a fury, to fight back. But Bad Boy stopped screaming the moment the hood was on. He shook it, scratched it violently, then sat quietly in the sudden night. As good falconers, John and Frank intended that Bad Boy should be hooded when not hunting. But I could not bear the thought of my sky-loving bird sitting in darkness. I unhooded him and took him to my room. If I was too busy to keep him in training, then I would make a pet of him. And Bad Boy as a pet—although a breach of falconry rules—was a satisfying arrangement for me. He sat

on my head or the back of my chair while I studied. And when there was company, he always caused such a sensation flying around the house that I forgot my own awkward embarrassment in the midst of adults.

One evening my father was having a colleague to dinner, and by the preparations under way I knew Mother wanted me to look particularly nice. I went to my room and dug out those hidden garments. Shyly I put them on, and when I was dressed I remember standing a moment at the door. An exciting pride came over me. I turned back to Bad Boy. But this time, instead of whistling him to my shoulder, I slipped the hood over his head and watched the calm descend, with some vague understanding that the hood wasn't so cruel after all. The mention of this in my diary was brief: "It's not scary at all," I wrote, and walked calmly downstairs. My need for the falcon seems to have ended here.

The following summer Bad Boy was so tame that he was rarely leashed. He would go out to the meadows to catch his own food and bring it back to his perch to eat. I began to notice, however, that each time he went he stayed away longer. Once, as he winged over my head, I whistled and called in vain. When night came I saw him huddled against the chimney for warmth, so I crawled out on the roof and got him. Not long afterward Bad Boy was gone for three days, then a week.

He came back to the chimney a wild bird. I climbed up to get him but he flew away from me. Leaning against the chimney, watching him spurn me, I suddenly didn't want it to end like this. There was something so final, at once sad and exciting, about the parting. I could smell the bricks through my sobs. "Did I know then," I said to myself in the attic, "that those tears were for the farewell to my childhood?" I recall having been

a little surprised that I was not more upset over the absences of my falcon.

But other things were clamoring for attention—canoeing races on the creek, baseball games, campfire picnics. Then one day, when he had been gone two weeks, I came home to find a yellow gown on my bed, so romantically bouffant it took my breath away. Holding it up to myself, I looked dreamily into my mirror. Suddenly a movement in the mirror caught my eye. Bad Boy was in the tree outside my window, looking at me. I could get him by merely stepping out on the roof. I would—but first I turned slowly before the mirror, admiring the dress. When I had completed the circle, the falcon was gone. I ran to the window. I could see his pointed wings against the sky as he circled the chimney, the house, the yard. Then he turned and flew like a wild bird. This time, I sensed, he would not be back.

I dropped my head in the yellow organdy and waited for the tears. They did not come. In the blue-leather diary I wrote: "Now you belong to the sky—good-bye, my pretty friend. How different the winds that carry us will be."

The falcon and I were free.

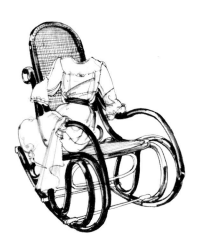

Lobo, King of the Currumpaw

Condensed from Trail of an Artist-Naturalist

by Ernest Thompson Seton

YEARS AGO a friend who owned a cattle ranch in the Currumpaw Valley of northern New Mexico, and who knew that I had once been a wolf hunter, urged me to come there and rid the region of a marauding pack of gray wolves which, in defiance of local trappers and cowboys, was taking a terrible toll of valuable cattle. I was in the Southwest at the time and I accepted the invitation, setting out for the Currumpaw with a wagon and team, two helpers—Billy Allen and Charley Winn—and some wolf traps.

On my arrival I learned that the pack was led by a giant wolf which local Mexicans had named Old Lobo, the King. All the ranchmen knew Lobo well, though few had ever seen him. His voice, an octave lower than that of his fellows, was unmistakable, and his track was easily recognized. An ordinary wolf's forefoot is four and a half inches long; Lobo's was five and a half. The old outlaw's wiliness and strength were in proportion to his size. Under his diabolically cunning leadership the pack avoided all

efforts to poison or trap them. The ranchmen had finally set a price of a thousand dollars on Lobo's head—an unparalleled wolf-bounty. But he and his band seemed to possess charmed lives, and in five years had destroyed more than two thousand cattle. They were so fastidious about what they ate that they touched nothing except the tenderest parts of yearling heifers, one of which they killed almost every night.

Lobo feared only one thing—firearms. Knowing that all men in that region carried them, he would never face a human being, and permitted his band to roam abroad only after nightfall. For such an adversary the traps I had brought were too small, and pending the arrival of larger ones, I tried to get him with poison. For bait, I cooked a mixture of cheese and kidney fat from a freshly killed heifer. To avoid tainting it with the odor of man I wore a pair of gloves steeped in the hot blood of the heifer, and was even careful not to breathe upon the meat. After it cooled I cut it into lumps with

125

a bone knife and inserted in each lump an odorless capsule of strychnine and cyanide, sealing it with a bit of the cheese. I put this bait into a rawhide bag rubbed all over with the blood, and rode forth on horseback, dragging the bag at the end of a rope. Making a ten-mile circuit, I dropped a lump every quarter of a mile, taking care not to touch it with bare hands.

Next day I rode the circuit, eager to learn the result. From the wolves' tracks in the dust I found that they had scented my drag and had followed it. At the spot where I had dropped the first piece of bait, Lobo had sniffed about and had finally picked it up. Now, I thought, I've got him. But I could see no dead wolf on the plain. Proceeding to the second and third baits, I found that they also were gone. At the next one I discovered what had happened. Lobo had not eaten the baits but had *carried them in his mouth* and dropped them when he came to the fourth. There he scattered filth all over them to express his utter contempt for all my stratagems.

Obviously the King was too clever to be taken with poison, so I obtained a hundred heavy, double-spring steel wolf traps. My helpers and I worked a week to set them out properly in all the trails leading to the watering places and canyon crossings of the region. Each trap was chained to a short log and rubbed with fresh blood; at strategic spots I buried four traps about a foot from each other. I placed the logs on each side of the trail, and after concealing them with dust and grass we smoothed the ground with the body of a rabbit. The traps were so well hidden that no man could have detected them even in daylight, but Lobo was not fooled. When I inspected my traps a few days later I read again, from the tracks in the dust, the record of his doings. When he had come upon the first trap his keen nose

had warned him that there was something suspicious ahead. Cautiously scratching around, he had exposed trap, chain and log. Then, passing on, he had treated a dozen more traps in the same manner.

Studying his moves, I found that when he detected a trap he invariably moved off the trail to the downwind side. That gave me a new idea. Setting one trap directly in the trail, I placed three others on each side of it, forming an H. Now, I thought, when he comes to the middle trap which forms the crossbar of the H, he will certainly get into one of the side traps. But he was too smart. Upon encountering the trap in the trail, being warned of it by his incredible sense of smell, he had stopped. Then, instead of moving off to one side as was his custom, he had *backed up, carefully putting each paw in its old track,* until he was beyond dangerous ground. Once clear, he had made a wide circuit around my H—and had triumphantly gone on to kill another heifer a few miles away.

For four months I had pursued the wily old reprobate and his band, to no avail. I was at my wit's end. And he might have roamed and marauded to the end of his natural span if he had not made a mistake— the one mistake of his life. He married a young and incautious wife. Some Mexicans, who occasionally caught glimpses of the pack, told me his mate was pure white. They called her Blanca.

Now at last I believed I had found a weak spot in the old warrior's armor and planned my strategy for a final campaign. Killing a heifer, I placed two traps near the carcass so they would be fairly obvious, then cut off the head and laid it on the ground a short distance away, as if it had been carelessly thrown aside. To it I fastened two deodorized traps and buried them. I then brushed the ground smooth with the skin of a coyote and made tracks over the trap with one of its paws.

The next morning, to my delight, the head was gone. The tracks revealed that Lobo had come, decoyed by the delicious odor of fresh beef. He had walked around the carcass at a safe distance. The rest of the pack, except one, had sensed his usual warning and had stayed away from the spot. That one—a small wolf—had heedlessly trotted over to examine the beef head, had set foot in one of my traps, and had run off, dragging head and all.

About a mile away we overtook the hapless wolf. It was Blanca! She was the handsomest wolf I had ever seen. Lobo was with her, and only when he saw men coming with guns did he leave her. Making off up a

hill, he called to her to follow, but the horns of the big beef head caught in the rocks and held her. Turning to fight, she raised her voice in a long howl that rolled over the canyon. From far away came Lobo's deep response. That was her last call; quickly we closed in on her and killed her and rode back to the ranch with her body.

All that day we heard Lobo calling. It was no longer the old, defiant howl; there was a note of sorrow in it now. As evening fell, his voice sounded nearer and I could tell that he was not far from the place where we had overtaken Blanca. When he reached the spot where his mate had died, he seemed to know what had happened and his wailing was piteous to hear. Even the stolid cowboys said they had "never heard a wolf carry on

like that before." In the night Lobo followed the tracks of our horses almost to the ranch house, and next morning we found our watchdog torn to bits.

I went feverishly to work to catch him before he might abandon his search for Blanca. My helpers and I placed traps in sets of four on every trail leading to the home canyon. Each was fastened to a log, every log-and-trap was buried, and with one of Blanca's paws I made tracks over every trap-set. The second day afterward I saw a great gray form in a trail of the north canyon. There, helpless, lay the King of the Currumpaw. He had come to the tracks I had made with Blanca's forefoot, and had forgotten his customary caution.

When he saw me, the old hero—worn out from struggling for two days and nights—arose valiantly to give battle. His eyes glared green with fury and his powerful jaws snapped viciously as he tried to reach me and my trembling horse. But the traps held him fast and, weak from hunger and loss of blood, he soon sank down exhausted. Now that I had him at last, pity came over me. "You grand old outlaw," I said, "I'm sorry to do it, but it must be done." I threw my lasso, but as the noose was dropping on his neck he seized it and with one chop cut the thick rope. I had my rifle but did not wish to spoil his royal hide, so I galloped back to the house to get another lasso—and Billy Allen. We flung a stick to the wolf and be-

fore he could drop it our lassos tightened on his neck. It was easy to lash his jaws tight over the stick with a rope.

As soon as he was bound he made no further resistance and uttered no sound. He merely looked at me calmly as if to say, "You have got me at last; do as you please with me." From that time on he took no further notice of us. We tied his legs and released the traps. Our strength was just sufficient to lift his 150-pound weight across my saddle. At the ranch house I put a strong collar on his neck, fastened it to a post by means of a chain and removed his bonds. I put meat and water beside him but he paid no heed. He did not even move a muscle when I touched him, but turned his head away, gazing past me down the canyon to the open plains—the kingdom where he had so long hunted and triumphed. Thus he lay until sundown.

It is said that a lion shorn of his strength, an eagle robbed of his freedom or a dove bereft of his mate will die of a broken heart. Who will say that this grim bandit could bear the loss of all three? This only I know: When morning came he was lying just as I had left him; but his spirit was gone— the king-wolf was dead. A cowboy helped me carry him into the shed where the remains of Blanca lay. As we placed Lobo beside her, the cattleman looked down at him and said, "There—you *would* come to her; now you are together again."

A Pelican Called Peter

by GORDON GASKILL

ON A SEPTEMBER day in 1955, as they have done for countless ages, great flocks of pelicans flew high above the Aegean Sea in migration from the Balkans to Africa. About a hundred miles east of Athens, one young bird—weak, tired and lamed—gave up and fell behind. Far below him lay an island. He glided down to it and settled on a rocky point to rest, perhaps to die. No prophet could have foretold what this single weary bird was to mean to the island of Mykonos. "Nothing had happened here for five thousand years," one Mykonian remarked. "And then our pelican came."

It is true that Mykonos shares little history or legend with other Greek islands. Close to two famous neighbors—Delos, once sacred as the birthplace of Apollo, and Tenos, shrine of the Greek Orthodox world and known today as the "Lourdes of Greece"— Mykonos was a humble Cinderella among islands until the pelican came. The exhausted bird, too crippled to fish for itself, might well have died. But a fisherman happened along in his boat and carried it into port, where it aroused much curiosity and sympathy. Everybody soon came to agree on the solution: "Give it to Theodoros."

Theodoros Kyrandonis, a stalwart, huge-mustached boatman who was decorated for valor in World War II, loved all wildlife. His two-room house at the moment sheltered several birds and even a baby seal that he was nursing back to health. Theodoros was glad to add the pelican to his charges. He named him Petros (Peter) in honor of a Mykonian hero, Petros Dracopoulos, who had been executed by the Nazis. Peter, petted and spoiled by Theodoros, fattened by everybody, grew strong and healthy. Soon the Mykonians began to consider him a sort of mascot. Somebody said, lightheartedly, that perhaps it was significant that the bird was turned back in flight over sacred Delos. Maybe, after so many centuries, the god Apollo had pronounced another oracle—that Mykonos would prosper as long as it had Peter. Fishermen began to wonder if their catches hadn't been bigger lately. All in jest, of course. Still . . .

One spring, in the migration season, Peter vanished. Anxious queries went out via radiotelephone to the other islands. Soon the Mykonians got an answer which at first cheered them: Peter was safe and sound, in Tenos. Then they turned purple with anger. Tenos refused to give him back! Thus began a teapot tempest celebrated throughout Greece, where it was called the Pelicanesian War. Eventually the Mykonians appealed to the prefect of the Cyclades Islands, who has jurisdiction over both Mykonos and Tenos. His Excellency listened to impassioned arguments from both sides.

Insisted the men of Tenos: "This is no tame bird; it is a wild migrant, free to go where it likes. It obviously decided it did not like Mykonos—for reasons we are too polite to suggest—and has of its own will come to us, seeking asylum."

Retorted the men of Mykonos: "What nonsense! We saved Peter, fed him, cared for him as for our children. He is a young bird, easily confused. It was only bad navigation or, more likely, a strong wind that carried him to Tenos against his will. By Zeus, he is ours!"

The prefect thoughtfully stroked his mustache before he announced his decision: "The bird rightfully belongs to the people of Mykonos. Tell the police in Tenos to let them have him."

Peter returned home in glory. Practically everybody on Mykonos (population 3600) dropped work and crowded around the harbor. Church bells rang in triumph. The minute the gangplank was lowered, Peter pushed ahead to walk down it first—solemnly aware of his own importance.

The Mykonians took no more risks. Around one of Peter's legs they put a light silver nameplate reading *"Dimos Mykonion"* (Municipality of Mykonos). Further, to make sure he could never fly away again, Theodoros pulled out a few feathers from one wing. Theodoros explained, "He is not hurt, and he can fly a little for exercise, but not far." Peter on the wing became, in fact, quite a sight. The missing feathers altered his balance and control. He staggered around in the air like a drunk and soon plopped back to earth or water, looking puzzled and thoughtful.

Thus far, Peter's fame was largely confined to Greece. But on a warm July evening in 1961, it began to spread around the world. Here is how it happened. Theodoros was haranguing a crowd in a harbor-front café about his favorite bird. "Peter is not happy!" he said. "He goes off by himself; he stands on the shore alone, staring out to sea. What is wrong with him? Every man here knows! He needs a mate!"

By great luck one of his listeners was an official of Magcobar (Magnet Cove Mining Corporation) of Houston, Texas, which provided the only industry on Mykonos. (It mines barite, used in drilling oil wells.) And I. W. Hoskins, the Magcobar official, is a native of Louisiana, which proudly calls itself the Pelican State. "Hmmm," said Hoskins when he heard of the problem, and got in touch with the then governor of Louisiana, James H. Davis.

The governor, all helpful smiles, sent out an order to his wildlife people: "Find a mate for this Greek pelican." Game wardens combed the swamps and bayous and came up with two white pelicans, which they named Alphonse and Omega. The birds made the 6500-mile trip by air, in fancy cages proudly emblazoned: "Magcobar's Playmates for Peter." When they arrived in Mykonos on December 2, the island celebrated all day. Again church bells, this time plus fireworks.

At the wedding party Peter appeared decked out in a red bow tie. The acting mayor charged all three pelicans to be "faithful unto each other" and read telegrams from Greek admirers wishing the birds long life and many little pelicans. For Alphonse, unfortunately, this was not to be: He had become ill during the long journey and soon died. When Omega looked bad, too, she was rushed to a veterinarian on a neighboring island. Weeks later, her health restored, she was returned to Mykonos—only to find a rival. A French film company, come to make a short film on Mykonos and Peter, had also worried about Peter's lack of *l'amour* and generously brought their own mate for him, named Irene—"Peace" in Greek. The question now: Would Peter prefer an American mate or a European? Mykonians settled down to watch and wait.

They were to wait in vain. For Omega disappeared and Irene was destroyed after attacking a child. Peter remains alone, paddling in the harbor, snoozing on the sandy beach, strutting around the quays with authority. He is a true extrovert, a clown and a ham. Let anybody lift a camera within a hundred yards of him, and he freezes in a photogenic pose. Says an admiring merchant who has made a small fortune selling film to tourists: "If that bird could talk, by now he'd be correcting their lens settings."

In the old days Pete sometimes wandered around the cafés begging food, or into butcher shops, or even into private homes (once lifting the latch with his beak). Householders were honored by such visits, considering them good omens. When thirsty, he tries to open the spigot on the communal waterpoint on the docks. He has never succeeded, but he doesn't need to: Anybody who sees Peter tugging vainly at the spigot with his beak rushes over and draws him enough to drink. In his clumsy, jovial way, Peter sometimes plays "football" with Theodoros, batting around a small balloon. If anybody attacks Theodoros (or pretends to), Peter dashes up with ruffled feathers and jabbing beak to defend him. "If I had another son," says Theodoros, who has had eleven children so far, "I'd name him Peter."

Peter occasionally takes a sudden strong liking to an unsuspecting tourist. This happened with a young Englishwoman. Peter not only gave her a lot of admiring awk-awk-awks, but insisted on flopping into her lap whenever she sat at a café table. Since the pelican is one of the largest of all web-footed birds, weighing not far from twenty pounds, the honor of this attention soon wore off. Tourists often buy fish for Peter, and fishermen vie among themselves to throw part of their catch to him.

"It's only right that Mykonos should feed Peter, because Peter helps feed Mykonos," people say. And the mayor, whose office is adorned with Alphonse—reverently stuffed —nods agreement, for a good part of the island's recent tourist boom can be credited to Peter. Seventeen years ago, Mykonos was known only to a handful of tourists, who liked its quiet, friendly charm and low prices. They liked its ancient windmills, some of them still turning to grind out wheat for the islanders' bread. They liked the beautifully simple, cubelike houses, all dazzling white. (Most of them are whitewashed afresh *every week*. Even the streets are regularly whitewashed, with broad white outlines painted around the large flagstones that serve as paving.) Now everybody seems to know about Mykonos. As a press agent, Peter has been beyond rubies. I have seen a folder advertising Aegean cruises which ranks Peter almost on a par with Greece's famous art treasures. In Mykonian shops you can find him on bronze medallions, dishes and seashells, or woven into the Mykonians' popular woolen bags.

Visitors sometimes wonder what Mykonians would do if Peter died. Yet here the scientists have a word of cheer. Peter is only about seventeen, and his species can reasonably expect a lifetime of forty years or more. Peter should be ruling his grateful kingdom for many a year to come.

The Saga of Patsy and Oscar

by HARLAND MANCHESTER

Driving up the hill to open our Vermont farmhouse one spring day some years ago, my wife, Laetitia, and I stopped to say hello to a neighbor who kept a friendly eye on the place. He looked a little gloomy. After matters of health and weather had been settled, he gave us the bad news. "Your dam washed out," he announced.

We went and looked. The shimmering five-acre mirror which once reflected the red sunset and the wind-tossed pines and birches was now a dim eye of water sunk in a murky socket of mud and sedge. Freshets from the winter's melting snows had chewed a gaping hole around the concrete core of the earth dam. We turned away from the dismal sight, speculating about contractors and repair costs.

For the next two weeks we stayed away from the lake. Then early one morning Laetitia returned from a walk. "Something odd is happening at the dam," she said.

Sure enough, the washout was partly blocked with rocks, mud, bits of log and twigs, and the water was a little higher. Fresh green leaves showed that the work was only a few hours old. Next morning we noticed that the dike was higher, and water covered more of the marshland. Apparently the mysterious engineers were working at night. At sundown I smeared myself with insect repellent, took the binoculars and crawled through the bushy pines to a point overlooking the dam.

The repair crew was hard at work. A big beaver was plastering mud over the break. Another beaver was pushing a rock into place, and a third, only his nose showing, was swimming down the lake with a section of log. Each night at dusk they came and did their stint. The water crept over the flats to the forested shores. I painted and launched our small rowboat and repaired the pier. Once more we had our shining bit of sea.

At first we hardly ever saw our hydraulic maintenance crew. The only evidence of their presence was their lodge—an island hummock built of sticks and earth—and occasional fresh twigs on the dam. Then one hot afternoon when we were lying on the pier near the dam my wife suddenly grabbed my arm and pointed down the center of the lake. A curious dark-brown dot, just skimming the surface, was coming toward us, leaving a long wake. Behind the leader, to left and right, two other dots appeared, trail-

ing their rippling Vs. Assured and precise, the committee advanced in symmetrical formation. Soon we could see the noble head of the chairman. He looked enormous. When he was some fifty feet away, his entourage submerged and gave him the stage. He turned and described a wide circle, completing the maneuver with an arrogant tail slap which rang against the hills.

It was a magnificent picketing job. Obviously they wanted to inspect their project, so we meekly took our towels and slunk to the other side of the lake like gate-crashers ordered from a beach club. But it was not enough—the leader followed us and repeated his circle-and-slap demonstration. Emboldened by his example, the others copied his routine, and the three-ring beaver

circus proceeded to put on a fifteen-minute act that lesser beasts would have spent whole winters rehearsing in Sarasota. They would submerge, leaving the water still and quiet for long minutes, pop up in unexpected places, circle again, slap and recircle. Finally, having made their point, they swam off into the sunset, three fading dots.

"Maybe they don't like summer people," I said.

"You can't tell about Vermonters," said my wife. "Maybe what they really want is to be friendly."

She turned out to be right. They never lost a certain aloof poise, but on days when they had no pressing chores they came down the lake to see us. Sometimes the chairman came alone. We thought he should have a name, so we began to call him Oscar, first behind his back, then to his face. He became more jovial and frisky, until one day when Laetitia was swimming I saw Oscar serenely escorting her, only a few feet away.

About this time Patsy, our black retriever-clipped poodle, discovered the beavers. Patsy was fervently egalitarian. Some of her best friends were cats, and not even sad encounters with skunks and porcupines could dent her grinning faith in all God's creatures. We had been told that beavers distrusted dogs and had been known to drag them underwater and drown them. But Patsy, true to her breed, loved to swim. The inevitable happened—she took to chasing the beavers.

I was working in my study one day and my wife had gone to the lake when I heard a triple blast from the jeep horn—a family signal of distress. I ran puffing to the pier. Halfway up the lake, Patsy was pursuing Oscar. Whenever she got close, Oscar would submerge, leaving the bewildered poodle splashing about at her wits' end. Jumping into the boat, I rowed to the rescue.

Little good it did—the next day Patsy was back for another round. The wily Oscar, with three dimensions at his command, evaded her with infuriating ease. But it became clear that he meant her no harm—he was having the time of his life. While Patsy was swimming west toward his last vanishing point, he would pop up in the east, deal the water a resounding crack and lead her off on another wild beaver chase.

This went on day after day. When Oscar was late, Patsy climbed to the top of the beaver lodge and barked, tapping an impatient paw. After time enough had elapsed for a beaver to rouse from his siesta and exit through his subterranean tunnel, the familiar brown dot would break the surface, and the chase was on.

When Oscar finally got bored and retired to quarters, Patsy would stagger home, eat her supper and go to sleep. As the summer progressed, she slept more and more. She seldom barked at birds anymore or dug for woodchucks beneath pasture walls. She seemed to be living only for her daily workout. One afternoon it lasted longer than usual, and my wife got worried. "Let's go and get her," she said. "She's an old dog—she'll wear herself out." So we got into the boat and broke up the act by hauling her in with us.

After that, we tried to keep Patsy in the house when we went swimming, but she scratched the paint off the door and appeared miserable. One day she disappeared and came back wet and exhausted. That night she didn't touch her food. The next morning she lay in the kitchen and didn't rise when we called her.

The vet shook his head. Her heart was leaking, he said. We put her away beneath a young birch tree. The next spring Oscar was gone. Our neighbor said he had seen men with traps.

For several years, although the dam was kept in perfect repair, no beavers came to see us. From time to time we spoke about another poodle, but during winters in town they have to be taken out on a leash, and somehow or other . . .

Then one spring when we arrived we jeeped down to the pier and looked at the fresh, gleaming water. Far down the lake, a brown dot appeared—then another and another. A veritable armada of five submersibles advanced in a stately procession. At their head swam a majestic young beaver, worthy heir to Oscar the Great. Up on the hill the young birch tree had shot high against the dark pines. Its lacy foliage, swaying in the breeze, seemed to take the shape of a retriever clip.

FIRST LADY
OF THE
SEEING EYE

Condensed from the book

by MORRIS FRANK, as told to Blake Clark

PERHAPS THE CLOSEST brush I have ever had with death came in a hotel corridor in Dayton, Ohio. The near-disaster occurred because I am blind. But it need not have happened at all, and it was solely my own fault. I was scheduled to address a large convention in Dayton that evening, the train had arrived late and I was pressed for time. With Buddy, the Seeing Eye guide dog who served as my eyes, I rushed up to my room on the fourteenth floor. After I had freshened up I had only fifteen minutes to get to the convention hall. I had to hurry downstairs and find a cab.

With my ever-present German shepherd companion I hustled along the corridor to the elevator foyer. There Buddy stopped stock-still. She, who always walked up to an elevator and pointed with her nose to the call button for my convenience, would not

approach this one. She ignored completely my "Forward" command. Then, in my great haste, I did what no Seeing Eye owner should ever do—I dropped the harness and started forward alone.

Buddy immediately threw herself across my legs, pushing so hard against me that I could not move ahead. At that moment a maid coming out of one of the rooms let out a terrified shriek.

"Don't move!" she shouted. "The elevator door's open, but the elevator's not there! There's only a hole!"

My knees all but buckled. Had Buddy let me take two more steps I would have disappeared down the empty shaft!

In that grateful and revealing instant there flashed through my mind an acute realization of just how much the loyalty and intelligence of that beautiful German shepherd

137

lady had meant to me. And not only to me, but to all of the American blind who had secured freedom and independence through the use of trained guide dogs. For Buddy was the first Seeing Eye dog in America— the pioneer who opened the way for all the others. All her actions were attended by the widest publicity and were watched with a curiosity which was at first profoundly skeptical. Had her performance not been brilliant and flawless, it is quite possible that the Seeing Eye program would never have got under way in America.

A few years earlier I had never heard of trained guide dogs for the blind. Then one day—I vividly remember the date, November 5, 1927—I was downtown in Nashville, Tennessee, where I was born and raised. An attendant was leading me from my bank on Church Street, and as I haltingly felt for the curb with my cane, a newsstand vendor called out:

"Hey, Mr. Frank, there's a piece in this week's *Post* you oughta read! It's about blind folks like you."

I felt in my pocket for a coin and bought the magazine. And that evening when my father read that momentous *Saturday Evening Post* article to me I listened with mounting excitement.

It described how the Germans had trained shepherd dogs to take the place of a blind man's eyes. These intelligent and highly tutored animals, it said, responded to commands with almost human perception, and led their charges safely through city traffic, around obstacles, up stairs, into elevators. In short, the author maintained, the blind with the help of these wonderful dogs could go any place they wished and could lead almost normal lives. If this were true—and I alternated between cynical disbelief and wild hope as I listened—it meant that I and

hundreds like me could break out of the prison of blindness. Those dogs could liberate us all.

I was then twenty years old and had been blind for four years. I lost my right eye at six when I ran into a tree limb while riding horseback. Then, at sixteen, came an unfortunate blow during a boxing match, and within two days I saw no more.

I had no intention of becoming one of those pitiful blind people one sometimes sees, dependent on others for their slightest needs. For some time I had been attending classes at Vanderbilt University and selling insurance after school hours. But I had great difficulty in getting around. Once, tapping along with a cane, I fell into a ditch that was over my head and spent a humiliating hour there before someone came along and hauled me out. On another occasion a driver crashed into a curb to keep from hitting me, overturned his car and only by good luck escaped unharmed. Such nerve-racking experiences made it plain that I needed something more than a cane.

Nor was my experience much better when I hired a boy to guide me. Many mornings he failed to show up and I had to miss classes. Sometimes, when he took me around to sell insurance, people would signal to him that they were "not in," and he would fall in with their subterfuge. Thus I was desperately ready to try any expedient which offered a measure of independence.

After mulling over that hope-inspiring magazine article for a sleepless night, I wrote the author, Dorothy Harrison Eustis, in care of the *Saturday Evening Post*. "Is what you say really true?" I asked. "If so, I want one of those dogs! And I am not alone. Thousands of blind like me abhor being dependent on others. Help me and I will help them. Train me and I will bring back my dog and show people here how a blind man can be absolutely on his own." My hand was trembling as I signed my name to this most significant letter of my life.

After an agonizing month of waiting, the answer came. The letter bore a bright blue and red Swiss stamp. Mrs. Eustis explained that she was a Philadelphian but now lived near Vevey in the Swiss Alps. On her estate there, Fortunate Fields, she herself raised German shepherds and trained them for police and Red Cross work.

She had never trained any guide dogs for the blind, she said. (As my father read me this, my heart sank.) However, if I really had the courage to come all the way from Tennessee to the mountains of Switzerland in search of a dog, she would find me one and line up a qualified trainer for me. There was never any doubt in my mind. To achieve independence I would willingly have gone anywhere in the world.

Family circumstances were such that I had to make the trip alone. So in April 1928 I went to Switzerland as if I were a parcel— by American Express. The experience both angered and frustrated me and made me all the more determined to win my freedom.

I was put in the charge of a steward who was less an attendant than a jailer. Each morning I was a prisoner in my locked-from-the-outside cabin until he came to escort me to breakfast. As soon as I finished my coffee he led me back to my quarters. At ten he exercised me as if I were a horse, methodically trotting me around the deck. Then he deposited me in a steamer chair. If some friendly passenger invited me to take a stroll, we got only a few feet before my keeper ran up, breathless, grasped my elbow and steered me to my seat again, where he could keep an eye on me.

I met a delightful English girl with whom I would have liked to spend the evening.

But that sleuthing steward always ferreted me out at nine o'clock, took me in tow and locked me in my cabin for the night. American Express and the captain of that ship certainly took seriously their responsibility to the blind man aboard!

How different it was when I stepped down from the train into the warm sunshine and fresh cool air of spring in the town of Vevey, Switzerland.

"Mr. Frank, here we are!" were the first words I heard. It was Mrs. Eustis' lovely voice. She shook my hand warmly, then introduced the others.

"With me are our director of training and genetics, Jack Humphrey, Mrs. Humphrey and their little George, who's four."

As I listened, I guessed that Mrs. Eustis was small, perhaps five feet two. By the way she spoke, she impressed me as being considerate yet firm, one who had high standards of conduct for herself and for others. And obviously she knew exactly how to get what she wanted—a good person to take up one's cause.

After dinner at Fortunate Fields, Jack Humphrey told me that Mrs. Eustis was interested in breeding a strain of German shepherds with high teachability. Most of them were trained for sentry, police and rescue work, but one of the finest of the breed had been selected as my guide dog. Jack, who was to be my instructor, had trained her himself. He had spent a month in Potsdam learning the highly specialized technique of training guide dogs, then had studied ways of teaching the blind to use them. I was to be his first pupil.

The next afternoon Jack brought my dog to me, first putting a bit of ground meat into my hand so that I could start winning her affection. I heard the door open and the soft fall of the dog's paws on the floor. I held out the morsel, which she accepted with dignity; then I knelt and stroked her coat.

How lovely she was! Mrs. Eustis had described her as a beautiful dark gray with a creamy patch at her throat. Her sensitive ears were always alert, her soft brown eyes brilliant and full of understanding. I felt a surge of affection for her. How I hoped I'd look as well to her as, in my mind's eye, she already did to me.

Her name was Kiss. But when I pictured my embarrassment at calling out "Here, Kiss! Come, Kiss!" in a crowd of strangers, I knew it wouldn't do. I put my arms around my new friend and told her, "I'm going to call you Buddy."

I took Buddy's leash and made a fuss over her all afternoon. Already attached to her trainers and fond of her playmates in the kennel, she merely tolerated me. She was pleased that night, however, to be taken to sleep beside my bed in my warm room, instead of to the dogs' quarters.

Cold air racing off the snow-capped mountains next morning made me snuggle under the blankets until, suddenly, a warm tongue licked my face. Then I remembered I was in Switzerland, on top of Mount Pelerin, and this was Buddy. All that had happened to me in the past few weeks had not been a dream.

That morning my training began. I buckled on Buddy's harness, with its rigid U-shaped leather handle which was to be my vital link with her, and met Jack at the front door.

"Pick up your handle in your left hand—the dog always works on your left side, between you and pedestrian traffic," Jack said quietly. "Keep your shoulders back and walk with the stride of a soldier.

"Now give the command 'Forward,' and give it clearly. As soon as the dog responds, praise her."

I took the harness, my heart pounding, and said somewhat shakily, "Forward!" The handle almost jerked out of my hand, and we simply flew to the gate. Buddy stopped before it and for a moment I teetered back and forth, off balance.

"She's showing you where the latch is," said Jack.

I put my hand on her head and slid it down her nose. She could not have indicated the location of the latch more accurately if she had been a teacher with a wooden pointer. I lifted it and we started.

"Keep your free arm close to your side or you'll hit the gatepost," warned Jack.

Following Jack's instructions, I gave the commands "Right" and "Forward"—this time a little less timidly—and down the road we went at a clip I had not gone in years. I heard, "Keep your shoulders back." As I straightened, I threw out my chest. My stride lengthened and I heard Mrs. Eustis' voice saying, "Look, his head has gone up!"

No wonder! It was glorious—just a dog and a leather strap linking me to life. We were bound for Vevey—a funicular ride away and down the mountainside from Fortunate Fields. I was keenly aware of the people, the dogcarts, the horses and wagons on the sloping road leading to the depot. As I was visualizing the jostle and enjoying the crisp air, Buddy abruptly stopped. "The funicular steps, probably," I thought and slid my foot forward. Sure enough, there was a low platform. How exciting! "Forward! That's a good girl!" I cried. I felt Buddy's harness tilt, giving me a gentle pull, and up we went.

Jack sat with us when we found places on the cable car. "Put the dog under your knees so no one steps on her," he said. I felt the car start jerkily, and twenty minutes later we had grated our way down the hill to the center of the little city.

My first blurred memory of Vevey is a mélange of commands and swift, exhilarating walk, of the sound of horses' hooves on stone streets and the chatter of people whose language I could not understand.

As we walked down the narrow sidewalk the feel of the harness told me Buddy was swerving to the right and I swerved with her. "She just took you around a man carrying two big bushel baskets," said Jack.

At one point Buddy deftly swung out to the left, then back in line again. I felt no presence of person or building nearby. "Why did she do that?" I asked Jack.

"Put your hand up," was his reply.

I did and at about eye level hit an iron pipe, the framework support of an awning. It would have struck me right in the face but for Buddy. This to me seemed the most amazing guiding she had done. Traveling alone she would hardly have noticed that heavy structure, so far above her. But with me in tow, her eyes had measured it against my six feet. She had received no command, she acted entirely on her own responsibility. When she did that, she was thinking! Hers were, indeed, my seeing eyes. *That's a good girl!*" I said, with feeling.

Each new experience gave me more the feel of the harness, the ability to relax and put my trust in Buddy. For two hours Jack constantly interpreted the movements of my dog, reminding me to walk erectly and not grip the lead rein too tightly. Buddy worked with a gay air, tail wagging, as though she enjoyed knowing so much more than I did.

It was so exciting that not until I reached home and sank into a comfortable chair did I realize how exhausted I was. My feet hurt, the muscles of my legs ached from the unaccustomed exercise, my left arm was sore and my back hurt from pulling against the harness. But these aches added up to the best feeling I had in years.

For five days we took an excursion every morning and afternoon. Then Jack said, "Tomorrow you're on your own. I'll follow behind you but I won't interfere."

I trembled inwardly. With every trip Jack had become more strict. He did not tolerate mind wandering. If I were carried away by the exhilaration of a brisk walk he would bring me back to earth with a gruff prompting that I was in training. He was an excellent coach.

"You'll get no more reminders," he warned. "If you don't do what I've tried to teach you, you may get a good bump. That'll penetrate that thick skull of yours!"

I listened, thinking hopefully, "He wouldn't dare let me get hurt."

When Buddy and I appeared next morning Jack carefully reviewed for me every turn and block of the route to the city. Then for the first time we set out on our own.

At the gate, instead of stopping immediately when Buddy did, I took two steps and ran smack into the post. There was Jack's big laugh and a hearty, "I told you so!"

I lifted the latch, pretending I had only brushed the gatepost, and laughed back.

"Forward and right," I commanded. Buddy did not move. Jack said not a word. "Oh, I mean—Right, forward!" I corrected myself, disconcerted to have made another error. I felt Buddy's tail wag, and on we went.

Buddy paused as usual at the steps to the funicular, but I was nervous and once more failed to halt promptly. This time I stumbled and fell, giving my knees a good thwacking. Again Jack just laughed. Brushing off the dust, I clenched my teeth and thought, "That's a mean way to treat a blind man."

As the cable car bore us down the mountain, my resentment of Jack's callousness grew. "Why does he laugh?" I thought. "He could have saved me from falling."

In Vevey, discouraged and angry, I followed Buddy lackadaisically down the sidewalk. By the time we reached our first corner I was in a boiling rage. Instead of listening for the sound of traffic as Jack had instructed, I rashly gave my command, "Forward." Halfway across Buddy made an abrupt stop, then hurriedly backed up, dragging me with her. I felt a car zoom past, so close that its wheels threw gravel in my face. That brought me to my senses. When we reached the safety of the opposite curb I gave Buddy a big, heartfelt hug.

On the return trip to Fortunate Fields I did better. I relaxed more and followed my guide with an easier gait. But I was still angry at Jack.

When we got back I went to my room and threw myself resentfully on the bed. Presently I heard the door open.

"Look, boy"—it was Jack's voice. "You have your choice: You can be just another blind man or you can be a man on your own with Buddy's eyes to help you. You can't lean on me. If I have to follow you and tell you everything, you aren't going to depend on your dog."

I didn't answer.

"When you go back to America," Jack continued, "I won't be there. Your future is up to you." He had quietly closed the door before I realized he was gone. I was ashamed. Jack wasn't unsympathetic; and he was absolutely right.

That night I went to bed feeling lonely and discouraged. What if I couldn't learn to use a guide dog after all? What a fool I'd feel returning to Nashville and admitting failure. The other blind I wanted to help would never even know that I had tried. I felt miserable.

Then, as if she knew how low-spirited I was, Buddy got up from her place by my bed. She crawled up on top of the covers beside me, nuzzled the back of my neck and snuggled as close as she could, giving a grunt of contentment and companionship.

Her warm affection completely changed my attitude. In reviewing the morning I thought it had not been so bad, really. I had made mistakes, but I had learned from them. I had done fairly well on the last part of the trip. Even Jack had said so.

Most important, Buddy had shown me that if I did my part we two would walk together in safety. My heartache gone, I dropped off to sleep with the comfort of Buddy close beside me.

That night a partnership was born, the beginning of a life together—a man and a dog, a man whose dog meant to him emancipation, a new world and still other worlds to conquer.

Our training trips became more difficult. Jack mapped out trial runs for Buddy and me that forced us to learn to move together under all conditions. One day we had an unexpected test of our responses. As we trudged up the narrow way from the cable car, my ears were assailed by a wild clatter of hoofbeats.

"Runaway horses!" I thought, as the turmoil bore down upon us. I was helpless to know which way to turn to escape. But not Buddy! She lunged off the road with such force that she almost bowled me over. Then the harness handle tilted until I was reaching up over my head to maintain my grasp, and she had me stumbling up a steep embankment. She literally hauled me up the seven-foot rocky slope. We stopped, panting, at the top—out of the way just in time as the team of snorting mad animals careened past, dragging a crashing wagon.

When it was all over and I had patted and praised Buddy, I suddenly realized that Jack had seen the whole episode. Too far behind to help, he had simply held his breath and prayed that we would escape. Thanks to Buddy, we did.

As the lessons progressed, my powers of concentration increased so that when listening to directions I never had to ask that they be repeated. I gave my commands in a loud, clear voice, aimed straight at the back of Buddy's head. I became more sensitive to Buddy's communications. I could even tell if she moved her head to the left or right.

I had been at Fortunate Fields several weeks when one morning I said to Mrs. Eustis, "I'd like to get a haircut. I guess I'll ask Jack to take me to the barbershop."

"Take yourself," she answered. "You have your dog."

What a challenge! I had never made the complete round trip to the city alone. My hands became moist with excitement. It would be the first time I dared set out on my own initiative, without the knowledge that Jack was always there if the worst should happen.

"Forward, Buddy!" my voice rang out.

My senses seemed sharpened as she and I followed the familiar paths. Now I repeated over and over to myself the directions I had been given. I felt like a child trying to find his way through a maze—only this wasn't a game, this was in earnest.

I counted the curbs as we passed the village shops. The clucking of hens told me I had arrived at the poultryman's corner. I turned left. Soon the fragrance from the

crusty loaves at the bakery assured me that we were on the right track.

"Right, Buddy," I said.

Then, suddenly, borne on the heavenly scent of bay rum, I heard the barber's cheery "Good morning, monsieur!"

Never did a haircut please me more, and Buddy and I made the trip home as if on wings. Then I sat down in the living room, threw back my head and laughed, roared until the tears came to my eyes.

"What's got into you, Morris?" asked Mrs. Eustis.

"Ma'am," I said, "I've been blind since I was sixteen. For years someone has had to take me to the barbershop. I've been left waiting there like unclaimed luggage for hours at a time. Today when Buddy took me to the barbershop and then brought me back it convinced me, for the first time, that I am really going to be free. That's why I'm laughing—because I'm free!"

No sighted person could ever understand the magnitude of my relief. I felt like a bound eagle who had been loosed to soar again. I had maintained a smile on my face since I was a teen-ager, to keep up a false front. This was my first genuine laugh in four years.

As the time drew near for me to "graduate" and go back home, Mrs. Eustis, Jack and I talked about my hopes for bringing guide dogs to the blind in America. Eventually, with their help, I wanted to organize an instruction center where others could be given such training as I had received. But where would we begin? Who would provide the money? Could we find a sufficient number of intelligent dogs in the United States? And who there would train them and teach the blind to use them?

Since Nashville was my home, we decided to begin with an office there. Fortunate

Fields could supply the first few dogs and trainers. Then if we could get help from established charitable agencies for the blind, we could begin the training of as many blind people as available dogs and instructors would permit.

"Whether any school for guide dogs can ever get started at all depends upon two things," Mrs. Eustis warned me. "Number one, since few people will believe that a dog can give you complete freedom of movement, you and Buddy will have to go from city to city and prove beyond a doubt that, whatever the traffic, it is practically as easy for you to get about as for any sighted person."

That was indeed a large order. I shuddered as I visualized the traffic bedlam of Chicago's Loop.

"Number two," Mrs. Eustis continued, "you must not forget that signs saying 'No dogs allowed' are almost everywhere—in restaurants, hotels, office buildings and stores, and on trains and buses. If the blind man's dog can't be with him wherever he goes, of what value is it to him? So your second task is to get Buddy accepted all over America with no more fuss than if she were a cane."

This, too, was a sobering task.

"If you and Buddy can meet these two challenges," she concluded, "I will guarantee ten thousand dollars and will send a staff to help you start the guide-dog school."

Immensely thrilled, I suggested that we call my proposed organization The Seeing Eye, which was the title of Mrs. Eustis' *Post* article.

"I think that would be appropriate, Morris," she said. "It's from a book that has been an unsurpassed guide itself for centuries: Proverbs 20:12, 'The hearing ear, and the seeing eye, the Lord hath made even both of them.' "

The trip back on the boat could not have

offered a greater contrast to my voyage over. I was not just a blind boy herded hither and yon. I was a free man, able to attend the concerts, listen to the dance music, participate in social affairs. Buddy and I were all over the ship at all hours. Some nights we hardly got to bed.

Buddy's brilliance, affectionate nature and responsiveness won everyone's heart. Through her I made more friends the first hour on deck than during the entire crossing to Europe.

As we neared the end of the voyage, I went to the purser's office to exchange my French money for U.S. currency. Leaving, I put my wallet inside my coat pocket and started back to my cabin, a labyrinthine journey that took us through the entire length of the ship.

As I lay down on my bunk to nap, Buddy touched me on the arm with her paw, but I paid no attention. Again I felt her, but ignored her. Then she put her forefeet up on me and dropped something on my chest. It was my wallet. Evidently it had missed my pocket and fallen on the floor. She had picked it up and carried it while guiding me all the way. I was deeply touched by the fact that she had acted entirely on her own initiative. She certainly realized that I belonged to her and was her responsibility.

Our first real challenge came when one of the reporters who met the boat in New York dared me to cross West Street. I had never heard of West Street. If I had, I would not have answered so confidently. Almost two hundred fifty feet wide, this waterfront thoroughfare carries the heaviest kind of traffic. But it was just another street to me. "Show us where it is," I assured him, "and we'll cross it."

"It's right here," he said.

"Okay," I replied. "Buddy, forward."

We entered a street so noisy it was almost like entering a wall of sound. Buddy went about four paces and halted. A deafening roar and a rush of hot air told me a tremendous truck was swooshing past. She moved forward into the earsplitting clangor, stopped, backed up and started again. I lost all sense of direction and surrendered myself entirely to the dog. I shall never forget the next three minutes. Trucks rocketed past, cabs blew their horns in our ears, drivers shouted at us.

When we finally got to the other side and I realized what a magnificent job she had done, I leaned over and gave Buddy a big hug and told her what a good, good girl she was.

"She sure is a good girl," exclaimed a voice at my elbow—one of the photographers. "I had to cross over in a cab, and some of the other fellows are still on the other side!"

Thereafter, Fifth Avenue, Broadway and other of New York's traffic mazes were almost easy by comparison. Throughout our stay in New York photographers and newsmen trailed us constantly and chronicled Buddy's every move. Everywhere people spoke to her and petted her. Buddy refused to be distracted and continued to do her work magnificently and with obvious pleasure. In a week she had conquered the biggest city in the world. She was a celebrity, in a town that loves nothing better.

Before leaving New York I visited an important agency for the blind. The director, a blind man himself, listened politely while I tried to enlist his support for an organization which would supply guide dogs.

"Mr. Frank," he said coldly, "it's bad enough to be blind, I feel, without being tied to a dog."

This was the first of a series of disillusioning interviews, there and later in other cities, with professional workers with the blind.

145

Many did excellent work, but others simply represented the kind of blind who could not or would not accept the challenge of getting out and doing for themselves. Our work, it was clear, would appeal only to that special breed of men and women who would put up a real fight to regain self-reliance. I gave up hope of help from the charitable agencies. We were going to have to start from scratch.

The small hotel where we stayed in New York made Buddy completely welcome, and we did not come up against the "No dogs allowed" ban until we set out for Philadelphia on the first lap of our journey home. When I started to board the train, the conductor put a restraining hand on my arm. "You can't bring that dog on the train."

"You're right," I told him. "The dog is going to bring *me* on. Buddy, forward!"

Buddy went right in, found me a seat and curled up under it. Angrily the conductor followed us and reached down to take her away. Buddy just looked at him and showed her beautiful white teeth. He hesitated, hastily punched my ticket, then prudently retreated. Obviously Buddy could handle any situation intelligently—with or without orders from me!

I discovered later, however, that not all train officials had to be intimidated. On the final lap of our journey to Nashville a new conductor boarded our train. "No dogs allowed!" he said loudly, when he saw Buddy. "It's against regulations. I'll have to call the police!" Then, having made this gesture, he leaned over and whispered, "Keep the dog's feet out of the aisle so she won't be stepped on," turned his back and headed for the dining car.

By the time we reached home Buddy had given triumphant and highly publicized demonstrations of her prowess in Philadelphia and Cincinnati, as well as in New York.

Jubilantly I sought out Western Union. "I want to send a cable. Address it 'Eustis, Mount Pelerin, Switzerland,' " I told the clerk.

"Yes, sir. What is the message?"

"SUCCESS!"

"Just one word?" he asked incredulously.

"Brother," I answered him, "that one word tells everything."

My family took to Buddy immediately. When she greeted Mother by licking her hand, as much as to say, "I bring you, ma'am, a new son, a seeing child again," Mother's eyes were wet with tears. As for my father, the dog could do no wrong. It was hard to keep him from spoiling her.

Life in Nashville was quite different for me now, for I could go anywhere at will. Buddy loved her work. She loved her harness. I had merely to hold it out to her and she would bound to me and wriggle into it all by herself. Together we spent many happy hours exploring familiar streets, which I could visualize clearly from memory. And on these walks I regained my sense of identity. Formerly, if I wandered off the sidewalk a few blocks from my home people would call out from their windows to a passerby, "Put the blind boy back on the walk." Now, I heard them say, "Oh, look, there come Morris and his dog."

"Morris!" Once again I had a name and was a person in my own right.

With half a dozen old friends, boys I'd known since prep school, I now went out on dates and shared many other normal activities. Strangers, too, spoke freely to me. I had often envied the ease with which sighted persons fell into conversation at bus stops and other casual meeting places. They rarely included me because they did not know how to get my attention. Now, however, it was the most natural thing in the world for them to say, "What a lovely dog you have!" and thus start the ball rolling.

146

My insurance business prospered, for I no longer had trouble getting to talk to potential clients. They gave no secret signals to my guide to dodge my visit. My prospects welcomed me. They were eager to ask about Buddy and watch her work. When word went in to a vice-president that Mr. Frank and his dog were here, the answer was a cordial, "Tell them to come in. Come right on in, Morris!"

From the start, however, it was evident that it was going to take a long campaign to buck that "No dogs allowed" slogan displayed in so many public places. The first set-to occurred at my insurance office, in the First and Fourth National Bank Building. The bank's attorney was so concerned about having a dog riding in the elevators that he spoke to the president, Mr. James Caldwell, about it.

"Mr. Jimmie" called in the attorney and me. "Percy," he said to the lawyer, "you have three children. You don't know what will happen—some of them may become incapacitated. This boy, once helpless, has found a way to come and go as he needs to, without being dependent on others. You and I have no right to stand in his way."

The attorney started to protest, and Mr. Jimmie's temper flared. "I don't give a damn what the law says. For God's sake, man, don't put obstacles in the way of people handling their problems with spirit and dignity!" We had no further trouble at the First and Fourth.

The streetcar company was another institution which frowned on dogs. On the West End car, which we rode by special permission, Buddy did her best to break down this prejudice, delighting the passengers by recognizing our home stop. They watched her to see if she knew when to get off and were always astonished by her "intuition." Even at night, when she couldn't see landmarks, she would invariably rise shortly before we reached our station, shake herself and nudge me to attention.

Being blind and alert to sounds, I realized how she did it. Just before our stop the car wheels made a special click-click sound, passing over a dead switch. When she heard this, she got up. Buddy kept so many secrets for me, however, that until now I never gave away this one of hers.

It was not long before all Nashville had taken Buddy to its heart. When a newsreel was taken of her at work, the Paramont marquee announced in big lights, "Buddy, Seeing Eye Dog," and in smaller ones underneath, "Also, Greta Garbo in *Camille.*" Nashville knew a great star when it saw one.

As newspaper and magazine stories about Buddy spread over the country, many fellow blind wrote to me. One touching letter came from the Reverend R. A. Blair, a clergyman who had lost his sight three years previously from an attack of malaria.

"I can read Braille and use the typewriter," he wrote, "but I cannot visit my flock. My wife, who took me on calls at first, is now an invalid. Thus I am badly impeded in my work. If only I had a dog to take me about my parish, it would overcome this handicap. When I heard your story I wondered if there would be any chance of getting help."

What spirit! Here was just the kind of stouthearted person I was eager to assist! Soon my desk was piled high with equally urgent appeals, and I felt that the time had come to start our school. Mrs. Eustis agreed. Fortunate Fields now had two trained guide dogs ready, and Jack had developed some promising instructors, among them a twenty-year-old girl, Adelaide Clifford, who displayed a genius for the work. Mrs. Eustis thought I could safely plan beginning classes for February. "Jack will arrive soon, and I will follow as quickly as I can."

One cold morning in January, when I left my house to go to work, Buddy for no apparent reason suddenly stopped dead in her tracks. I strained my ears to discover why. Then I heard familiar footsteps and noticed that Buddy's head was up in that alert way that always meant "Jack" in Switzerland.

"Jack," I called out. "It can't be anyone but you!"

Jack's hearty laugh pealed out, and he strode forward to shake my hand. But his first words were to Buddy. He patted her fondly and said, "Well, congratulations, old girl. You got us here!" And, to me, "Now, Morris, it's time to get to work."

Things moved fast after that. We opened a small office, rented an old building for kennel space, set up schedules for classes and arranged housing for students. The remarkable Miss Clifford arrived from Switzerland and took care of a thousand and one details that would have otherwise swamped us. And W. H. "Uncle Willi" Ebeling, a breeder in Morristown, New Jersey, who proved to be a first-rate source of supply for German shepherds, became so interested in our project that he joined us in Nashville and was soon an indispensable member of our staff.

Shortly after Mrs. Eustis arrived, late in January 1929, we incorporated The Seeing Eye as a nonprofit organization with Mrs. Eustis as president and myself as managing director. Three friends pledged twenty-five hundred dollars apiece for one year, though Mrs. Eustis cheerfully offered to pay all our expenses herself. And finally, exactly one year and three months after I had come across her blessed article, we opened the doors of our school.

Our first class, which consisted of two doctors, absorbed our entire resources in finished guide dogs—the two that Jack had brought from Switzerland. But others that we had acquired were in training, and for our second class a month later we had five dogs ready. Each guide dog was given three months of intensive training, and its intelligence and judgment were tested thoroughly before it was finally trusted with the responsibility of being a blind man's eyes. For the final examination Jack or Uncle Willi put on a blindfold and required the dog to lead him under archways, around mailboxes, in and out of revolving doors and through all manner of heavy traffic.

The training period for the blind themselves was four weeks and was of course equally strenuous. But it was immeasurably rewarding. The trainees came to Seeing Eye hesitantly and timidly, shuffling and feeling their way along. They strode briskly away from our doors with heads up—reborn. It was hard to believe they were blind.

The difference it effected in their lives made reading the correspondence from our graduates an inspiring pleasure. A few months after we opened the school we received another letter from the Reverend R. A. Blair, who had written earlier about his difficulties. Now an alumnus of our March class, he sent us greetings from Dot, the beautiful German shepherd he had already come to love. "I am sure it is due to Dot," he wrote, "that our church membership has steadily increased. She is my beloved companion on visits to my parishioners. She is so eager, so full of life that if she had her way we would be paying calls all the time. I must continually hold her back, for now that I've found my eyes, I certainly don't want to wear them out!"

By the end of our third year, when we moved to our present site near Morristown, New Jersey, our school had given new hope to fifty men and women, and not one of our students had ever had a serious accident. In New Jersey, Mrs. Eustis had found an ideally situated fifty-six-acre estate, which she purchased and gave to The Seeing Eye. Its large Victorian house and other buildings provided room for office space, student lodging and kennels. Our staff was increased, and we felt we could now expand so as to help more of the several hundred applicants who were impatiently awaiting enrollment.

The chief bottlenecks were the difficulty of finding suitable dogs, the even greater difficulty of obtaining good instructors and the perennial problem of money. On this last count Buddy gave us invaluable aid. She was a born fund raiser.

People all over the country had now heard of The Seeing Eye, and our work seemed to fascinate them. We received numerous requests for a speaker to come and talk about it, often with offers of substantial payment. But what most audiences really wanted was to see Buddy, the star of our establishment, in action; so Mrs. Eustis decided that I should turn lecturer.

I shall never forget our first appearance. It was in Louisville, Kentucky, before the International Lions Clubs, with seventy-five hundred members present. I knew nothing of public speaking and was faint with nervousness. Buddy, on the other hand, behaved as if she had been born in a theatrical trunk. With superb stage presence, she sat ramrod straight, her head high, her eyes snapping with excitement.

At the close of the introduction, when Buddy heard the chairman speak my name and the huge audience applauded, she joined in with a rousing round of barks. The crowd roared with delight, and their laughter helped get me off to a fine start. As I told them the story of The Seeing Eye, they were most attentive and sympathetic.

Of course Buddy stole the show. We gave a demonstration of how we work together and she obeyed my commands with clockwork precision. The strangeness of the huge hall, the unprecedented situation, with thousands of eyes focused on our every move, rattled her not one whit. Indeed, the electric atmosphere seemed to stimulate her.

For an hour after the scheduled talk, the questions fairly flew. What chiefly puzzled people was how we knew where we were going. "What if you're in a strange city and don't know your way to a certain place?" one questioner asked.

"Then you do as any stranger does—ask directions. You'll be told 'Four blocks straight ahead, then make a right turn and go on a block and a half,' for instance. All you have to do is give the commands and your dog guides you. When you think you are just about there, you check on it by asking someone."

I recalled following this procedure once in Chicago. I thought, but wasn't quite sure, that I had reached the People's Gas Building. When I asked a man where it was he replied, "What's the matter, are you blind? You're standing right in front of it!" Before I could give Buddy the command to go in, a young man came up to me and said, "I beg your pardon, but where is the People's Gas Building?" I could not resist the temptation. "What's the trouble? You blind?" I asked triumphantly. "It's right there in front of you!"

This first lecture was the beginning of a career that took us into many states and to the speaking platforms of countless clubs and conventions. Early in our appearances Buddy made it quite clear that she was a guide dog, not a trick dog.

One time a group asked me to have Buddy fetch my handkerchief, which she did. Within a few days a second audience, and then a third, requested the same trick. By this time Buddy could tell that I did not really need that blasted handkerchief. When I gave the command "Fetch!" she decided to demonstrate once and for all that she was no vaudeville performer. She picked up the handkerchief with her teeth, stepped on the trailing corners with her front paws, and tore it neatly in two. Then she carefully brought me the two separate parts.

To make our talks more graphic, The Seeing Eye shot a movie of Buddy leading me through traffic, and around low awnings and the like. It was so impressive that audiences burst into spontaneous tribute to her skill. When I showed the film, my procedure was to set up the projector in the center aisle of the hall. At the proper time Buddy would take me from the stage and lead me down the aisle to the machine, largely to illustrate her guiding ability.

On one occasion in Washington, D.C., the people in charge, without informing me, quietly blocked the aisle with chairs and other obstacles, and even erected an overhead hazard. They wanted to test Buddy's efficiency to the utmost.

When I stepped off the stage I gave the proper command, which was "Right!" To my consternation, Buddy refused to obey. The audience was absolutely hushed. I had no idea what was wrong, but I trusted my dog. I gave her her head. She had watched the whole proceeding from the platform and had seen the complicated series of impediments set up for us. Without a second's hesitation she simply took me the quickest, safest way to our destination. She led me up the *outer* aisle, across the back of the auditorium and down the rear of the center aisle to the projector.

The audience went wild with applause. By taking the commonsense way out of our predicament, Buddy had given a far more remarkable demonstration of her prowess than they had ever anticipated.

Buddy loved our lecture trips. When I began packing she would stand and watch. If I put her currycomb and brush in first she would wait contentedly. But if I arranged everything else before including them she would pace around me, pressing against my knees, as if to say to me, "Put my things in too."

She was immensely fond of traveling by car. She arranged herself in a position of extreme elegance, one front paw draped over the armrest, and her eyes at just the right level for effortless sight-seeing. Not only did she take keen interest in everything we passed but she expected others, except me, who had a good excuse, to do likewise. This was clearly demonstrated when a young lady riding in the back seat closed her eyes to relax after a long Seeing Eye meeting. Buddy looked at her dozing companion disapprovingly for a few minutes; then she took careful aim with her wet nose and knocked her hat off. It was just a hint that, in this big, bright, wonderful world, people who have precious eyes should use them.

On our tours I learned something from or about Buddy every day. She showed a special sympathy for anyone who was handicapped. If a blind person or someone with a crutch sat on the aisle as we proceeded to the lecture platform, she would stop and give them a friendly lick. On the street she would pull me several feet out of our way to greet a spastic in a wheelchair, or to thrust a sociable nose at a maimed beggar.

She was tenderhearted with animals too. On one train trip Buddy had to ride in the baggage car. I was concerned about it and went back the first thing in the morning to ask if she was all right.

"You needn't have worried," said the baggage man. "She had company. A forlorn little bulldog puppy taking its first ride was whimpering and trembling enough to break your heart. I could see Buddy wasn't going to let that go on long. She reached over and pulled it to her and mothered it. That contented little pup slept between her paws all night. Both of them got along fine!"

A man could not have a better traveling companion than Buddy. She showed her intelligence in all kinds of situations. Once when we got off the train in New York and started to follow a redcap into Pennsylvania Station, Buddy suddenly stopped and refused to go any farther.

"She's lookin' at the bags, sir," the redcap said. "She's eyin' 'em mighty peculiar."

Buddy led us back to our car. There we found the conductor trying to pacify an irate passenger who was insisting that someone had taken his bag. We exchanged suitcases and everybody was happy, particularly Buddy. She cavorted all around in little leaps, wagging her tail furiously and accepting the praise heaped on her as if she knew how richly she deserved it.

Buddy was extremely hotel-wise and could get around in strange establishments very well by herself. In Atlantic City I once asked a bellboy to take her out and exercise her. Instead he sought to amuse his friends by having her show off. Buddy, quickly bored with the purposeless "fetching" and other aimless commands, slipped her collar and ran away.

Worried almost sick, the bellboy came up to my room to confess what had happened. I never heard such relief in a person's voice as when he saw Buddy lying in the corner. She had been home for some forty-five minutes, having come straight to the hotel and stepped on the elevator. The operator, who knew her, let her off at the fifth floor and in a few seconds she was scratching at

our door. She regarded the bellboy with a stare that seemed to say, "I guess that will teach you!"

No emergency found her judgment at fault. One sultry summer night when I stopped over in Nashville en route to a speaking engagement, my mother put me in a first-floor bedroom. During the night I awoke with an odd feeling to find that Buddy was not in her usual place beside me. As I came to full consciousness, I became aware of an ominous sound—someone was carefully cutting through the window screen. Then I heard a piercing, terrified yell, followed by the racket of running footsteps.

Buddy then calmly came back to bed. Apparently she had heard the burglar before I had, and had quietly padded over to the window. When he cut the screen and felt for the latch, he found instead a set of sharp, businesslike teeth. Buddy might have handled the situation differently. She probably could have frightened the intruder away sooner by barking. But the silent-treatment strategy she decided upon added an element of terror to his surprise.

Wherever Buddy and I went I always looked up the local Seeing Eye graduates. I knew all of them well. Part of my work as a traveler was to interview and screen applicants, and I had called on most of them before they came to Morristown. Almost without exception, the change was thrilling to observe. The poise and self-reliance they had achieved confirmed the wisdom of The Seeing Eye's approach to the problem of blindness.

Suspecting that some groups exploited our graduates and their dogs in order to publicize their own "generosity," we soon ruled that all contributions had to be made directly to The Seeing Eye and could not be tagged for any one person. We further decided that, to encourage his confidence and pride in himself, each student must pay for his own dog. We lowered the price from $375 to $150, and allowed a student years, if necessary, to settle the account; but we wanted him never to feel beholden to anyone, not even ourselves, for his most precious possession.

A young mother, Mary, in Milwaukee, was only one of our graduates who showed us that our decision was absolutely right. Despite her blindness she held down a job in a factory. She rose early every morning to make breakfast for herself, her baby and the dog before leaving for work. She placed the baby in a two-wheeled stroller and, holding the guide dog's harness with her left hand, pushed the baby with her right. Six blocks they walked to the bus stop.

Just to board the bus was a major undertaking. She had to fold the stroller, hang it over her right arm, hold the baby securely in the same arm, keep a tight grip on the dog's harness with her left hand and show her pass at the same time.

She delivered the baby to a day nursery, then walked one mile to her job. The evening routine was the same, in reverse—to the nursery and then home again to cook, feed the baby, clean the house, wash clothes and get ready for the next morning.

"Mary," I said, "you know there are state and federal funds available to mothers and children in cases like yours. Why don't you apply for assistance?"

Her answer made me very proud. "When I came to Seeing Eye and got Sara," she said, "I paid for her out of my own earnings. It was the first thing I ever earned. That gave me a feeling of self-respect. Just because things aren't going well for me right now, I'm not going to sacrifice that feeling. I've got Sara—I don't need charity."

Another graduate of whom we were proud was Anne. When I visited her she had had Lady for three years, and was endlessly grateful to her and to us. People had always been kind to her, but she had been cut to the quick when they referred to her as "the blind girl" and seemed to think she was also deaf and feebleminded.

Thanks to Lady, Anne was able to take a typing course and secure a job. She was highly successful in it. The first Christmas after she was earning her own money she was thrilled to be able to shop alone and bought her family the most lavish gifts she could afford. But she gave the nicest present to Lady.

After I had visited her Anne wrote me, "A young man in my office, sighted, proposed to me. When I asked why he wanted to marry me, a blind girl, he said, 'What's the difference between you and anybody else? You can go everywhere and do everything. Besides, I want Lady, and the only way I can get her is to take you both!' So now I am married, just like any other girl, and entering a new phase of my life."

Most Seeing Eye owners loved their dogs almost to a fault. When I visited one couple in Arkansas, the wife told me that in fifteen years of ideally happy marriage the only time her husband had ever yelled at her was in defense of his guide dog, Jerry. She had just finished waxing the living-room floor when Jerry dashed over it. "Keep off my floor!" she reprimanded him, in annoyance.

"Don't you dare speak ugly to that dog!" her husband shouted at her. "He just saved my life!"

Then he told her the story. A few minutes earlier he had slipped and fallen while crossing an ice-covered intersection. A car was bearing down on him, its brakes useless on the icy pavement. Being blind, he knew nothing of the danger. But Jerry saw the terrifying situation in a flash and dragged him by the harness handle until he was out of the automobile's path.

When he told her this, his wife sat right down on that freshly waxed floor, called Jerry to her, took him in her arms and cried.

A Washington, D.C., girl had equal reason to feel gratitude to her dog, June, for her amazing, quick thinking. She was out walking near Dupont Circle when, without any warning, June, in harness, rose on her hind feet, whirled around and knocked her down.

Some workmen ran to her assistance and told her what had happened. A crane was being moved through the streets and a fastening had given way, freeing a giant iron hook. She had been directly in the path of its lethal swinging arc. Had it not been for her dog's split-second reasoning and action, her stroll would have ended tragically.

Between tours I managed to get back to Morristown for at least part of every month. There Buddy, the veteran, enjoyed sitting at the window and watching the current class of dogs being put through their paces. She took everything in so completely that I half expected her to give me a detailed report on the pupils: "That blond Suzie isn't heeling correctly." Or, "Tom the Second did well on the long leash today."

She disdained the company of such neophytes. If we started down the street in a group of blind students and their dogs, she would either stall and hold me far in the rear or increase her pace until she passed all the others. She was not going to be mistaken for just another guide dog. *She* was Buddy, the first and foremost of them all!

We often spent weekends at the hospitable nearby farm of Uncle Willi Ebeling, the dog breeder who had devoted himself to The Seeing Eye since its Nashville days. Buddy adored these holidays. There was the lake to swim in, a flower bed that was a grand place to bury bones—dogs came before roses at the Ebelings'—and a room to ourselves with a large double bed that held us both comfortably.

On one of our visits there Buddy gave another clear demonstration that she was a thinking being. A new flight of stairs to the second floor was under construction. The treads were finished but the railing was not up. The passageway was wide, however, and by keeping close to the wall I anticipated no difficulty going up or down.

Buddy was never expected to do anything for me when she was not in harness; she was free to romp and play, forget her duties. But the first time I started up that uncompleted staircase she dashed to my side. She could see that the protecting barrier was missing, so she provided my safeguard. Up she went with me, step by step, keeping herself between me and the open ends of the treads. She spent very little time out of doors that weekend. During our entire stay she never let me out of her sight, rushing to my side to escort me each time I went upstairs or down.

On another occasion at the Ebelings' Buddy's help was more needed. I had started to swim out to a log raft anchored in the middle of the lake. I missed it and, in circling around trying to locate it, lost all sense of direction. Finally I realized, with some panic, that I was almost exhausted.

I wanted to return to shore, but did not know which way to head. And as usual when I needed help, I thought of Buddy. I called for her, hoping she would not be out of voice range. She gave the most welcome answering bark I ever heard, hit the water with a resounding splash and was soon at my side.

I reached for her collar and almost before I could say, "That's a *good* girl!" she had led me back to the shore and safety.

Such priceless guardianship demands affection in return and is not to be won without it. Jack always emphasized this to his students and constantly exhorted them, "Praise your dog! Reward your dog!"

The fight to make the guide dog acceptable in public places was not easily won. But Mrs. Eustis and Buddy made formidable adversaries in that continuing battle.

Mrs. Eustis mapped out a brilliant strategy for winning blanket permission for our dogs to ride in the passenger cars of railway trains. After months of scheming, she arranged for us to attend a dinner party at which—just by coincidence—General Atterbury, president of the Pennsylvania Railroad, would be present.

After dinner, the General was patting Buddy, who had made a beeline to him when coffee was served, and Mrs. Eustis joined them.

"You know, General," she said, "these dogs must stay at the sides of their masters all the time to give them full service."

Now the Boss, as we called her, was an extraordinarily capable woman with a redoubtable will and a mind like a steel trap. But on occasion she could open her big brown eyes and seem the epitome of helpless femininity. When she brought her problems to a big, strong businessman, there were few who passed up the opportunity to make those little problems disappear.

"We have a perfectly dreadful time," Miss Innocence continued, "with the railroads crating our dogs in baggage cars."

Buddy, all coöperation, raised her head at the hated words "baggage cars" and gave a low growl.

"I just don't know how to go about getting railway officials to coöperate to let these indispensable, well-behaved companions of the blind ride as passengers instead

of packages," the Boss concluded. "Can you help us?"

Five days later she telephoned to tell me the good news. "Morris, you can now step on the Pennsy with Buddy like a man, not a smuggler!"

General Atterbury had sent out an order authorizing that Seeing Eye dogs be permitted throughout the entire Pennsylvania system. This was the first road officially to give full "right of way" to our guides.

After the Pennsylvania gave us the green light, one railroad after another was opened up to our dogs. Finally the only major holdout was the New York, New Haven & Hartford. And here pure chance—and Buddy's winning personality—turned the trick.

We were invited to Thanksgiving dinner at a lovely home in Connecticut. A most engaging young lady at my right showed great interest in the story of The Seeing Eye, and after dinner simply fell in love with Buddy. I mentioned our struggle to get Buddy and others like her accepted by the railroads, and she seemed outraged that a single line was still boycotting these wonderful animals.

"You mean to say Buddy can't travel with you?" she asked indignantly. "That she has to be tied up six or eight coaches away?"

"It's worse than that," I assured her. "We blind can't even use local and commuting trains—the ones that would do us the most good—because those short-haul lines don't carry baggage cars."

On January 1 the New York, New Haven & Hartford announced that guide dogs could now travel on it freely. I called a friend in the road's public-relations department and asked how it happened.

"Remember that girl who sat next to you at Thanksgiving dinner?" he replied. "She is the daughter of one of the chief executives of the line. I don't know whether it was because of you or Buddy, but all through December she gave her father no peace. She pestered him until the twenty-fifth and finally said, 'I won't take a bite of Christmas dinner in this house until you promise to treat those dogs like the human beings they are!' "

Thus, by 1935, one of our major objectives was won. Thanks largely to Buddy, the independent blind could now travel freely anywhere in the United States that an engine and two steel rails could take them.

To further our work, Mrs. Eustis arranged for Buddy and me to spend several weekends with her at the homes of her wealthy and fashionable friends. The host would ask a group in to see our movie and hear the story of The Seeing Eye. Buddy and I were Exhibit A—the end product of the organization—and it was important for us to make a good impression. For these people could help us financially, could give jobs to our blind in factories and invaluable aid in opening streetcars, buses and hotels to our dogs.

We need never have worried about Buddy. In these high social circles she always behaved with the greatest decorum. Even her occasional peculations were conducted with immense dignity.

Once at an elegant tea party in Boston, amid a buzz of polite conversation, the butler served sandwiches from a tea cart. When it rolled up to me its lower tray was right on a level with Buddy's nose. Though her head did not move nor an eye flicker, in less time than it takes to tell, a stack of sandwiches disappeared. Only one person, Mrs. Eustis, who happened to be watching Buddy, saw the snatch. It was, Mrs. Eustis said, as if a dowager, in a moment when she thought herself unobserved, without even so much as lowering her lorgnette, surreptitiously put out a well-shod foot and scraped a fallen wallet under her skirt.

Even her departures from acceptable canine behavior seemed to be well-timed. I once secured an appointment with the president of a big insurance company to ask him for a contribution. He welcomed us, gave me an armchair, then sat down at his desk. I told him all about our work and how his money could help. He was most attentive and gave me a much-appreciated check. As I thanked him and rose to leave, I heard Buddy's feet hit the floor with a thud. Reaching over, I found she had been making herself comfortable on a luxuriously upholstered sofa.

When I started to scold her the donor said, "Oh, no. Don't say a word to her. All the time you were talking she had her head on the arm of the sofa, gazing straight at me. It wasn't what you said that made me give you the thousand dollars; it was looking into that dog's eyes—I just didn't have it in my heart to refuse her."

During one of our stays in Detroit we had a gracious note from Henry Ford. "I have often read of Buddy," he said. "I'd like to meet her."

The great industrialist gave us a warm welcome, shaking hands with Buddy and watching our demonstration with genuine interest. Buddy assumed an attitude appropriate for the executive suite. She sat erect, her back straight as a Prussian soldier's, her fine head poised and alert. Mr. Ford said with a laugh, "She looks exactly like one of my vice-presidents."

Buddy was much impressed with Booth Tarkington. Often at his boathouse in Maine she would go over, put her head on his knee and look at him as if asking, "Are you the fine writer who has brought so many people such great pleasure?" And then, while he was drinking his tea and not looking, she would nibble his own graham cracker right out of his hand.

Sitting by a cozy fire at Mr. Tarkington's

one autumn afternoon, I dropped a box of matches. Buddy got up from where she had been snoozing, ambled over, picked up the box and returned it to me. As I patted and thanked her, our host said, "I know it sounds absurd, but something about the way Buddy looked at you when she handed you those matches made me think, 'Why, that dog knows her man is blind.' "

The idea amazed him, as it does many people. We at Seeing Eye, however, have long been convinced that it is true. I told him that our trainers often remark that our dogs lying on the floor let the kennelmen and other sighted persons walk around them, but get up and move for the blind students. And of course many of my experiences with Buddy showed me that she understood perfectly the special reason she was with me.

When Buddy and I had been together about five years, a growth appeared on the underside of her stomach. I did not want to depend upon the advice of a veterinarian only and was relieved when Vanderbilt Hospital in Nashville accepted her as a patient. There some of the best specialists in the South examined her and found that the growth was cancerous.

Dr. Alfred Blalock, the surgeon now famous for his "blue baby" operation, removed it. I waited for Buddy's reappearance from surgery with almost unbearable apprehension. But all went well, and at my parents' home, where no human convalescent ever had more devoted care, she was soon herself again. Indeed, she was apparently rather proud of what she had been through. For when company came she would lie down, roll over and show off her scar.

For the next two years Buddy continued her full and useful life. We spent every waking moment introducing The Seeing Eye across the length and breadth of America.

But in the third year she began to slow up. And the following year, though her zeal for her work remained unflagging, it was sometimes beyond her strength. She was then twelve years old and was having difficulty getting around, breathing harder and having to rest often. One night in Chicago, where we had a talk scheduled, it became apparent that the end was near.

Though she was sick and weary, when the time came to go before the audience she spruced up, guided me to the platform and barked at the proper moments—and at some not so proper. Afterward she stood quietly so her admirers could pet her. But when they had all left, this trouper hunched down on her forepaws, tired, old and worn. That night she could not get up on the bed so I slept on the floor with her.

She had one more public triumph. Although we had often flown on the airlines, we had always had to secure special permission in advance. Before we left Chicago, United Airlines announced a change in the company policy: Henceforth the blind would be allowed to bring guide dogs aboard their planes simply as a matter of course. It meant that Buddy had finally completed the job assigned to her.

The trip East was made with suitable fanfare. United Airlines tipped off the newspapers and wire services that a Seeing Eye Dog was taking its first official regular trip by air. When we came down for a stop at Cleveland, reporters and photographers met the plane and asked for pictures.

Buddy did not reveal her illness going down the ramp, because she leaned forward in the harness and I held her up. I did not want it known that she was reaching the end of the road. When the time came to return to our seats I held back, waiting for the newsmen to leave, because I knew Buddy could not make her way under her own power up that steep gangplank. I would have to carry her and I did not want to hurt her sense of dignity.

I stalled as long as I could; then one of the photographers said, "I'd like a shot of her leading you back to the cabin, if you don't mind."

I was licked. I had to confess that Buddy was old and ill and would have to have help getting up the ramp. Immediately several newsmen stepped forward and gently helped me carry her aboard. And, although such a shot might have made them a reputation for sensational "human interest" photography, not one of those hard-boiled photographers took a picture of Buddy in her time of trouble.

That night we joined the Ebelings for a quiet dinner at their farm. Buddy, usually so full of vitality, simply flopped down on the living-room floor when we arrived. "I have brought him home safely," she seemed to say. "I have finished my journey. I am through." There she lay for the entire evening without moving.

We took her some food. She seemed glad to have it and was weakly responsive. We could all see that she was tired, very tired. When we returned to our apartment in Morristown, she seemed glad to be home and threw herself on the bed which we had made for her since it had become so difficult for her to get on mine.

We did everything to make her comfortable. Our veterinarian gave her heat and violet-ray treatments each morning and afternoon. I couldn't bear to leave her alone and gave in to her insistence that she come to the office with me. I was really too distracted to do any work, but at least her bed at the office was a change of scene for her. She would lie there and look through the glass partition to watch everything going on. She was glad to see those who came by to pay their respects.

On the last morning, she led me from the apartment to the car. I had to help hold her up with the harness, because she was too weak to stand alone. At the office, she would not stay in her place but kept coming over to me. She wanted to be near me all the time, so I took her back to her bed and sat by her, stroking her lovely head. There in the sunshine that streamed in through a window, the gallant creature shivered with cold. We put a blanket around her and I patted her. She reached up, gave my tear-stained face a loving lick and then dropped to well-earned sleep.

Her death brought more than thirty-four hundred letters and telegrams of tribute from every part of the world.

At that time—1938—three hundred fifty dogs were already guiding blind men and women under all conditions, in town and city, farm and factory, all over America. Today there are some thirty-five hundred guide dogs, and their owners, who represent nearly one hundred occupations, have traveled all the way from Hawaii, Alaska, Puerto Rico and Canada to get them. I am convinced that it was Buddy, my beloved companion of ten years, and a true pioneer, who made this great service to the blind possible.

My Friend, The Mouse

Condensed from The Happy Time

by ROBERT FONTAINE

I MADE A FRIEND of a mouse. I had never known a mouse before, and this new comradeship taught me a sad lesson in love and loyalty.

Sometimes I took shortbreads to bed to keep under my pillow and munch while I read fairy tales. This was forbidden, but I knew that *Maman* expected me to do it anyway, and that her only interest in the matter was keeping her conscience and record clear. So I disregarded the injunction. The Mouse, I soon discovered, was gnawing on the shortbreads while I slept. I caught him in the act one morning. Fortunately, *Maman* had not yet had time to teach me to fear mice. I wished him to remain with me so that I might have him for a pet. Fervently I asked the Lord to make it so that no one would see The Mouse and set a trap.

But *Papa* entered my room one night and saw The Mouse. *"Hein?"* he said as a gray streak flashed across the room. "What was that?"

"Qu'est-ce que c'est?" I asked naïvely.

"What was that which just now appeared and disappeared?"

"Me, I saw nothing. You promised to fix my skates."

My father frowned and sat down slowly on the bed. But in a moment he suddenly arose with a bad light in his eyes. He was, I could see, no longer a good, kind man with music in his heart; he was now a fierce hunter. He had discovered the doorway to The Mouse's home. It was a very small hole near a corner.

"Oho!" he shouted like a savage.

"Is something the matter?" I inquired.

"Aha!" *Papa* exclaimed. He kneeled down and peeked into The Mouse's home.

"Don't let him kill The Mouse," I demanded silently of the Lord. "Fair is fair. I have learned already twice the number of Bible verses I am supposed to learn and You have hardly noticed *me* at all. *Papa* is *Papa* and I love and respect him, but You know and I know The Mouse is my friend." This was the first time I had ever given the Lord orders, and I was not so sure I had used the most politic method.

I tried to engage my father in conversation. "What do you think I learned in school today?" I asked eagerly. My father replied without looking up, "Very little, no doubt. And that little of more harm than good."

I tried hard to think of something else to

158

talk about when suddenly *Papa* jumped up, holding his nose, and cried, *"Nom d'un nom!"* The Mouse apparently had scratched *Papa's* long nose. I could not help but laugh. "You, too, would be angry if someone stuck his nose in your house," I said.

Papa rubbed his nose and came back to the bed, a little confused. He began to repair my skating boot, and I sighed happily, thinking that he had abandoned his wild-game hunt.

Perhaps he had, but The Mouse had not given up *Papa.* Foolish Mouse! As soon as my father became comfortably seated on the bed, The Mouse walked right out. Not only did he walk out; he stood up on two legs and looked my father calmly in the eye. It was as if he wished to say, "Look here, I did not mean to hurt your nose. It was an accident. The Boy and I are friends. It is not easy to find a true friend in this world. For a small boy it is difficult; for a mouse it is almost impossible. Can we not talk this over, man to man?"

Alas, my poor father, who understood so many lovely things so well, did not understand The Mouse. He saw only a wild animal and lunged for it. The Mouse, who apparently knew something of human nature, was intelligent enough to disappear.

The next day there was a trap with some cheese. I stole the cheese in the name of my friendship with The Mouse. I could not do otherwise.

The following day, *Papa,* seeing neither cheese nor mouse, remarked pointedly, "Aha! What a remarkable mouse it is we have here, eh? He eats the cheese and yet he does not spring the trap!"

I rolled my eyes and tried to look as much as possible like a cherub in the Sunday-school pictures. "Such a thing is possible— for a very smart mouse."

Papa looked me in the eye. "It is not possible," he said firmly. "But what is most possible is that a small boy with a vacant head is removing the cheese from the trap."

"What small boy would do such a thing?" I inquired.

"You will find him in the mirror," said *Papa.*

He then forbade me to touch the cheese. It was a direct command of the first degree and had to be obeyed.

Once more I prayed for The Mouse. "Dear Lord, I saved The Mouse once. What I can do, certainly You can do. If the worst comes to the worst, remove The Mouse from the temptation of the cheese. Lead him not into temptation, but deliver him from the evil trap."

Nevertheless, I awaited, with terror in my heart, the end of *mon ami,* my proven friend. I opened the subject with *Maman.* "If you have a friend whose loyalty is proven, you stand by this friend when others wish him harm. *N'est-ce pas?*"

My mother was working a large gourd into one of *Papa's* socks. *"Mais oui,"* she replied.

"Aha!" I shouted triumphantly. "Then why do we have to catch The Mouse?"

My mother opened her eyes wide and stood up quickly. "Mouse?" she repeated nervously. "What mouse? Where is The Mouse?"

Papa sipped his wine and put down his newspaper. He looked at me across the room with a wise smile. I could see I had made a fatal strategic error. *Maman* was afraid of mice.

"The Boy," my father said quietly, "has in his room a mouse. They are friends, these two. So the Boy claims. The Mouse has said nothing."

"Set the trap!" cried *Maman.* "Set the trap!"

"The trap was set," my father explained patiently, "but The Mouse removed the cheese without springing the trap."

"C'est impossible!" my mother said. She turned to me. "I forbid you to remove the cheese. You understand?"

"I will not remove the cheese," I promised sadly. "But it is only a coward who stands still while his best friend is killed with low tricks."

"Listen to him sing!" *Papa* exclaimed, a little upset.

"Maman herself has said this is one of the things one does not do," I argued.

"But a mouse," my mother countered, "is different."

"A friend is a friend," I said. "At least, if you wish to fight my friend you could fight fair—not with traps."

"Ho! Name of a thousand and one names!" *Papa* cried. "Shall I make a tail for myself and get down on my hands and knees and bite The Mouse with my teeth?"

Papa went upstairs and set the trap with an unfairly large and unusually attractive piece of cheese.

I sighed. I could see it was no use. The Mouse could be saved now only by the good Lord.

When I awakened in the morning the cheese was still there. I jumped out of bed, kneeled down and told the Lord: *"Merci bien, Monsieur!"* Then I dressed and bounded joyfully down to breakfast, humming gaily. I ate my oatmeal in bliss. Just as I had finished, there was a scampering above us.

"Is that," *Papa* asked, "perhaps The Mouse?"

I held my breath and prayed one more time. *Maman* was busy making toast and said nothing. In a few moments there was the sound of scampering again. This time it seemed very close.

"Does The Mouse know even the way downstairs?" *Papa* asked in surprise.

I did not answer him. I busied myself putting jam on my toast. Halfway through the toast I felt as if something soft had touched my feet. I looked down. There was The Mouse, reeling, wobbling, struggling toward my feet.

When he saw my friend, my father stood up hastily. I do not know what he intended to do—perhaps protect *Maman.* It does not matter. In a few seconds The Mouse rolled over at my feet, dead. He did not die, however, before he had said something to me with his eyes.

My father rushed upstairs and came back exclaiming, "Astonishing! The cheese was removed from the trap. One imagines the trap then sprang and struck The Mouse in the jaw. Imagine it, this is a mouse who has died from a punch in the jaw!"

The wonder of it did not impress me. I knew The Mouse was a brave one. But I did not know about myself, for, with his eyes, The Mouse seemed to have said to me, "Look, I was your friend and you have killed me. But here is the wonder—I am still your friend. See, I come to die at your feet and to forgive you. It is easy to love those who are kind to you; it is a terrible but necessary thing to love those who have betrayed you."

Ah, perhaps The Mouse did not mean anything of the sort. Maybe it was my own heart speaking, learning, growing up.

"Papa," I asked quietly, "is there a heaven for The Mouse?"

"Yes, yes," *Papa* said unhappily, "there is for everyone a heaven."

Maman, who had been white and silent through the tragedy, now spoke meekly, "After this, let us get a large cat, so that such matters will be out of our hands."

Was There a Horse with Wings?

Condensed from West with the Night

by BERYL MARKHAM

MY FATHER'S first love was horses, and on our farm at Njoro, Kenya Colony, he raised and trained some of the best racehorses to come out of Africa. One of them was Coquette, an Abyssinian, small and golden-yellow with pure white mane and tail. I remember Coquette especially because she gave me my first foal.

It was the year I was fifteen. Coquette had been bred to Referee—small, perfect, gallant as a warrior, smooth as a coin. Now almost eleven months had gone by. I called in my personal staff of two: Toombo and Otieno.

Nothing in this world is rounder than Toombo's belly, nothing broader than his smile. Otieno is tall, somber-eyed, dependable as daylight.

"The day for Coquette is very near," I told them. "We must begin the watch."

To Toombo, birth and success are synonymous; the hatching of a hen's egg is a triumph, his own birth is the major success of his life. Now he grins until his eyes disappear. Otieno accepts the duty with pious gravity. I follow them down to the stables.

Ah, Coquette! How could a creature deserving such a gay name have become so dowdy? Once she was small and pert and golden; now she is plain and shapeless with the weight of her first foal. Her twinkling hooves are of lead; the bright, wise eyes are dulled. Her foaling box, large as a room, is ready, its earthen floor covered with deep grass bedding gathered fresh from the pastures; the smell of a mowed field is gathered with it. Coquette looks at me as she enters the box—to wait, and wait. All of us know what she is waiting for, but she herself does not. None of us can tell her. I leave Toombo and Otieno to take turns on watch.

Nineteen long days pass, and on the evening of the twentieth I make the rounds of the stables, ending, as usual, at Coquette's foaling box. Otieno the Vigilant is there— and Toombo the Rotund. The hurricane lamp has already been lighted. Coquette stands heavily under its gentle glow, her evening feed not finished. She lowers her exquisitely fashioned head as if it were an ugly and tiresome burden.

I lay my head against the mare's smooth, warm belly. The new life is there. I hear and feel it, struggling already—demanding the right to freedom and growth.

"Watch carefully," I say. "It is near."

"This is a good night," Toombo says, his fat face filled with expectation.

I return to my hut. Soon Otieno knocks. "Come quickly. She is lying."

I snatch up my foaling kit, with its knives, twine and disinfectant, and run to the stable. Coquette is flat on her side, breathing in spasmodic jerks. Horses are not voiceless in pain, but Coquette's groans—deep, tired and a little frightened—are not really violent. I kneel in the grass bedding and feel her soft ears. They are limp and moist, but there is no temperature. She labors heavily, looking at nothing out of staring eyes.

The time is not quite yet. We three sit down cross-legged and talk, almost tranquilly, about other things while the little brush of flame in the hurricane lamp paints experimental pictures on the wall.

The laboring of Coquette ebbs and flows in methodical tides of torment. There are minutes of peace and minutes of anguish, which we all feel together, but smother, for ourselves, with words. Suddenly Coquette groans from the depth of her womb, and trembles. Otieno reaches at once for the lamp and swells the flame with a twist of his fingers.

"Now." Coquette says it with her eyes

and with her wordless voice. "Now—perhaps now—"

I kneel over the mare waiting for the first glimpse of the foal's tiny hooves, the first sight of the sheath—the cloak it will wear for its great debut. It appears, and Coquette and I work together. Otieno at one of my shoulders, Toombo at the other. No one speaks because there is nothing to say.

But there are things to wonder. Will this be a colt or a filly? Will it be sound and well formed? Will its new heart be strong and stubborn? Will it breathe when it is meant to breathe? Will it have the anger to feed and to grow and to demand its needs?

I have my hands at last on the tiny legs, on the bag encasing them. It is a strong bag, transparent and sleek. Through it I see the diminutive hooves, pointed, soft as the flesh of sprouted seeds.

Gently, gently, but strong and steady, I coax the new life into the glow of the stable lamp as the mare strains with all she has. I renew my grip, hand over hand, waiting for her muscles to surge with my pull. Nose, head, at last the foal itself slips into my arms, and the silence that follows is sharp as the crack of a whip—and as short.

"Walihie!" says Toombo. Otieno smears sweat from under his eyes; Coquette sighs the last pain out of her.

I break the shining bag, giving full freedom to the wobbly little head. The soft, mouse-colored nostrils suck at their first taste of air. With care I slip the whole bag away, tie the cord and cut it. The old life of the mare and the new life of the foal run together in a quick christening of blood, and as I bathe the wound with disinfectant I see that he is a strong colt, full of the tremor of living.

Coquette stirs. She knows now what birth is; she can cope with what she knows. She lurches to her feet without gracefulness or balance, and whinnies once—So this is mine! So this is what I have borne! Together we dry the babe.

When it is done, I turn to smile at Otieno. And now I see that my father stands beside me, with the air of a man who has observed more than anyone suspected. This is a scene he has witnessed more times than he can remember; yet there is bright interest in his eyes.

"A fine job of work," he says, "and a fine colt. Shall I reward you or Coquette—or both?"

Toombo grins and Otieno respectfully scuffs the floor with his toes. I slip my arm through my father's and together we look down on the awkward, angry little bundle, fighting already to gain his feet.

"Render unto Caesar," says my father. "You brought the colt to life. He shall be yours."

For years I had handled my father's horses, fed them, ridden them, groomed them and loved them. But I had never owned one. Now, because my father said so, I owned one for myself. The colt was mine, and no one else could ever touch him, or ride him, or feed him, or nurse him. I do not remember thanking my father; I suppose I did, for whatever words are worth. I remember that when the foaling box was cleaned, the light turned down again and Otieno left to watch over the newly born, I went out and walked beyond the stables.

I thought about the new colt. What shall I name him?

Who doesn't look upward when searching for a name? When one looks upward, what is there but the sky to see? So, how can the name or the hope be earthbound? Was there a horse named Pegasus that flew? Was there a horse with wings? Yes, once there was—once, long ago, there was. And now there is again.

The Ape
in Our House

Condensed from the book

by CATHY HAYES

My husband, Keith, and I were curious about chimpanzees. How intelligent are they, in comparison with man? Why shouldn't an ape, raised in a human family, learn how to talk? So, after Keith had become research psychologist at the Yerkes Laboratories of Primate Biology in Orange Park, Florida, three-day-old Viki joined our family.

Viki looked like a monstrous four-pound spider as we put her in her tiny crib. Long, skinny arms and legs thrashed out from a solid potbelly. Stiff black hair stood out from her head and cheeks, conspiring with wide, vacant eyes to give an expression of terror and resentment. And always her right hand swept the air, searching for a mother to cling to. In order to put Viki down I had to undo her grasp on my clothing, hand by hand, foot by foot, then hand by hand again. A chimp's ability to hang on is no doubt partly responsible for its survival in the native arboreal life.

Before she was a month old, Viki, clasping my thumb, could suspend her own weight by one arm for more than a minute. In her eagerness for food, she began to raise her whole body free of the bed pad and wait trembling on hands and knees as I ap-

proached with the bottle. So voracious was her appetite that sometimes she clutched my hand which held the bottle and pushed her feet against my lap until she was actually standing up to eat—this at only four weeks of age!

Viki never cried. She had an apprehensive little *oo oo, oo oo,* which burst into a scream under stress, but she did not whimper or give any vocal indication that she needed food. Being a quiet baby is probably also essential for jungle survival.

We made Viki "work" for her food. As I snuggled her close to me, I held the bottle in my hand with my thumb sticking out from it like a handle. She quickly learned to grasp my thumb and pull the bottle toward her. Now we made the chore a little harder. Instead of pulling my hand toward her, she had to pull a string which was tied around the bottle. When she had learned this, we held the bottle farther away so that she had to grasp the string, pull, let go, take a second grip nearer the bottle and pull once more. In a few weeks she learned to pull hand over hand, sailor fashion. Later, at the table Keith had built for her, the bottle was mounted on a little cart to which was attached a long string. Then we placed a second, unbaited string alongside the first. She had to select the correct string to get her reward.

Although she obviously preferred being carried, Viki could walk on all fours when she was four months old. She also discovered that she could climb. One of her first "games" was to climb up the edge of the sofa, clasp her hands to her head, then hurtle off the cliff.

At six months Viki was apprehensive of all people and most things. But when Keith's mother came to visit we showered upon her and Viki rides, adventures, people and a party almost every night. Never again did Vicki fear people in general. She grew more sociable until she became at her best in the company of human adults. At these parties Viki showed some very human qualities, including contrariness. One day she ignored completely a woman who was "just dying to squeeze her." After this woman had become very unhappy about Viki's snubs, the little ape went up to her sweetly and seemed about to give her a kiss. As the woman smiled at her tenderly, Viki's kiss turned into a raucous Bronx cheer and off she ran.

Keith's mother was at first amused by our chimp child, then enchanted and finally downright fond of her. One day I was shocked speechless when she picked up Viki's elfin cap, turned it over tenderly in her hands and said, "I must send Viki the little bonnet Keith had when he was a baby."

Soon Viki discovered, to her great delight, that she could walk upright. Holding out her arms for balance, like a child walking a fence, she toddled along, a huge grin on her face. New confidence now came to Viki, and she began to challenge the right of any other animal to walk the earth. Her first reaction to a cat was to bristle and stand silently tense. As the hair stood up on her

back, head, arms and legs, she seemed to become more massive, and rather terrifying on a small scale. Next she would slowly rise to her feet and stick out her chest. Then with a great show of bravado, stamping her feet down hard, waving her long arms, she would charge her enemy. The cats ran for their lives. Dogs, bewildered by this strange organism, did not always run. Viki would advance just so far—still threatening—and if the dog did not retreat she would turn and race back to my legs. Clutching me, she would rock back and forth "soaking up security," as Keith called it, then try her bluff again. Should the dog advance so much as a paw toward her, her retreat became a screaming rout.

In the hot high noons we came indoors to bathe, nap and give Viki her "schoolwork." She had outgrown the kitchen sink for her baths, so to get her accustomed to the great expanse of a bathtub I went into the tub with her at this time. The procedure was to bathe her, rub her dry, then turn her loose while I finished my own bath. Viki's sociability and her love of fabrics here led to a dire consequence. While I sat marooned in the tub, she would carry away all my clothes, maybe even the towels. Then, perching atop the bookcase at her favorite window, she would wave my things at any passersby. Naturally they stopped to investigate. Viki pounded and hooted her hello, while the visitors said, "Well, Ah declare!" or "Did you evah!"

When Viki was about a year old, I glanced up from my writing one day to see her sitting on the couch soberly turning the pages of a book. It was Clarence Day's *This Simian World*. It became her favorite book.

Viki was now somewhat ahead of a child her age in physical capabilities. She liked scribbling, bead stringing and take-apart-and-assemble toys. But as she learned to put round pegs in round holes, she also began to put odd bits of rubbish into my cooking. As she learned to pile blocks, she made towers of glassware which was never intended for that purpose. Then there was the more serious nuisance of her biting. One day she bit *me*. It hurt and something primitive flared in my blood. Grabbing her furry little arm, I bit down as hard as I could. She yelped and clung to me in surprise. It was not a thing I had intended to do, but never again did Viki so much as threaten to bite me. This method is not to be recommended, however, for use on just any old chimpanzee.

Punishment is a real problem with a chimpanzee. Its skin is tougher than ours and cushioned with hair, so that when I slapped Viki she generally laughed as if I were tickling her. For a while, when I gave the command "No! No!" she stuck out her chest, made a sassy, hooting noise and returned to her mischief. Finally, I reluctantly cut a switch. When she opened a bottle of ink and began to pour it onto the carpet I switched her twice across the shoulders. From that time on I was compelled to use the stick very seldom. Before long, simply wagging it at her or even the word "stick" brought instant obedience.

At eighteen months Viki's everyday activities were much the same as those of a child that age. She built impressive towers of six or seven blocks. She could draw a straight line in imitation, changing to a scribble as the tester did so. She could feed herself with a spoon, open doors, wave bye-bye, and was showing some promise in washing and dressing herself. As a child does at about this time, Viki also began "aping" us. She helped with the dishes in a very businesslike manner. She dug at her fingernails with a nail file, patted a powder puff over her face with startling results and insisted on being given a dab of lipstick, which she smoothed on, as I do, with a little finger.

During the early months of our experiment Viki wore a T-shirt most of the time. So many visitors referred to her as "he," however, that I bought her a pretty white dress printed with tiny rosebuds. When Keith saw it, he clapped a hand to his head. But Viki was definitely pleased. She held very still as I slipped it over her head; then she sat smoothing the skirt out around her. The first time she climbed a door jamb in her dress and leaped down, the skirt flew up into her face. She grinned and tried the jump again and again.

The rear of her skirt poked up in an intriguing way as she ran about the house on all fours, but she kept tripping over the hem until she devised a simple precaution: She began holding the front of her dress in her mouth as she ran. Her first dress caused people to treat her more gently, and this reacted favorably on Viki. After that, until her death in 1955 at the age of seven, she often amused herself by rummaging through her bureau and dressing herself in odd assortments of clothes.

Viki fell behind a human child most noticeably in the use and understanding of language. She was five months old the day I first held out a portion of milk and said, "Speak!" She looked at the milk, then at me, and of course said nothing. I waited for fifteen minutes, then rose to leave. As I moved away, worried little *oo oo's* broke the silence and I quickly rewarded her for making the sound. Each time I rose to leave she cried, and thus she earned her supper. For several discouraging weeks we struggled to make Viki "speak." Suddenly one day when she was ten months old she began making a new sound—ugly, hoarse and strained, like someone whispering "ah" as loudly as possible and with great effort.

She then confidently reached for the milk, so we concluded she had at last gotten the idea of speaking for food. From then on, whenever we told her to speak, she replied with this straining *ah*.

When Viki was fourteen months old, Keith began holding her on his lap, slipping his hand around her head so that his thumb was on her upper lip and his other fingers cradled her chin. In this position he could press her lips together and release them, to form an "m." Then, with food in his other hand, he would tell her to speak. As she made her *ah* sound, he pressed her lips together and apart, and she said, *"Ma ma."* Then he fed her. Only two weeks later, Viki said her first unaided "mama." As yet she did not know that *I* was "mama," but she had many other uses for this new "asking sound." She awakened us each morning by calling "mama" hoarsely from the depths of her crib. She begged to be fed with this

valuable word, and to be extricated from each day's many crises.

In the hope of enlarging Viki's vocabulary we started what we called our Imitation Series when she was a year and a half old—an age at which a human child already commonly uses ten words. We would clap our hands or blow a whistle, meanwhile saying, "Do this!" To get a jelly bean Viki had to repeat our actions. She picked up the idea quickly. Later we would introduce sounds and mouth movements. Perhaps after enough sessions of "do this," Viki would be able to "say this" in imitation.

We soon learned that imitation can be a headache. I had taught Viki how to turn a key in a padlock, forgetting that our brand-new car was started simply by turning the ignition key. I was washing the car one day—having first parked it in reverse and put Viki inside it to keep her from getting wet and dirty—when suddenly I heard the motor turn over. To my horror the car lurched backward, headed straight for the fishpond! I threw the door open and dived headfirst to press the brake pedal with my hand. Luckily the motor stalled. Viki and I were both shaky—but safe.

As Viki approached two years of age, the Imitation Series paid off by giving her a second word—a whispered but perfectly audible "papa." She immediately used "mama" and "papa" interchangeably in asking for food or favors. One day I was talking to a friend about the possibility of using Viki's play sounds to give her more words. "She has a 'k' sound," I said, "which she can repeat after us, and a 'p' as in 'papa.' If we could teach her to string 'k' and 'p' together, we would get a primitive 'cup.' "

Viki had been listening and she immediately said, "K-p." "She did it!" my friend exclaimed. This third word immediately became Viki's best. It meant "I want a drink," and since her thirst was practically unquenchable, she said "cup" a hundred times a day.

We found it hard, however, to teach Viki language *understanding*. After more than eighteen months of coaching, we had not yet taught her to identify, unfailingly, her nose, ears, eyes, hands and feet when we asked her. Some days, to be sure, she could point to all these parts without error, but at other times she was completely lost. When we tried to teach her a few new words, she might start to learn them, but then, suddenly, she couldn't remember the old ones. For Viki a very few words were too many.

A human being can become educated without being able to talk. Listening and understanding open to a man the wisdom of the ages. But where does that leave one small chimpanzee who couldn't quite remember which were her ears and which were her eyes?

Hector, the Stowaway Dog

by CAPTAIN KENNETH DODSON

Second officer Harold Kildall of the S.S. *Hanley* noticed the dog first. The *Hanley,* an Admiral-Oriental Line freighter, was one of five ships loading at the Government Dock in Vancouver, British Columbia, on April 20, 1922. Inspecting chain lashings, Kildall glanced up to see a large, smooth-haired terrier, white with black markings, coming aboard by the gangplank. Once aboard, the dog stood perfectly still, listening and looking all about the deck. He sniffed at the fresh-sawed timbers of the deck load and at the sacked grain being loaded into the last hatch. Then he returned ashore, only to board the next ship, which was loading apples, flour and fir logs for England. Here the terrier again sniffed at the cargo and about the decks and living quarters, then slowly went ashore.

The inspections seemed so deliberate and purposeful that Kildall's interest was roused. Now he watched the dog board a freighter loading paper pulp for East Coast ports. The dog boarded the other ships in turn, examining each in the same intent fashion. After that, busy with preparations for sea, Kildall forgot the episode. And at noon the *Hanley* got under way to Japan.

Early the next morning the dog was found lying on a coco mat outside the cabin of the *Hanley*'s captain. Unseen, he had come aboard again and stowed away for the voyage. The captain, who loved dogs, tried to be friendly, but the terrier would not warm up to his overtures. Kildall and others tried, too, to win him over. To all of them he remained dignified and cool. He merely walked about the captain's deck, sniffing the salt air. Late that first morning, when Kildall went below to eat, the dog followed him and stood at the galley door, waiting expectantly. The cook gave him his best morsels, which the dog ate as if they were his due. When Kildall climbed to the bridge to take over the watch, the dog followed close behind, walked through the pilothouse, took a turn through the chart room, then ran up the ladder to the flying bridge and stood beside the compass binnacle. Apparently satisfied, he lay down in a comfortable corner. Obviously this stowaway was an old sea dog.

For eighteen days the *Hanley* plowed across the northern rim of the Pacific. Day after day her officers and men tried to make up to the dog, but he was exasperatingly aloof. He allowed his head to be patted but showed no return of affection. When not "on watch" with Kildall, he remained at the captain's door, going belowdecks only for his meals. When the coast of Honshu was sighted, the stowaway sniffed the land breeze and watched intently as the land came abeam. His interest grew as the *Hanley* proceeded through the Yokohama breakwaters to her anchorage near the Customs Jetty. Here the freighter found herself among a number of anchored ships that were unloading cargoes.

While supervising cargo work, Kildall noticed that the dog was remarkably alert, his tail switching from time to time and his nostrils quivering nervously as he peered at the other ships. The nearest of these, the S.S. *Simaloer* of the Nederland Line, was, like the *Hanley,* unloading squared timbers into the harbor. Soon the *Hanley* swung with the tide so that her stern pointed in the direction of the Dutch ship, now some three hundred yards distant. At once the dog's interest centered on her. He ran aft to the fantail, as close to her as possible, and sniffed the air with rising excitement. While Kildall watched, a sampan came alongside the *Simaloer,* took two men aboard, shoved off and sculled for the Customs Landing on a course which carried the craft close under the *Hanley*'s stern.

Whining softly, the dog watched. Suddenly he began prancing back and forth in wild

excitement, barking madly. This caught the attention of the two passengers in the sampan. Shading their eyes against the sun, they stared at the *Hanley*'s stern. Presently one of them jumped to his feet and began shouting and waving his arms, motioning to the sampan man and slapping his companion on the back. His excitement matched the dog's. Now, as the sampan came alongside the *Hanley*'s accommodation ladder, the dog became so worked up that he jumped into the water. The shouting man pulled him aboard the sampan and hugged him close. The dog whined with joy and licked his face. Obviously a dog and his master had been reunited.

The reunion of the stowaway and his happy owner became the talk of the crews of both ships. The dog's name, it turned out, was Hector. His owner, W. H. Mante, sec-

ond officer of the *Simaloer,* had the same duties as Kildall had on the *Hanley*. Leaving Government Dock in Vancouver, the *Simaloer* had shifted berth for bunkering while Hector was off for a last run before the long voyage. Mante's frantic search of the waterfront failed to locate Hector in time—and the *Simaloer* sailed without him.

What mysterious instinct could have governed Hector's methodical search for the one ship out of many which would carry him across an ocean to rejoin his beloved master? Did the character of the *Hanley*'s cargo and perhaps other signs tell him that the *Hanley* was bound for the same destination as his own ship? Did he then attach himself to the officer whose duties were like his master's? Any answers would be the guesswork of men, who know only what happened.

The Saga of Moby Doll

by DAVID MacDONALD

ON JULY 16, 1964, at the eastern tip of British Columbia's Saturna Island, Samuel Burich hunched over a harpoon gun, while thirteen huge dorsal fins knifed toward him through the dark water. Burich, a bearded sculptor of thirty-eight, had been commissioned to kill a killer whale—the fiercest thing that swims—and to make a model of it for the Public Aquarium in Vancouver, British Columbia. Easier said than done. The killer (*Orcinus orca*) is a mammal as smart as his playful cousin, the porpoise, and far more elusive. But Sam was lucky. As the black-and-white hulks slid by, spouting high, he fired. Then, pulling in his nylon rope, he found he had a whale on the end of it—alive.

Burich and a helper, Joe Bauer, quickly set out in a light boat to finish the job. As the killer pack circled, uttering high-pitched bleeps, the captive leaped out of the sea. It was a sleek fifteen-footer with a hole where the harpoon cut through its shoulder. When Burich aimed a rifle at the whale, the three-thousand-pound beast looked him right in the eye. "I just couldn't do it," Sam later confessed. "It would have been an execution." Instead, he radioed Vancouver and suggested trying to save the killer's life. Thus began one of the most improbable sagas since Jonah. It made headlines around the globe, revealed many unexpected things about the ocean's champion predator and perhaps even more about people.

Burich's radio call was to Dr. Murray Newman, at the time the curator of the Vancouver Public Aquarium. Dr. Newman promptly flew to Saturna Island. Newman was as excited as a kid at Christmas. Small wonder. Only one other killer whale had ever been captured, and it died in eighteen hours. This *Orcinus orca* could be a living laboratory for scientific research. En route to Saturna, Newman worried about the whale and its captors; angry killers had been known to overturn sizable boats. But this killer surprised him. Newman found it swimming quietly around on its six-hundred-foot leash, so docile that Burich had dubbed it Hound Dog. Newman asked Burich to tow Hound Dog to Vancouver, forty miles away.

"And where do we put it?" Sam inquired.

"Never mind," replied Newman. "I'll think of something."

That night he phoned David Wallace, manager of the Burrard Dry Dock Company, and asked to use the dry dock as a swimming pool for his leviathan. "Of course," he added, "we can't pay." Wallace, surprisingly —and generously—agreed.

Before starting for Vancouver, Burich spliced a rubber tire into the harpoon line as a shock absorber, so the towboat's heaving wouldn't hurt the whale's wound. On the seventeen-hour journey, Burich timed the whale's spouts and stopped whenever it tired and started blowing too fast. "Right from the start," he says, "I wanted that animal to get well." He wasn't alone. When the curious convoy entered the two-hundred-foot dry dock in Vancouver harbor amid cheers from thousands on shore, Dr. Newman had a medical team standing by. Chief physician was Dr. Pat McGeer, a neurochemist. He was assisted by several biologists, a heart specialist, a bacteriologist, a mammalogist, a dermatologist, a pathologist and a veterinarian. "We called in everyone but a psychiatrist," says McGeer. "And no one was too busy to help."

Lowered into the dry dock in a box, two biologists removed the harpoon and injected a massive dose of penicillin with a hypodermic syringe mounted on a twelve-foot pole. McGeer thought that the whale was a female, so she was promptly named Moby Doll. However, some of the scientists, not so certain of the whale's sex, called her Moby Maybe.

Her capture roused wide interest. From London, New York, Los Angeles, Boston and Philadelphia, scientists queried Newman about his unique pet. Some flew to Vancouver, hoping to test her intelligence, her voice and the uncanny built-in sonar with which killers are thought to home in on their prey by bouncing echoes off it. Vancouverites themselves were so taken with Moby Doll that when the dry dock was opened to the public for one day, more than

fifteen thousand people queued in the rain to see her.

Ironically, the first human being Moby warmed to was the man who had harpooned her. Day after day, Burich went to her pen at 6 a.m. and stayed until dark, sitting on a flimsy float that she could have smashed with one flip of her tail. "Killer whales aren't used to being alone," he explained. "And I want her to know that she has a friend." But though he offered her chunks of meat and fish, Moby Doll wouldn't touch a bite.

Meanwhile, in searching for a place to improvise a sea pen, Newman had found an old dock across Vancouver harbor at the Jericho army base. He quickly won over the chief of staff, Lieutenant Colonel William Matthews. While defense officials in Ottawa pondered the curious request—"wharf, one, Moby Doll, for the use of"—Matthews sought troops to work on the pen after hours. Eighty men volunteered. "To us," says Matthews, "she wasn't just a whale. She was our whale."

Her Majesty's Royal Canadian Navy assigned six frogmen to Operation Whalepen. The army donated wire fencing and steel decking. Various Vancouver firms supplied timber, cargo nets and labor, all without charge. One company provided five tugs to haul the dry dock across the harbor, while another sent a power scow to raise and lower it. But the biggest benefactor was Burrard Dry Dock Company, which housed Moby Doll for eight days, at a cost in forgone contracts of about fifteen thousand dollars. Said manager David Wallace, "It was the least we could do for a lady in distress." When the move was completed, the Vancouver City Council sent thank-you notes to all the firms and individuals who had helped.

Though her wound healed, Moby still

wouldn't eat. Through weeks of suspense the Vancouver press ran daily reports on her health, while thousands of people phoned television and radio stations for further news. As one cabby remarked, "It was like a member of the family was dying." To get her to eat, Newman offered her horsemeat, salmon, lingcod, flounder, octopus. Yet, despite vitamin injections to perk up her appetite, she refused them all.

As the weeks wore on, scientists arrived from as far away as Florida. Among them was William Schevill of Harvard, the world's foremost authority on whale "talk." From his recordings of Moby's beeps, grunts and squeals for a dictionary of the deep, he suspected that she could scan a vast tract of ocean with her clicking sonar—better than any devised by man—or even beam it like a flashlight.

A caller on September 9 was Edward Griffin, director of the Seattle aquarium. "While I was talking to Dr. Newman," Griffin later recalled, "Moby Doll began flapping her tail as if to attract our attention. So we threw her a fish, and she ate it!" While the onlookers cheered, she wolfed down three more, her first meal in fifty-five days. The event was front-page news. "When that whale finally began eating," says Stuart Keate, publisher of the Vancouver *Sun,* "the whole city seemed to heave a great sigh of relief."

Once she was dining regularly—a hundred pounds of fish per day—a remarkable change came over Moby Doll. Shy and lethargic before, she now leaped and frolicked in her pen and drew closer to her keepers. On one occasion, Vincent Penfold, then assistant curator, summoned her to lunch by slapping the water with a Pacific cod. Three times Moby glided up, opened her great toothy jaws and gently took it from him. Next time, Penfold held the fish high,

inviting her to jump. Instead, Moby promptly dived, came up in the middle of her pen and flapped her tail flukes indignantly. Then, after serving more cod in the approved way, Penfold substituted an orange rockfish. When Moby Doll saw it, she again smacked her tail with obvious annoyance. But as soon as Penfold cut off the rockfish's sharp fins, Moby ate it. "By gosh," he cried, "she's training me!"

Moby turned out to be a very clever whale indeed. When recordings of other killers' calls were piped into her pen, she squeaked excitedly. Yet she coldly ignored the playback of one voice—her own. But the most amazing thing about Moby Doll was her tame way with man. Once, for example, Penfold donned scuba gear and went down in a wire cage to observe her underwater. When his back was turned, Moby playfully nudged the cage, then darted away with a squeal. Terry McLeod, one of the whale's feeders, spent many hours on a float beside her and actually taught her to roll over while he scratched her stomach with a brush. "At times," he said, "she seems like a big cocker spaniel."

Her fame spread far. On a special radio program Moby's voice was heard by millions across Canada, while the National Film Board released a movie about her in forty-four countries. She was visited by reporters from Texas to Toronto, and by two Canadian cabinet ministers. In Vancouver, an alderman proposed making her the city's official emblem, teachers assigned essays on her and several stores used her picture to advertise "A Whale of a Sale." Although, for safety reasons, the public was not admitted onto the old army wharf, Vancouverites were determined to see their whale. Some climbed over six-foot fences, some floated past the open end of the pen in boats and on rubber rafts. A few even swam up, an exploit that might have proved interesting if any other killers had answered Moby's calls.

In time, Dr. Newman began to worry about Moby's health again. Because of low salinity in that part of the harbor, a fungus infection was turning her glossy black skin to gray. "We've got to get her into saltier water," he told the aquarium board. But on October 9, before a floating pen could be built, Moby Doll took a sudden turn for the worse. Newman found her swimming erratically. After barely nibbling at her 3 p.m. feeding, she rolled over to have her tummy scratched, then dived. She never came up again. The first person to be told the sad news was Burich, who was then preparing a life-size model of Moby Doll.

Moby's death was headlined in the Vancouver *Province* next day, and even the *Times* of London gave her obituary a two-column heading, the same size as the one given to the outbreak of World War II.

An autopsy showed that Moby Doll died chiefly from exhaustion, resulting from the harbor water's low buoyancy. In death, the killer revealed one parting surprise: It was really a two-year-old male.

In eighty-five days of captivity, Moby received a hundred thousand dollars' worth of volunteer care. Was it worth it? Dr. Newman thinks so. "Moby made a definite contribution to human knowledge," he says. Dr. H. D. Fisher, a University of British Columbia zoologist, feels that the whale's greatest value went beyond the scientific. "For a little while," he says, "people found something better to worry about than the bomb and themselves. It was very refreshing."

LIFE AMONG THE ELEPHANTS

Condensed from Elephant Bill

by LIEUTENANT COLONEL J. H. WILLIAMS

I HAVE ALWAYS got on well with animals. I like them and, with one or two notable exceptions, they always seemed to like me. When I was a boy in Cornwall my first animal friend was a donkey. He had free range over the moors, but I always knew where to find him. During the World War of 1914–1918, I was in the Camel Corps, and then, later on, transport officer in charge of a lot of mules. These experiences taught me much about animals, for both camels and mules are temperamental beasts; and mules have also a remarkable sense of humor, so that in dealing with them one gets plenty of exercise for one's own. That was valuable. My life has been spent east of Suez in places where if you lose your sense of humor you had much better take the first boat home.

Like millions of other fellows, when World War I was over I began to think about finding myself a job. A friend told me that he knew of a man who did something with elephants in Burma. This sounded as though it would be what I wanted. My friend wrote to the man, introducing me as a candidate for elephant management, and I wrote to the head of the Bombay-Burma Trading Corporation, the company concerned. It was 1920 before I got back to England, but my letter led to an interview and before the year was out I was in Burma.

My first vivid memories of Burma are not of the pagodas and rice fields and all I had read about, but of my first "jungle salt," Willie, the man under whom I was to begin my training. I met him at his camp on the banks of the Upper Chindwin River, Upper Burma. He was, in his own words, down with fever, but he was sitting at a table, about midday, outside his tent, drinking a whisky and soda and smoking a Burma cheroot.

His welcome was icy, and I immediately guessed that he jealously resented anyone sharing his jungle life. About four o'clock in the afternoon I asked for a cup of tea—and was laughed at for not drinking whisky and soda. I vowed, privately, that I would see him under the table later on. About five o'clock seven elephants arrived in camp and were paraded in line for inspection. Willie did not speak to me as he walked off to inspect them. However, I followed him, uninvited. Judging by appearances, there was one worn-out animal which looked as though

179

it might be the mother of the other six. Each animal was inspected in turn and Willie entered some remark about it in a book. This took up about half an hour, during which he did not address a single word to me. I was careful not to ask any questions, as I saw that I should only be called a fool for my pains. However, when the inspection was over, Willie turned on me, saying: "Those four on the right are yours, and God help you if you can't look after them." For all I knew, I was supposed to take them to bed with me. (The next evening, when Willie told me to inspect my own four and to see that their gear was on their backs comfortably, I followed a lifelong rule when in doubt: I trusted to luck.)

That first night, as my tent had been pitched near his, I joined Willie at his camp table. On it were two bottles of Scotch—one of his and one of mine. After half an hour or so Willie thawed sufficiently to ask me, "Are you safe with a shotgun?"—not "Do you shoot?" as is more usual.

Silence reigned after my answer. Willie emptied and refilled his glass several times. At last he opened up and, passing his empty bottle to me, remarked, "I drink a bottle a night and it does me no harm. There are two vices in this country. Woman is one and the other the bottle. Choose which you like, but you must not mix them. Anything to do with the jungle, elephants and your work you can learn only by experience. No one but a Burman can teach you and you'll draw your pay for ten years before you earn it. Tomorrow I'll give you some maps and the day after you must push off for three months on your own. You can do what you damned well like—including suicide if you're lonely —but don't come back until you can speak some Burmese." After this speech he walked off to his bed without even saying good-night.

After four and a half years' service in the army I believed I was past the age of adventures; but leaving on my first jungle trip, two days later, I experienced a new thrill. With four elephants carrying my kit, a cook, two bearers and two messengers, I was on my own again. My life in charge of elephants had begun. I had been on the march less than two days when the ancient female elephant known as Ma Oh (Old Lady) was discovered dead an hour before I was due to move camp. Willie had, I now know, somewhat unscrupulously palmed her off on me— and his terrible words, "God help you if you can't look after them," now rang in my ears. Seeing her enormous carcass lying in the jungle—just as she had died in her sleep—was a terrible sight, and it was awful that she had died within a few days of my being made responsible for her. How on earth, I wondered, should I get out of this mess? "At the worst," I thought, "I can only lose my job. I'm damned if I'll buy them a new one!" It was a bad business but as I had no one to help me out I had to help myself, and I decided that the best thing I could do was to hold a postmortem.

The Old Lady was scarcely cold before I was literally inside her, with her arching ribs sheltering me from the sun. I learned a good deal about elephant construction from her. Her carcass proved to be a cave full of strange treasures such as the heart, the gizzard and the lungs. The only snag was that I could not find any kidneys, and I was almost tempted to conclude that she must have died for lack of them. However, when I came to write out a report that evening I decided that "no kidneys" might not be an acceptable cause of death—so in desperation I left it at "found dead" and did not even mention my Jonah's journey.

Ma Oh's load was easily divided among the remaining three animals, and on I went. My instructions were to march to a certain village in the Myittha Valley, where I was to meet a head Burman named U Tha Yauk. I was on foot with my messengers and the two bearers, and we had outdistanced the elephants by several miles by taking a shortcut up the bed of the creek. U Tha Yauk had come some way out of the village to meet me and was squatting on a rock beside the creek up which we were traveling.

I greeted him with my three words of Burmese and laughed because I could say no more, and he laughed back; we marched on in single file until we came to a clearing around which there were about ten bamboo huts, all standing on bamboo stilts and thatched with grass. One of them was assigned to me, and after a bath and dinner I went to bed.

Next morning a new life began—my life as a pupil of U Tha Yauk. With the aid of a good map of the Indaung Forest Reserve, he made me understand I was to go on a tour with him from the valley, crossing five parallel creeks flowing from east to west into the Myittha River. On the sides of each of the watersheds he had a camp of elephants, ten camps altogether, each with an average of seven elephants, or seventy working animals all told. Judging from the map, the distance between the camps was six to seven miles, with hills three to four thousand feet high between. At the first camp we reached I found about twenty Burmans, including a carpenter of sorts, erecting a set of jungle buildings. It was explained to me that this camp was to be my headquarters during the coming monsoon months.

I soon realized that the elephant was the backbone of the Burmese teak industry. Teak is one of the world's finest hardwoods, partly because of the silica it contains. As it grows best in country inacessible to tractors and machinery—steep, precipitous terrain two to three thousand feet in elevation —elephant power is essential for hauling and pushing the logs from the stump to the nearest stream.

The history of the Bombay-Burma Corporation went back to the time of Burma's King Theebaw, when a senior member of the firm who visited Burma appreciated the great possibilities of the teak trade and was able to obtain a lease of certain forest areas. Sawmills were established at the ports, a system of rafting teak logs down the creeks and rivers was organized and elephants were bought on a large scale.

The health, management and handling of the elephants in this enormous organization impressed me as the factor on which everything else depended. The routine work of elephant management in camp consisted of checking up gear-making, getting to know the "oozies," or elephant riders, inspecting elephants and dressing any galls caused by gear rubbing, wounds caused by bamboo splinters in the feet, and other common injuries. For my early training in all these tasks I am indebted to U Tha Yauk. After our first trip we spent several days in camp. I mixed with everyone, forever asking questions and being given answers packed with information I had to remember.

One day, on my way back to my hut for lunch, I watched a most fascinating sight. About a hundred yards below my hut was a large pool in the brook. Two elephants, each with its rider sitting behind its head, entered the pool, and, without any word of command that I could hear, they lay down in the water. The riders tucked up their lungyi skirts so that they were transformed into loincloths, slipped off their mounts into the water and began to scrub the elephant from head to tail with a soap which lathered freely. Then they washed it off the animals, splashing water over them with their hands.

The soap they used turned out to be the soapy bark of a tree. Soon I was standing on the bank of the pool and from there I watched other elephants being washed in the same way. Two of them were cows with young calves which rolled over and over and played in the water like young children. There were also two large males, with gleaming white tusks which were scrubbed with handfuls of silver sand.

After they had all been washed and dried off, the elephants were paraded for inspection—all drawn up in line abreast, each rider dressed in his best. U Tha Yauk advanced with military precision and, after bowing instead of saluting, handed me a set of ragged and torn books. On the cover of each an elephant's name was written.

I looked at one book and called out the name of the elephant; and the rider rode it toward me at a fast, bold stride, halting the animal just before me. He was a splendid beast with his head up, his skin newly scrubbed but already dry in the sun, a black skin with a faint tinge of blue showing through. The white tusks, freshly polished, gleamed in the sunlight. The motionless rider was sitting on one leg while the other leg dangled behind the elephant's ear. On his face was an expression of intense pride—pride in his magnificent beast. Suddenly, he gave an order and the elephant swung around to present his hindquarters, on which there was a brand, made with phosphorescent paint when the animal was six years old. I opened the book and read a number of entries, each with the date the elephant had been inspected during the last ten years. On the front page was the animal's history with his registered number and other details—such as that he had been born in Siam, bought when he was twenty years old, badly gored by a wild tusker, but had fully recovered after being off work for a year. Thus

I inspected each of the animals in turn and read their histories. As each inspection was finished, the rider and elephant left the clearing and disappeared into the jungle.

When they had all gone I was taken around the harness racks—just a row of horizontal branches of trees, on each of which hung the gear of one of the animals. All the harness except the heavy dragging chains was handmade by the riders. There were great cane panniers (baskets), laibuts (woven breast straps of fiber), wooden breeching blocks, padding from the bark of the banbrwe tree, ropes of every kind twisted from the bark of the sha tree.

In those first three months on my own I did most of the things worth doing in Burma. U Tha Yauk helped me to achieve my ambition—to shoot a wild bull elephant. My main reason for shooting him was not to secure the tusks, much as I coveted them, but to carry out a postmortem to see what the organs of a really healthy elephant looked like, and to make another attempt to find the kidneys. This second postmortem taught me a good deal about what had been wrong with Ma Oh. In fact, it showed me half a dozen reasons sufficient to explain her death.

After three months, which passed all too soon, I returned to Willie, having learned a great deal. When I arrived I got the greeting I expected: sarcastic remarks about my having let one of my elephants die in the first two days—no doubt by overloading her with all my blasted new kit. I replied that I was surprised that she had lived as long as she had: her liver was riddled with flukes and her heart was as big as a football.

"How do *you* know how big an elephant's heart ought to be?"

"I shot a wild tusker that was forty years old, and I did a postmortem on him to see how the organs of a healthy elephant compared with hers. His heart was only the size of a coconut."

Willie's whole attitude to me changed after I said this. What pleased him was that I had shot an elephant, not for its tusks, but in order to learn more about elephants. For Willie, like most men who live long in the jungle, deplored the shooting of big game. He felt far more sympathy toward any creature which was part of his jungle than for a new arrival armed with all his fresh kit. That evening I became a companion with whom he could enjoy rational conversation instead of an interloper who had to be bullied and kept in his place. His great ambition had been to get someone who would take up the subject of elephant management seriously, and it seemed to him that I might be the man he wanted. Before I left him two or three days later, he had advised me to take up elephants and to make them my life's work. I thus owe a great debt of gratitude to Willie.

The job of extracting teak and delivering it a thousand miles away has many aspects, and up till that time none of the European assistants had specialized in trying to improve the management of elephants. Most of the details had been left to the Burman. The average European assistant joining any of the large teak firms in Burma was put in charge of a forest area bigger than an English county. In it were scattered a total of about a hundred elephants, in groups of seven. By continually touring during all the seasons of the year, he might be able to visit every camp about once every six weeks. Under such conditions it would be a long time before he learned to know his elephants even by name, still less by sight; and it would be a very long time indeed before he knew their individual temperaments and capacities for work.

I was fortunate, as I was responsible for seventy elephants, all working in a fairly small area. I was thus often able to visit my camps twice a month and to spend a longer time in each of them. What follows is largely the result of my having the luck to start in conditions that enabled me to get to know my elephants really well.

It is impossible to understand much about tame elephants unless one knows a great deal about the habits of wild ones. The study of wild elephants usually entails shooting a few of them at some period, either deliberately, for sport or ivory, or in self-defense. Most men who have shot elephants come afterward to regret having done so—but "to hunt is to learn."

Wild elephants normally live in herds of thirty to fifty, and during the year cover great distances, chiefly in search of fodder. During the rainy monsoon months—from June to October—they graze on bamboo in the hilly forest country. After the monsoons are over they move into the lower foothills and the swamp valleys, feeding more on grass and less on bamboo. It is at this time that the full-grown tuskers join the herd, though they seldom actually enter it, preferring to remain on its outskirts. At this season they do their courting and mating, in the course of which an older bull often has to fight some youngster who is pursuing the same female.

Wild elephants hate being disturbed on their feeding grounds but they do not usually stampede suddenly, as do many other herds of big game. With an uncanny intelligence, they close up around one animal as though they were drilled and their leader had decided on the best line of retreat. He leads and they follow irresistibly, smashing through everything like steamrollers.

Most wild-elephant calves are born between March and May—the hot, dry season.

183

I believe that if the mother elephant is disturbed she will carry her calf during its first month, holding it wrapped in her trunk. I have often seen a mother pick up her calf in this way.

For many years I could not understand the bellowing and trumpeting of wild elephants at night during the hot weather when most calves are born. The fuss is made by the herd in order to protect the mother and calf from intruders—tigers in particular. The noise is terrifying. The grazing herd will remain in the neighborhood for some weeks until the new arrival can keep up with them. The area may cover a square mile, and all day the herd will graze over it, surrounding the mother and her newly born calf, and closing their ranks around her at night. The places chosen are on low ground where a river has suddenly changed its course and taken a hairpin bend. These spots are thus bounded on three sides by banks and river.

The mating of wild elephants is very private. The bull remains, as usual, outside the herd, and his ladylove comes out where she knows she will find him. She gives the herd the slip in the evening and is back with them at dawn. Sometimes a rival tusker intervenes and a duel ensues. This is why elephant fights are always between two bulls. There is never a general dogfight within the herd.

Elephant bulls fight head to head and seldom fight to the death without one trying to break away. The one that breaks away, however, may receive a wound which can be mortal, for, in turning, he exposes the most vulnerable part of the body. The deadly blow is a thrust of one tusk between the hind legs into the loins and intestines, where the testicles are carried inside the body. It is a common wound to have to treat after a wild tusker has attacked a domesticated one.

Some males never grow tusks, but these tuskless fellows are at no disadvantage in a fight. From the age of three all that the animal gains by not having to grow tusks goes into bodily strength, particularly in the girth and weight of the trunk. The trunk becomes so strong that it will smash off an opponent's solid ivory tusk as though it were the dry branch of a tree. From the time that a male calf is three years old there is always interest among the oozies as to whether it is going to be a tusker with two tusks, or a tai (with one tusk either right or left), or a han (a tuskless male but with two small tushes such as females carry), or a hine (which has neither tusks nor tushes).

I arrived in Burma just as a determined effort had been started to improve the management of elephants and their calves. In order to do this, it was first necessary to improve the conditions of the oozies, who must be considered as part and parcel of the Burmese timber-working elephants which they ride. These men have an uncanny knowledge of elephants. Their homes are in camps in the most remote parts of the jungle. They can sit an elephant from the age of six, and they grow up learning all the traditional knowledge, the myth and legend, the blended fact and fiction which is attached to this lovable animal.

At the age of fourteen the average boy in an elephant camp is earning a wage. He starts life as a paijaik—that is, the man who hooks the chains to the logs, a ground assistant of the oozie. There is no more lovely sight I know than to see a fourteen-year-old boy riding a newly trained calf elephant of six. It is a proud day in that boy's life when he is promoted to oozie and has an elephant in his own charge. The understanding between them is equaled only by that of a child with a puppy, but the Burmese boy is not as cruel to his elephant as most children are to puppies.

The Burman oozie has a pretty hard life. In the first place, he has to catch his elephant every morning and bring it to camp. Catching his elephant involves tracking the animal a distance of about eight miles, starting at dawn through jungles infested with all types of big game. That in itself is a lonely job, and to do it successfully the oozie has to become as alert and wary as one of the jungle beasts.

He knows the shape, size and peculiarities of his own elephant's footprints with certainty. Once he has picked up the trail, he sets off following her. While he is doing so he notices many things: He finds the spot where the animal rested in the night; he observes her droppings, and can tell from them that his elephant has been eating too much bamboo and for that reason will probably have headed for a patch of kaing grass that grows on the banks of the creek over the watershed.

When he has gained the ridge he will halt and listen, perhaps for ten minutes, for the distinctive sound of his elephant's kalouk, or bell, which the oozie made himself. Elephant bells are made with two clappers, one on each side, hanging outside the bell, which is made from a hollowed-out lump of teak. No two bells ever have the same note, and the sound of fifteen or more can only be compared to the music of a babbling brook.

As the oozie approaches his beast he begins to sing so as to let her know that he is coming. Then, instead of bursting through the kaing grass that stands nine feet high, he sits down on a boulder beside the creek and fills his homemade pipe and lights it. Between the puffs he keeps calling: *"Lah! Lah! Lah!* [Come on! Come on! Come on!]" But no sound comes from where his elephant is grazing, so he changes his words to *"Digo lah! Digo lah!* [Come here! Come here!]" And he will sit and smoke and call some

fifteen minutes without showing impatience. He gives her time to accept the grim fact that another day of hard work has begun. If he hurries her, she may rebel.

Presently the elephant emerges from the kaing grass, and, chatting away to her, he says, "Do you think I've nothing else to do but wait for you? You've been eating since noon yesterday."

Then his voice rings out with a firm order: *"Hmit!"* Dropping first on her haunches and then reposing with all four legs extended, she allows him to approach her.

"Tah! [Stand up!]," he orders, and she does so, keeping her front legs close together. He bends down and unfastens her hobbles and throws them over her withers. Then the oozie orders her to sit down, climbs onto her head and away they go. When they reach camp the oozie has his first meal of the day, washes his elephant in the creek and harnesses her for work. Their job for the day is to climb a ridge two thousand feet above the camp and to drag a log from the stump to the creek.

When the oozie reaches the log with his elephant and his paijaik, he will trim it of knots so as to make it easier for dragging and fasten chains around it securely. Then begins the wearisome task of dragging a log twenty-nine feet long and six or seven feet in girth—that is to say, over a hundred cubic feet of timber, or four tons deadweight. For a mile the path follows the top of the ridge. "Patience! patience! patience! *Yoo! Yoo! Yoo!* [Pull! Pull! Pull!]" calls the oozie. As the elephant takes the strain, she feels what power she must exert besides that of her enormous weight. The ground is ankle-deep in mud, and there are dozens of small obstructions which must be leveled out by the log's nose—sapling stumps, bamboos, rocks.

The elephant puts out her first effort and,

bellowing like fury, pulls the log three times her own length and stops. She rests then to take breath, and her trunk goes out sideways to snatch at a bamboo. It is her chewing gum as she works, but it earns her a sarcastic comment from the oozie: "My mother, but you are forever eating!" However, his patience is quite undisturbed. The elephant takes her time. "*Yoo! Yoo! Yoo!*" calls the oozie, but there is no response. "*Yooo! Yooo! Yooo!*" Then the elephant pulls again, but this time as it is slightly downhill, she pulls the log six times her length before she halts. So it goes on until they reach the edge of a precipice—a four-hundred-foot drop. The elephant knows the exact margin of safety, and when the log is ten feet from the edge she refuses to haul it any closer.

The chains are unfastened, and the elephant is moved around behind the log. The oozie gives his orders by kicks and scratches with his bare feet behind the elephant's ears. So he coaxes her to bend down her massive head in order to get a leverage under the log with her trunk. Working like that, she moves it first four feet at one end, then rolls it from the middle, then pushes the other end until she has got it onto the very edge of the cliff, almost trembling on the balance. She will then torment her oozie by refusing to touch it again for ten minutes. Finally, when the oozie's patience is almost at an end, she puts one forefoot out as calmly as if she were tapping a football, and the log is away—gone. There is a crash in the jungle below, and then a prolonged series of crashes echoing through the jungle as the log tears down bamboos until it comes to rest four hundred feet lower down, leaving the elephant standing on the edge of the precipice above with a supercilious expression on her face, as though she were saying: "Damned easy."

Half an hour later elephant and oozie have reached the log again, having gone around by a circuitous game track to the foot of the precipice. Once down there, she has again to drag the log with the chains along a ledge. Dragging a log weighing four tons while negotiating a narrow ledge is a risky business, for the log might roll. But the elephant can judge what is safe to the inch—not to the foot—and she works with patience, patience, patience. Both oozie and elephant know that, should the log start to roll or slide over the ledge, all the gear and harness can be got rid of in the twinkling of an eye. The elephant has only to whip around in her tracks, step inside her chain and bend down her head for all the harness to peel off over her head, as easily as a girl strips off a silk slip over her shoulders. For this reason it is very rare indeed for an elephant to be dragged over a precipice by a log suddenly taking charge.

After the ledge, there is an easy downhill drag for half a mile to the floating point on the side of the creek. By that time it is about three o'clock in the afternoon. The oozie unharnesses his elephant, puts on her fetters, slaps her on her backside and tells her that she must go off in search of food. For neither of them is the day's work really over. The elephant still has to find her fodder, not only to chew it but to break off, pull down or pull up every branch, tree, creeper or tuft of grass that she eats. The oozie has to repair his gear, trim logs or weave a new breast strap of bark. This bit of harness takes the full strain of the elephant's strength when dragging.

Living under such primitive conditions, not only the oozie but also his wife and family need frequent medical attention, and they have no one to look to but the European assistant who lives nearest. Apart from all the diseases, accidents are constantly occurring in the jungle; the assistant has to be ready to make decisions which would make an ordinary medical man's hair stand on end. One may come into a new camp and find sick people down with beriberi—women with their breasts split like ripe tomatoes from the swelling characteristic of that disease—and one has to decide at once what to do. One has to be ready to treat a girl with an afterbirth hemorrhage or a man scalped by a bear. Malaria is more common than head colds are in England. Dysentery and even cholera and smallpox epidemics are all likely to break out in the jungle. I am convinced that life in such conditions would be unbearable if it were not for the elephants, which exert a fascination over the Burmese, a fascination which Europeans soon begin to feel as well.

Europeans tell and even believe the most fantastic tales about the mating habits of elephants, but the lovemaking of elephants as I have seen it seems to me more simple and more lovely than any myth. It is beautiful because it is quite without the brutishness and the cruelty of the matings of so many animals.

Without there being any appearance of "season," two animals become attracted to each other. Most females first mate between the ages of seventeen and twenty. She shows no sign of any particular season but apparently feels some natural urge. Days and even weeks of courtship may take place. Eventually the mating is consummated, and the act may be repeated three or four times during the twenty-four hours. For months the pair will keep together as they graze, and their honeymoon will last all that time. After the day's work they will call each other and go off together into the jungle. My own belief is that this close relationship lasts until the female has been pregnant for ten months

—that is, until she has become aware that she is pregnant.

The companionship of the male is then replaced by that of a female friend or "auntie." From that time onward they are never apart and it becomes difficult to separate them. Indeed, it is cruel to do so. Their association is founded on mutual aid among animals, the instinctive knowledge that it takes two mothers to protect a calf elephant against tigers which, in spite of all precautions, still kill 25 percent of all calves born. Gestation lasts twenty-two months. After the calf has been born, the mother and the auntie always keep it between them as they graze—all through the night and, while it is very young, during daylight hours as well. To kill the calf the tiger has to drive off both the mother and auntie by stampeding them. To do this he will first attack the mother, springing on her back and stampeding her; then he returns to attack Auntie, who defends the calf, knowing that in a few moments the mother will return. On many occasions I have had to dress the lacerated wounds of tiger claws on the backs of both a mother elephant and her friend.

A baby calf follows its mother at heel for three or four years, being suckled by the mother from the breasts between her forelegs. This position, between the forelegs, affords the calf perfect protection. At birth the calf's trunk is a useless membrane growing rather to one side so as to allow the calf to suck more easily through the mouth. It does not become flexible and useful for three to four months.

At the age of five or, at most, six years, the calf has learned to gather its own fodder and gradually gives up suckling its mother. Female elephants have an average of four calves in a lifetime. Twins are not uncommon, and two calves of different ages following their mother at heel is a usual sight.

After their weaning, young elephants go through an awkward stage, becoming a bit truculent owing to the desire for independence—much like human boys and girls. At fifteen or sixteen they become very much like human teen-agers. Young male elephants do a lot of flirting with the females from the ages of sixteen to twenty, sometimes being most enterprising. But the average animal does not show any signs of musth until the age of twenty. A male elephant will mate when he is not "on musth," in fact he usually does. But when he is on musth all the savage lust and combative instincts of his huge body come out.

From the age of twenty to thirty-five musth is shown by a slight discharge of a strong-smelling fluid from the musth glands near the eye, directly above the line of the mouth. In a perfectly fit male it occurs annually during the hot months, which are the mating season. It may last about two weeks, during which time he is very temperamental. From the age of thirty-five to forty-five the discharge increases and runs freely, eventually dribbling into his mouth, and the taste of it makes him much more ferocious. He is physically in his prime at that age, and unless he is securely chained to a large tree while on musth, he is a danger to his oozie and to other elephants. His brain goes wild, and nothing will satisfy him. From forty-five to fifty, musth gradually subsides. Tuskers between the ages of thirty-five and forty-five that have killed as many as nine men will become docile during musth in their later years. But no elephant on musth can be trusted unless he is over sixty years old.

Poo Ban was normally a friendly animal and would let me walk under his tusks, but he went on musth in the Taungdwin Forest area, killed his oozie and another man, then killed two female elephants and attacked all men on sight. Finally he entered villages, tore rice granaries open and became the terror of the valley. I offered a reward of three hundred rupees for his capture and decided it would be necessary to destroy him if he could not be captured.

He was marked down in a dense patch of bamboo jungle in Saiyawah (the Valley of Ten Villages), four marches away. With Kya Sine, my gun boy, I set out, lightly loaded with two traveling elephants as pack. The evening before I was to tackle Poo Ban I was testing my rifle when Kya Sine begged me to let him go ahead and attempt to recapture the elephant without shooting, so that he could earn the three hundred rupees. Unfortunately I gave in, and before dawn he had gone on ahead. I arrived at 3 p.m. next day to be met by men who said, "Kya Sine is dead." Poo Ban had killed him.

That night I bivouacked in an open place which had at one time been paddy fields. It was a brilliant moonlit night and before I went to sleep I made my plans to recapture Poo Ban. I intended to wound him in the forefoot, break his spirit and then heal the wound.

I was asleep, lying in the open, when I was wakened by a clank, clank, clank! Luckily for me, a piece of chain had been left on Poo Ban's off forefoot. Two hundred yards away, in the open, a magnificent tusker was standing, head erect in challenge, defiant of the whole world. He was a perfect silhouette. I did not dare move an eyelid, and while I held my breath he moved on with a clank, clank, clank, which at last faded away like the far sound of the pipes over the hills.

At dawn I tried to put my plans into action. When he had been located, I took up my position, while twenty Burmans with four shotguns among them tried to drive him past me. At last Poo Ban came out of the jungle with his head held high. He halted and then made a beeline across my front, traveling fast over the open ground. Kneeling, I took the shot at his foot on which all of my plans depended. The bullet kicked up a puff of dust in front of his near forefoot as he put it down in his stride. I had missed!

Poo Ban halted and swung around to face me, or the bark of my rifle which he had heard. Then he took up the never-to-be-forgotten attitude of an elephant about to charge, with the trunk well tucked away in his mouth, like a wound-up watch spring. As he charged, I took a chest shot at twenty-five yards. His tusks drove nine inches into the ground, his head dropped. For a few seconds he balanced himself and then toppled over dead.

I dropped my rifle and was sick, vomiting with fear, excitement and regret. Poo Ban was dead, and I had failed to catch him alive. There was no court of inquiry. My report was accepted and I was given the tusks as a souvenir, a souvenir of a double failure that I bitterly regretted, and of the death of the finest and bravest Burman hunter I have known.

Doubtless there is cruelty in breaking the spirit and training wild elephants after they have been captured by kheddaring. The ideal age at which to capture a wild elephant is considered to be from fifteen to twenty, as it is then only a few years away from sufficient maturity to do heavy work and earn its original cost. But the spirit of a youngster of that age, whether male or female, takes a lot of breaking—often a matter of weeks, during which the animal is tethered to a tree with chains. Its continual struggling and fighting to break free cause the most shocking galling of the ankles and neck. Food is thrown to the elephant, but it is insufficient and unsuitable, and it leads to great loss of

condition. The wounds are almost impossible to treat, and they become flyblown and ulcerated. In the end the young animal becomes heartbroken and thin. Finally it realizes that it is in captivity for the rest of its days and, after one last struggle, will put up with a man sitting on its head.

But a calf born in captivity is far more easily trained. From the day it is born until it leaves its mother at five years old it is in contact with its mother's oozie. It flirts with him like a child; it pretends to chase him, then runs away again. But though so playful, it seldom trusts him beyond accepting a tidbit of fruit or a handful of rice from his hands. In November of its fifth year the calf is weaned and from that moment becomes more independent. Five or six calves are trained at a time in one camp. An area of a hundred yards square is cleared, except for a few trees to give shade. In the middle a "crush," or triangular-shaped pen, is built of logs about the height of the average five-year-old calf. The logs are fastened with wooden pegs; no nails are used. The bark is stripped from the logs, which are rubbed smooth and smeared with grease—all precautions against galling the calf's hide. In camp, in addition to the calves with their mothers, is an elephant known as the koonkie (schoolmaster). This animal is usually a tuskless male between forty-five and fifty years of age, chosen for his docility and patience.

On the morning when the first calf is to be weaned, the mother and the calf are brought into the clearing and made familiar with the crush and its surroundings. Once the calf has been lured into the crush with a bit of fruit (or butted into it by the koonkie), the attendant Burmans quickly slip in two stout bars behind its hindquarters. It will usually struggle and kick for about two hours. Then it sulks and finally it will take a banana from the oozie out of sheer boredom and disgust.

Meanwhile, the calf's future rider has been attached to a pulley a few feet over its head. Two men on the ground, on either side of the crush, control this pulley and on a signal from the rider he is lowered slowly onto the calf's head.

"Damn you, get off!" screams the calf, bucking like a bronco. The would-be oozie has soon to be hauled up again, but no sooner has the calf quieted down and accepted another banana than the rider is lowered once more—and so on, until the poor little calf seems to say, "All right. Sit there if you must."

So far so good. The poor calf is tired, but the Burmans, stripped of all but their tucked-up lungyis, are thoroughly enjoying the game, though they are dripping with sweat.

Suspended from another pulley above the center of the calf's back is a heavy block of padded wood. This is also lowered onto its back and provokes more bucking-bronco antics. A moment or two later the block is lifted, but as soon as the calf stands still, down it comes again. Once more there are determined struggles to get free. So it goes on, and all the while the calf is being offered food and spoken to with kind and soothing words. Finally, in utter disgust the calf sits down with its front feet straight out, hoping that it will get rid of the pests.

A cheer goes up from the Burmans, a cheer which soon becomes a chant of *"Tah [Get up]! Hmit [Sit down]!"* As the weight is lifted, the calf gets up and all the Burmans chant, *"Tah!"* As the weight comes down, and the calf sits, all of them chant, *"Hmit!"* in chorus. After a time the rider, still attached to the pulley, remains comfortably seated on its head. By evening, unless the calf is a really obstinate young devil, the rider can turn and, putting his hand on its

back instead of the log of wood, order the calf to sit down by exerting pressure and by saying, *"Hmit."*

Once that is possible, the calf is considered broken. Often it takes less than twelve hours with no cruelty whatsoever. Sometimes, however, in dealing with obstinate and truculent young tuskers, the game has to be kept up, by the light of bamboo torches, far into the night. Occasionally it may last even till the next morning. But however long it may take, the Burmans never give in and never give the calf any rest until their object is achieved. The great lesson is that man's willpower is stronger than the calf's and that man will always get his way.

Before the calf is taken out of the crush on the following morning, it is hobbled with well-greased buffalo-hide thongs, and it is then tied to a tree for twenty-four hours, being caressed and cajoled all the time by its future rider. He makes it sit down each time he approaches. He mounts on its head, remains there ten minutes, orders the calf to sit again and dismounts, and sometimes keeps it in the sitting position for five or ten minutes. Extraordinary patience is needed throughout. Once the Burman starts, he goes on until he gains his point. He never lets the calf win a victory, however temporary.

The calf is then taken for its first walk, attached to the koonkie by a buffalo-hide girdle. The koonkie thinks the whole thing a bore but he stands no nonsense. If the calf jibs, sits down or lags, he gives him one wrench that pulls him along. On occasion he will give him a real welt with his trunk. It soon becomes a decorous walking out, and at a later stage the koonkie can manage two calves—one on each side.

From the age of breaking, young elephants are kept under training until the finishing age of nineteen. For about two years they remain in the camp nursery, merely being caught daily and taught the simple words of command and the "aids" of the rider and his foot controls behind their ears. The aids are simply movements of the rider's body by which he translates his wishes, almost instinctively, to his mount. Thus an intense stiffening of his limbs and leaning back will be at once understood as halt. A pressure on one side will be understood as turn to the left, on the other as turn to the right. Leaning forward and forcing downward will mean stoop or kneel. A dragging up on the right side will be correctly interpreted as lift the right foot—on the other, as lift the left.

At about eight years old, young elephants carry their first pack and become "travelers," accompanying a European assistant when he tours the forest. They thus become accustomed to going over mountains and down streams, carrying light weights, such as camp cooking pots or bedrolls. During the early years the elephant never really earns its keep or does enough to pay the wages of its oozie, but it is learning all the time. Up to the age of nineteen or twenty it will have cost about twenty-five hundred dollars, when the wages of the oozie, training costs and maintenance are added up. But thereafter the elephant has on the average a working life from its twentieth to its fifty-fifth year.

Each working year consists of nine months' work and three months' rest, necessary both to keep the animal in condition and on account of the seasonal changes. Each month consists of only eighteen working days and twelve rest days, three days of work alternating with two days of rest. Thus, during the nine months of the working year there are only 162 working days. Each day averages about eight hours. Thus an elephant works 1300 hours a year. During this time an average animal delivers a hundred tons of timber from stump to a floating point in a creek.

By the time it is twenty-five years old, a well-trained elephant should understand twenty-four separate words of command, apart from the signals, or "foot aids," of the rider. He ought also to be able to pick up five different things from the ground when asked. That is, he should pick up and pass to his rider with his trunk a jungle dah (knife), a koon (axe), his fetter or hobble chain, his tying chain (for tethering him to a tree) and a stick. I have seen an intelligent elephant pick up not only a pipe that his rider had dropped but a large lighted cheroot. He will tighten a chain attached to a log by giving it a sharp tug with his trunk, or loosen it with a shake, giving it the very same motion with his trunk as that given by a human hand.

An elephant does not work mechanically; he never stops learning because he is always thinking. Not even a really good sheep dog can compare with an elephant in intelligence. If he cannot reach with his trunk some part of his body that itches, he doesn't always rub it against a tree; he may pick up a long stick and give himself a good scratch with that instead. If he pulls up some grass and it comes up by the roots with a lump of earth, he will smack it against his foot until all the earth is shaken off, or if water is handy he will wash it clean. And he will extract a pill the size of an aspirin tablet from a tamarind fruit the size of a cricket ball in which one has planted it, with an air of saying, "You can't fool me."

Many young elephants develop the naughty habit of plugging up the wooden bell they wear around their necks with good stodgy mud or clay so that the clappers cannot ring, in order to steal silently into banana groves at night. There they will have a whale of a time, quietly stuffing, eating not only the bunches of bananas but the leaves and indeed the whole tree as well, and they will do this just beside the hut occupied by the owner of the grove, without waking him or any of his family.

I have personally witnessed many remarkable instances of the quick intelligence of elephants. An uncertain-tempered tusker was being loaded with kit while in the standing position. On his back was his oozie, with another Burman in the pannier filling it with kit. Alongside on the flank, standing on the ground, was the paijaik attendant, armed with a spear which consisted of a five-foot cane, a brightly polished spearhead at one end and a spiked ferrule at the other. Another Burman was handing gear up to the Burman in the pannier, but got into difficulties with one package and called out to the paijaik to help him. The latter thrust the ferrule of the spear into the ground so that it stood planted upright with the spearhead in line with the elephant's eye. Then he lent a hand. The oozie, however, did not trust his beast, and said in a determined voice, "Pass me the spear." The tusker calmly put its trunk around the cane at the point of balance and carefully passed it up to his rider. But unthinkingly he passed it headfirst. The rider yelled at his beast in Burmese, "Don't be a bloody fool—pass it right way round!" With perfect calm and a rather dandified movement, the elephant revolved the spear in midair and, still holding it by the point of balance, passed it to his oozie, this time ferrule first.

One of the most intelligent acts I ever saw an elephant perform occurred one evening when the Upper Taungdwin River was in heavy spate. I was listening for the boom and roar of timber coming from upstream.

Directly below my camp the banks of the river were steep and rocky and twelve to fifteen feet high. I was suddenly alarmed by hearing an elephant roaring as though frightened and, looking down, I saw three or four men rushing up and down on the opposite bank in a state of great excitement. I ran down to the edge of the near bank and there saw Ma Shwe (Miss Gold) with her three-month-old calf, trapped in the fast-rising torrent. She herself was still in her depth, as the water was about six feet deep. But there was a life-and-death struggle going on. Her calf was screaming with terror and was afloat like a cork. Ma Shwe was as near to the far bank as she could get, holding her massive body against the raging torrent and keeping the calf pressed against her. The swirling water kept sweeping the calf away; then, with terrific strength, she would encircle it with her trunk and pull it upstream to rest against her body again.

There was a sudden rise in the water and the calf was washed clean over the mother's hindquarters. She turned to chase it, like an otter after a fish, but she had traveled about fifty yards downstream and crossed to my side of the river before she caught it and got it back. For what seemed minutes she pinned the calf with her head and trunk against the bank. Then, with a really gigantic effort, she picked it up in her trunk and reared up until she was half standing on her hind legs, so as to place it on a narrow shelf of rock five feet above the flood level.

Having accomplished this, she fell back into the raging torrent and she herself went away like a cork. She well knew that she would now have a fight to save her own life, as less than three hundred yards below where she had safely stowed her calf there was a gorge. If she were carried down, it would be certain death. I knew as well as she did that there was one spot between her and the gorge where she could get up the bank, but it was on the other side from where she had put her calf. By that time my chief interest was in the calf. It stood tucked up, shivering and terrified, on a ledge just wide enough to hold its feet. Its little, fat, protruding belly was tightly pressed against the bank.

While I was peering over at it, wondering what I could do, I heard the grandest sounds of a mother's love I can remember. Ma Shwe had crossed the river and got up the bank and was making her way back as fast as she could, calling the whole time—a defiant roar, but to her calf it was music. The two little ears, like little maps of India, were cocked forward listening to the only sound that mattered, the call of its mother. As darkness came on, a torrential rain was falling and the river still separated the mother and her calf. I decided that I could do nothing but wait and see what happened.

At dawn Ma Shwe and her calf were together—both on the far bank. The spate had subsided to a mere foot of dirty-colored water. No one in the camp had seen Ma Shwe recover her calf but she must have lifted it down from the ledge in the same way she had put it there. Five years later, when the calf was christened, it was named Ma Yay Yee (Miss Laughing Water).

During my years in Burma all elephant surgery was on old and primitive lines. It needs confidence to walk under an elephant's jaw and tusks, armed with a heavy knife in one's left hand and a six-pound wooden club in the right hand, and then to tell him to hold up his head while, with one blow of the mallet, you drive the knife up to the hilt into a huge abscess on his chest. One blow is all you get; if you try another you must look out for squalls. But if you do the job properly and make a quick and quiet get-away to his flank, he will let you go back ten minutes later to clean out the abscess and syringe it with disinfectant.

Wounds caused by tigers are exceptionally difficult to heal and often do not respond to modern antiseptics. The Burman has cures for all the ills that may befall an elephant. Some are herbal, some are mystic spells and incantations and some of them have had to be vetoed as being definitely harmful. But I have so far found no treatment for tiger wounds that comes up to the traditional Burmese method of plugging the wounds with sugar. The Burman also used maggots to clean up gangrened wounds for centuries before the method was rediscovered in modern surgery.

It has been quite truly said that once an elephant goes down because of exhaustion or severe colic, he has only a 25-percent chance of getting onto his legs again unaided. Any method of keeping him on his legs improves a sick elephant's chances of survival. The Burman will do this by putting chili juice in his eye—a counterirritant that must be agony. But it is effective and about doubles the animal's chances of recovery. No matter how far modern veterinary research goes, we shall always rely to a certain extent upon the Burman's knowledge.

I know without question that an elephant can be grateful for relief given to it from pain and sickness. For example, I remember Ma Kyaw ("Miss Smooth," an expression often used to describe any Burmese girl with a strikingly good figure). She had fearful lacerations on the barrel of her back from tiger claws, and I treated her for them every day for three weeks. In the early stages she suffered great pain, but although she made a lot of fuss she always gave way and let me go on. When she was sufficiently healed I sent her back to camp under a reliable Burman with instructions that she was to be given light dressings of fly repellent on the wounds. Two months later I was having a cup of tea in camp outside my tent while seven elephants were being washed in the creek nearby, preparatory to my inspecting them. The last animal to come out of the creek was Ma Kyaw. As she passed me about fifty yards away, with her rider on foot, I called, "How is Ma Kyaw's back?"

Her rider did not reply, as he had not caught what I said, but Ma Kyaw swung around and came toward me. She walked straight up to where I was sitting, dropped into the sitting position and leaned toward me so as to show me her back. Having patted her, I told her to *"Tah* [get up]," and away she went, leaving me with the agreeable conviction that she had come over to say thank you.

As regards sleep, elephants are rather like horses. They get most of it standing up and they will only go down when they think that, for a brief period at night, all the world is asleep. The time is never the same, but it is always at that eerie hour when even the insects stop their serenades. It never lasts longer than half an hour if the animal is fit, but while it lasts he sleeps very soundly. For an hour previously the elephant stands absolutely motionless without feeding. Then he seems satisfied that all is well, and down he goes in a slow, silent movement, as if overcome by some unseen jungle god. In bright moonlight it is a beautiful but uncanny sight.

Elephants are not usually frightened by natural phenomena without very good reason. They do not mind thunderstorms in the way that dogs do, and they remain calm in the face of forest fires. I have only once seen elephants really frightened by natural phenomena, and that was because of their realizing that they were in a gorge where water was rapidly rising in a spate.

Rain was coming down as though it would never cease. I had decided to take a short cut through the Kanti Gorge. I was traveling with eight young pack elephants, and it would save us a climb of two thousand feet from one watershed to another. After passing down the gorge, I meant to move up a side stream. My spirits were high, the oozies were singing and our circus was traveling in Indian file down the hard, sandy bottom of the stream. Both banks of the gorge were sheer rock, to a height of about thirty feet. The gorge was three miles long, and the stream was about ankle-deep when we started down it. By the time we had gone a mile one could hear the unmistakable sound of a heavy thunderstorm breaking in the headwaters of the stream. The elephants showed their nervousness by half turning around. The bore of water eventually overtook us, and it was soon lapping under the bellies of the smaller calves.

By some instinct not shared by man, the elephants knew there was more water coming down. They began what would soon have become a stampede if they had not been hindered by the depth of the water and kept under partial restraint by their riders. It became a terrifying experience, as there was no possibility of turning back and no hope of getting up the sides. During the last mile all the elephants began bellowing; that, with the sound of the torrential rain and the raging, muddy water around, made it seem a pretty grim situation.

I never knew a mile to seem longer. Bend after bend came in view, with never a sign of the mouth of the creek I knew, which would provide for our exodus from the black hole in which we floundered. Logs were floating past and, though I had no time to be amused then, I noticed how the elephants' hindquarters seemed to have a magnetic attraction for them. Just as a log was about to strike its hindquarters, the elephant would swing its rear end to one side, giving the log a glancing blow so that it caromed off like a billiard ball from the cushion and passed on to the chap in front—and so on all down the line.

We were fortunate, really, as the smaller animals were just afloat when we went around the bend to go up the side creek. The water was up to my armpits, and I was holding my rifle in both hands above my head. The side creek came down in spate only half an hour after we had started up. If we had met the combined spates at the confluence, all our kit would have been lost. The elephants scrambled up the first feasible bank after turning in off the main river, and at a general halt they seemed to look at me as if to say: "And you call yourself a jungle man!"

Savage elephants are as rare as really wicked men, but those that are not savage sometimes give way to moments of bad temper. Their most tiresome and dangerous habit at such moments is to pick up a large stick or stone with the trunk and throw it with great force and accuracy at some onlooker. One has to be prepared to jump when this happens.

Of course, during the musth period all males are of uncertain temper. My interpretation of musth is that it is an instinctive desire in the male elephant to fight and kill before mating. The mere act of mating does not cool his passion. He would rather drive off and kill an intruder—fighting for his chosen mate before he has won her.

The great majority of cases in which oozies are killed by their elephants take place when their charges are on musth. For some unknown reason, the animal may then suddenly attack his rider, first striking him with tusk or trunk, then crushing him to death with a knee when he is on the ground. Strange as it may sound, there is very little difficulty in finding a new rider for such an animal. Many oozies take pride in riding an elephant known to be dangerous. Such men find life easy; they care nothing for anything or anyone. They are usually opium eaters, but in spite of that they work well.

In addition to the rider, a dangerous animal has a really good type of spearman attached to it as an attendant, whose duty is to cover every movement of the rider when he is entirely at the mercy of the elephant— undoing his fetters, for example. Although the spearman carries a spear, the secret of his control is by the eye: He keeps his eye fixed on the elephant's. The two men can usually control a savage elephant.

I have known one case of what seemed like remorse in an elephant. He was a tusker who killed his rider. But he guarded the body and would let nobody get near it for a whole week. He grazed all around it, and charged in mad fury at anyone who came near. When the body had quite decomposed he wandered away from it; ten days later he was recaptured without any difficulty and behaved quite normally. He was not on musth.

The wickedest elephant I ever knew was called Taw Sin Ma (Miss Wild Elephant). She was about twenty-five years old when I first knew her, and there was nothing in her recorded history which gave any explanation of why she should loathe every European she saw. Even at inspection she had to be chained to a tree, and when one was a hundred yards away she would begin to strain at her chains in order to attack.

I had a nasty experience with her, when she first attacked me and then chased me, following me by scent for four miles. I met her by chance when walking from one camp to another. I came on her suddenly and she went for me at once, so I raced off, not knowing for two miles whether I was on the right track back to the camp I had left. There would have been no hope for me if her hobbles had snapped or come undone, unless I had found refuge up a tree. As she was hobbled, my pace was faster than hers. She wore a brass danger bell around her neck (docile elephants wear wooden bells). Often the bell sounded as though she were nearly up to me.

I dropped a haversack, hoping she would halt and attack it, but I heard no check in the sound of her clanking bell. When I had climbed to the top of a ridge I halted for a few moments to locate her. Then on I plunged, trying to act on the law of the jungle that one must never hurry and always keep cool. Once one breaks that rule every thorny bush that grows reaches out a tentacle to impede one, to tear and scratch. My relief was great when I met two men, busy with a crosscut saw on a fallen teak tree. But I had only to shout out the words "Taw Sin Ma!" and they joined me in my flight without asking questions. They soon took the lead and, as I followed, I at least had the satisfaction of knowing I was on the right track to camp and safety.

One of them got into camp well ahead of me and gave the alarm on my account. When I got in I met a chattering group of elephant riders and their families, all of them doubled up with laughter or smacking their hands on their hips in mirth at the sight of me—all, that is, except Maung Po Net (Mr. Black as Night), who prepared to go out and meet his "pet." There was no alternative but to join the Burmans in their joke—for I often wanted them to share in mine. So I joined in their laughter and their hip smacking.

Within an hour a rider came back with my haversack, quite undamaged and not even trodden on, and Po Net rode Taw Sin Ma back into camp. The expressions on

both their faces seemed to indicate that the same incident might be repeated next day. It was not, as I at once issued twenty-five feet of chain for Taw Sin Ma to trail behind her whenever she was at large grazing.

Some riders teach their charges tricks that give a wrong impression of the animal's real disposition. Bo Gyi (Big Man), a young elephant, always charged his rider as soon as he appeared to catch him and bring him to camp. But at ten paces the animal would stop dead and sit down for his fetters to be undone, as gentle as a lamb. Any other rider would bolt.

The secret—that it was just a matter of standing one's ground—was only discovered after the rider who had taught him the trick had been killed by a bear. The elephant was at large for a month after his rider's death; nobody would face him. Finally a reward of three hundred rupees was offered for his recapture. A young village lad turned up one day, saying he could capture him. Two days later he came into camp riding the animal and smiling gaily and was paid his reward. Two of my own men had gone with the lad and had watched the whole procedure from a hiding place nearby. The secret had come from a young Burmese girl, a former sweetheart of the dead rider. The young lad was her new lover and no doubt boy and girl found the three hundred rupees a useful start in life.

Young calves, if they have not been properly trained, are apt to get savage if not well handled afterward. One particular calf named Soe Bone (Wicked Bone) delighted in chasing me whenever he got an opportunity. We decided he was not too old to learn his manners. "Shoot him in his toenails with roasted rice," was the suggestion. So I emptied two cartridges and, after filling them with rice instead of shot, I wandered out of camp to find Soe Bone. He was standing in a sandy creek throwing wet sand over his body and was under a bank only three feet high.

"Hullo, little chap!" I said, greeting him.

"Little chap to you," he seemed to reply, and charged.

I stood my ground and gave him a left and right in the forefeet so as to sting his toenails. Did it stop him? I nearly lost my precious shotgun as I made my getaway. He was up that bank with his fetters on almost as quickly as I could turn to run. And he did not love me the next time he saw me either.

We decided to put the little devil back into a crush and cane him. A substantial crush was made, and into it he was enticed and trapped. My head Burman came to fetch me, carrying in his hand a six-foot whippy cane. At least a dozen Burmans were there to witness the caning of this naughty school-boy, as even Soe Bone's own rider had no use for his chasing game. I was asked to give him the first twenty strokes. And what a behind it was to whip! I went to his head first and showed him the cane. He showed me the whites of his eyes as if to say: "Wait till I get out of here," but I changed his mind for him, and he squealed blue murder. Then everyone present, except his rider, was ordered to give him half a dozen, whereas his rider was permitted to stay behind and give him tidbits after we had all gone.

I saw him next morning, being loaded with some light kit as we were moving camp, and he looked rather ashamed of himself. Suddenly he saw me, carrying a stick, and instead of pricking his ears as he did when he was going to chase me he gave one shrieking trumpet and bolted into the jungle.

One of the most remarkable incidents I ever had with savage elephants concerned a young Shan woman of about twenty. I was sitting in my hut near the camp one evening, very worried over a seriously injured spearman, Maung Chan Tha, who had been gored that afternoon by an elephant named Kyauk Sein (Jade Eyes). Maung Chan Tha had been trying to save the life of the rider, Maung Po Yin, who had been killed instantaneously by the elephant; the beast had then attacked the spearman. The animal had gone on musth and was roaming at large in the neighborhood.

I was discussing the case with my head Burman when suddenly, quite unannounced, a tall, fine-looking girl walked into my bamboo hut and I immediately recognized her as the widow of the dead rider. She was not wailing or weeping, or carrying her youngest child, which is the custom on such occasions. She just stood erect and in a firm, unemotional voice said, "May I have a dismissal certificate for my husband, Maung Po Yin, who was killed today by Kyauk Sein?"

"Yes," I replied. "And your compensation, if you will wait till tomorrow, as I am busy arranging to get Maung Chan Tha to hospital." I added how grieved I was and asked her if she had any children.

My head Burman answered, instead of her, that she had none, and then, addressing her as though he were most displeased with her for coming to see me in such an unceremonious way, said, "You can go now. I shall be coming back to camp soon."

She moved quietly out of the room, a tall and graceful figure.

When she was out of earshot I turned to my head Burman and asked, "Is that Po Yin's wife?"

"Yes," he replied. "She takes more opium than Po Yin did and that is the reason why she has no children."

I was very much surprised, as it was the first time I had ever heard of a Shan girl taking opium. Then my old Burman said in a quiet voice, "Give me ten ticals of opium

197

tonight, and she will recapture Kyauk Sein tomorrow. She has often caught him for Po Yin when he was in a heavy opium bout."

I gave him the opium he asked for, but I went to bed that night with a very disturbed conscience. To add to my troubles, Chan Tha died before dawn.

About ten o'clock, my old Burman came to me saying, "Kyauk Sein is coming in with Ma Kyaw riding him."

I could scarcely believe my eyes: Kyauk Sein was passing through the camp with the Shan girl riding him, oblivious to everything, her eyes fixed straight in front of her. Her long black hair was hanging loose down her back and she wore her blue tamain girdled above her breasts, leaving her beautiful pale shoulders bare. I did not interfere and was soon informed that Kyauk Sein was securely tethered to a tree.

That evening Ma Kyaw was brought to me to receive the compensation due to her. She was dressed in her best, wearing a multicolored tamain, a little white coat and a flower in her jet-black hair. She knelt and bowed low three times and then sat down in front of me. She kept her eyes lowered. After paying her the compensation due to her for the loss of her husband, I gave her an extra bonus for recapturing Kyauk Sein. When I told her this, I could see a wisp of a smile at the corners of her mouth. I then wrote for her a certificate such as is customarily made out for all men killed in accidents. These certificates are for the benefit of the jungle nats (gods), who require them before admitting the spirit of the dead rider to their domains. The certificate ran, "I hereby give leave to Maung Po Yin, rider of Kyauk Sein, to go where he wishes, as he has been dismissed from my service," and I signed it. When I had risen from my table and given the money and the certificate into her hands, she wiped

away two crocodile tears, got up and went quietly out into the dusk.

Next day, when I asked my old Burman about finding a new rider for Kyauk Sein, he told me: "Oh, that is all arranged. Maung Ngwe Gyaw is an opium taker, too. He has taken on [not married] Ma Kyaw, and they tell me that the biggest opium taker of the lot is Kyauk Sein, the elephant. Another ten ticals of opium would be useful." By that time I would willingly have given him twenty if he had asked.

I do not believe to this day that the girl took opium, but she was a resolute character and the elephant Kyauk Sein knew her well enough to take opium out of her hand. I think she completely stupefied the animal before she caught him.

The ways of the jungle are strange, but all is not savage, hard and cruel in it. For every savage elephant that attacks or kills his rider there are ninety-nine that are docile and friendly.

I find it hard to realize, after living for twenty-five years in the jungle with the most magnificent of all animals, that for the first three and a half years my eyes were blinded by the thrill of big-game shooting. I now feel that elephants are God's own and I would never shoot another. However, I can still live over again the thrill when I was young enough to take any opportunity that offered which gave me even chances of life or death.

I remember how for two whole months I spent day after day near the mouth of the Manipur River trying to get a solitary wild bull elephant—and every day was hard, and ended in disappointment. He was well known by the name of Shwe Kah, which my elephant riders had given him. Shwe Kah had gored two of my tuskers badly and had continually worried my elephants. Many of my riders had seen him and they described the dimensions of his tusks outside the lip by stretching both arms out horizontally to show their length and by encircling their legs above the knee with the outstretched thumbs and forefingers of both hands to indicate their girth.

I had numerous opportunities to bag other wild elephants at that time, but I was set on getting Shwe Kah. I saw him twice but not in a position for a shot. I then went on leave for a month, knowing I should be back in the same area during May, the best month in Burma for big game.

One night during my leave I met a very pleasant major who told me he was more than keen to bag an elephant before he left Burma. I said, "I'm going back on the twenty-fifth for a tour of jungle camps, during which I hope to get in some big-game shooting myself. Can you get a month's leave?" He jumped at it. I explained that I would do all I could to put him on to the track of a decent wild tusker, but that Shwe Kah was to be mine only. He joined me on the appointed date and we set off, poling up the Myittha River in a country dugout. Shortly after we reached Sinywa (Wild Elephant Village), a Burman arrived to say there was an enormous wild tusker, believed to be Shwe Kah, not three hundred yards from their camp, a mile away.

Without any hesitation I was off. My companion candidly admitted that he was far too tired to leave camp. By 3 p.m., under a sweltering tropical sun, I had got near enough to this wild elephant to hear an occasional flap of his ear. There was no other sound, as he was browsing in elephant grass twelve feet high, through which I had ventured, following up his tracks. I knew that the riverbank could not be far to my left. I stopped and took a quick swallow from a water flask, as that was probably the last refresher I should get.

I was suddenly alarmed by the realization that my presence had been detected by the elephant, probably, as so often happens, by scent. There was a never-to-be-forgotten noise of the animal cracking the end of his trunk on the ground—it makes a sharp, clear, metallic, ringing sound, owing to the trunk's being hollow. Then there followed an awful silence. I had no alternative but to stand my ground. Both of us were left guessing, but the elephant broke first and made away from where I was standing, whereupon I made direct to where I imagined the riverbank to be. Not many seconds passed before I heard a tremendous splashing, and through the tall grass I saw a magnificent tusker elephant crossing the river fifty yards below me, moving fast.

Without hesitation, I jumped down the eight-foot bank, landing in three feet of water but sinking into the mud to the tops of my boots. I was bogged. It was now or never. I decided on a heart shot, as he was moving quickly and I was unsteady. Crack! He was quite seventy-five yards away when I fired. He stumbled a bit, recovered and then swung around like a polo pony and came back, not twenty-five yards below me. He was wild with rage—so wild that he did not see me. I was stuck and had no hope of regaining the bank. As he climbed up where he had slid down before, I realized that he was mortally wounded and noticed that his tusks did not appear to be as large as those of Shwe Kah.

I gave him another heart shot and there was no mistake this time. He collapsed stone-dead against the top of the bank. Before I had extricated myself from the mud, my gun boy, who had remained behind in a tree on the bank, went off to inspect him and came rushing back to me yelling excitedly, *"Amai* [Oh, Mother]! *Amai!* You have shot a Kyan Zit."

I was far too excited and occupied to appreciate what he meant. It was about half past four in the afternoon and sweltering hot. I well remember my feelings when I realized that I had not bagged Shwe Kah, as I could not now get a license to shoot another wild elephant for a year. However, all my disappointment vanished as soon as I saw the head of the magnificent beast I had shot. For he was something very rare and was already causing great excitement among all the elephant riders who had come rushing along from their camp.

"Kyan Zit! Kyan Zit! Kyan Zit!" was all they could repeat.

I could not have been more astonished if I had shot a unicorn. The words "Kyan Zit" describe a rare type of elephant tusk that has grown in rings or corrugations like the sections of a piece of sugarcane. The Burmans speak of such an animal as an almost mythical rarity, a king of elephants to whom all other elephants do obeisance, in terror of his strength.

Long discussions followed among the riders standing around and admiring the rare tusks. A head man arrived from camp to supervise their removal. Then the women of the camp arrived with children and babies in arms, all to be shown Kyan Zit. Up to this time I had not allowed any of them to touch him as I knew that once they started on a dead elephant, they would combine the qualities of souvenir hunters and vultures after flesh.

I then heard someone yelling my name. It was my guest, who on hearing my two shots in camp had hopped off his bed and, without waiting to put on his shoes, had come along with two or three of the men from my camp. "Lord, how magnificent!" he said as he opened up his camera and took several snapshots. Then we settled down to supervise the removal of the tusks.

The human vultures now began operations. Whole baskets of meat were carried off to camp to be dried in the sun. There was enough to last them many months. It was my Burman hunter's perquisite to have the coveted aphrodisiac snips, which consist of the triangular tip of the trunk and the big nerves out of the tusks, which are also a native medicine for eye troubles. By the time we had removed the tusks and the forefoot it was almost dusk. More men and women from Sinywa Village had arrived to carry away meat.

That was my last elephant, and I never shot big game again. I have no regrets in regard to those early years. For it was those years that laid the foundations of a love and understanding of the jungle and the elephants in it. I shot four elephants, but on the other side of the account is all I have tried to do for hundreds of their fellows.

The Day Grandfather Tickled a Tiger

Condensed from The National Observer

by RUSKIN BOND

TIMOTHY, OUR TIGER CUB, was found by my grandfather on a hunting expedition in the Terai jungles near Dehra, in northern India. Because Grandfather lived in Dehra and knew the Siwalik hills so well, he was persuaded to accompany the hunting party, consisting of several very important persons from Delhi, to advise on the terrain and the direction the beaters should take once a tiger had been spotted. A tiger, of course, was the hunters' chief target.

The sportsmen never got their tiger, but Grandfather, strolling down a forest path some distance from the main party, discovered a little tiger about eighteen inches long hidden among the roots of a banyan tree. After the expedition ended, Grandfather took the beast home to Dehra, where Grandmother gave him the name Timothy.

Timothy's favorite place in the house was the drawing room. He would snuggle down comfortably on the sofa, reclining there with serene dignity and snarling only when anyone tried to dispossess him. One of his chief amusements was to stalk whoever was playing with him, and so, when I went to live with Grandfather, I became one of the tiger's pets. With a crafty look in his eyes, and his body in a deep crouch, he would creep closer and closer to me, suddenly making a dash for my feet. Then, rolling on his back and kicking with delight, he would pretend to bite my ankles.

By this time he was the size of a full-grown golden retriever, and when I took him for walks in Dehra, people on the road would give us a wide berth. Nights he slept in the quarters of our cook, Mahmoud. "One of these days," Grandmother declared, "we are going to find Timothy sitting on Mah-

moud's bed and no sign of Mahmoud."

When Timothy was about six months old, his stalking became more serious and he had to be chained up more frequently. Even the household started to mistrust him and, when he began to trail Mahmoud around the house with what looked like villainous intent, Grandfather decided it was time to transfer the animal to a zoo. The nearest zoo was at Lucknow, some two hundred miles away. Grandfather reserved a first-class compartment for himself and Timothy and set forth. The authorities at the Lucknow zoo were only too pleased to receive Timothy.

Grandfather had no opportunity to see how Timothy was faring in confinement until about six months later when he and Grandmother visited relatives in Lucknow. Grandfather went to the zoo and directly to Timothy's cage. The tiger was there, crouched in a corner, full-grown, his magnificent striped coat gleaming with health.

"Hello, Timothy," Grandfather said. Climbing over the railing, he put his arm through the bars of the cage. Timothy approached and allowed Grandfather to put both arms around his head. Grandfather stroked the big tiger's forehead and tickled his ears. Each time Timothy growled, Grandfather gave him a smack across the mouth, which had been his way of keeping the animal quiet when he was living with us.

Timothy licked Grandfather's hands. The tiger showed nervousness, springing away when a leopard in the next cage snarled at him, but Grandfather shooed the leopard off and Timothy returned to licking his hands. Every now and then the leopard would rush at the bars, and Timothy would again slink back to a neutral corner.

A number of people had gathered to watch the reunion when a keeper asked Grandfather what he was doing. "I'm talking to Timothy," said Grandfather patiently. "Weren't you here when I gave him to the zoo six months ago?"

"I haven't been here very long," said the surprised keeper. "Please continue your conversation. I have never been able to touch that tiger myself. He is very bad tempered."

Grandfather had been stroking and slapping Timothy for about five minutes when he noticed another keeper observing him with some alarm. Grandfather recognized him as the keeper who had been there when he had delivered Timothy to the zoo. "*You* remember me," said Grandfather. "Why don't you transfer Timothy to another cage, away from this stupid leopard?"

"But—sir," stammered the keeper, "it is not your tiger."

"I realize that he is no longer mine," said Grandfather testily. "But at least take my suggestion."

"I remember your tiger very well," said the keeper. "He died two months ago."

"Died!" exclaimed Grandfather.

"Yes, sir, of pneumonia. This tiger was trapped in the hills only last month, and he is very dangerous!"

The tiger was still licking Grandfather's arm and apparently enjoying it more all the time. Grandfather withdrew his hand from the cage in a motion that seemed to take an age. With his face near the tiger's he mumbled, "Good night, Timothy." Then, giving the keeper a scornful look, Grandfather walked briskly out of the zoo.

A Summer with Wendell

by FRED SPARKS

I'VE ALWAYS disliked seeing in captivity any creature born to run, fly or swim free. I won't visit a zoo; I won't even keep goldfish. So you will understand the shock I received when I arrived at the New York apartment a friend was letting me have for the summer. "Everything's okay," he said. "Say—I forgot to write I've got a parrot. Name's Wendell."

I stared, dumbstruck, at a caged young fifteen-inch green parrot with yellow blotches above his beak and on the back of his neck, and with red tail-fender feathers. "He's no trouble," my friend added, grabbing his valise. "Leave him in the cage. Cover it nights and toss in some seed. There's a ton in the pantry. Have a nice summer."

Except for a bleak "Hello," Wendell was ominously quiet. But he haunted me like Edgar Allan Poe's raven, as if I had kidnapped him from his Amazon rain forest. The next morning, feathers ruffled, he began a dirge: "OHHHHHH. OHHHHHH. . . ." He beat his wings, then buried his face in his shoulder feathers, a broken bird. I surrendered unconditionally. This apartment could not survive half-slave, half-free! Wendell would share it.

When I opened the cage, Wendell hopped to the carpet and walked around, grim and defiant. Gradually he unwound, whistled a few merry bars of "Get Me to the Church on Time" and prattled, "Good morning. What's up? *Some* kid!" With the pleasure of a spring stroller, he flew about in easy circles, then settled on a lamp. He chirped, sang, gabbled jolly tidings, stretched: He was *free, free, free.*

Our first difference occurred when I recaged him for the night. I advanced a hand and baby-talked, "Nice Wendell, nice bird." He bit my thumb. High on a venetian blind, he swayed on the cord like a sailor in the rigging. I donned protective gloves, climbed a chair and offered a peanut. He extended a claw and I pinned him. En route to his cell he bit again, clipping through the glove like a railroad conductor's ticket punch.

Next day my sister dropped in. As she pulled off her gloves, Wendell went berserk. He flew into the bar, shattering four highball, three wine and two cocktail glasses. He rocketed back into a vase, splattering water, carnations and feathers. I shouted to my sister, "He's afraid of your gloves!" Petrified, she dropped the gloves into her purse. Immediately the tantrum ended. A few days later Wendell had hysterics again when a plumber took out a pair of work gloves. I posted this sign on the door:

BEWARE THE PARROT
Please Hide Gloves
Before Entering

I discovered a peaceful way to cage Wendell. I'd extend a broom handle to him. He would mount and ride home, dignified as a dowager in her limousine. He loved broom travel and, twirling like a ballet dancer, I'd swing him around as his wings worked for balance.

In the living room Wendell sampled many perches—doorknobs, picture frames, cornices—but decided the telephone receiver was best. Unfortunately each ring startled him and he popped up like bread out of a toaster. As I answered, he would hover

overhead, scolding: "Grahhhh. Grahhhh. . . . Scratch. Scratch. Scratch," a devil's symphony of skidding railway wheels, buzzing dentists' drills, grinding garbage disposals.

Shortly after Wendell's owner left, he wrote to tell me to bathe Wendell twice weekly. In a pet shop I bought an aerosol shampoo with directions: (a) Dampen bird. (b) Spray bird. (c) Soak bird. After one messy struggle to bathe Wendell in the sink, I lured him aboard the broom, drew the curtain in the bathtub and man and parrot showered together. Wendell loved the shower, thinking it was a monsoon. After that, whenever he was pesky I'd park him in the tub, plug out. He'd stay put, whistling gleefully in the lukewarm drizzle.

Regardless of the hour, whenever I returned to the apartment Wendell would greet me with "Good morning!" Then he would wing to my shoulder and work his beak gently into my ear in the manner of true love. Hanging on a lapel, he'd pry into the handkerchief pocket where I kept gifts—a carrot, celery stalk or pecan. He poked into everything—cupboards, drawers, even shoes.

One Saturday morning I took some soiled linen in a pillowcase four blocks to a laundromat. As I entered, my wash came to life. "Where's the body? Don't hit me! Hello, hello, *hello!*" said the pillowcase. I hurried back toward the apartment as the bird's howls boomed down the street. Children began skipping behind me. A grocery boy pedaled alongside. "Grahhh. Grrrrahhhhh!" protested Wendell. "He's got a baby in there!" cried a woman. Wendell's beak clipped through the fabric. "It's a wild animal!" shouted the cyclist.

As I trotted down the street, mob astern, a policeman joined us. "What's this?" he demanded. "Follow me," I pleaded. Out-side my apartment I handed him the squirming pillowcase while I unlocked the door. Wendell got a firm grip on the policeman's pistol holster. "Let go," said the Law, "whatever you are!" I stammered an explanation. The officer enlightened the crowd. After that, whenever the children saw me they chanted, "Parrot man! Parrot man!"

My feathered rubbernecker never suffered serious hurt, but he did have a few close calls. Once he dunked his bill in liquid cement. I sent him, almost lockjawed, to the showers. As he was inspecting my work at the typewriter one morning, a flying key caught him in the face. Another time, playing Tarzan on the venetian blind cord, he tied a hangman's noose around his neck and was choked limp before being rescued.

Anything recalling his native Brazilian wild activated Wendell. The day my brother brought orchids from his hothouse Wendell, enthralled, watched the vased flowers for hours, prodding them like a bee. He chewed up one of the maid's hatpins that was shaped like a butterfly. Since his ancestors eternally battled snakes, he snatched four of my favorite neckties from their rack and bit them to death, apparently mistaking them for serpents. Another time he jerked out my typewriter ribbon and draped it all around the furniture.

Now back home, I miss Wendell, one of whose feathers brightens my fedora. But there is good news from New York. His owner has agreed to let the parrot accompany a botanist friend on a forthcoming expedition to the Amazon. There Wendell will remain, home again. Meanwhile, he still flies free in my friend's apartment, with all breakage charged to me. I have just mailed a forty-dollar check to replace a mangled gold tie clip. It was shaped like a snake.

Savage Dog

by J. L. WOLFF

THE TEAM jogged along the hard clay surface of a northern Kansas road as we approached a lone farmhouse. At the driveway my horses turned in. They were thirsty. I unfastened their checkreins, but suddenly they seemed to forget their thirst. They were highly nervous. Afraid.

I too sensed danger close at hand and looked quickly toward the barn. Every door was closed—not a sign of life. In each window of the house a faded curtain hung all the way down. It was eerie. I wanted to run.

Then I saw it. A tremendous dog, of mastiff breed, stood just inside the house gate, straining powerfully against a heavy chain, trying to reach the intruder. Bloodshot eyes fixed upon mine, wanting to kill.

For several minutes I looked at this ferocious specimen, whose shoulders stood better than three feet high. The chain seemed secure. Slowly, I walked toward him, talking all the while in a low tone. He neither barked nor growled. He merely stood straining every muscle of his mighty body to snap the leash.

Approaching the gate and this apparition of frozen hate, a chill tingled down my spine. Still talking, I opened the latch and very slowly walked toward this formidable guardian. Not by the faintest quiver did he show any movement except with his burning red eyes that followed mine. I talked about the weather, the size of his doghouse, the weight of his chain, the terrific strain against his collar. And I was exceedingly careful to size up the strength of his collar before gradually, inch by inch, settling down to my haunches with my head but two feet from his.

Ten minutes must have passed. Never for an instant did I stop talking. I began to wonder if this huge beast was utterly devoid of friendliness. Minute followed minute. Almost imperceptibly, the chain started to slacken. On and on I talked. "It's a shame to be left alone on this Kansas prairie, where the nearest house is miles away; it must be lonesome to be a savage dog of whom everyone is afraid—to have them walk in wide circles around you, to have no one say one kind word to such a magnificent animal as you are. Your heart, if it's in proportion to your body, must be gigantic. How long has it been since any man or child has played with you, has stroked your fur or tickled you behind your ears?"

As I continued to sympathize with him, he gradually relaxed, loosening his chain. Our eyes never parted. Neither of us moved until carefully I lifted my hand and reached gradually toward his nose. A foot, eight inches, five, two—barely one inch! Not by the slightest twitch of his nostrils did he show any interest.

"Why don't you smell my hand; don't you want to be friends?"

My arm began to ache and I feared my overtures were doomed to failure. And then his head moved slightly toward my fingers as he gently strained against his chain, trying to reach them. Softly I stroked the side of his nostrils. Now he was looking at me with only a questioning gaze, all viciousness gone. Farther and farther back along the side of his face my fingers scratched, until his jaws could easily have crushed my wrist.

My legs were falling asleep. So, patting his head, I arose cautiously. The great animal swung his rear quarters over toward me and I scratched his shoulders. For a long time we stood, while I kept up my low-voiced conversation. My fingers never rested. I was ready, of course, instantly to jump well out of reach.

Ever so imperceptibly I edged closer until his shoulder rested against my side. All thought of danger disappeared and I was filled with compassion for this majestic creature. He never looked up, his tail never wagged. He was content to lean against me, to be stroked, to hear my sympathetic voice. But this could not go on. There were miles ahead of us and the afternoon was getting late. Yet I hated to leave him, after friendship so laboriously gained. And his final surrender to the delight of my fingertips was complete.

As I moved away he looked up in wonder. And when I reached for the latch, he whined —just a little—and looked at me pleadingly. I couldn't run out on him this way. Quickly I returned and without hesitation dropped to my knees and put my arm around his neck. He rubbed his nose against my cheek. I no longer talked—merely stroked and patted his neck and shoulders.

It almost broke my heart when once more I started for the gate, this time going through resolutely, not even turning to look back. I got in the buggy and swung the horses around. As I drove past he was whining—whining. I couldn't leave him so. Again I jumped down and ran back.

His immense tail slowly moved from side to side as eagerly he put his head against me and looked into my eyes. It was unbearable to think of his lonesomeness, the utter loneliness that belongs to a savage dog, scolded and cursed, whose longing for a friendly gesture no one can guess.

In his deep brown eyes, looking understandingly into my own, I saw a newborn loyalty. Steadfast. Eternal. Tears streamed down my cheeks as I left him, straining to follow me, his whines cut short by the collar that was choking him. As my horses clogged down the road he howled. . . .

Many, many years have passed. I can't even remember the town. But every detail of the friendship forged that afternoon is seared deep in my memory.

The Divided Life
of a
Canada Goose

by CHARLES T. DRUMMOND

JANE WAS a Canada goose. Her full name, Calamity Jane, arose from her strange and inauspicious birth: She came into this world on the back seat of an automobile, born prematurely as the result of a collision between that vehicle and a roadside pine.

I had fallen asleep at the wheel while returning from an expedition on which, under government permits, we had gathered flooded-out goose eggs. A maelstrom of flying glass, snow and dirt was followed by sudden silence; then came a tiny, insistent "peep, peep" from the rear seat. I looked to see a broken egg and a newly hatched gosling, still wet. To shelter it from the freezing temperature, I thrust the downy mite under my shirt, next to my skin. The peepings gradually quieted, and the uncomfortably clammy object turned warm and dry and almost unnoticeable. The car would still run, and we limped home. The baby goose was put in a cardboard box and introduced to a diet of mash and chopped greens.

Jane flourished, and soon graduated to an outdoor playpen of wire mesh. When she wanted attention, she would peep raucously. But once satisfied—usually with either warmth or food—her protestations turned to the young Canada goose's fluty "chirr," certainly one of nature's most charming sounds. With fierce loyalty she attached herself to my wife and me. Released from her pen, she would follow us wherever we went, a ball of olive-and-yellow fuzz toddling along on jet-black legs and feet.

When she was half-grown we began taking her with us about the ranch in the pickup truck, letting her graze on grass while we inspected cattle or fences or tended to irrigation. Periodically my wife took Jane for a dip in the stream which ran past the fenced enclosure protecting twenty or thirty crippled geese of different species (our place has always been run as a private wildlife refuge). But the fledgling who lived with humans paid them no attention, considering herself a thing apart.

The day came when Jane was too large to

fit into the truck cab with us. We placed plenty of feed in front of her and started off without her. Suddenly my wife exclaimed, "She's coming!" I glanced in the mirror to see Jane running wildly after us, her not-yet-fully-grown wings spread. In her frenzy she actually began to fly a little, and this was such a surprising experience that it threw her off and we were able to draw out of sight, behind some trees. In a moment we glimpsed Jane coming cross-lots, half running, half flying, and gabbling in near hysteria. We took her in, moved almost to tears by the neck weavings with which she greeted us.

The next time we tried to sneak away, Jane took to the air. Flying unsteadily, she pulled ahead of us and landed in the road. We were forced to stop and take her aboard. Within a few days Jane was flying alongside the truck wherever we went, honking and gabbling companionably. A speed of about fifteen miles an hour seemed to suit her best.

We let her fly freely through the summer, but as the shooting season drew near we decided Jane would be safer in the enclosure with the other birds. So we clipped her right wing and during an evening feeding period walked her down to the duck-and-goose pond. Seeing the others, she clung close to us like a child being taken to school for the first time. When I picked her up and threw her over the wire-mesh fence, she paced back and forth, trying to return to her human friends. Ultimately she settled down contentedly with the other Canada geese and spent the winter with them. But she was always the first to greet us at feeding time, and she never gave up honking disconsolately as we climbed the hill toward her former home.

The next spring an especially large wild Canada gander began to light daily in the marsh, clearly interested in something within

the fenced area. A lordly chap, he was at first content to stalk the marsh and honk in stentorian tones. Then one day we spotted him inside the three-acre enclosure, sitting with another goose. His companion was Jane! Although she was really too young, by Canada goose standards, for the honor and responsibility, her human parents raised a toast that evening to her somewhat premature marriage.

We spied on the connubial pair shamefully, first with a pair of binoculars, later moving in for a closeup. Jane, on the nest, would lower her head and neck at our approach, but not to the same extent as a wild bird. The gander would withdraw to a far corner, fixing us with outstretched neck and beady eye. Then one afternoon we came upon both birds sitting together at a distance from the nest. We had a premonition of disaster. Sure enough, at the nest site we discovered scattered and mangled eggshells, torn feathers and general dishevelment. No bird could have done it; the gander was more than a match for any of the feathered tribe. Some predator must have leaped the fence to break up the nest. "Poor Jane!" we exclaimed, but she eyed us calmly, sitting on one leg in philosophical content.

Jane and "the wild one" remained together—the Canada goose usually mates for life—and when Jane's clipped wing feathers were shed and replaced, the gander lured her to far corners of the ranch. We saw them frequently, and invariably Jane would gabble and honk in recognition and waddle toward us. But the gander would sound warnings and make off in the opposite direction. Rather than cause domestic difficulties, we went our human way.

With the coming of spring we noticed that Jane was acting strangely. After eating grain at the back door, with the gander looking on disapprovingly from a distance,

she would circle the house on foot, gazing at it speculatively. Then one morning at daylight my wife and I were awakened by the sound of measured footsteps on the roof.

"What in the world?" my wife gasped. She jumped from bed and ran outside. "It's Jane!" she called. That evening, seated in the living room, we were astonished to see Jane's head and neck appear suddenly over the edge of the roof. Her dark eyes were directed not at us but at the space under the eaves. Of course! Her previous nest, fashioned in the duck-and-goose enclosure, had proved too vulnerable. Now she was looking for the securest possible spot, and what could be more secure than the top of the house in which her people lived? The idea apparently was not entirely agreeable to "the wild one"; during this house-hunting period he stood at a distance and honked reprovingly, but his wife merely talked back with great cheer and confidence.

"If she wants to nest on the roof, why don't we fix her a place?" my wife said. I found a wooden box, stuffed it with marsh grasses and fastened it at a spot where two roof lines converged—a site which would offer maximum protection from wind and sun. Next morning we were awakened by honks and gabbles and by the sound of Jane landing on the roof. She walked here and there, gabbling to herself. Suddenly sound and motion ceased. "She's found the box!" we exclaimed to each other. After some seconds of silence Jane flew down to join her mate and gabbled earnestly with him. This time he rubbed necks with her, and the pair flew to the stream for a dip.

Early each day now both geese landed on the hillside near the house, and the gander assumed a watchful stance while Jane flew to the roof, entered her box and stayed an hour or so. After each visit I climbed a ladder and found that an egg had been laid.

When there were four, Jane came for her "confinement." For four weeks all we could see of her was the head and part of the neck projecting above the nest box. The gander spent this period half a mile upstream.

There was one daily interruption of this routine. About midmorning Jane would start honking, and immediately, from half a mile away, would come the gander's answer. We learned from observation that at the same instant he would start flying. Jane would leave the nest and fly to the marsh, where the two birds arrived almost simultaneously. Their meeting was transparently joyful: They honked and gabbled, rubbed necks and "billed" each other in true lover fashion. Jane then dipped and flapped in the water. A few minutes of sitting together while she preened her feathers and prinked concluded the morning's reunion.

We, meantime, were marking each day on the calendar. The eggs should hatch twenty-eight to thirty days from the beginning of incubation. Jane had to get her babies from the roof to the ground, a distance of some twelve feet, and we didn't want to miss the event. It is not unusual for Canada geese to nest in trees, but few human beings have witnessed the descent of the fledglings. At dawn on the morning of the twenty-ninth day we heard Jane honk softly. This was a break in the usual pattern. Surely it signified something. I ran out to look, and there, standing on Jane's back, was a mite of a gosling! While I stood watch, my wife prepared breakfast, and we ate by separate windows. Another baby appeared, and then another. Presently four goslings were scrambling about in the nest.

Suddenly Jane stood up and honked, full voice. The gander answered from the meadow, and soon he landed only fifty feet from the house. Spying Jane and his offspring at the roof's edge, he broke into redoubled honkings. Jane answered back. The result was bedlam. Now Jane flew to the ground, and both of them walked close to the house, looking up at the babies. These balls of fluff were running about in some distraction, but it was evident that one of them was a creature of decision. He simply walked to the roof's edge and jumped off. He hit the ground with no indication of shock. We realized that his weight was so slight and his down so thick that he probably hardly felt the impact. He scuttled under his mother's body, and that was that.

Three remained. One of them approached the edge, looked down, drew back. He did this again and again until he was inadvertently bumped by one of the others and he had to go, quite unprepared. He hit the ground headfirst, but quickly righted himself and hurried to mamma. The third gosling stepped off purely by mistake. The fourth and last was a showman. Stepping well back and pausing dramatically, he made a run for the precipice and launched himself into space in a veritable swan dive—head well up, tiny wings working madly. He landed well and walked sedately to join the family group. It was done. Jane turned downhill and led for the water. The gander trailed behind her by several feet. Between them trotted the four fuzzy moppets, single file. It was a touching tableau.

We saw Jane, the wild one and their four youngsters on the lakes fairly frequently through the summer. Toward fall, we spied them flying together several times. Then the wild geese came in from the north, and for several months there were too many birds around to distinguish our friends. After the shooting season, Jane did not reappear. That winter the wild one came around alone. For a week or so he sat with head under wing or stood on some vantage point and honked. Then one day we discovered his dead body, unmarked by violence, not far from the site of Jane's original marshland nest.

His death is hard to explain. It is possible that it was an affair of the heart. But Jane, we feel sure, came to grief through her divided personality. She regarded humans as her friends and protectors, and may well have flown within murderous range of a hunter's gun. Since Jane, I have never shot at a Canada goose.

The Jackasses and I

by ARCH OBOLER

In MY LATE TWENTIES, happily married and out of the arroyos of the city for the first time, I looked at and then bought four hundred acres of California mountain and meadow. One day, impressed by my acreage, I decided that now I would become a horse owner. As if fated, that very evening I noticed a classified ad in the two-sheet local weekly: "Two brrs. Chp. Eves. Rcky. Rnch."

That eve I telephoned the Rcky. Rnch. "About those burros you advertised. Are they healthy animals?"

"Yep!"

"Burros run around in the open and don't need any exercise boy or stables, do they? And they forage off the country?"

"Yep!"

"Twenty-five dollars for the pair?"

"Nope!"

"Thirty dollars?"

"Nope!"

At forty-five I got into the "Yep" dialogue again, and the following day a trailer tail gate clanged on the road and the burros came into my startled view. Instead of the small burros I had expected, within the trailer sat (both animals were definitely sitting) one small-horse-sized gray individual with huge rabbit ears and one long-eared brown creature the size of a big dog and covered with the unmistakable fuzz of animal infancy. Mr. Rcky. Rnch. informed me, as he pocketed my check, that the gray animal was named Peter, he was between eight and ten years old, and the Great Dane with the skyscraper ears was Peter's two-month-old son, Tony. The seller also reassured me I needn't worry, them animals would stay put.

This was a true statement: We had no trouble with the critters' staying at home. Papa Peter, trailed by his fuzzy papoose, conducted a tour of inspection of the house worthy of an appraiser for a second-mortgage loan. After a few hours Tony got bored with his father's route and chased Jeanie, our sedate cocker spaniel, until she hid in a closet. Then he found his own reflection in the swimming pool and spent a fascinating three hours looking at himself, until he fell in. Having been evicted from the kitchen for the tenth time, Papa Peter stationed himself at the living-room window. There he critically contemplated our evening activities until we turned off the lights. After that, it developed the following morning, he had moved in among my fledgling orange trees,

216

decapitating and digesting about a hundred and fifty dollars' worth.

He announced this fact proudly at sunrise with his opening concert—the first of many years of such sun salutes. Boy and man, I have heard most of the loud sounds of our time, but I say unequivocally that the bray of a full-grown jackass outside one's bedroom window is a sound that ranks high among the psychological weapons of all time. Son Tony joined in that first paean to the Oboler arising—on a more youthful note than Father, of course, but with a fullness of tonality that foreshadowed future greatness. This pair of vocalizing equines followed us around like dogs, they gamboled like lambs and, above all, they ate like goats. Everything on the place was Three Star Duncan Hines on their menu. I consulted Mr. Rcky. Rnch. by phone. He told me that any blamed fool knew that an old car axle was the only kind of tie-out stake to use on jackasses. I drove to the closest junkyard and returned with a pair of old axles and chains which cost enough to have been silver-plated.

First I staked out Junior, and then Papa. Papa put his weight against the chain. A link unfolded like an earthworm stretching out in a rain puddle, and with one triumphant kick of his heels Papa was off to the fruit trees, while his son squealed in frustration. It took me a week to find the right combination of massive logging chain, forged-steel truck axle and case-hardened lock before Papa was safely moored. Meanwhile our landscaping had attained a naturalistic look—back to the original sagebrush, ribbonwood and manzanita, all our expensive plantings having gone by way of Peter's insatiable gullet.

"You're not going to keep those animals chained up all the time!" said Mrs. O.

I told her it was my firm intention to restrain the jackass family until Papa learned the difference between hay and orange trees.

My wife said, "What are you going to do, give him botany lessons?"

The following morning I summoned a local contractor and crew to build a corral, a king-sized enclosure worthy of my wife's insistence on Freedom for Jackasses. Between munches of rolled oats and Danish pastry left over from our breakfast, Peter and Tony watched every detail of the process as the hand-hewn redwood poles were nestled into pools of concrete and coils of barbed wire whipped around the landscape. By noon the new enclosure was done and I managed to herd the animals into their open-air Alcatraz. As I began to show them the details of their expensive suite, Peter, with a wild flail of heels, began racing around the block-long corral, son Tony squealing in close pursuit.

I said, "They're looking for an escape route," and then laughed, because hadn't the expert said it was jackass-proof?

That night two mournful heads gazed into our bedroom window. The morning light revealed that somehow they had managed to paw a couple of strands of wire loose and climb through.

Next I consulted our mail-order catalogue. There I discovered an apparatus which, by charging the fence wire with a jolting flow of electricity, would keep even the most amorous bull in docile containment. Operation Shocking, including the high-voltage injectors and the waterproof extension to the closest AC line, cost me well over the original price of the beasts, but no matter—we had to have it because Tony was munching on the laundry and Papa Peter was pruning the flowering eucalyptus.

The fence completed, I proceeded to plug in the current. Mrs. O. said, "You should test it."

I said, "How?"

She said, "You're not afraid of a little shock, are you?"

Tony guffawed and headed for the shreds of the lemon trees.

I said, "The instructions say it's not harmful to man or beast, but you'll find my will in the cookie jar." I lightly touched the wire and picked myself up off the ground six feet away.

The electric fence was a triumph for forty-eight hours. But on the next morning there were brays outside our bedroom window, and father and son did a merry pirouette as I gaped in unbelief. Suddenly I knew—the fuse must have blown and the current was off. I tore out to the corral, grabbed the wire—and landed flat on my back again.

For three nights those donkeys got out of the electrified corral. The gate and wires were intact, and the jolt was strong enough to smelt one's gold fillings, yet those animals got out. The mystery was solved one frosty 4 a.m. when I came out just in time to see Peter get down on his forelegs and squirm under the charged wire. Junior then went through the same maneuver, his small rump wriggling out of reach of possible shock.

Fifteen years and many coils of rusted barbed wire have gone by, and my jackasses and I have long since established a truce in the matter of containment. Our agreement is this: As long as they get sufficient alfalfa and oat hay by eight in the morning with enough left over to snack on through the day, and as long as someone goes to the corral before nightfall to talk to them man to burro and scratch their ears, Peter and Son stay put. But should we forget that ear-stroking routine, or should the pitchfork fail to deliver a

sufficiently elevated pile of plant life, away they go unerringly to the laundry line.

As the children arrived and began to grow, the jackasses took on new stature—as combination jungle gyms, roller coasters and king-sized kiddy cars. The sight of one small boy sliding off Peter's broad derriere, to land within inches of those massive hooves, while another youngster was busily examining Tony's jagged teeth, was definitely not covered by the book on children's care, but I remained calm. I had found out that, intertwined with that fence-breaking perseverance, patience and common sense were also heraldic devices on the jackass escutcheon.

My jackasses have only one pet hate—the Jeep. Every fender of this inoffensive ranch vehicle has felt the impact of their dislike;

they decapitated the original canvas top and ever since have been working on the aluminum enclosure that I substituted. I have puzzled over this feud and have come to the conclusion that in the Jeep Peter and Son see the terror of the Mechanical Age, which sets a pattern of work all day, leaving no time to heehaw or raise one's head to watch a hawk gliding above, a peculiar cloud formation, the fall of rain, a branch swaying in the wind—all the things around them that are head-lifting wonders to my jackasses in this remarkable world of theirs.

They prefer to live each day for the day; when trouble comes along they simply become immovable objects. Sometimes, listening closely, I fancy I hear them mutter to themselves the credo of all jackasses since jackasses began: "This, too, shall pass."

Million-Dollar Show-Off

by ROSCOE MACY

I T MAY surprise those who follow the ponies today to learn that some sixty years ago a crooked-legged mahogany-bay harness horse—a pacer named Dan Patch—had the largest and most faithful popular following of any animal in racing history. At the height of his career there was a Dan Patch cigar, and toy stores everywhere featured Dan Patch sleds, coaster wagons and hobby-horses. One manufacturer advertised the Dan Patch washing machine, a two-minute performer, like Dan.

Even after The Patch was retired to stud, throngs made pilgrimages to his stable outside Minneapolis on the Dan Patch Railroad. "Men, women and children," said the magazine *Harness Horse,* "seemed content just to see him—as if he were George Washington or Abraham Lincoln."

The saga of Dan Patch had its beginning in an ill-judged wink. Big Dan Messner, village storekeeper at Oxford, Indiana, flickered his eyelid in greeting to his friend the auctioneer at a dispersion sale and was astounded to hear him shout, "Sold to Dan Messner for two hundred and fifty-five dollars!" A "dead-game sport," as they said in 1894, Messner paid up, then ruefully inspected his purchase—a lame, decrepit old plug named Zelica. She had a good pedigree but she had lost the only race in which she had ever been entered. A few miles away in Illinois the famed Joe Patchen, brief holder of the world's harness record, was at stud. Dan decided to invest a hundred and fifty dollars in breeding his mare to the former champion. Joe Patchen was a coal-black horse with a heart to match—a vicious brute and would-be killer.

Zelica foaled in March 1896. Dan studied the gaunt, scraggly colt and sighed. The things that were wrong, he saw, were not the sort an animal outgrows. The knees were too knobby, legs too long, hocks curving. He had neither the looks nor the temperament of a racer. Unlike his sire, he was a friendly little cuss. Dan thought he might make a pretty fair delivery horse some day.

Messner christened his colt Dan Patch, after himself and Joe Patchen, then left the colt's handling to Johnny Wattles at the livery barn. Johnny soon came to set great store by his charge, often neglecting his business to see that young Dan had his daily workout. The first time the gawky colt was harnessed to a racing sulky, Johnny

221

clucked, Dan Patch started, there was a crash and the sulky collapsed. The horse had kicked the spokes out of the left wheel. Messner thought it was the sire's temper showing up—especially when it happened a second time. But Johnny finally caught on; a crooked hock made Dan throw his left foot far out when he took a full stride. So the rest of his life he had special sulkies, with axles eight inches longer than standard.

The Patch was a four-year-old before his owner put him in a race. Worn down by Johnny's persistent urging, Messner finally matched the horse with two local nags in the summer of 1900. Only a few neighbors were present to see the bay stallion win in straight heats under wraps. Dan Messner shook his stopwatch and looked again. "Hm-m! Reckon mebbe we got something here after all, eh, Johnny?"

Johnny reckoned so.

The following spring, the Messner stallion was entered in his first big-time match. At Lafayette, Indiana, there was real competition—seasoned pacers with wide experience around the Grand Circuit. Top-heavy favorite was the rugged Milo S. No one even looked at Dan Patch. The track would not accommodate a single-tiered start with so many entrants, and Dan drew a position in the rear rank. The big bay, hemmed in by so many other horses, was lost in the ruck at first. Then, near the halfway mark, Dan Patch moved to the outside of the thinned-out line and sped past horse after horse. But the spurt was too late. Milo S. nosed out a victory.

And that, as it turned out, was a historic loss. Dan Patch won the next heat in the remarkable "maiden" time of 2:16, then went on to win the third and fourth heats, and thus the race. Never again did the pacer lose a heat, except one in which the circumstances were so suspicious that the judges

grilled Dan Patch's driver severely. After half a dozen of those effortless wins, Messner began to suspect that he was beyond his depth. The poisoning of a well-known colt helped to convince him that ownership of a miracle horse was precarious business for a country storekeeper. He was offered twenty thousand dollars, and Dan Patch became the property of C. F. Sturgis. Johnny Wattles wept openly.

In 1901 and 1902, The Patch had an unbroken winning streak of eighteen races around the circuit. At Providence, Rhode Island, on August 29, 1902, he became the second harness horse to go a mile in less than two minutes. His mark was 1:59$\frac{1}{2}$; the world mark set by Star Pointer in 1897 was 1:59$\frac{1}{4}$. With the aging Star Pointer in retirement, no horse anywhere could give Dan Patch a run for the money. Track managers shifted uneasily in their chairs when Sturgis came in to file his entry. The fans loved The Patch, but they clamored for real races. Nobody even thought any more of betting against him. Amazingly, though, Dan Patch's days of greatest fame were still ahead.

Throughout the latter part of the 1902 season a quiet, soft-spoken man in frock coat and black derby had trailed the horse around the circuit, holding a stopwatch but deaf to gamblers' tips. He neither smoked nor drank, and he never visited the track on Sunday. The stable boys took to calling him the Parson. Then one day in December, the Parson was identified in an electrifying news item: Marion Willis Savage, the Minneapolis stock-feed manufacturer, had bought Dan Patch for the stupendous sum of sixty thousand dollars! That is still the record price for a pacer. "Another good churchman has lost his head over fast horses," his fellow Methodists grieved.

Sturgis had a hunch that he had given the purchaser a mild shellacking. But three years later he pleaded with Savage, "Look, M. W., you gave me three times what I paid for the horse. Say the word, and I'll write you a check today for three times what you paid me." The offer was turned down.

Farm-bred Marion Savage, founder and owner of the International Stock Food Company, a million-dollar concern, had an uncanny flair for profitable publicity. He bought Dan Patch to promote his product; it was a brand-new advertising technique. On opening day of the 1903 Grand Circuit, Dan Patch was entered in a trial against time at Brighton Beach, New York. Such events were notoriously dull, but a surprise was in store for the spectators.

The pacesetter, a running horse hitched to a "speed cart," galloped along in the lead, with The Patch immediately behind. A second running horse ran neck and neck with him on the outside—and the big bay matched both, pace for gallop. The crowd sat up. As the three horses swept around the final turn into the straightaway, the second runner began to drop back. Dan Patch edged up, foot by foot, to overtake and pass the pacesetter. Suddenly a fresh runner charged onto the track. The steady clop-clop-clop of the pacer never faltered. The crowd was in a frenzy as The Patch crept into the lead and crossed the finish line ahead of the pack.

The Eastern campaign was a triumph. With his eye on a wider audience, Savage then entered the horse at state fairs in the Midwest and Southwest, cheerfully accepting opening day—traditionally poorly attended —as Dan Patch Day. He would take a percentage or all of the gate receipts above the highest for the corresponding day of any previous year. Fair managers considered the arrangement a bonanza either way.

To each area Savage dispatched advance men to plaster the countryside with bills describing "Dan Patch, the Wonder Horse."

Advertisements in farm journals invited readers to send postage for the pamphlet *The Racing Life of Dan Patch* (stock-feed literature included free). Before the campaign ended, every villager and every farm family had determined to see the Miracle Horse. Come Dan Patch Day at the fair, trains were jammed and dust clouds swirled over the roads leading to the fair grounds. After one such day the managers discovered that they owed Marion Savage twenty-one thousand dollars as his share of the gate!

Evenings the local folk congregated in barbershops, drugstores and pool halls to sing the praises of the pacer that not only had shown his heels to the best horses the Eastern slickers could round up against him, but was "gentle as a woman and wiser than most men."

And wise The Patch was. There were no starting judges in exhibition races, the take-off being left to the judgment of the driver— in theory. But driver Harry Hersey, who held the reins in some of Dan Patch's fastest races, said that *he* never controlled the start. "When Dan was ready, he just gave a certain jerk on the reins, and that was my cue." His trick of bowing right and left—"If you've been there before, he'll recognize you and bow," the advance agents promised— made spectators come back and back. He had his pride, too. On a muddy track at Oklahoma City he "broke" (into a gallop) for the first time in his track career. He was so humiliated, the story goes, that he refused to finish the race in front of the grandstand, swerving through a gate before he reached the homestretch.

In 1904 The Patch traveled ten thousand miles in his private railroad car, played to six hundred thousand people. On his return home that winter he was met at the Minneapolis station by a brass band and escorted down Nicollet Avenue by two thousand parader. The Patch reveled in his gaudy role. He was known as an out-and-out camera hound, but with such frankness and naïveté that nobody ever held it against him. Among the thousands of still shots of the horse, it is almost impossible to find one in which he is not facing the camera. The stable crowd, playing up to this weakness, would approach him pretending to shield a camera. Invariably he would stand stock-still, turn full-face and wait for the snap of the shutter. "Why, you almost had to take the gad to him to get him past a photographer," said his trainer.

Fast horses are proverbially high-strung. Dan Patch was as easy to get along with as an old shoe. Savage's twelve-year-old son used to hitch the great racer to a sleigh and jog him around the streets of Minneapolis, delivering Christmas packages and doing errands. The horse was never startled by flags or sudden sights or sounds; he never wore blinders and he loved band music. It was even safe to let him stand unattended in a noisy crowd. He just loved people!

As he stepped onto the track, the band playing, Dan Patch liked to turn his head and scan the crowd. "You know what he was doing?" said Ed Hanson, long his handler. "Counting the gate. Just go through the books and see how he always made his best marks before the big crowds. There were eighty thousand at the Allentown track the day he set two world records for a half-mile course. At Lexington, Kentucky, in 1905, some forty-five thousand saw him do 1:55¼, for thirty-three years the fastest accepted mile in harness. Then there was that day in 1906 in St. Paul. . . ." That was the day—

some say there were ninety-three thousand in the crowd—when Dan Patch stepped off a mile in 1:55, a racing mark which was not broken until 1960 and wasn't equaled until 1938. Meanwhile, harness-racing officials had ruled against exhibition trial records behind a windshield—the sailcloth stretched between the wheels of the pacesetting sulky. So the 1:55 mile done behind a dirt-shield was never officially recognized.

Down the years, record after record fell beneath the hooves of the intelligent, lovable bay. As the hero walked off the track after a triumph, people tried to shove through the ring of bodyguards to pluck hairs from his tail as souvenirs. Old Man Nash, his "official" farrier, sold thousands of "genuine Dan Patch horseshoes" at a dollar each. "Dan Patch," exclaimed the *Horse Review,* too excited to mind its grammar, "is so phenomenal as to absolutely defy comparison."

Finishing an exhibition mile at Los Angeles in 1909, Dan Patch went lame. Next day, in a newspaper piece headed "THE CURTAIN CALL OF A CHAMPION," a reporter wrote a tender story of the hush that settled over the multitude when the great pacer limped up to receive the floral wreath, of the tears that swam in many an eye as he hobbled off toward the stables. In 1910 Dan Patch was retired to stud on Savage's farm. There he held court in a palatial stable, steam-heated and electric-lighted, with fourteen hundred windows and an enclosed training track. And there, by a curious coincidence, Marion Savage and Dan Patch were both stricken ill, each with a mysterious heart ailment, one July day in 1916. One week later they passed from this world together.

Tiger Bait

Condensed from Fang and Claw

by FRANK BUCK with Ferrin Fraser

JOHNSON'S EYES were serious, a bit wistful, as they followed a little yellow dog running past. "Frank," he said, "want to come up on my plantation and get a tiger?"

We were on the terrace of the Keppel Harbor Golf Club, and just behind the club a sheep-laden Australian mail boat was coming into Singapore.

"Don't tell me that pup reminded you of a tiger!" I exclaimed.

"Yes, it did. And if you really want a live tiger—" He took out cigars and handed me one.

"You know Dick Scott?" he asked. "Well, Dick's got two kids, and he had the idea of getting them a dog. Last time he was on vacation he got one—an Alsatian, strong, gray and lean as a wolf. They named him Binji. Well, he turned out a marvelous dog; gentle and a grand watchdog, a wonderful playmate for the children."

"You're putting all this in the past tense," I said.

Johnson's eyes moved across to the ship. "Yes," he said, "and boats like that are the reason. After the voyage, they fatten up those sheep on the grazing land near where Dick lives. One night the flock was stampeded, and in the morning they had six dead sheep with torn throats."

"Binji?"

"Yes, it was Binji. No doubt of it. He had shreds of wool and blood on his muzzle, and his chain was broken. After that, at night, they kept the dog on a chain strong enough to hold a leopard.

"But Binji was powerful, Frank—and he'd tasted sheep's blood. One night he broke loose again, and that time a cool dozen sheep were slaughtered. Of course, this was the last straw. Dick didn't want a killer dog. So that afternoon he took Binji down to the hotel. This is where I come in.

"I'd never seen Binji until I walked into the hotel bar. Dick was there, and the dog, curled up at his feet, was a beautiful animal. I admired him. 'You can have him if you want him,' Dick said. 'He's a killer. I've paid for eighteen sheep and I don't intend to pay for any more.'

"Well, I didn't want a 'killer' either. But then all at once I remembered something a dog *would* be good for. 'All right,' I said. 'I'll take him.'

"Dick handed me the chain without a word. The dog looked first at Dick and then at me. His eyes weren't reproachful—just questioning. He went off with me easily—seemed rather pleased."

Johnson paused. Then, without looking at me, "You know what I wanted that dog for, Frank? Tiger bait. I told you there's a tiger on my plantation. You know all the red tape about getting permission to shoot one. But there's no law against trapping one alive, so I had had a log trap built. But I had to have good bait—something that would howl and make a racket at night. So I decided to use this sheep killer.

"You've got to understand, Frank, that I'd never seen this dog before. I thought he'd be savage. And now it seemed to me impossible that this gentle, loving dog was really a sheep killer. You know my plantation's eight miles across and up the river. Well, I didn't have to coax Binji into the launch; he came as if he trusted me—as if he'd been hoping all his life for this ride. He barked at the waves and caught bits of foam in his teeth. Then he'd slip his muzzle under my hand and gaze at me as if to say, 'We're having a swell time, aren't we?'

"I had supper. Binji lay on the floor looking up at me. He didn't beg for food—he just sort of hoped. I'm afraid I threw him a few scraps, something I never do with dogs at table. It was—well, he was going to die, you see, but even condemned criminals have a last meal. And it was nice to see the grateful look in his eyes when he caught a scrap. On the porch afterward I lighted my pipe and sat watching the stars. Presently Binji's head was on my knee. He didn't ask to be petted; he just put his big head there for companionship. I got hastily to my feet and called my houseboy. 'Come on,' I said. 'We're going to bait that trap.'

"Binji came gladly. He delighted in this unlooked-for walk up the jungle trail. I could see the white-gray of his tail waving as his nose explored the underbrush. I think a dog loves that more than anything—to be loose, free, but with a man behind to call his name in the dark. We finally got to the trap. You know the kind: heavy, log type, with a sliding door that works when a trigger is pulled. It was only after the boy had left him tied in the cage that Binji realized there was something queer in this business. He started to whine.

"Binji was a killer—a bad dog. Dick had been going to shoot him anyway. I told myself this as I walked back. Behind I could hear Binji, howling now, loudly. 'Dog make very fine tiger bait,' my boy said. 'He howl loud. Tiger come sure.' Somehow that didn't comfort me very much. That beautiful Alsatian alone in the dark, and somewhere nearby a tiger that could silence him with one blow!

"I went to bed, but I couldn't sleep. I thought of all sorts of queer things and through them all I saw that dog: great brown eyes, wrinkled nose, big paws warm and friendly against my leg. I began to reason. I hadn't a dog on the place. Binji might be a sheep killer, but here there were *no sheep* to kill! Why shouldn't I keep him?

"It's strange how quickly a man can change his ideas. Until then, I had wanted to trap that tiger. Now I hoped I hadn't trapped him! Call it sentiment; call it Binji's wet muzzle on my knee in the car, his eagerness in the boat, the look in his eyes as he lay at my feet—or call it plain dog consciousness. I routed out my boy: 'Come on! We're going to get the dog out of that trap!' We covered that half mile on a dead run. You'll understand if you've ever had a dog.

"As we neared the trap there was no sound; to me that meant the tiger had got him. Then I heard a low whine—the whine I imagine babies make when left alone. Ahead I saw Binji, his black nose through

the bars of the cage, his eyes shining straight into the torch's beam and that gray-white tail wagging friendship and confidence, as if to say, 'Well, we've played *this* game long enough—let's try another!' Untied, he came bounding out. He didn't jump on me. He just came running up, eager, his tail swishing and his red tongue hanging out. 'Come on,' I said, 'we're going home, Binji!' He ran down the trail just as he had come up it, frisking, investigating everything, now far ahead, now close up just under my feet, sniffing and pure dog.

"Suddenly something happened—so quickly and so close that I couldn't even get the torch up. A dusky, rushing movement in the dark. I saw two spears of gleaming ivory coming straight toward me—cruel, sharp as needles! I had stumbled on a wild boar protecting a sow with a litter. Two hundred pounds of fierce animal dynamite about to gore me! There was no getting my rifle up. It was all so quick—so sudden. And then a gray streak sprang from the black. I heard the boar grunt with the impact. I saw two gleaming tusks disappear in the dark. And then I heard Binji's cry of pain, followed by his low, savage growl—his sheep growl!

"I shot the boar," said Johnson slowly. "And I found Binji—both those tusks through his breast, but with his great, white teeth firm and fast in the boar's throat."

The Indomitable Akbar

Condensed from Birds Against Men

by LOUIS J. HALLE, JR.

THE MATING of the wild red-shouldered hawks who were Akbar's parents was a natural phenomenon comparable to an earthquake or a storm at sea. The two big birds were so absorbed in their courtship that my presence went unnoticed. For a time they flew back and forth through the woods in a series of dashing maneuvers, turning abruptly to avoid collisions, intermittently repeating the wild two-syllabled cry of their kind. Then the male, having proved his skill at obstacle flying, suddenly left the female for a display of power flight, rising on beating wings in a steep spiral into the sky. The female settled on a dead chestnut tree and attended the fateful moment of his descent.

The male shot up so high that I momentarily lost sight of him, but the unbroken series of screams still invaded every corner of the landscape. Silent and receptive, the earth seemed, like the female, to be waiting with suspended breath for the thrill of the plunge. This moment was entirely his. While it lasted he was the repository of all passion, the resplendent guardian of the seeds of creation. Suddenly his wings collapsed against his body as he began his dive. The speck grew like a storm cloud, accelerating as it approached, until the male hawk shot below the treetops and swung up screaming behind the quivering female. In the white heat of that union all of Akbar's nobility, the unequivocal jealousy of his dignity and the fierceness of his pride had its catastrophic inception.

Even when I first retrieved the baby Akbar from the nest in the silver birch three months later, he was the perfect expression of sheer hawk. He posed rigidly erect, his head set well back, his eyes fixed in a stare of unrelenting fierce wildness. One guileless human, deceived by the ludicrous topknot of feathers on his head, smilingly reached out his hand but immediately withdrew it with a gasp. So quickly that the eye could not follow the movement, the young hawk had struck with one of his talons and torn a gash right across the man's palm.

I installed Akbar in an empty garage and made him a bed of straw on top of a large wooden box. I attached leather jesses to his legs so that I could keep him in leash when we went out. But I never succeeded in reducing his wildness.

Akbar always took his raw meat from the sharpened end of a stick which I held. He

230

would strike with one talon, transfixing the meat with his sickle claws as though it had been a live mouse which might dart away. Being a true hawk, he never began to feed on his prize without allowing at least a minute to elapse after its capture; for in the hawk world it is not proper form to devour one's prey until there has been time for its quivering to stop.

My books on falconry stated that as soon as a young hawk is able to fly he may be given liberty, since, accustomed to being fed at a certain time and place, he will return there at that hour. But when I released Akbar for the first time he flew to the top of a butternut tree and sat there gazing fiercely at the wide world. When I called him to dinner he merely stared at me with steely eyes, and when I climbed up after him he soared away. The next day, after a desperate

search, we found Akbar high up in an oak tree. We captured him by means of a long pole, to the end of which we had fastened a bent nail, garnished with a hunk of meat. Akbar stabbed the meat with his foot, and we caught the hook in one of the jesses. In a moment we had pulled him down.

We did not realize then that we had injured him. But the next time Akbar tried to fly he suddenly collapsed, one wing lifeless. Experts told me that Akbar's wing would never again be of use to him, but his ancient stamina defied science. After a few weeks he could once more fly; not as he had flown in his one moment of freedom, powerfully rising far up in the sky, but on a level course and for limited distances. His spirit was never crushed by this adversity; somehow this broken-winged god seemed grander for the touch of ruin. But he began to accept our relationship, and I no longer kept him on a leash.

It did not take long for him to associate my whistle with feeding, and soon he came to me whenever I gave the signal. Along the ground he could proceed with a swift, hopping gait, and his powerful legs enabled him to leap vertically to my hand. But when starting from a height he was the equal of any sound hawk, and on such occasions it took fortitude to face his charge. Most birds reduce their speed when alighting by backing their wings hard before they touch; but Akbar belonged to a race of hunters whose livelihood depends on their striking power. When I called him from his perch in a tree a hundred fifty yards away he would start like a shot, beating his wings for the first few seconds to gain momentum, then coast downhill at an accelerating pace and strike my gloved hand without any reduction in speed, his talons extended straight before him. Since he weighed several pounds, the impact of the blow sent me staggering.

For several weeks Akbar did not engage in any hunting of his own; the killer instinct had not yet come to him. When it did come, it made its appearance first as a desire to play games. He began with a certain bump on his perch. Eyeing it with concentrated fury, he would suddenly stab at it, sinking his long claws deep into the wood. Then he would try the other foot, and at last would pounce on it with both feet at once. After annihilating the bump several times, he would change the game and begin falling like a thunderbolt onto the big yellow butternuts scattered on the lawn. There was never any frivolity in these games; he was always in deadly earnest.

Our walks were now habitually interrupted because Akbar attacked sticks and stones that lay in our way. He would swoop from my hand on a broken piece of branch, strike it with both feet, stab at first one end and then the other, maul it and even roll over on his side, holding the stick clear of the ground in a mock struggle.

One day a chipmunk darted across our path. Akbar fell from my hand and struck in one movement, grazed his quarry, struck again and missed as it dodged into a bush. Another day, when a woodcock was flushed from the grass ahead it was as though a string attached to its tail had jerked Akbar from my hand; but the woodcock was gone. From such failures Akbar came to know that grasshoppers, toads, frogs, snakes were his game, but birds and squirrels were not.

Akbar's power of vision was astonishing. I had had no conception of the many hawks which migrate at such altitudes that they are beyond human sight. But Akbar, with a hawk's jealous determination to protect his hunting ground, always saw them. His gaze would be fixed toward a point just above the northern horizon. I might strain my eyes to their utmost and still see only the empty sky. But slowly, steadily, Akbar would follow the invisible point until it fell below the southern horizon. By pointing my binoculars in the indicated direction, I could make out a little swarm as of particles of dust. Akbar not only saw them but identified them as hawks. He rarely bothered even to glance at other birds; no robin or crow, swooping across his field of vision, ever managed to attract his interest.

In one respect the power of Akbar's eyes was completely mysterious: He could follow the course of a passage hawk right across the face of the sun without being dazzled. I understand that when birds look into the sun they draw up over their eyes their thin transparent inner eyelids. But Akbar invariably looked at the sun with his naked eyes.

Akbar could not see in the dark half as well as I, however, nor could he identify a motionless object as a living animal. Any little beast was perfectly safe as long as it did not move. Akbar invariably overlooked the big bullfrogs at the edge of our pond, however close over them I held him; he would not see them until they jumped.

Akbar had the solitary disposition which was in keeping with the noble independence of his spirit. On his own terms he was willing to accept the presence of others; but he contained himself in serenity only as long as his rights were not infringed.

I had, at this time, a pet crow, a raucous urchin who was constantly plaguing us, landing on our heads from behind, mussing our hair, tweaking our ears and robbing us of whatever possessions we left lying about loose. One day this troublesome and tactless bird approached Akbar with the loud, defensive quarrelsomeness of a consciously inferior being.

If you have ever seen a ragamuffin danc-

ing about in the street before a rival of whom he is secretly afraid, threatening with his fists but ready to run, you have some conception of how the crow danced about on Akbar's perch. His guttural squawks seemed to call upon heaven to witness his quarrel. Akbar stood at ease, paying not the least attention to the challenges. Gradually the crow became emboldened to dance up closer along the perch, weaving his head back and forth in mock heroics. But he went too far. Akbar turned his head, and before the crow had time to make a move in defense one yellow talon had shot out and caught him firmly by the throat, in the middle of a derisive caw that abruptly fell to a weak, rattling gurgle. For a moment he was shaken helplessly back and forth; then he was flung sprawling to the grass, his feathers rumpled, his feet in the air. Akbar remained impassive as ever while the crow picked himself up, gave a few plaintive caws which implied that he had been unfairly attacked, and departed in disgrace.

Akbar had risen above and remained untouched by the ignorance and petty hostility of a crow; but the ignorance and petty hostility of a man destroyed him. Most men believe that all hawks are vermin, although the great majority of species, of which Akbar's is one, are beneficial to mankind. This tragic error is responsible for the slaughter of thousands yearly.

One evening during the hunting season, after a day disturbed by the continual explosion of guns, I could not find the noble hawk who had lived with me for two hundred days. I never saw any sign of him again. Some hunter, I suppose, proudly held that limp body up, its eyes now glazed and without character. I hope his poor triumph was at least tinged with shame.

SAMMY, THE SOCIABLE SEAL

Condensed from The Seal Summer

by NINA WARNER HOOKE

On THE SOUTH Dorset coast, not far from my village, there is a cove called Chapman's Pool. It is a wild place, frequented in summer by fishermen and holiday makers, deserted for the rest of the year. The Pool is a quarter of a mile at its widest point and lies in a half circle of shale cliffs. To reach it you must start from the headland four hundred feet above and make your way down a ravine by slippery tracks. The beach is of coarse sand and pebbles thinly spread over the ledges of slate. It is strewn with boulders and the flotsam of the tides.

In wintry weather the scene is somber and desolate. But on a bright day in summer the Pool can be a place of enchantment, the water intensely blue, a jewel in a silver setting. It is a timeless, quiet place. Nothing moves but a leaping fish or a plunging cormorant. There is no sound but the rumbling talk of the fishermen working at their gear, or the scream of a falcon from the hill.

This was once, of all places hereabout, the most dear to me. But now I hesitate to go. I miss too painfully the friend I once had here, a sea creature who used to come arrowing through the water at my call. Eight years ago, this cove was the scene of a friendship as rich and strange as any ever recorded. For my friend was a wild seal.

It was first seen by Sid Lander, a fisherman, early in May 1961. Sid and his son Alan were dropping crab pots a half mile out from shore when a seal bobbed up near their boat. It seemed startled and swam off to a safer distance, then sat up on its tail with part of its body out of water and watched the men. Had either man shouted or made menacing gestures, this story would never have been written. But they did not. Instead, Alan tossed the onlooker one of the whitings he used for bait. Instantly the seal dived for it.

Two days later the men saw the seal again, this time stretched on a ledge near the beach. Knowing of my interest in wildlife, a friend telephoned me, and I went down to the Pool. It was a raw, gray spring afternoon with tatters of mist hanging on the hills. A small group of people stood on the beach looking chilled and disappointed. There was no sign of the seal. Percy Wallace, a coast guard who does a bit of fishing in his spare time, shouted from a nearby boat shed. "It came in this morning and then made off again. I doubt it's far away. Try hollering."

235

Our cries rolled back at us from the cliffs. Some startled gulls rose from the rocks. Nothing else happened. We tried again. "Hullo-oo!"

Then suddenly someone pointed. "Look!"

Far out in the Pool a gleaming, round object had surfaced. At first it was stationary; then it slowly moved toward us. It came to a halt within four or five yards of where we stood. The heavy body was half out of water, supported by the front flippers. The large eyes were benign and calm, the blunt nose very black against the sleek, pewter-gray head.

I was overcome by the strangeness of the occurrence, oblivious to everything but the creature in front of me. He measured roughly four and one half feet from the end of his nose to the tip of the small tail between his hind flippers. The broad nostrils opened and closed, and the long white whiskers were wiry and thick. The ears were round holes without external parts. The eyeballs seemed oddly flat, with large pupils and very thick lenses. When he opened his jaws, I saw a formidable set of teeth. Each of the flippers was fringed with five shiny-black, non-retractile nails. They resembled the claws of a bear, though neater and less sharp. (Later I discovered how adroitly they were used, for holding fish, for grooming the coat and for gripping slippery rocks.)

"It won't stay, of course," Percy said. "Seals like lonely places. When the season starts, the tourists will scare it off." He was totally mistaken. For the thing which brought the seal to the cove—and which was to keep him there for almost six months—was human society. Why this should have been so is a mystery we were never able to fathom.

Most seals are protected only in the breeding season, but even this small mercy is often disregarded by fishermen, who have slaughtered them in countless numbers. So whether my friend was unusually trusting, or whether his curiosity was stronger than his fear of men, I do not know. I do know that he gave to me and to many others that summer a joyous comradeship, and a unique opportunity to learn his nature and his ways.

"The seal was on the beach all day yesterday," Mary Hickman told me early in the following week. "He came and lay quite close to me. His fur looks like moth-eaten velvet when it's dry. When Percy went out in his dingy, the seal flopped into the sea and followed. He kept diving under the boat and popping up on the other side. Then two more people arrived on the beach, and he came tearing back. They asked if it was safe to stroke him, but I advised against it."

This problem worried me, also; the seal had a threatening armory of razor-sharp teeth, the canines about an inch long. "Eventually," I said, "some fool's going to go pat it, and if he gets bitten you know what's liable to happen."

"Someone will put a bullet through its head," Mary said.

"Precisely."

The next day, when Mary and I went to the Pool, the seal came swimming up to the water's edge to meet us. A few minutes after we had spread rugs and settled ourselves, he hesitantly approached us on shore and flopped down within six feet of where we were sitting.

"Hullo!" I said. "How nice to see you! Are you all right?"

The absurd little tail wagged in response, and every line of his sleek body expressed pleasurable anticipation. From the first I talked to him in a normal tone, instead of the nonsense talk human beings commonly use with animals. Most others who met him did, too, possibly because he seemed more than half human himself.

As the seal lay quietly within touching distance, I put out my hand in a slow exploratory gesture, but his head jerked up, the eyes wide and alert.

"I wouldn't try it, if I were you," said Mary. "Not without wearing heavy gloves." I knew she was right. Those jaws could take a vicious bite, and the head could move like lightning. I gave up. The seal soon left us for a more comfortable patch of smooth rock some thirty or forty yards away.

A short time later, the Wrights, friends of Mary's, came down to the cove. Their four-year-old daughter was the first on the scene and, racing ahead of her parents, she aimed straight for the seal. Mary and I sprang up with warning shouts, but nothing could stop her. Horrified, we watched as the little girl flung herself down beside the animal and began hugging and kissing it. She evidently thought it was a kind of large dog, for when the rest of us caught up with her, she was crooning, "Dear doggie, good doggie." The seal responded with every appearance of delight. His flippers were clasped tightly around the child's body, and he was making a moaning sound. When we tried to pull her away, the seal showed quick resentment; it seemed safer to leave the pair of them undisturbed. They played together most of the afternoon, inseparable.

By the third week of May our friend was a familiar sight at the Pool, swimming from side to side, basking in the shallows or lying on a favorite ledge at low tide. I had learned now that he was a male gray seal (known scientifically as *Halichoerus grypus*), about eighteen or nineteen months old and definitely wild. He had a line of scars over his left shoulder, probably made by another seal, for they fight like demons, I was told, and even in play can be quite rough. However, he was so patently friendly that few now hesitated to fondle him. He liked to have his stomach rubbed and to be tickled under his fore-flippers. Never at a loss to make his requirements understood, he would flop over on his back and hold up a flipper until someone complied. To attract attention he would swivel around with both ends upturned till he seemed to be ballet dancing on his stomach. And when he was bored he chewed his fingernails or yawned, politely covering his mouth.

His amiability on shore was beyond doubt, but how would he react when swimmers invaded his own element? A group of us discussed this one windy morning while the seal lay at our feet, and decided that the only way to find out was to go for a swim and see what happened. We drew lots with colored pebbles, and the task fell to me.

I put on a swimsuit and walked to a ledge where the water was waist-deep. Immediately the seal flopped into the water and waited, as if he expected me to throw him a bit of seaweed or driftwood to retrieve. None of us had ever taught him this, but he did it voluntarily. When I failed to throw anything he looked at me inquiringly. I dropped off the ledge and stood beside him. His first reaction was astonishment. Plainly he had thought of us exclusively as land animals. His owlish stare changed to joy. He swam close, put his flippers around my waist and pushed his muzzle into my neck, at the same time making the queer moaning sound that seemed to denote emotion. Pushing him gently away, I began ducking and splashing to show that I was able to romp with him in the water as I had on land. When he grasped this, his excitement was uncontrollable. He dived, surfaced and rolled like a porpoise; he gyrated about me, pulled me along by taking my arm in his mouth and drew me down until our faces met underwater.

These antics caused such amusement on

shore that one by one the others ventured in to join the fun. Now almost beside himself, the seal raced from one to another, embraced and butted us, dived down and pretended to bite our toes, came up underneath and heaved us into the air. Snaking, gliding and somersaulting went the gleaming acrobat. The strong whiskers tickled us until we shrieked; the flippers suddenly clutched at ankles or calves. He discovered in a few minutes that a deft push at the back of the knees caused us to collapse, and as we sank he poured himself over our shoulders, turning over and peeping at us upside down, his black eyes shining with joy.

We had a flaming June that year, and, coupled with the newspaper publicity, it brought sightseers to the cove in increasing numbers. They came, they saw and were enraptured. The seal welcomed them all with the greatest delight. Now perfectly at ease amid crowds of strangers, he reveled in the admiration, the petting and fondling. In fact, it went to his head, and he behaved for a while like a spoiled child—rushing about and knocking over small children, flopping down soaking wet in the middle of picnic parties, snapping at dogs and frightening old ladies. "Why don't you call him off?" a visitor once asked, as if the seal had been an unruly dog.

Our friend was somewhat tiresome during this period. He demanded attention all the time and used various methods to obtain it. He tore off lumps of seaweed and tossed them into the air. He rolled on his back and clapped his flippers together, as sea lions do in circuses when applauding one another's acts. (It is always sea lions and not true seals like the Atlantic grays that are trained for circuses.) When this did not attract attention, he grabbed the nearest skirt, sleeve or trouser leg and tugged at it until either the owner complied with his wishes or the fabric gave way. If both these stratagems failed, he bawled. The noise, a kind of barking moo, designed by nature to be audible over the roar of wind and waves, brought everyone within earshot hurrying to see what was the matter with him.

I had been told that skilled animal trainers never scold or punish; they reward good behavior and ignore bad. With our friend, chastisement was useless—through his thick layer of blubber a hard smack must have felt like a gentle pat, for it only delighted him. So when we saw him annoying people, we told them to turn their backs to him. Quite often this proved effective. He was highly sensitive to a rebuff, and would flounce off, looking injured.

Fortunately, by the middle of June he had quieted down, causing no trouble except to yapping little dogs. And he was growing more selective about his company. Those humans who went into the water were preferable to those who stayed on the beach. Those with no fear of him in the water were preferred to the timid ones. Understandably, the latter were more numerous. When you are new to the experience, it is hard to believe in the harmlessness of a strange wild animal with huge teeth and an absent-minded way of mouthing your arms and legs. Yet the only time he ever bit anyone was when he was startled and involuntarily allowed his jaws to close on a man's arm. (The man, luckily, was one of his most devoted fans.)

He gradually acquired a sophisticated manner, which showed itself in his behavior with photographers. After a while he seemed to have grasped that the appearance of the little clicking metal object was a signal to stay where he was and keep still. And he did this impeccably—assuming the look of well-bred boredom so often seen on the faces of fashion models. He also showed a passionate love for music. One day a school-girl brought her recorder and began playing to him. When he heard the first notes, he immediately lay down with his head on her knee and his eyes half-closed, dreamily nodding. As soon as she stopped, however, he was as uproarious as ever, frisking and frolicking and begging for the games of which he never tired.

By this time, through the columns of the local newspapers, the seal had become known over a wide area as Sammy. Who first bestowed this name on him we never discovered. But Sammy the Seal he became and remained. At least it was better than *Halichoerus grypus.*

None of us liked being confined to the shallows when romping with Sammy. But we had no notion how he would behave with swimmers in deep water, and it seemed wise to experiment first. To obviate any risk we needed a life belt and a long rope, the use of a dinghy, and a party of five persons: three in the boat and two in the water. Everything was organized. But when we assembled at the Pool the third weekend in June, Sammy was missing.

His absence always alarmed us. A fishing syndicate operated in these waters with a powerboat and trawl nets, and the members were no seal lovers. The next day, however, I was relieved to see him floating in the lee of the rocks on the far side of the cove. I called, and he headed inshore.

The cove was empty save for us two. It was very early on a wonderful morning. The Pool shimmered like a sheet of glass under a flawless sky. I sat beside him at the water's edge, and he laid his head in my lap. The heat made him sleepy. I stroked him until he nodded off. His flippers twitched and his whiskers bristled as he hunted conger eels in his dreams. A shag plummeted into the water near the boat moorings. Sammy snored gently and squirmed farther onto my lap.

Suddenly I had an impulse to conduct the experiment *now,* without preparation, alone. It seemed to me that the other way, so hedged about with safeguards and precautions, was wrong because it was based on distrust. I thought: He knows that his teeth can hurt me if he does not restrain himself, because my skin is thinner and my body more vulnerable than his own. He can only have learned this through picking up a warning signal from me. In the same way he will know that when we swim together he must not cling to my legs.

Pushing him gently off my lap, I opened my beach bag, took out a swimsuit and changed. Also I put on my rubber fins. If I was wrong—if he did attempt to take me down with him in a deep dive—after kicking myself free I would be able to rise to the surface more quickly. He was still asleep when I waded in. I had swum fifty yards before he wakened and came after me. In a few seconds he bobbed up in front of me, looking perplexed. I went on at a steady crawl. He shot ahead again and stood up. His flipper held in front of his stomach and his eyes round with surprise, he looked like an anxious nanny. Without words he was asking, "Is this right? Are you sure you ought to come so far?"

And suddenly, as before, awareness of an altered relationship showed in his face. He barked joyfully, swam around me in rapid circles, turned a back somersault, crash-dived and performed a whole new series of triumphant aquabatics. I swam on to the center of the Pool where the depth is twenty feet or more, and he accompanied me, swimming about eight feet down. In the clear water I could see him looking at me. His eyes and nose were black points of a triangle in an aureole of white whiskers. Without appearing to accelerate he suddenly spurted ahead, then did a banking turn and a half-roll. This brought him directly underneath me again but upside down. In this position, he shot straight down out of sight.

By the time he reappeared I was resting, floating on my back. He joined me and did the same. Side by side we lay in the clear, still water. The cliffs looked small with distance, the beach was a far-off, tawny sickle. There was nothing but an immensity of sea and sky and the two of us in a communion of happiness. As the tide rocked us closer together I reached for his flipper and held it. He turned his head and gazed into my face. I was conscious of some powerful magnetism that emanated from unseen depths, reached out and touched some answering chord in myself. I had felt the same magnetism the first time I saw Sammy, but now I understood it. In that moment the curtain moved aside, and I looked back through time to the morning of the world, before man was shunned by other living things. It was a glimpse of Eden.

A flash of metal on the headland above the cove told me that other visitors had arrived. I could see a car parked beside my own, and by the time I reached the beach the owners were already on their way down. I quickly toweled myself and changed, packed the beach bag and hurried away, leaving Sammy to welcome the new arrivals, for I knew I could not share him with strangers just then.

Sammy had a definite, though somewhat crude, sense of humor, and we were not long in discovering it. One joke that he frequently practiced was a deep dive right underneath some unsuspecting bather, who would suddenly find himself hoisted into the air as if on a waterspout. A nip on the buttocks was another favorite joke, accomplished by a

lightning twist of the head as he sped by. He loved to streak toward a bather like a torpedo, and then come to a dead stop within half a yard by jamming on the brakes in a flurry of foam. The braking was effected by hurling his head and shoulders back and thrusting his flippers forward. This seemed to be tremendously enjoyable and was always followed by seal "laughter"—baring his front teeth and flattening his whiskers sideways.

He also liked to swim up behind bathers and hitch on with his teeth to the seat of their swimsuits or trunks. Out of this grew the hilarious idea of trying to remove the trunks. I was one of the first victims. One day, wearing an old two-piece swimsuit with a slack elastic in the pants waist, I was floating face downward off the shore in about five feet of water, intently searching the bottom for a child's lost sandal. Suddenly I felt his whiskers brush the back of my thighs, then a tug—and the next moment I heard howls of laughter. It transpired that my posterior was abruptly revealed to everyone on the crowded beach.

The success of any jest being measured in Sammy's mind by the applause it evoked, we knew that repetition of this masterpiece was inevitable. It soon became commonplace to hear one bather shout a warning to another: "Look out! *Hold onto your pants!*" From inside a derelict blockhouse I sometimes watched Sammy when he thought himself unobserved. Never at these times did I see him behave as he did before an audience. His antics were designed for the amusement of others, not himself.

He had an extensive range of utterances. When excited or impatient he barked, not like a dog but with a sound nearer to a bellow. He used a variety of grunts, chuckles and chortles to convey contentment, an equal range of wails, sobs and howls for venting grief. He was so emotional that we often refrained from a certain course of action for fear of precipitating a "scene." He liked, for instance, to lie sprawled over our legs when we sat on the beach. Even on a chilly day we would endure the contact of his damp, cold skin sooner than push him away.

When it was time to go home we would go to elaborate lengths to conceal our departure from him because of the wails and sobs that followed us up the ravine. A seal has no lachrymal ducts, so when Sammy cried the tears poured straight down his cheeks. The sight was so affecting that few remained indifferent to it. Alan Lander, who often watched him from the boathouse, says that after the last visitor had gone, Sammy would tearfully survey the deserted beach and shuffle to the ledge where he customarily lay. After a while he would cease crying and heave a great sigh. Then, as if saying, "Oh, well, there's always food," he would flop into the sea and go fishing.

Sammy bestowed liking indiscriminately, but his love he reserved for the special few who would swim with him in deep water. Perhaps because I was the first to do so, I seemed to come first in his affections. Our meetings now had a new significance. He trembled with joy, and his impatience to get into the water was conveyed in barks and whines. He always plunged in ahead of me and waited for me to decide which way we would go. Often we would swim to the mouth of the cove and beyond, around the eastern reef to the lonely bay under St. Aldhelm's Head, where few people come because there is no beach.

Here one day, after a long swim, I climbed out to rest while Sammy cruised about in the kelp and the rock crannies. The water was glassy-clear, and from my vantage point on a high boulder I could watch him and marvel at his sinuous grace and the effortless speed with which he chased a fish. Small prey he ate underwater, swallowing them at a gulp, without slackening speed. He could store enough oxygen in his blood system to enable him to stay submerged for as long as ten minutes.

After a while I lay back and dropped off to sleep. Some time later, the heat of the sun wakened me. I looked for Sammy, but he was nowhere to be seen. Of course he was free to come and go as he chose; all the same, he did not generally leave when we went on expeditions together. Then I noticed a deep channel undercutting the boulder on which I stood. At the near end it dipped to a cup-shaped hollow where the depth was about eight feet. And at the bottom of this hollow there was a gray shape, its outline blurred by the ruffled surface of the water.

My heart turned over. It was Sammy lying face down, motionless, his flippers asprawl. With every insurge of water from the seaward end his body lurched to one side, then fell back. I cried his name again and again, not with any hope that he would answer me but in the futile certainty that he was dead. What had happened while I slept? A rifle shot from a passing boat? But there was no blood, no mark of injury. Poison in the fish he had eaten? Unlikely. As I was about to dive in, I noticed that the position of his body had changed. The head and torso were raised, and rising still. He was being slowly lifted as if by an invisible agency. When the top of his nose broke surface the upward motion ceased and he hung suspended. More certain than ever that he was dead, I poised myself again to dive and retrieve him. But again I stopped, halted this time by a minute movement. Though his eyes were closed, his nostrils had opened, and there was a movement, a fractional expansion and retraction, in the region of his lungs.

241

He was asleep! The marvelous safeguards of his diving mechanism had lifted him, without conscious volition, to the surface to replenish his oxygen supply. He breathed in and out very rapidly for about ten seconds and then, still without opening his eyes or giving any other sign of life, sank to the bottom again.

Lowering myself into the water, I swam down and touched him lightly on the neck. Instantly he was awake. There was no transitional stage. He rolled over and welcomed me. His eyes were clear and shining-black. I put my arms under him and carried him with me to the surface. He lay inert, his head and hind flippers dangling. Being carried in the water like this was one of the things he most enjoyed. Then, pushing him in front of me and thrashing with my legs, I worked my way out of the channel into the open sea, and together we swam back to the Pool.

During the summer I occasionally visited Seacombe Cove, another of the many inlets within reach of my home, and on one memorable September day there I noticed a familiar retriever-like head nosing around a rock in the water. It was Sammy, either fishing or come in search of me. I had been busy and had not seen him at Chapman's Pool for three weeks. I dived in to meet him, and he nuzzled me affectionately, then raced off. It seemed clear that there was something he wanted to show me, and it was important.

He led the way to a tiny, white-pebbled beach, a few hundred yards to the west of the cove, that can be reached only by boat or by swimming. I had explored it many times. There was a cave here, running from the beach deep into the cliff, and screened from above by an overhang. It had always seemed to me an ideal place for a seal. Sammy hauled out and stretched himself flat on the pebbles. Pretending to be very surprised and pleased, I walked about examining the interior of the cave, picking up various bits of flotsam and all the time talking to him, expressing my appreciation in glowing terms. "It's wonderful, a marvelous place. How *clever* of you to have found it!"

He watched me with beaming complacency. Finally I splashed into the sea. "You've shown me your secret place," I said. "Now I'll show you mine."

He shot ahead, as he always did, waiting for me to catch up. At times he was so far ahead that he had time for a dive and a look around. If the water was clear I might see him far below, coasting along with no more effort than a flick and a wriggle. His body swerved in arcs of incomparable grace. Sometimes he was a bird in lazy flight, a hawk banking in the wind; then he would quicken speed and vanish like a silver arrow into the waving tresses of the weed we call mermaid's-hair. At such moments I longed unspeakably for an aqua-lung, so that I could join him in his weightless flight through the peacock-green firmament.

There is another cavern on the eastern side of Seacombe Cove. The interior is of smooth basalt whose rosy tint permeates the translucent water. Rising up in the center of this pink grotto is a wedge-shaped rock on which the Lorelei herself might have sat combing her sea-green hair. It is a proper place for a mermaid—and also perfectly adapted for a chute. The gentler incline is rough, offering good foothold, and the steep side is very slippery.

I swam to the back, climbed up and slid down feet first with a tremendous splash. Sammy's eyes opened wide with excitement. He tried to climb up the front but could not get a grip. I pulled him off and maneuvered him around to the other side. He was grunting with impatience. It was not easy for him even at the back because the rock was coated with algae, so I had to help him. At first I shoved from behind, then I stood on the ridge and hauled him up by his flippers. He panted with the effort and, just when I had got him into position, blew such a blast of fishy breath into my face that I fell over backward. We shot down together in a tangle of arms, legs and flippers, and had to start all over again. It did not take him long, though, to master the technique. At the third attempt he clambered up unaided and went whizzing down the slide with an expression of pure ecstasy on his face.

After that he was not to be distracted for a moment from this glorious game. I was only able to take a turn myself if I could get up while he was coming down, but this was seldom because he was so quick. Barely had he plummeted into the water than he would twist like an eel around the base of the rock and start climbing up again. I was nearly always caught in a highly vulnerable position at the summit and butted off head first. When finally I went to the entrance he ignored my call, giving me a look that said, "You go if you like. I'm quite happy here." I called again several times, and at last he came, glancing back yearningly at the wonderful rock but evidently unwilling to let me leave without him.

This was the only time I met him away from the Pool. He was showing less and less inclination to leave it. Summer was ending. Already the children had gone back to school, and the flood of visitors had dwindled to a trickle. Somehow, Sammy seemed to be aware that he must make the most of the time that remained.

October is for us the best month of the year. The sun shines, the sea is still warm and we revel in the peace of our coves and beaches after the departure of the holiday crowds. However, in October of 1961 the

gales came early, and before the month was out our lawns were white with frost. I knew Sammy must be lonely, but I managed to get down to the Pool only rarely. Alan Lander found him one day at the top of the slip, and next day right up on the green, one hundred yards from the sea. Plainly he had gone to look for the playmates who had vanished so unaccountably. Percy Wallace noticed a change in the seal's temperament: he got fits of the sulks. One day several of us congregated at the Pool. We called him and he came, and for a while we played with him. The wind was blowing hard, and before long the others left.

Soon there occurred one of those abrupt changes to which the weather in this region is liable. From the edge of a pall of cloud the sun burst out. The Pool turned from gray and dun to blue and gold. The beach pebbles glittered as if strewn with diamond dust. This joyous transformation galvanized Sammy into one of his archly playful moods. He came to me, rolled over onto my feet, frisking, wriggling and making mock snaps. When I stopped to fondle him he grabbed the sleeve of my jacket and began to tug in the usual direction, down toward the water. What he wanted was written in every line of his urgent body.

I looked at his pleading eyes; I looked at the cold sea. I said, "No." And then I thought, it will be the last, perhaps the last time ever. So I took off my clothes and slid into a pool between the rocks. The water was cold. I stayed in for about five minutes, and we played the best of the familiar games with uproarious splashing and laughter. It was the more perfect because so short and because I knew, as he knew, that it was the last time.

Next day the weather worsened. Gales and thunderstorms raged for a week. I telephoned Percy twice during the early days of

November. The second time he said, "Yes, the seal's still there. But if you want to see him again, you'd better go quick."

I drove down to the Pool. The day was gray and very cold. The sullen sky looked full of foreboding. From above, the cove looked deserted, but finally I saw Sammy mounted on a rock and staring at the horizon. The tide was high. There was a big sea running. I had to edge along close under the cliff to reach the slipway. He gave me a welcome that was full of affection, but his eyes were troubled. He kept shaking his head and whining. I sat down and took his head in my hands, stroking it until he quietened. All the time I talked softly. "Stay with us. Winter will pass, and another summer will come. Don't go. Stay here with us."

He was heavy. My legs were cramped, and the wet stones were icy cold. I got up. Directly I did so he moved away from me a little, then a little more, down toward the water, looking searchingly at me as I followed. While I stood irresolute, a wave ran up the slip and he became water-borne, but he held his position and continued to watch me out of flat-black, tormented eyes. The next wave licked at my feet. I turned and ran, scrambling from rock to rock between the seas that crashed and tore at the stones, until I reached the ravine.

Nearing the top, I looked down, muddied and gasping for breath, and saw the gray shape, small with distance, swimming through the breakers. The head, now visible, now lost, pointed westward into the haze over the center of the Pool. There he paused and turned, and I felt his relentless gaze on me as I went on and up over the lip of the headland. When next I looked, the sea had taken him. He has never returned.

Where Sammy came from and where he went I was never able to discover. If he has survived, he will now be about nine years old. In the pride of his potency and the lust of battle, he will have forgotten the months he spent and the games he played on a far-off Dorset coast. But we will never forget. He came like a messenger from a distant, happier world, and when he departed he left all of us the richer for having known and loved him.

Queen
of the Coop

by GERALD MOVIUS

WE DIDN'T CALL her Elizabeth at first. She was just "that little Brown Leghorn pullet." And she had some right to the pedigree because her neck feathers were light orange and her breast was a rich salmon; but one of her ancestors must have been a Bantam, for she never weighed more than three pounds.

Elizabeth had hardly feathered out before it was obvious she had an eye for the men, and every rooster in the yard was in raptures about her. She had the manners and grace of an educated courtesan and the instincts of a floozy. Elizabeth was less than five months old when she held an announcement party over her first egg, giggling and gushing until her flashy little red comb danced. A committee of cockerels met in honor of the event, and there wasn't one of them without a high fever. Later that day, Louis XIV, a cockerel of great promise as a future roast, met an untimely death. It seemed Elizabeth had looked upon him with special favor and the rest of the boys ganged up on him.

It was my younger sister, just then exposed to high school history, who hung the monickers on the denizens of our backyard,

and she eventually named Elizabeth in honor of the Virgin Queen because she was the only one among the yearlings who showed no evidence of wanting to raise a family. The rest of the girls turned short-tempered and peckish in late spring and lost interest completely in their boyfriends. But Elizabeth was strictly a bachelor girl—carefree of family ties, the little love bug of all the lads at home and visiting gallants who came from miles around.

Elizabeth was a career girl, too—she must have rattled out more than 250 large white eggs in her first year, a prodigious production in any chicken yard. We could well afford to overlook her habit of roaming the surrounding countryside in pursuit of rooster trouble. The first time this happened was when a brace of swaggering young roosters came calling outside our poultry run and exchanged insults with our headmen. Elizabeth was enchanted. She cocked her small head coquettishly, poised herself and sailed over the six-foot mesh fence as easily as a barn swallow, screeching girlishly and invitingly. Then she was off at a swift pace for the bush, her swains in ardent chase. We debated the advisability of clipping Elizabeth's wings, but she always came home promptly at feeding time, as innocent-looking as if she'd been someplace for tea.

Old age began to catch up with her contemporaries, but Elizabeth remained the perennial pullet, forever young, forever desired. At the ripe age of three she had laid enough eggs to pave the yard, without the slightest maternal interest in one of them. She looked on her sisters with contempt, and they hated her.

That year the Earl of Leicester came into Elizabeth's life, the biggest, loudest-mouthed, gaudiest cock we had ever seen. He came calling as a score of others had, and Elizabeth went over the fence without even waiting long enough to stir up a rumpus between the visiting challenger and the local talent. The Earl was worth a woman's time at that. Magnificently built, he moved

with a swagger that would have suited a star of adventure movies. When he threw up his head to crow, you got the idea that he had flung his cape over his shoulder first, hitched up his rapier and laid one claw on his dagger.

He and Elizabeth became inseparable. At least, she disappeared with him morning after morning and trailed home alone at night, occasionally escorted by the Earl as far as the turn in the road. A few weeks of this daily rendezvous and we noticed a definite weariness about Elizabeth. She wasn't laying, but we put that down to an approaching molt. Then one evening when we went out to scatter corn, Elizabeth wasn't there. We beat on a pan and called. But no Elizabeth appeared on the scene.

A few days later Samuel, our collie, and I were sloshing across the soggy ground when Samuel paused to investigate a clump

of tall grass in a fence corner. There was Elizabeth, squatted so low and flat you could have used her back and wings for a checkerboard, soaking wet, bad-tempered and obviously in the process of hatching out a family! Samuel shoved his nose against her beak in recognition and got well pecked for his interest. Easylike I picked her up, and lo, Elizabeth, thin as a splinter by now and designed by nature to set on not more than eight or nine eggs, had fifteen under her small breast and pathetic little wings. I let her down and legged it for home.

I was all for bringing her in out of the wet and cold, but my brother wisely suggested we build her a shelter with an old box and some tar paper, and let her be. Half the town came to look at Elizabeth in her trial by motherhood. Chickens may be empty-headed, but even the dopiest of them know better than to go broody in October in North Dakota—all except Elizabeth. After a fortnight we'd about decided she was sitting on a "cold deck"—a clutch that would die in the shell. Then one dark, damp afternoon, in she dragged, clucking inexpertly and wearily at a little platoon of wet, stumbling, wailing chicks. Every last one of them was gaily dappled with the sort of down which would have convicted the Earl of Leicester in any court. And Elizabeth had hit the jackpot. She had begun with fifteen eggs and she had finished with fifteen chicks. We fenced off a corner of the coop for her, while the rest of the flock muttered among themselves. They didn't like it. It wasn't natural. But as off-season chicks will sometimes do, the small devils thrived and feathered with amazing rapidity.

One morning we took down the barrier. It was a mistake. At noon we found Elizabeth half dead: Her sisters, half sisters and cousins had condemned this houri of the henyard to death and had almost carried out the execution. She had always had all the attention, and now she had performed the impossible by producing a family when respectable biddies were preparing for a long winter's rest. Elizabeth spent the winter in the woodhouse, finally recovering sufficiently to sing a little and scratch weakly in the straw. When the combs of her sisters were beginning to show springtime blushes and their feathers were taking on new sheens, Elizabeth's remained dull and colorless.

We were dubious about putting her back with the flock. But nothing happened. Nothing at all. Her little head jerked with its same come-hither air—and nothing happened. She rolled her eyes at Attila, but he was busy talking to a plump little pullet. Mark Antony, most gorgeous of the cockerels, stumbled over her without so much as a "pardon me." The truth was a long time dawning on Elizabeth: She was an old woman.

Then one day the Earl of Leicester sauntered arrogantly along the fence. Our hens stole admiring looks at him and were sternly shushed by our roosters. Suddenly, with a swoosh, Elizabeth leaped the fence and landed neatly in the Earl's path. It looked like old times. But the Earl's head jerked back in fright. His swagger faded, his tail feathers dropped. And then straight at him, wings spread, head stretched out, sprang our Elizabeth, fury and outrage in every quirk of her feathers. She pecked him on a wattle, and the blood came. She pecked him again —and again and again. She was everywhere inside his guard.

Of a sudden, the Earl picked up his cape and his rapier, his dagger and his gallant feathers, and headed for open country. Across the fields he fled, with Elizabeth in swift pursuit, catching him now and then and whaling all hell out of him. We never saw either of them again.

Ben
Got His Man

by JAMES MONAHAN

Not long after World War II ended, Scotland Yard produced a new hero to captivate British hearts and minds. His exploits made headlines; television and radio programs highlighted his career; his fan mail exceeded that of many movie stars. His greatest distinction was to be patted fondly by the Queen herself—an honor which, according to some of his friends at the Yard, turned his head completely. They admit, however, that it never once affected his way with criminals.

This spotlight-loving hero was Ben, a Labrador retriever who, in three years alone, captured more than a hundred lawbreakers. "Old Ben," said Chief Inspector S. E. Peck of Scotland Yard, "set a better record than most police constables achieve in their entire service."

Ben came to Scotland Yard in 1947, when he was one year old. Since the war the Yard had been experimenting with a new order of police dogs—peaceful but knowing animals, as gentle but firm as the traditional "bobby" himself. These dogs patrol the byways of London and provide the constable on the beat with an extra pair of eyes and ears plus that "sixth sense" which the hu-

man patrolman can only admire and envy.

That first day on the training grounds at Imber Court, Ben's sleek black coat quivered with excitement as he watched the other animals—mostly German shepherds and Labradors—being put through their paces. The broad green acres were dotted with false buildings, odd-looking shacks, simulated backyards, strategically placed walls and hedges—duplicating conditions that the team of constable-and-dog would encounter on their rounds.

Ben seemed impatient to get into the show. His handler, a cheerful man with an enormous Old Bill mustache, was Police Constable Herbert Shelton, and in those first moments a spiritual adoption was sealed. Together they watched as a veteran German shepherd, playing the part of "instructor," demonstrated the supreme importance of obedience. A police constable enacted the role of sneak thief or purse snatcher, tempting the animal in a variety of ways. Yet each time the dog, tense and growling, sprang to action only when he heard a command from his handler.

The rookies of Ben's class watched this performance time after time. Then, indi-

248

vidually, they were confronted by the same situations, and called back repeatedly when they acted without the master's command. Only after demonstrating absolute obedience were they allowed to pass on to more advanced training.

Following a scent, they tracked a "fugitive" over fields and along city pavements, through abandoned buildings, into all kinds of hideaways. They learned to "capture" a heavily padded constable, who would try every trick of resistance and escape, and to hold him at bay until help arrived.

Ben quickly became the star pupil. His obedience was flawless, his intelligence remarkable and his tracking superb. But when it came to "arresting" a man, Ben was openly critical of the prescribed routine. The dogs were trained to seize a man by the right arm, firmly, yet without tearing a sleeve or leaving even a tooth mark. Ben, having shown that such a trick was a pushover, made it clear that he preferred methods of his own. For a time he favored thrusting his head between the runner's legs and throwing him off balance. Then (having had his nose kicked a few times) he adopted a maneuver of encirclement, during which he fixed his man with a beady eye and growled assertively.

After three months at Imber Court, Ben was ready for active duty. He and Constable Shelton were assigned to a beat in London's Hyde Park. Each night they patrolled the pathways; ignoring lovers spooning in the darkened shrubbery, but always alert for the sneak thieves who slip off their shoes, pad quietly up to a preoccupied couple and snatch a neglected purse.

Ben early showed a remarkable awareness of guilt. Often, as man and dog strolled through the park, Ben would come to a sudden halt and growl deeply—a warning that trouble was afoot. Shelton learned to respect Ben's judgment. "Ben can sense the physical reaction of the culprit," he explained shortly after he and Ben started working together. "If a man is guilty, he feels fear at the sight of a policeman and a dog. Ben smells this fear."

At Shelton's command, Ben would be off into the bushes. When the constable caught up in the chase he would usually find a thief, quaking in his socks. Having delivered his prisoner, the dog would fetch the handbag that had been cast away, making as many return trips as were necessary to retrieve its scattered contents.

Ben became the unrelenting enemy of the London "spivs," who dealt in black-market cigarettes and nylons. Catching a spiv in the act of trading was one thing for the police; spotting him on the prowl was quite another problem.

The spivs learned to fear the constable and his dog, and to avoid their beat. Ben could spot a spiv at fifty paces. His growl became Shelton's signal to stop the man for questioning. "Sometimes Ben caused me to wonder if he didn't know precisely whether it was hosiery or tobacco the chap was concealing," Shelton says.

Ben's uncanny ability to detect fear or a guilty conscience became legendary at Scotland Yard. Once he went along merely for the ride when Shelton drove into the London suburbs to question a witness about a series of crimes committed in the vicinity. The witness proved difficult and uncommunicative, and finally Shelton suggested that he come to the police station for a talk with the sergeant.

"When the man got into the car, Ben growled from his tail up," Shelton recalls. "He was restless during the station interview, and when the chap departed Ben howled indignantly. I didn't like the man either, but we hadn't a thing against him."

Weeks later, the reluctant witness broke

down under persistent questioning and confessed himself the perpetrator of the puzzling crimes. He was sentenced to ten years.

Ben's exploits began to make spectacular headlines in the press. He never "savaged" a captive—"although there have been times," says Shelton, "when he was sorely tried." One criminal kicked Ben viciously when overtaken, and fled again. This time when Ben outran him he reverted to his old "obstructive" trick—head down, nose thrust between the man's legs.

"When I arrived the chap was sprawled on the ground and Ben's teeth were playing a tattoo up and down his shinbone," Shelton relates. "But he never harmed the man."

Shelton claimed proudly that Ben never "muddled" a scent. "One morning, for example, a call came in from the suburbs: Six houses had been burglarized, the last one only a few hours earlier. Constables had combed the neighborhood without success. When Ben and I arrived there were twenty or thirty police on the scene and the search had attracted a lot of onlookers. Ben completely ignored the crowd. He picked up the scent and in a few minutes had his man cornered in an orchard half a mile or so outside of town."

Ben won his greatest plaudits from both police and public in 1951 for his capture of a dangerous young criminal, Frederick Poole, who escaped from jail and was believed to be hiding somewhere in Middlesex. Warned that he might be armed, police patrolled the area while householders lived in terror. Then, on a Saturday night, the alarm sounded in Sunbury. Poole had broken into a house and stolen food and a suit of clothes—and had dropped a handkerchief bearing prison marking.

Police threw out a cordon; three police dogs were rushed to the scene. For hours the teams combed Sunbury, but Poole eluded them. Late on Sunday the call went out for Shelton and Ben.

They arrived just before dawn on Monday. Ben sniffed the captured handkerchief and was off. He led Shelton through cluttered backyards, over hedges, across fields. Finally Shelton heard Ben's warning bark and saw a figure run from behind a clump of bushes. A few minutes later he saw the figure fall with Ben on top. Frederick Poole was captured without a shot being fired.

By now Ben was a familiar figure in the police courts—as a party to the arrest he was required to appear at the hearing. Wherever he went he was besieged by admirers. His press clippings filled scrapbooks. His fan mail, formerly acknowledged by Shelton, required the services of a clerk in Scotland Yard. At the Police College near Coventry he gave a command performance for the King and Queen.

When he appeared on a BBC television broadcast, his sleek coat shimmering under the klieg lights, he put on a polished performance. For the fade-out, he looked directly into the camera and gave what Shelton insists is "Ben's characteristic smile."

Success, of course, had some drawbacks. Ben was sent back to Imber Court, where, for more than a month, he served as instructor. He demonstrated his tricks for the other dogs, obedient, but obviously bored. He seemed relieved when he and Shelton went back to pounding the beat again.

Before retiring in 1956, Ben had caught 199 miscreants. After one spectacular arrest, the presiding judge said: "I regret that the court cannot communicate its appreciation to this remarkable animal. If it were possible to promote police dogs for performance of duty, this dog should certainly be elevated in rank."

It would be enough, perhaps, if Ben could have sensed the gratitude of London's worshiping citizens. For years they felt safer knowing that their hero was around.

Elijah, the Hermit Horse

by BILL HOSOKAWA

ONE CLEAR, cold day in February 1955, Wallace Powell, a young commercial pilot, was jockeying his single-engine plane over the massive Collegiate Range of the central Colorado Rockies. Suddenly he saw a pair of horses where no horses should be. Tails to the frigid wind, hemmed in by huge snow-drifts, they were standing forlornly on the desolate ridge that connects the peaks of Mount Harvard and Mount Yale. Powell estimated the elevation of the ridge at 12,800 feet, far above the timberline. At his home base in Gunnison, forty miles south-west of the ridge, Powell told his boss, Gordon "Rocky" Warren, what he had seen. "They'll starve to death," Warren said. "Guess we'd better see if any ranchers are missing a pair of horses."

Eventually the news reached Gunnison's Mayor Ben H. Jorgensen, who had been a volunteer officer of the Colorado Humane Association for sixteen years. He hurried down to the airport. "Rocky," he said, "I want those horses fed. The Humane Association hasn't funds for this kind of thing, so I'll take care of the bills myself. What will you charge?"

"The least I can do is take the job at cost," Warren answered. "I'll fly hay up there for twelve dollars a bale."

"Fine," said Jorgensen. "Let's get going."

When Warren flew over the ridge with the first load, only one horse was there; apparently the other had died and been buried under drifting snow. The survivor, a bay, was in pitiful condition, barely able to totter around. Warren dropped the hay as close to the horse as he could. The bay was munching away when he headed back to Gunnison. Warren and Powell took turns flying the haylift, making two trips a week. "When the air was smooth," says Warren, "we could come in fifteen or twenty feet above the ground. But when the wind was high we'd have to stay a hundred feet off the ridge and drop the hay with a hope."

Soon delivering the hay got to be a personal thing. The horse would be waiting for them. "We hated to disappoint the old boy," says Warren. "Several times Wally and I flew up there when hundred-mile gusts were bouncing our tiny plane all over the ridge. That horse was getting the kind of flying out of us that money can't buy."

Early in April, six weeks after the haylift had been launched, Ray Schmitt, a Colorado

252

Air National Guard pilot, happened to touch down at Gunnison. Schmitt saw pictures of the hermit horse which Warren had snapped, and borrowed the photos for a friend, George McWilliams, Denver *Post* reporter. McWilliams excitedly telephoned Warren for details. "Incidentally," he asked, "have you got a name for the horse?"

"No," Warren replied. "If you can think of one, you're welcome to tag it on him."

McWilliams turned to a fellow reporter and said, "What was the name of that fellow in the Bible who was fed by ravens?"

"Elijah," the reporter said.

"That's the perfect name." McWilliams turned to his typewriter and hammered out the story of Elijah, the hermit horse.

The response was immediate. Ivan Thomas, manager of Centennial Race Track on Denver's outskirts, suggested a "Hay for Elijah" fund, started it off with a hundred-dollar check, and offered oats and a stall for life. Dozens of youngsters sent letters offering Elijah a home. One boy wrote, "I love horses next to my family and relations. If you are wondering how he would eat, I would mow lawns in the summer and shovel snow off the sidewalks in the winter." Next day some thirty horse lovers, mostly youngsters, sent in a total of sixty-seven dollars for Elijah's hay. Newspapers all over the country picked up the Elijah story. The pilot of a New York-to-Los Angeles airliner requested the horse's position so he could point it out to passengers as he flew over. Letters came from virtually every state and from England, Portugal, Switzerland, France, Holland, Germany, Canada and Japan. The London *Daily Mail* correspondent in New York interviewed Mayor Jorgensen by telephone. The Army offered helicopters for hay transport, if needed.

One day while piloting a television crew over the site, Warren saw what he described as a pair of winter-gaunt wolves stalking Elijah. Hurrying back to Gunnison, he picked up a shotgun and Wally Powell as copilot. The animals were still on the ridge when they got back. Warren shot and killed one, chased the second down the ridge. The American Humane Association in Denver announced that silver medals would be presented to Warren and Powell.

Meanwhile, in Colorado Springs, Bill and Al Turner, brothers who during the summer and fall guided pack trips in the mountains, read about Elijah with more than ordinary interest. Studying the photos, Al Turner said, "That horse must be our Bugs, the one that got away from the pasture last November." Bugs had been born in the shadow of the Collegiate peaks and ran wild until he was four years old. He was captured by a wrangler, from whom the Turners bought him in 1946 for fifty dollars. He turned out to be one of the best animals in their pack string. When Bugs disappeared through a break in the pasture fence, taking a gray horse named Smokey with him, the Turners hired a cowboy to look for the runaways. The cowboy made nine trips into the high country before snows forced him to quit. The horses were given up for lost.

"If Elijah is Bugs," they now wrote Mayor Jorgensen, "he has quite a history. He hates parked cars and women in skirts, which would certainly be motive enough for heading for the high country."

Entry of the Turners into the picture aroused new public interest. The *Post* published a straight-faced editorial which called the attention lavished on the hermit horse "a hideous invasion of privacy. If Elijah," the editorial continued, "is an unclaimed nag of uncertain history, then rescue efforts must continue. But if Elijah is really Bugs, leave him alone. He's using his good horse sense in seeking solitude away from a noxious

civilization." A newscaster wrote a song about Elijah, and a disk jockey sang it to the tune of the Davy Crockett ballad.

But efforts to rescue Elijah, regardless of his feelings about the matter, continued. The Turners led a party on snowshoes up the seven-mile climb to Elijah's hermitage. When they reached the windswept ridge, Elijah regarded them nervously.

"Come here, Bugs," Bill Turner commanded. The horse waited motionless as the Turners approached close enough to drop a halter over his head. It was Bugs, all right, and thanks to the haylift he was in good shape. But taking him down across the snow-drifts, where he would bog down to his belly, was out of the question. A month later the Turners made two more attempts to bring Elijah down. The last time, accompanied by two friends and equipped with shovels, they cut a path through drifts ten to twenty feet deep, working hours for yards of progress. Elijah was led down these paths, but darkness overtook them several miles short of the road. The men staked Elijah out and returned to town for the night. Next morning the Turners found him wandering a mile up the mountain. But now that he had had his last fling at freedom, Elijah took amiably to being rescued.

The welcome that was touched off as Elijah rolled into nearby Buena Vista aboard a trailer was fitting tribute to one of Colorado's most famous sons. The high-school band led a parade down Main Street. There was a float depicting the haylift, and behind it came Elijah himself. More floats followed, and then marchers and cars with horns honking. It was a great day for Buena Vista, population 783. More than a thousand persons watched the parade.

That afternoon Elijah enjoyed a trailer ride to Denver for the opening of Centennial Track. While seven thousand spectators cheered, Mayor Will Nicholson of Denver presented him with a red blanket bearing his name in white letters. Later there were radio and TV interviews. Elijah even visited the famous old Brown Palace Hotel. He was met at the entrance by the manager, led over a red carpet to the reception desk and escorted to a straw-filled enclosure set up in the lobby—the first horse to be thus housed.

After two weeks of high living Elijah went home to get in training for the summer's labors—carrying fishermen and dudes into the high Rockies. Bill and Al Turner were astonished by an offer of fifteen hundred dollars for Elijah, but they weren't selling. "Elijah is a simple mountain critter, just like us Turners," Al told me. "He has five or six more working years ahead of him. After that, I'll let him retire to pasture—and not on top of a mountain either."

BLIND JACK

Condensed from Blind Jack: A Responsibility

by STEPHANIE RODEN RYDER

JACK JOINED our family quite by chance. I was on line at our local fish market in Godalming, Surrey, England, when I overheard the woman ahead of me mention that her husband had found a helpless bird. "We think it's blind," she said. "We don't know how to look after it, yet we can't bear to have it destroyed."

"What kind of bird?" asked the man behind the counter.

"A jackdaw," she said.

A jackdaw! I had wanted one for years, and I broke into the conversation and secured a promise that the bird was mine, although I had a busy life already, what with a hardworking doctor husband, two young daughters, irregular mealtimes, a constantly ringing telephone, the gardening to do and a collection of birds and animals that included ducks, doves, budgerigars, guinea pigs and a cat. I almost regretted my impulsive offer.

But the large cardboard box delivered to my door three days later drove all misgivings from my mind. It quivered with the frenzy of the captive creature inside, and when I opened up the flaps it revealed a thin, incredibly dirty, panic-stricken jackdaw. As I slipped my hands under his feet, he ran straight up my right arm and onto the top of my head, where he wobbled precariously.

I put a small block of wood on the kitchen table as a makeshift perch and managed to persuade the trembling bird to stand on it. Then I held a cup of water to him. He took no notice, so I splashed a little on his beak. Instantly he began to drink thirstily, throwing up his head after each gulp as farmyard fowls do. There was something touchingly defenseless about his raised throat.

Having drunk he remained still, spent, and I sat looking at him. A more utterly pathetic creature I had never seen. Where his right eye should have been he had a gray, pus-edged socket. His left eye appeared normal but was colored an ominously brilliant yellow.

Should I destroy him? I had taken life many times—a diseased duck, insects, a chicken for dinner. It would have been so easy to press my thumb to that little throat and wrench the head around. As a fully grown wild bird, suddenly dependent on human care, he probably wouldn't survive longer than a few months anyway.

Just then, Jack bent down his head awkwardly, as though searching. He opened his beak. I pushed an earthenware dish of bread toward him. He found a large crusty slice, then with unexpected vigor tossed it into the air, placed his foot on it when it

257

landed and tore it apart, eating as if he'd never eaten before.

Here was my answer. Here was a need to live. I who had considered taking his life must now accept the responsibility for keeping him alive—even happy—in a world of humans. It was a challenge I accepted gladly.

Jack's first few days with us were precarious ones. His wings dragged, his body drooped, and his claws gripped my finger weakly. He was living in perpetual darkness, and I couldn't gently explain to him, as to a human patient, that his sight had gone and a new life must be accepted. It was heartrending to see him repeatedly rubbing the sides of his head against his perch, as if trying to remove the scales that obscured his vision.

Why was Jack blind? What had happened? It being March—a month for springtime quarrels over mates and territories—I suspected a fight. Later I formed a different theory. I read in a newspaper about a gardener who went temporarily blind after a long session of spraying a weed killer. Jackdaws find food on ploughed land, and often farmers spray such land with a weed killer before planting.

I made Jack a perch by nailing an alder branch to a short plank and putting it on a table in the bay window of the dining room. To give him an anchor in his darkness, everyone was asked to call "Jack!" on entering the room. I kept up a soft, ceaseless chatter while performing domestic chores and deliberately scraped my nail on the side of his dish when bringing him his food.

On the third day our efforts were handsomely rewarded. He lowered his head at the scrape of my nail and groped for contact with the edge of the dish. Suddenly he was eating ravenously. The household noises and human sounds didn't seem to worry him anymore. I managed to give him a bath, sprinkling him with tepid water over the kitchen sink and standing him out in the sun to dry. Then he shook himself vigorously and began to preen his plumage. Another step forward!

I put penicillin ointment into his eyes to clean away the pus and anesthetic cream to stop the irritation, but by the end of the first week I had to give up hope for a return of sight to his left eye. Its pupil was crinkled and fallen in. But the full impact of Jack's blindness didn't hit me until I came home late one evening. I looked in on him in the dark, shining a flashlight full in his face from a distance of two inches. He was quiet and at ease, completely unaware of the light. He stepped on my finger, and there was no change in his grip when the flashlight was switched off. Poor Jack; he couldn't even tell light from darkness.

I was prepared for Jack to take a turn for the worse at any moment, in which case I would destroy him. But after six weeks he was a different bird altogether. Gone was his dull, dusty look. His legs shone like sticks of polished jet. He was a beautiful glossy black all over, except for a white patch behind his head, navy-blue wing tips and a single white feather in his left wing which gave him a distinguished appearance.

Jack now preferred to be independent about baths, taking them himself in a shallow dish. On cold days I stood him on my hand in front of an electric heater to dry. Steam rose like little ghosts from his skinny frame, and he slapped his wings with pleasure at the unexpected heat.

After about three months there came a mealtime when Jack showed a new kind of behavior toward me. Instead of the gobbling that is typical of wild birds he began to eat slowly, appearing to savor every beakful. I was trying to persuade him to put his left foot, as well as his right foot, on the edge of his feeding dish, when he hesitated. Then without pausing in his meal he put back his left foot, gently gripped my thumb again and would not let it go. I gasped with pleasure at the significance of this tiny gesture. For the first time since he was blinded, Jack was fully relaxed. At last he was happy and confident in the company of a human he had never seen.

To ensure that Jack had a balanced diet I tried him on just about everything. He had his preferences. Shredded cheese he adored; also hard-boiled egg yolks, mealworms (supplied in cans by a pet-supply firm), and the cat's boiled meat and fish. Once I proudly offered him a slug from the garden, feeling sure he would relish it, but he was disgusted. Slices of apple, too, he picked up and threw across the dining room. (His reaction was surprising, for sighted jackdaws love apples. When Jack refused ripe red cherries—irresistible to all normal jackdaws—I knew that color has much to do with jackdaw taste.)

I took him out for walks twice daily. My hand ached with his weight, and his claws dug into my skin unmercifully, but he seemed to be perfectly content. One day he even let me carry him along the main road, past busy traffic, to the fish market where I first heard about him.

Vigorous wing flapping after breakfast became his regular exercise. His tense stance on his perch and little croaks as he sent the dining-room curtains flying were acts of sheer joy in living. By June he did his wing flapping when I held him. It was an exhilarating sensation—the pull on my thumb, the breeze in my face, and Jack's open-beaked delight.

But the most dramatic progress came when Jack determined to explore beyond his perch. For days he kept "peering" upward.

Then suddenly, without warning, he leaped into the air and flew to the ceiling. He hit his head hard and plummeted to the floor. I picked him up and replaced him on his perch, but again he took off, straight upward, struck his head and fell like a stone. The sight unnerved me, but this time I sat still. Slowly, probingly, Jack started to feel his way around the floor. His beak discovered the width of the chair legs, after which he carefully walked around them, and from then on he explored the dining room and kitchen floors daily. I never interfered, feeling it would be wrong to deny him the chance of regaining his confidence in his own way.

Jack's flights became a matter of trial and error. From his perch he discovered, and remembered, where the nearest wall was and where the windowsill could be found. I saw him fly straight toward the side window, turn in midair before he could knock against it, lose height and land neatly on the floor, without having hit anything.

His nighttime perch, reached by climbing the nylon net curtains, was a wooden extension on the metal curtain rod in the dining room. Usually, however, he was too full of energy to settle down for sleep at once. He played what looked to us to be a little game. He turned around on the perch so that his tail was pressed uncomfortably against the wall behind him. Then he leaned toward the center of the room and launched himself into space. He would fly in a tight circle of about a yard in diameter, with his head just scraping the ceiling (to check that he wasn't losing altitude) and his feet stretched straight out from his body (an extraordinary position for flying which took hours of practice) until he landed firmly back on the perch again. Even when we had switched off the light and left the dining room, this was Jack's evening routine during winter.

When he had completed his little circles

for perhaps an hour he preened himself and went to sleep, as always, on one leg. My last duty of the day was to lay newspaper on the floor beneath him. Then I breathed a prayer for his welfare and climbed the stairs to my own roost.

Our cat was the first animal member of the household to have a part in Jack's life. From the beginning she was extremely curious, and we had to be vigilant in case the two met when no one was watching. As soon as Jack had gained strength and confidence I took him on my hand and let the cat sniff him face to face. Jack heard and sensed the danger. I felt him stiffen. He listened most carefully, then slowly he took aim with his beak—and caught Pussy a splendidly accurate blow on the nose!

From then on, the cat showed him great respect and Jack walked in safety. An unusual relationship—a friendship, almost—developed between them. The cat took to sleeping in a dining-room chair close to Jack's curtain rod. She opened her eyes in the morning to watch him eat breakfast, but that awful bird-hunting expression which can appear on a cat's face was entirely absent. If he fell to the floor after a bad takeoff she would crouch near him, aware of his plight, until rescue arrived.

Except for walks, Jack spent the daytime in our large wire-mesh aviary in the garden. To help him find his way around inside I arranged three perches, each diagonally above the other and of a different thickness. When I put him on the lowest perch he quickly scrambled to the others. But if I left him on the ground, his method of reaching a perch was at once ludicrous and amazing. He flew blindly into the wire mesh and clung there squawking and fluttering. Then he began to stretch out for a perch with his beak, then with one foot, then with

his tail, and as a last resort with his left wing.

His use of a wing as a "feeler" was the most extraordinary of all. He would arch the wing up, down and around until, with its long reach, the tip brushed a perch. This was all he wanted. Gingerly he eased himself along the wire, keeping the perch between a couple of wing-tip feathers (as if between two fingers) until he could lurch down to it. If the perch was above him, he used the wing to hoist himself up.

As long as Jack's dishes in the aviary were filled with fresh food and water he was all right, and I needed to talk to him only once or twice a day. Thus he became much less of a tie. When a sudden shrill call let me know that he was in trouble, I would drop everything and rush out to find him lost in a far corner, or wobbling dreadfully on a lump of loose brick, afraid to step off it.

Particularly heartening was Jack's acquaintance with his own species. Three pairs of jackdaws nesting in a nearby chapel spire began calling out when they flew overhead. Soon Jack was sending up an "All's well!" cry to them as they passed. One day he became excited because a lone jackdaw called. It didn't belong to the chapel group and must have been a female, traveling from territory to territory, looking for an unattached male. The two birds answered one another for some minutes. In jackdaw etiquette, it must have been Jack's duty to go to her, for he made desperate efforts to get out through the wire, scrambling all over it and pushing his beak in search of a hole large enough to take his body. She waited for him, then flew away. And Jack was left alone in his darkness once more. This was the only time I ever saw him try to escape.

The Ceylonese necklace dove and the stock dove in the aviary took little notice of Jack. The budgerigars, Binkie and Belinda, flew around wildly at his wing flapping at first but later lost their anxiety, and the trio grew attached to each other. On winter days Jack stood on the top perch, acting as a black bulwark against the cold wind. A bright green Binkie nestled close to him on one side, a pale blue Belinda kept warm on the other.

In mid-September we celebrated the end of Jack's first six months with us. It never occurred to me that we would be together as long as this. His ready acceptance of my care had far exceeded my expectations, but there were still occasions when he seemed unfriendly toward me. Sometimes it was because I had noisy shoes or wore a dress that rustled. At other times my thoughts were far away, perhaps in a turmoil over a domestic upset, and my movements were not as gentle as usual. Conscious of my state, he couldn't settle to feeding. He was fidgety and uneasy. Because my attempts to caress him had only made him thoroughly frightened, I avoided touching him on the body unnecessarily, although we all longed to express our affection for him in the way that humans do, by fondling and stroking.

However, after his feed one sunny day in October, I was seated on a log outside the aviary with him, and he became sleepy. Noting his lowered wings and fluffed head, I spoke very quietly indeed and scratched the soft feathers of his nape. He did not shoot up nervously this time, but fluffed his feathers a little more. When I continued the caress he gave a loud call—"Tchack!"—and lowered his head contentedly. This was yet another infinitely rewarding moment in my gentling of Jack.

I conceived the idea of encouraging him to fly at the end of a long piece of wool. Each time I threw him into the air he flew higher and more confidently, but the irritation of the wool around his legs made him frantic.

String was too heavy for him to manage when he was fifteen yards from me, and nylon fishing line, though virtually weightless, tangled too easily. After five attempts at tethered flying I gave up. Jack had to rely for exercise on his stationary flapping—a dangerous thing on windy days.

Once he was blown onto the high roof of the local undertakers'. They had to bring out their longest ladder and hold it while I climbed up and carried him down. Another afternoon he was swept into a tall willow and had to stay there all night, clinging to a twig in a savage storm. I really thought I had lost him.

I determined, therefore, to teach him to answer my call. So I placed him on the ground and walked away, calling. His uncertainty was pitiful. Having grown used to standing and waiting for *me* to approach *him,* he was totally bewildered. Eventually the significance of my continued calls seemed to get through to him: he took a wavering step toward me, then a tiny spurt of two steps. After a few more practice sessions we were able to keep contact through mutual calls—a vital precaution that was achieved none too soon.

At the end of our garden, just beyond the aviary, ran the river Wey. About fourteen feet wide at this point, it had always seemed such a friend before. In summer we rowed on it, searching for moorhens' nests. In the autumn its swollen waters yielded up posts and even whole trees which reduced our fuel bills. In winter it flooded and froze, turning the field on the far side into a giant skating rink. But from the moment Jack started using his wings the river filled me with fears. It was positively waiting for him.

Eventually, one November afternoon, the inevitable happened. Jack was suddenly filled with an overwhelming desire to fly. He fluttered up from my hand, crashed into the surgery wall and fell onto the aviary roof beneath. My daughter Frances, then aged ten, climbed up and took him on her hand. But the madness of freedom was upon Jack. After fluttering into a bed of stinging nettles, he lost his head completely and set out across the swiftly running river.

At my desperate call he made an effort to return. Unfortunately, I made the mistake of running toward him, and this made him think I was near enough for safety. He came down only a few feet from me—but in the river. Instantly he shot into the air again, and even in the anxiety of the moment I was thrilled to notice that he tucked his feet into his body and flew like a normal, sighted jackdaw. It was the first time we had seen him fly properly. Frances still remembers it with pleasure.

Jack circled over the water without touch-ing the trees or bushes on either bank, then lost his nerve. His head went up, his tail pointed downward, his feet threshed the air and again he fell into the river. I told Frances, "Run and fetch my landing net!"

I remained on the bank, calling and call-ing, simply begging Jack to come to me. By now he was about six feet from the bank, lying motionless with both wings and his tail fanned out to their fullest extent on top of the water. His head was upright, his neck well stretched. As the current carried him farther away from me I called again, in growing despair. Our dinghy was out of the river for the winter; I looked at the icy water. Dare I go in? I had just made my decision to jump after him, arthritis and all, when Jack flung his wings strongly down-ward and kicked his feet hard. This threw him forward, nearer the bank.

I called with increasing firmness. He repeated the action, again and again. And with this wonderful swimming movement of wings and feet he actually worked his way upstream, to only a yard from where I stood. Frances arrived panting with the net as I was kneeling in the mud to reach him. Frances and I were shaken for the rest of that day, and nine days elapsed before Jack ventured to flap his wings again in the open.

In 1963 we moved from Surrey to Ross-on-Wye, Herefordshire. Jack's new outdoor aviary was so sheltered that he no longer needed to be brought into the house at all, even in winter. A cold night left him with a delicate frosting of rime over his back, very lovely to look at.

By now the entire family agreed that of all the pets we had ever had, Jack was the best. The children were attracted by the beauty of his shape in repose, the thrill of his spread wings and his air of contentment. He never pecked at them, however clumsy they were with him, but readily accepted their proffered little hands when he was lost. He liked to perch on the arm of our younger daughter, Betsy, and listen knowingly as she chatted to him.

Jack was seldom ill. Once, though, he worried us by developing a bad cough, and the vet recommended cod-liver oil at night. Jack had different ideas and wouldn't open his beak. At long last I managed to get a teaspoon of oil into his mouth, but, unfortunately, in the concentration of coaxing him to open his beak I had opened my own mouth wide. Jack gave a huge sneeze—and the whole lot went down *my* throat.

The most common question asked by visitors was, "Can he talk?"

"No, thank goodness," I would reply and go on to explain my dislike of useless mimicry in birds.

But what I did endeavor to do was to understand Jack's noises and teach him to understand mine. We progressed far enough for a complete understanding in simple everyday matters. He put down his head when I said, "Have a drink?"; waited quietly with his beak open when I asked, "Mealworm?"; fiddled his beak around the food dish at "Have some bread?"; and if I murmured, "Poor Jack, poor Jack," he would nibble my thumb affectionately, or rub his head along my fingers.

Jack, for his part, had several calls in his vocabulary, but only two distinct ones: "Tchack!" and the squeaky twitter he made to keep others away from chosen perches. Thanks to his teaching, I developed an ear for the tiny variations in tone and volume which meant different things.

He used his "gentle" voice to a female one spring. He tried hard to bring her down to him, but being wild, she was afraid of the cage. Thereafter Jack occasionally honored me with this sound, and since it had previously been used only to a female of his species, I took it as a compliment.

His territory-claiming "Tchack!," vigorous in springtime, had a harsh tone and was evidently much respected, for no daws came near him when he was making it. And there was his questioning "Tchack?," with a slight rise at the end, used when he heard unfamiliar footsteps approaching, or when the door opened and no one spoke to him. His cheerful, light-toned "Tchack!," short and friendly, always returned my greeting of "Hello, Jack!"

I called, "Hello, Jack!" to him, as usual, on the morning of January 9, 1967. There was no answer. Jack, who had been with us for nine years, and was probably twelve years old—doubtless twice the life-span of a wild jackdaw—lay on the aviary floor on his side. We warmed him up, and he ate a few mealworms, but his movements were dull. His labored breathing told of a tired heart.

Brought indoors, he kept falling off his perch. Ten days later he was unable even to eat. His last pleasure gone, there was only one thing left to do. Frances tactfully stayed out of the way while I kept the promise I made to myself when Jack was brought to me. I placed him in a large, soft polyethylene bag, together with a pad of cotton wool soaked in chloroform.

For months afterward the silence was heartbreaking. No bright "Tchack!" greeted my every coming and going; no Jack leaped about on his perch flapping his wings, opening his beak and sighing, "A-a-ah!" as I took him on my hand. I had no one to run to with juicy grubs found during gardening.

I keep among my most treasured possessions, though, a small bunch of feathers I removed from Jack's body. Their beautiful silkenness makes me think of Jack's woebegotten state when he first came to us. It also makes me wonder if we are often too eager to destroy creatures that may be injured. For all such unfortunates I make a plea for mercy. They are well worth saving —and the reward of trust and gratitude more than repays the trouble taken. This was abundantly true with Jack. The call of a jackdaw will mean something special to me for the rest of my life.

The Life and Love of Ivan the Terrible

by LESLIE T. WHITE

I FIRST MET him on a jungle trail in Brazil. He was in an argument with a native, and his temper fascinated me. Swelled up in barrel-chested majesty, his tiny yellow eyes ablaze with fury, he was fulminating at the top of his lungs. But the odds were against him, for he weighed a total of only three ounces. I interceded and, upon the transfer of fifty cents, became the custodian of Ivan the Terrible.

He was not grateful; he acted as if I had cheated him of a victim, and proceeded to give me a piece of his mind. Then his temper subsided and he went to sleep in my pocket. I sawed a coconut shell in half to make a house for him and took him back to the ship on which I was to return to the United States.

Ivan is a *saguim de noite,* a nocturnal monkey—a species of small marmoset. On his forehead is a luminous white fur that, in the darkness, lures moths and bugs, which he captures with bewildering rapidity. He is three and a half inches tall, with a tiny human face and hands, a brown-and-yellow squirrel-like body and a long, furry tail. His temperament is warm and sentimental when he has his way, but when crossed he will fly into a temper—which, however, quickly burns itself out.

Raising him was a matter of trial and error. At the first port I purchased a doll's milk bottle with a rubber nipple; Ivan handled it like a veteran tippler. One of the women on board knitted him a tiny turtle-neck sweater that made him look like a midget prizefighter. In his personal habits he was unbelievably clean. Ivan's intelligence amazed me. Once I left him in his cage in a too strong sun; upon returning I found that he had rigged a shade with his blanket. When I removed the blanket, Ivan promptly replaced it.

Home in California I built him an ornate little cage, painted red and yellow and fashioned like a circus wagon, about three feet long and two feet high. The ends were glassed, the back was hinged as a door and

265

the front was covered with wire mesh. His bedroom was a small cigar box, over which I installed a bed lamp with a 25-watt bulb to heat the cage at an even temperature. His coconut shell was suspended from the ceiling, and there were swings, dangling bells and a trapeze. Ivan loves civilization. One of his major thrills is traveling by automobile. We hang his coconut shell from the windshield mirror and in this vantage point he surveys the countryside. He chatters excitedly like a small boy when something unusual catches his attention.

He has come to adore the American breakfast. He demands his orange juice immediately on rising although his *pièce de résistance* consists of three mealy worms. He now weighs over five ounces. He is the most fastidious animal I have ever seen. He will take a whole grape in his little mouth, then tilt his head back and squeeze all the juice out of it, rather than get his hands sticky and soiled.

We thought that Ivan was destined to go through life a bachelor, but a friend of mine in Rio sent me a tiny female *saguim,* and romance entered the life of Ivan the Terrible. Tonita, an incredibly tiny little hoyden, was only about half the size of Ivan. We gave her liquid vitamins and exercised her

by forcing her to climb a walking stick. I did not think it wise to put her in with Ivan until she was larger, but one day I held her up to the glassed end of his cage so that he might see her. At first he turned away, thinking that it was just another mirror trick, but when she spoke, he nearly fell off his trapeze. His obvious excitement made me fear for her safety, so we postponed the "wedding" for a while. Eventually we built her weight up to three ounces.

Meanwhile, Ivan was consumed with curiosity and desire. He would pace his cage, swelling his chest like a miniature gorilla. Tonita thought him magnificent, and whenever we turned her loose she headed for his cage. But every time Ivan found her looking at him, he'd turn his head away just to show her that he didn't care. Yet when she wasn't watching, he'd follow her every movement. Finally we set the date for the marriage. I built them a tiny ivory-colored cottage, trimmed with blue, to go in the cage. My wife presented a pair of small pink blankets as a wedding gift.

Knowing Ivan's volatile nature, I was apprehensive for Tonita, and when I steered her into his lair I wore leather gloves so that I might rescue her if Ivan lost his head. Ivan's teeth are something to reckon with. Ivan, the little dope, took one look at the lady, then his courage evaporated; before I could close the door of the cage he dived outside and ran all over the house, while the tiny bride looked hurt and bewildered. When we put Ivan back in his cage he was completely embarrassed and walked around in a daze. Tonita, evidently a female of experience, took the initiative. Boldly cornering Ivan, she grabbed him securely by his ears and kissed him hard.

Ivan was stunned. Tonita stroked him and tried to be affectionate, but the reluctant bridegroom climbed to a corner of his screen and stared indifferently into space. That evening I put their bright new cottage into the cage. Tonita was bewitched by the splendor, and promptly climbed inside. After a brief examination she stuck her head out the door and called to Ivan, but the little ninny was afraid to go in with her. When he finally peeked inside, Tonita grabbed him and kissed him. He nearly swooned and raced to a corner. She remained in the cottage cooing at him and acting coy. Disgusted with Ivan, my wife and I went to a movie. When we came home I raised the removable top of their cottage and peered in. They were cuddled up together for the night. On Tonita's ugly little face was an expression of smug content.

Now that marriage was an established fact, Tonita set out to show Ivan who was boss. We could no longer talk to Ivan without her crowding him aside and giving us an argument. She never stopped talking. She took the food out of his mouth; she made him go to bed and rise on command. A mere male, caged with this vitriolic, blowtorch amazon, Ivan had no chance. He became a pocket Mr. Milquetoast. Yet he thrived on it.

Promptly after dinner each evening Tonita would retire alone into their cottage and pull the blankets over the door. For an hour she would remain in privacy. What she did in there we shall never know, but it reminded me of a woman retiring to remove her makeup. Eventually, she would brush aside the blanket and summon Ivan. He would bound inside and the blanket would cover the door for the night. To aid him regain his old independence I would take him out of the cage, leaving Tonita penned up, but he kept glancing nervously toward the cage as if wondering if he was going to catch hell when he got home, and soon headed back to his wife.

At last Tonita was going to become a

mother. Ivan knew it, too, for he began to worry if she was out of his sight for a moment. They would sit together atop their tiny cottage in the sun and he would comb her soft fur by the hour. He became particularly solicitous about her teeth. Every so often, he would tilt her head back so that the light was just right, open her mouth and peer intently inside. As gestation progressed, Tonita became ravenous and irascible, demanding her food in shrill, querulous tones. Several times she bit my hand when I was slow to place her dish within her cage, but immediately afterward she would be sorry. Then she would climb up her bar and make a funny little grimace of apology, or else chatter out a justification of her act. During this period Ivan gave her first chance at all the food, even to his beloved worms.

Toward the last they spent endless hours with their heads together, chattering softly, and if either got out of sight of the other there was much anxious whistling back and forth. Her cantankerousness faded, and she became sweetly mellow. We cannot know what dreams and ambitions these tiny atoms had, but it seems to me the rankest human conceit to think that they could not dream.

Unfortunately my wife and I were out of town when the tragedy struck. One morning when my aunt came in to give them breakfast, Tonita lay sick on the floor outside her cottage. Ivan was distraught, and when an attempt was made to remove Tonita, he attacked savagely. Finally, by wrapping an arm with a heavy cloth, my aunt was able to lift her out. Ivan hurled himself against the wire in a frenzy, so she laid Tonita on a blanket close by where he could watch her. A drop of whiskey and water perked the tiny monkey momentarily, but she grew steadily weaker and died. So fell the tiniest star in my firmament.

For a while Ivan was completely lost. Sometimes he would give a shrill, eerie wail, as if trying to call into the Beyond. Always he watched the door, hoping to see her scamper in with that funny little crabwise movement she had. He would stay up nights, a bewildered expression on his tragic face, dreading to retire, and it was heartrending to see him crawl alone into their little cottage. I took him out for romps, but he no longer cared to play. Instead, he would crawl down inside my shirt, and I could feel his tiny heart beating against my own.

Now that he is at last reconciled to the fact that Tonita is gone forever, he has transferred the bulk of his affections to my wife. She has taught him to blow kisses at her, but he won't do it when I'm around. If she kisses me, he turns his back and sulks in jealousy. He considers me his rival. He's a great little guy, Ivan the Terrible.

Old Dog by WILLIAM BRANDON

OLD DOG was a neighbor of ours when I was a small boy growing up on a ranch in New Mexico. He was a Russian wolfhound, or Borzoi, and he belonged to my friend Juan Izquierdo, who lived down the road from us.

Russian wolfhounds, long nosed, graceful, superbly elegant, are the aristocrats of the dog world, but Old Dog was the sorriest Russian wolfhound in existence. His coat was ragged and shaggy; he had cauliflower ears; he limped on one leg or another—it was immaterial to him which one; and the only thing he had any real enthusiasm for was sleeping. He would come with Juan to our place, collapse like a dropped rug and sleep until Juan shook him awake to go home. Then he would clamber to his feet and limp away, leaning against his owner so he wouldn't fall over.

Old Dog thought a great deal of Juan. He wouldn't wake up and move for anyone else. If you wanted him out of the way you practically had to pick him up and carry him—a job for a man and a boy, since he weighed close to a hundred pounds. As for Juan, he loved Old Dog more than anything in the world. Juan had no brothers or sisters, and there was a lot of trouble at his house. Except for Old Dog he felt pretty much alone.

Ironically, the unpleasant atmosphere at home was caused mainly by arguments about how Juan should be brought up. Mr. Izquierdo's mother-in-law, a leathery, angry-eyed little woman who spoke only Spanish, lived with the family, and she and Mr. Izquierdo had furious encounters over such questions as whether Juan should go to Sunday school or church; whether he should be forced to eat something he didn't like; what chores he should do.

One day Mr. Izquierdo said to my mother desperately, with tears in his eyes, "I tell her she raised her kids, now let us raise ours!" The result was that Juan didn't get much raising at all. Mrs. Izquierdo pitched into the fights too, sometimes on her mother's side, sometimes on her husband's, and sometimes from a new direction altogether—and all three gave scant thought to Juan in the process of quarreling over him.

Old Dog was undoubtedly the only reason Juan didn't run away. Juan used to say that he would like to cross the mountains and get a job over on the Pecos wrangling horses, but obviously Old Dog was too old and sleepy to run away with him, so he couldn't go. On the other hand, there was one thing that Juan's father, mother and grandmother were agreed on—they didn't like Old Dog. He was a nuisance: He was always in every-

269

body's way, and there was the extra expense of food for him. The Izquierdos were poor, and Old Dog ate as much as two people.

All these troubles simmered and boiled for a long time, and then one winter day they exploded. Juan had been sick with a cold and fever. Mr. Izquierdo had brought out the doctor, while his mother-in-law had taken all the correct precautions against the malevolence of *brujas*—witches. The older country people still clung to many such superstitions. Mr. Izquierdo himself took witches seriously enough to wrangle with his mother-in-law about the proper way to fling salt strategically here and there, and when she happened to find one of the little creatures called Child-of-the-Earth, a particularly dread omen, Mr. Izquierdo threw salt on *her,* as if she herself might be a *bruja*—which sent her into an almost hysterical rage.

The doctor said Juan would have to stay in bed—there was danger of pneumonia. And it was while he was lying there helpless that Juan's parents and grandmother decided to get rid of Old Dog. With all the worry about Juan and the expense of the doctor, Old Dog's presence in the house had finally become unbearable.

It was a leaden day, with a booming northwest wind and occasional rain and spitting snow, and Mr. Izquierdo's truck got stuck in the mud, going past our place. He had to confess why Old Dog was with him in the truck, away from Juan's side for the first time in years. Mr. Izquierdo was taking him to a friend who ran a gun club. The friend would do away with Old Dog. Mr. Izquierdo was shamefaced and defiant at the same time. He said over and over, with a sort of despair, "We got to, we got to. We'll all go crazy. We got to."

It seemed monstrous to us. After he had freed his truck and gone on, my mother had to restrain me from going down the road and

telling Juan what was happening. Here was real tragedy. What would Juan do when he found Old Dog gone?

I never did know who told Juan. Maybe he overheard something—or maybe he only sensed it. In any case he found out, and when Mr. Izquierdo came back in his empty truck, Juan had disappeared.

Mrs. Izquierdo ran all the way to our place. She arrived almost fainting from lack of breath. "Juanito! Juanito! Juanito is out in the rain!"

We all roared down the road to the Izquierdos' in our old Dodge. The grandmother was prostrate on the floor in Juan's room, sobbing, her outstretched arms rigid and quivering. Juan's window was wide open.

We learned that Mr. Izquierdo had gone out toward the foothills, looking for Juan. Then we went back to our place, and Mother telephoned the doctor and the sheriff. I caught up my horse, Buddy, and rode out on the mesa, but I didn't see anything of Juan. On the way back, I saw Mr. Izquierdo racing down the road in his truck, slueing wildly on the turns, the rear wheels throwing fountains of wet sand.

The doctor appeared a little later, with a deputy sheriff and an Indian to constitute a search party. Everyone drove down to the Izquierdo place, and soon Mr. Izquierdo returned in his truck. Old Dog was with him, sound asleep. Mr. Izquierdo explained that his friend at the gun club had not been home when he had left Old Dog there, and so Old Dog was still living. Mr. Izquierdo was excessively calm and very gentle. He spoke so softly you could scarcely hear him, but his eyes crackled like electricity. The doctor went to his car and came back with a bottle and said, "Take a long drink." Mr. Izquierdo said, "Thank you," his voice breaking. Then he picked up Old Dog and carried him into Juan's room.

Old Dog woke up and got to his feet and tottered to the empty bed. Everyone watched him. It was amazing for him to wake up without Juan calling him. He put his chin on the edge of the bed and whined. Mrs. Izquierdo buried her face in her hands.

Suddenly Mr. Izquierdo said, "Old Dog, where's Juanito? Find Juanito!"

Old Dog blundered excitedly here and there. The deputy sheriff said, "Wouldn't any dog have much nose with all this rain."

"It hasn't rained since noon," the doctor pointed out.

The Indian, a little, stump-legged old man, stepped forward and grasped Old Dog by the scruff of the neck and dragged him to the window, picked him up and dumped him out, and climbed out after him. Everyone else charged out the door and around the house. The Indian, his hand on Old Dog's shoulder, was already moving away through the mesquite. Old Dog's nose was to the ground. He began to run, a remarkable sight, and immediately fell down like a tumbleweed hitting a fence. The Indian set him on his feet again and ran beside him, holding the hair of his neck.

It was late afternoon by then and almost dark, and the mountains Juan had said he would cross looked high and black in the eastern sky, and a long way off. Old Dog and the Indian reached the first manzanita-dotted foothills. The rest of us followed, running as hard as we could. The Indian and Old Dog disappeared into a wash, and when we came up they were standing beside Juan, who lay asleep under a sheltering overhang of rock. He woke up and gazed at us in astonishment. Then he saw Old Dog and remembered what had happened, but he didn't say a word.

The doctor was the only one who had thought to bring a blanket. Mr. Izquierdo said, whispering for some reason, although Juan was wide-awake in Mrs. Izquierdo's arms, "He's all wet."

"Sweat," the doctor said. "It might be good for him."

The next day I left with my family for a visit with friends in the East, and didn't hear the rest of the story until weeks later. When we returned, we found Juan and Old Dog constant companions as before, and a great change in the Izquierdo family. They lived together without a whisper of dissension. Mr. Izquierdo was always polite to his mother-in-law, and she was very polite to everyone, and they never argued about anything. A miracle, everyone said. But Juan told us the truth. They believed Old Dog was a *bruja*, he said, and they knew they had to behave scrupulously to conciliate him.

For they had discovered, when Old Dog was searching for Juan, something Juan had known and kept secret for a long time. Old Dog was blind.

"The Mink's in the Sink!"

by IRVING PETITE

O N A RAINY June day I was helping a friend roof his ranch house in the Cascade Mountain foothills southeast of Seattle. Suddenly, over the noise of tack-driving and the steady drone of rain, I heard a squeaking scream of enraged bafflement. Peering down at the ground, I saw a humped-up gob of animated gray-brown fur doing a jitterbug step in the curtain of water falling from the roof's edge.

I backed down the ladder for a closer view. The bedraggled little animal had the size and, approximately, the slender shape of a gray squirrel, but with an extra little hump on its rear. Fur-drenched and soul-wrenched, it glared up at me, its wails interspersed with a high-pitched bark-squeak of fright or warning. Water got into its eyes. It pivoted to face the basement wall, screeching even louder and continuing its jig step under the cold shower—seemingly hypnotized by the drip and unable to leave.

"It's a baby mink," said my friend, "and only a female could make so much noise." Then and there we named her Mademoiselle.

I found an empty cardboard box and edged it under the skittering feet; even while being slipped inside, the little waif kept yowling. But finally, in an old toolbox with a scrap of carpet for a lining, and the lid down, the voice quieted. An odor took its place—a musty-musky smell, like the scent of toadstools in the leaf mold in the woods. The scent was an indication of Mademoiselle's fear, one of the few times in our long association that she showed any sign of fear (though later, occasionally, she did odorize rage). We estimated her age at four to six weeks, but she was about three-fifths her adult size. I took her home to get acquainted.

Mink are numerous in the swamps and along the streams of Washington. In one recent season, 6571 wild mink were taken by trappers; the pelts were worth more than $100,000. In addition, there are about three hundred mink ranches in the state. But Mademoiselle was destined to be perhaps the first mink to share a human being's home. I arranged temporary outdoor quarters for her, a large cage screened across the front. It was carpeted with layers of newspaper and fresh hay; there were drinking facilities and, for a den, a two-foot length of black pipe, some two and a half inches in diameter.

As her water-plastered fur dried off, there emerged from the bedraggled chrysalis of distraught infanthood a slim, lithe creature, more a lustrous russet-brown than gray, with an obsidian-eyed, delicately bewhiskered pixie face. She was eight inches long, including tail. When she made a circling climb on the front wire, a whitewash of short fur flashed under her throat. Her legs were short, her hind feet slightly webbed between the toes. When I opened the door and offered a slice of fresh salmon, Mademoiselle came for it in a rush, her mouth wide open, showing teeth as white as quartz sand. She gave a sharp yelp, grabbed the fish ungraciously and rushed behind the hay. Her trauma had not affected her appetite.

The following morning she seemed to have disappeared, but she had only tunneled under the newspapers. At the sound of my voice she thrust her head up, like a sleek periscope, in a far corner; then, a second later—quicker than sound—she popped out of the tunnel about an inch from me. And yelped! It sounded like "Where's breakfast?"

When one sees mink in the wild or in zoos, they are silent and seem almost sinister, like their cousin the weasel. But Mademoiselle, at close quarters, had many voices. A "thanks" for food was a prolonged *his-s-s-s*, with mouth wide open. Most common was her "yeak!," a scream which sounded throat-shattering for such a small creature. This voice she used for warnings, greetings or demands. Whenever a car drove up she would "yeak!" to challenge it. Or any domestic animal, from cat to horse, set off the cry.

The dogs were fascinated, Bozo especially. He and Mademoiselle would regard each other for long intervals in utter silence, but his first move would bring out a "yeak!" from her. Once he leaned against the screening and came away with his ear bleeding profusely where Mademoiselle had punctured it with her needle-like incisors. She did not attack humans, however; a fingertip held out to her received a quick gumming; then she would rush away, turn, and screech.

In order to observe her more closely, I trapped Mademoiselle in the pipe and brought her into the house to live. Her favorite places, quickly discovered, were—as befits a mink—the watering spots and cool, dark hidey-holes.

She took a sensuous delight in water, and a sink was always left full of clean water for her. A young visitor once put two orphan ducklings into the sink, then a minute later called in panic: "Come here quick! The mink's in the sink!"

Mademoiselle was indeed sharing her pool with the ducklings. She swam circles around them, a brown back and trailing tail slueing through the water. The ducklings bobbed in the middle like plastic toys. They made muted quackings while Mademoiselle, silent for once, enjoyed herself. Had she been hungrier or better trained as a huntress, she might have made a grab for the duck feet. But she didn't.

Mademoiselle slept for hours during the day. The night was her time to howl. Or to bowl. One of the first nights she was in the house I was abruptly awakened by a sound of rattling and rolling. I went to the bathroom door and flicked the switch. Mademoiselle, a front paw raised, was cuffing at one of the half-round porcelain knobs that cover bolt tops at the base of a bathroom fixture. The other knobs lay scattered about her on the floor. For an hour or more, that night and many nights thereafter, she continued "setting 'em up in the other alley."

I awoke one night about 3 a.m. with the uneasy sense of being watched. As I opened one eye, I looked directly into the black eyes and long, silky whiskers of Mademoiselle, who was regarding me intently from the other side of the pillow.

When guests were expected at the house, Mademoiselle was removed to her outdoor quarters. To catch and transport her I used a live trap. Such a trap has two compartments, one with a funnel-like hole which the animal enters. To get at the bait in the second section, he must push a small, sloping door, which drops under his weight and then is pulled shut by a spring. But Mademoiselle had the highest "trap IQ" of any animal I've known. The first time she was trapped it took her only three minutes to let herself out. Then she went in again, just to prove she could leave when she chose. (Besides, she loved small openings.) Though she let me carry her in the trap, she would sometimes go blithely in and out the door as we moved from one place to another.

Sometimes her outside-cage door was left open by a stranger, and sometimes the house door was left open. But though Mademoiselle was free to go, she remained near home base and would always willingly hump back into whichever home she was occupying at the moment. Come fall, I moved her cage down to the lowlands of the ranch, within a few feet of the stream—natural mink territory. She seemed to be intrigued by the running water, which has a different face and a different singing for every hour of the year.

It was on an October day that Mademoiselle was released to real freedom—a day when the red squirrel paused, head down, upon the lichen-silvered maple-tree bark, caught in an autumn dream, and the great blue heron lifted from the swamp, his wings ghostly and winter-presaging even at midday. This time she did not return to the cage. When I opened the door, she left, and I watched her slipping and sliding, gleefully splashing downstream—tasting, exploring, scenting. Seeking her own kind.

Nearly seven months passed before I saw Mademoiselle again. One May evening, when I was doing chores in the barn, a dark shape humped across the corner of the last of the hay. My heart leaped, for it looked like Mademoiselle's gait. Then I knew that it was Mademoiselle—she "yeaked" at me once, and disappeared beneath the hayloft floor. I took a mirror and flashlight and looked into her tunnel. There were four little-finger-size minklets in a grassy nest. They were nearly as naked and wiggly as baby mice, and Mademoiselle—certainly Madame now—stood this side of them, her pink-lined mouth open wide enough to swallow me.

Except for offerings of fresh fish, and a pan of milk after each milking, I left her alone. One mink bowling in the bathroom had been enough; I didn't need a team.

LIVING FREE

Condensed from the book

by JOY ADAMSON

For five anxious and exciting months now we had known that Elsa was pregnant. My husband, George, and I had raised her from a cub and returned her to the wilds only when she was grown, an affectionate and sometimes embarrassingly playful three-hundred-pound lioness. We knew the adjustment would be difficult, and to wean her of dependence on us we had released her a hundred and fifty miles from our home in Isiolo (from which George operates as senior game warden in the Northern Frontier Province of Kenya) and had tried not to interfere with her new life.

But according to jungle belief, a pregnant lioness who is handicapped in hunting by her condition is helped by one or two other lionesses who act as "aunts." And since poor Elsa had no aunts, we felt it was our job to replace them. So we established a herd of goats at the nearest game post and periodically put out a freshly killed carcass where Elsa could find it. She accepted this cafeteria service and in return often visited George and me in camp, stretching out on my camp bed as if she thought it the only suitable place for an expectant mother.

Like all expectant mothers, however, she was unpredictable. As her time approached, late in December, Elsa disappeared altogether, and we could find no trace of her. Had something bad happened? We were worried, the more so because we had just experienced another tragedy of the wild.

A few weeks earlier George had rescued and brought home a baby elephant that had fallen into a well. We called him Pampo, found him a most engaging creature, and fed him two gallons of milk a day, fortified with cod-liver oil and glucose. But we knew it would be difficult to rear him, since there is no substitute for elephant milk, which is richer than any other.

Housekeeping for two animals a hundred and fifty miles apart was a problem, but luckily a woman friend who is a great animal lover offered to act as an elephant-sitter. After returning from a visit of several days in Elsa's territory we were delighted to find Pampo well, though nervous because of the many admirers he had attracted. Strangers seemed to make him uneasy, but as soon as he and I were alone he trustfully moved his body against mine and went to sleep. Plainly this contact gave him a sense of security.

But when next we returned home after an extended stay in camp, I was horrified at Pampo's appearance. His face had fallen in alarmingly, especially around the eyes, and as he dragged himself up to us his bones stuck out. His milk consumption had suddenly fallen way off, my sitter friend said, which she first thought due to teething pains since he kept rubbing his gums against anything he could find. When his condition grew steadily worse she had called in the vet, who put Pampo on glucose and water only and treated him with a sulfa drug.

Pampo got weaker day by day, however, and a few days after our return he died very peacefully, leaning his head against me. I loved the little elephant and it was sad to lose him, but a postmortem showed both pneumonia and diseased intestines; we could not have hoped to save him.

It was with a heavy heart that, on Christmas morning, we went in search of Elsa. It was now five days since she had visited us, and on that occasion she was already moaning in the first pangs of labor. We believed that she must have given birth on the night of the twentieth, but we had not seen her

since. After hours of fruitless tracking we sat down in the shade of an overhanging rock and discussed her possible fate. We were depressed, and even Nuru and Makedde, the two Africans who were with us, spoke in subdued voices.

At midday we returned to camp and began a gloomy and silent Christmas dinner. Suddenly there was a swift movement, and before I could take in what was happening Elsa was between us, sweeping everything off the table, knocking us to the ground, sitting on us and overwhelming us with joy and affection.

Her figure was normal again, and she looked superbly fit. We gave her some meat, which she ate immediately. Meanwhile, we discussed many questions. Why had she come to visit us during the hottest part of the day, a time when normally she would never move? Had she chosen it deliberately as the safest time to leave the cubs, since few predators would be on the prowl in such heat? Or had she heard the shot when George had fired at a particularly aggressive cobra that morning, and taken it as a signal to her? Had the cubs died? And, whatever had happened, why had she waited for five days before coming to us for food?

After she had had a good meal and drunk some water she came and rubbed her head affectionately against us, walked about thirty yards down the river, lay down and had a doze. We left her alone, so that she would feel at ease. When I looked for her at teatime she had gone.

After this, Elsa often visited us in the afternoon. Each time she ate heartily, and sometimes hopped on the roof of the Land-Rover or rested in its shade. She seemed in no hurry to get back to her cubs and stayed until we were troubled by her neglect. When we tried to get her to leave by walking along the path on which she had come, she accompanied us nervously, but kept turning back toward camp. Only when it was completely dark would she slip away.

One evening when I saw her sneak into the bush upstream, I followed. Obviously she did not wish to be observed, for when she caught my scent she pretended to sharpen her claws on a tree. Then as soon as I turned my back, she jumped at me and knocked me over, as though to say, "That's for spying on me!" Now it was my turn to pretend that I had come only to bring more meat to her. She accepted my excuse, followed me to the carcass and began eating. But after this nothing would induce her to return to the cubs until long after dark, when she felt certain I would not follow.

We worried about her family, for zoo authorities had told us that the offspring of hand-reared lionesses often fail to live. Feeling that we must check on the cubs and rescue them if necessary, we set out early one morning and followed Elsa's spoor. It led us to a big rock that formed a landmark for what seemed to us an ideal lion home. Very large boulders gave complete shelter, and these in turn were surrounded by almost impenetrable bush.

We made straight for the topmost boulder and from it tried to look down into the center of the "den." We could see nothing. Then, suddenly, out of a cluster of bush only twenty yards away, a lioness appeared. It was Elsa. She seemed shocked at seeing us, looked at us silently and remained very still, as though hoping we would not come nearer. She moved slowly back toward the bush and stood for about five minutes with her back toward us, listening intently for any sound from the thicket. Then she sat down, still with her back to us. It was as though she were saying, "Here my private world begins, and you must not trespass." It was a digni-

fied demonstration, and no words could have conveyed her wishes more clearly. We withdrew as quietly as we could.

Despite this rebuff, we decided to take Elsa's meals to her, so as to reduce the time she had to spend away from her cubs. During the following days I left food near her supposed nursery. Whenever I met Elsa on these occasions, she took great pains to conceal the whereabouts of her lie-up, often doubling back artfully on her tracks.

One afternoon when I was passing at some distance from the big rock, I saw standing on it a large animal which I could not identify, and when it saw me it sneaked off; but it had obviously spotted the cubs, and I was much alarmed. After this, I determined to find and see about them in spite of Elsa's disapproval.

On the following afternoon, accompanied by our personal servant, the *toto*—the word simply means "boy" in Swahili—I climbed the big rock, calling repeatedly to warn Elsa of our approach. She did not answer. When we reached the top we stood on the edge of the cliff and raked the bush below with field glasses. There was no sign of her, though the place had the look of a well-used nursery.

As I was concentrating on examining the bush below us, I suddenly became aware of a strange feeling of danger. I dropped my field glasses, turned and saw Elsa creeping up behind the toto. I had just time to shout a warning to him before she knocked him down. She had crept up the rock behind us quite silently, and the toto missed toppling over the cliff by only a hairbreadth. Next, Elsa walked over to me and knocked me down, too. It was done in a friendly way, but it was obvious that she was expressing annoyance at finding us so close to her cubs.

Then she walked slowly along the crest of the rock, from time to time looking back over her shoulder to make sure we were following her. Silently she led us to the far end of the ridge, down into the bush, through thorny thickets and finally back to the road. She had made a wide detour, bypassing the lie-up completely.

When we walked together I usually patted Elsa occasionally, and she liked it, but today she would not allow me to touch her and made it clear that I was in disgrace. After we had got back to camp, even when she was eating her dinner on the roof of the car, whenever I came near she turned away. She did not return to her lair until it was dark.

It was George who first spied out Elsa's family. Silently peeping over the big rock one day, he saw Elsa below suckling two cubs. Her head was hidden by an over-hanging rock, and he went away quickly before she saw him. Again on the afternoon of January 14, while Elsa was visiting our camp, George slipped away and climbed to a vantage point from which he could see the cubs. There were three of them. Two were asleep, but the third was chewing at a sansevieria plant. The cub looked up with eyes that were blurred, bluish and apparently still unfocused. As George was taking photographs, the two sleeping cubs woke up and crawled about. They seemed perfectly healthy.

One afternoon two weeks later Elsa her-self brought the cubs out to show us. I was writing in my improvised camp studio when the toto came running to tell me that she was calling very strangely from across the river. I went upstream, following the sound, till I broke through the undergrowth at a fairly wide sandbank.

Suddenly I stopped, unable to believe my eyes. There was Elsa standing within a few yards of me, one cub near her, a second just emerging from the water, the third still on the far bank, pacing to and fro and calling piteously. Elsa looked fixedly at me,

her expression a mixture of pride and embarrassment.

I remained absolutely still while she moaned gently to her young—it sounded like "M-hm, m-hm." She walked up to the cub which was now on shore, licked it affection-ately, then turned back to swim across to the youngster stranded on the far bank. The two cubs with her followed immediately, swim-ming bravely through the deep water, and soon the family was reunited on the other shore. Elsa rested under a fig tree that grew out of some rocks, her golden coat showing up vividly against the dark-green foliage and the silver-gray boulders. The cubs hid, peeping at me through the undergrowth; but soon curiosity conquered their shyness and they came out into the open and stared inquisitively. Elsa "M-hm, m-hm'd" reassur-ingly, and they climbed onto her back and tried to catch her switching tail.

I had sent the toto back to fetch Elsa's food. When he arrived with it, she swam across quickly and settled down to her meal. One plucky chap swam over with her, but now started back to join the other cubs. As soon as Elsa saw it swimming out of its depth, she plunged into the river, grabbed its head in her mouth and ducked it thor-oughly, as a lesson not to be too venture-some. Then she brought it to our bank, still dangling from her mouth. A second cub plucked up courage and swam across, its tiny head just visible above the water, but the third timidly stayed on the far bank.

Elsa came up to me and rolled on her back as if to show her cubs that I was part of the pride. Reassured, the two cubs crept cautiously closer, their large expressive eyes watching Elsa's every movement and mine. Soon they were within three feet, and I found it difficult not to lean forward and touch them. But a zoologist had warned: never touch cubs unless they take the initiative. Meanwhile, the third cub kept up a pathetic meowing from the far bank. Finally its distress moved Elsa to go back to it, and she was accompanied by the two bold ones, which seemed to enjoy swimming.

I watched for about an hour as they all played together on the opposite bank. Elsa licked the cubs affectionately, talked to them in her soft, moaning voice, never let them out of her sight and quickly brought back any cub that ventured too far away. Then I called to Elsa. She replied and again started to swim across. This time all three cubs came with her.

On landing, she licked each cub in turn, then walked over and rubbed herself gently against me. To show the cubs that we were friends she rolled in the sand, licked my face and finally hugged me. They watched from a distance, interested but puzzled, and determined to stay out of reach. Next Elsa went back to the carcass the toto had brought and started eating, while the youngsters licked the skin and tore at it, somersaulting over it excitedly. It was probably their first encounter with a "kill."

They seemed about six weeks old. They were in excellent condition and though their eyes had a bluish film they could certainly see perfectly. I could not tell their sex, but I noticed that the cub with the lightest coat was much livelier and more inquisitive than the other two and especially devoted to its mother. It always cuddled up close to her and embraced her with its little paws. She was gentle and patient with all of them and allowed them to crawl all over her and chew her ears and tail. When it became dark Elsa listened attentively and then took the cubs a few yards into the bush. A few moments later I heard the sound of suckling.

I returned to camp—only to find Elsa and the cubs already waiting there for me. She followed me into my tent, flung herself on the ground and called to the cubs to join her. But they remained outside meowing; soon she went back to them, and so did I. We all sat together on the grass, and Elsa again began to suckle her family, meanwhile leaning against me and hugging me with one paw. Motherhood had left her as trusting as ever, and she clearly wanted me to share her happiness. I felt very humble.

Four days later George and I tried to make a return call, but Elsa obviously saw a difference between bringing the cubs to see us and our visiting them. As we neared her lie-up, talking loudly to herald our approach, Elsa suddenly emerged and stood gazing at us. There was no welcome in her greeting, and as we started forward she sat down abruptly, flattening her ears. Plainly we were not to come any nearer. We respected her wishes; we knew a lion "on guard" when we saw one.

On her visits to camp, however, Elsa was as affectionate as ever, though perhaps less playful than before the advent of motherhood. She was also less friendly with the Africans. If Nuru or Makedde approached the cubs, she flattened her ears and watched apprehensively through half-closed eyes. Me she trusted completely, and gave proof of it by sometimes leaving the cubs in my charge when she went to the river to drink. She demonstrated her affection for George by going into his tent, especially when it rained, and lying on his bed. Safe inside, she would call to the cubs to join her, but only the smallest was brave enough to accept. The other two stood shivering outside, their inbred fear of man evidently so great that they preferred the misery of the cold rain.

In time we learned that two of the cubs were male, one female. The Africans began calling the bold, plucky little fellow Jespah, a name which they said came from the Bible

(apparently after Jephthah, which means "God sets free"—a very appropriate name indeed). We called Jespah's brother Gopa, which in Swahili means "timid," and his sister Little Elsa.

Jespah was much the lightest in color, was perfectly proportioned and had a pointed nose and eyes so acutely slanted that they gave his sensitive face a slightly Mongolian cast. He was not only the most nonchalant, daring and inquisitive, but also the most affectionate. He followed his mother everywhere like a shadow.

Timid brother Gopa was equally engaging; he had dark markings on his forehead, but his eyes, instead of being bright and open like Jespah's, were rather clouded and squinty. His legs were short, and he was so potbellied that I once feared he might have a rupture. He was by no means stupid, but took a long time to make up his mind.

Little Elsa fitted her name, for she was a duplicate of her mother at the same age. She had the same expression, the same markings, the same slender build. Her behavior was so like Elsa's that we hoped she would develop the same lovable character. She was, of course, at a physical disadvantage compared to her two brothers, but she used cunning to restore the balance.

In the late afternoon the cubs' favorite playground was near a palm tree which had fallen at the edge of the riverbank. Here we took many pictures of them playing king-of-the-castle or wrestling over a stick. At times they played hide-and-seek and "ambushes." Often two of them would get locked in a clinch, the victim struggling on his back with all four paws in the air. Elsa usually joined in their games, and in spite of her great weight she sprang and hopped about as though she, too, were a cub.

282

When her youngsters were ten weeks old, Elsa started to wean them. In camp, if she thought they had enough milk, she either sat on her teats or jumped to the roof of the Land-Rover, out of their reach. The cubs soon caught on that they must either eat meat or starve. They tore the intestines of the "kill" out of their mother's mouth and sucked them like spaghetti through closed teeth, pressing out the unwanted contents just as she did.

Elsa was frequently rather rough with the cubs, holding their heads down with one paw so they would not interfere with her meal, biting them affectionately or pulling their skin. When she and I played together, however, she was always gentle. I attributed this partly to the fact that when I stroked her, I always did so very gently, talking to her at the same time in a low, calm voice. The cubs were most upset if I acted any other way. Whenever Elsa, persecuted by tsetse flies, flung herself in front of me, for example, and I squashed the flies by slapping her, Jespah in particular would come close and crouch, ready to spring to his mother's protection.

My impulse was to love and pet the cubs much as I had Elsa, but I resisted it. George and I were determined that they should grow up as wild lions. We both remembered the struggle it had been to give Elsa back to the wild world, and we did not want to go through such an ordeal again. Also these cubs had a mother and father to care for them; they were a true pride of lions. We must not risk weakening them.

When Elsa tried to bring her two families closer together, our attitude must have appeared heartless. One evening she entered my tent, deliberately lay down behind me, then called softly to her cubs to suckle her. This would have forced the cubs into the tent and near to me, but I made no move to encourage them. Elsa looked at me with a disappointed expression, then went out to join her children. She could not understand my lack of response, but gradually she became accustomed to it, and by the time the cubs were eighteen weeks old she appeared resigned to our "coldness."

The cubs' father was a great disappointment to us. No doubt we were partly to blame, for we had interfered with his relationship with his family, but certainly he was of no help as a provider; on the contrary he often stole their food. One night he attempted to get at a goat that was inside my truck. Another time when Elsa and the cubs were eating outside our tent she suddenly scented him, became very nervous, cut her meal short and hurriedly removed the cubs. George then went out with a torch; he had not gone three yards when he was startled by a fierce growl and saw the cubs' father hiding in a bush just in front of him. George retreated rapidly, and luckily so did the lion.

The nights when the cubs' father kept his distance were the happiest. After Elsa and the cubs had eaten heartily, they'd come to sit in front of our tent, facing the bright lamplight. The cubs were quite unperturbed by the glare; perhaps they thought it was some new kind of moon. After I had gone to bed, George turned out the "moon" and sat for a while in the dark. The cubs always came within touching distance of him, then, having had "a drink for the road," they all trotted off toward the big rock, from which immediately afterward we would hear Elsa's mate calling.

After *Born Free,* my first book about the lion, was published, Elsa found herself famous. People all over the world wrote, saying they'd like to come and see her. This posed a problem. We were earnestly trying to keep Elsa and the cubs wild, and we could not have them turned into a tourist attraction. We were afraid, too, that someone might unintentionally provoke Elsa and cause trouble. Reluctantly we discouraged all visitors except old friends who had known Elsa since she was a cub. One such had come to make sketches of the cubs, and Elsa raised no objections. Two wonderfully tactful cameramen from the London BBC-TV were equally well received. Although Elsa generally objected to picture-taking, she provided them with some splendid shots by obligingly playing with the cubs on the big rock.

But we were hardly prepared for the reception she gave William Collins, the London publisher who had launched *Born Free*. We chartered a plane to bring him from Nairobi to the nearest airstrip, and I drove him from there back to camp. We were relieved when Elsa welcomed us in her usual friendly manner and, after a few cautious sniffs, rubbed her head against Billy Collins while the three cubs watched from a distance.

We made a special thorn enclosure for Billy's tent and, having barricaded his wicker gate from outside with more thorns, left him for a well-deserved night's sleep. Elsa remained outside my tent enclosure, and I heard her softly talking to her cubs until I fell asleep. At dawn I was wakened by loud noises from Billy's tent. I recognized his voice and George's, both evidently trying to persuade Elsa to leave. She had squeezed through the densely woven wicker gate and hopped onto Billy's bed, tearing the mosquito net, caressing him affectionately and finally holding him prisoner under her three-hundred-pound body. Billy kept admirably calm, considering that it was his first experience of waking up to find a fully grown lioness sitting on him. Even when Elsa nibbled at his arm, her way of showing fondness, he did nothing but talk quietly to

her. Soon she lost interest, followed George out of the enclosure.

Before daybreak the next morning I was again wakened by noises from Billy's tent, into which Elsa had once more found her way to say good-morning. After some coaxing from George, who had come to Billy's rescue, she left.

George then reinforced the thorn barricade until he felt sure it was impenetrable. But Elsa was not going to be defeated by a few thorns, and at dawn the following morning Billy found himself again being heartily embraced and squashed under Elsa's weight. By the time George forced his way through the thorn barrier, Elsa had both paws around Billy's neck and was holding his cheekbones between her teeth. She often held her cubs in this fashion as a sign of love, but the effect on Billy must have been very different. Luckily he suffered only slight scratches, which I carefully dressed with disinfectant powder.

Now much alarmed at Elsa's unusual behavior, I remained with Billy in his tent until I hoped Elsa had taken her cubs away for the day. Despite this precaution she again forced herself through the wicker gate before either George or I could stop her. Billy was standing up this time. She approached him directly, then stood on her hind legs, rested her front paws on his shoulders and started to nibble at his ear. Being tall and strong, Billy braced himself against her weight and stood his ground. As soon as she released him I gave her such a beating that she sulkily left the tent. Outside, in a rather embarrassed way, she turned her attention to Jespah, rolling with him in the grass, biting and clasping him exactly as she had done with Billy. Finally the whole family gamboled off toward the rocks.

I do not know who was more shaken, poor Billy Collins or myself. Apparently

Elsa's extraordinary reaction toward Billy was simply her way of accepting him into the family. But it would be dangerous to risk a repetition of such demonstrations. So we decided to break Billy's visit short and left camp immediately after breakfast.

Early in June we were returning from Isiolo and near sunset were about six miles short of camp, when suddenly we found ourselves surrounded by elephants. The herd, which must have numbered some thirty or forty head, closed in on us from every direction. It contained many very young calves whose worried mothers came up to the car with raised trunks and fanning ears.

The situation was tricky. George jumped on the roof of the Land-Rover and stood there, rifle in hand, waiting while the elephant mothers continued their infuriated protests. After what seemed an endless time, the herd started to move away. It was a magnificent sight. The giants walked in single file, wedging their young protectively in line between them and jerking their massive heads disapprovingly toward us.

Every bush and tree around us was loaded with birds which feed on carrion, and when it was safe to do so, George looked around for the kill which had attracted them. Presently he found the carcass of a freshly killed waterbuck. There was lion spoor around it, but little of the buck had been eaten; plainly the lion had been interrupted by the elephant herd. Had it been Elsa who made the kill? This was far from her usual hunting ground, and tackling this fearsomely horned, four-hundred-pound beast while protecting her cubs would have been a dangerous enterprise. We felt sure Elsa would not have undertaken it unless she was very hungry indeed.

When we reached camp we signaled Elsa with a rifle shot, but she failed to appear that night. Next day we were greatly relieved to see her and the cubs on the big rock. She at once threw herself against George, squashing him with her affection, and afterward bowled me over, while the cubs quizzically craned their heads at us above the high grass. In camp, we provided a meal for them over which they competed with the hungriest kind of growls, snarls and spankings. Little Elsa had the best of it and eventually went off with her loot, leaving her brothers still so hungry that we felt obliged to produce another carcass for them.

That evening Elsa took her usual position on the roof of the Land-Rover, but instead of romping about—at this hour they were normally most energetic—the cubs flung themselves on the ground and never stirred. During the night I heard Elsa talking to them in a low moan and also heard suckling noises. They must indeed have been hungry, to need milk after consuming two goats in twenty-four hours.

In the morning they had all gone. When we followed their spoor, it led straight to the waterbuck kill. So it must have been Elsa who two days earlier had tackled this formidable beast. It was hard luck that the arrival of the elephant herd had given her and the cubs no chance to eat her kill. Now we understood why they had been so hungry.

We collected the waterbuck's fine horns and hung them in the studio, a proud record of the cubs' first big hunt with their mother. They were now five and a half months old.

At dusk, when their bellies were full, the cubs were always bursting with energy and played the most outrageous tricks on their mother. Jespah, for instance, discovered that when he stood on his hind legs and clasped her tail she could not easily free herself. In this fashion they would walk round in circles, Jespah behaving like a clown until Elsa had enough of it and sat down on him. He seemed delighted by this and would lick and hug his mother until she escaped into our tent. But the tent soon ceased to provide an asylum, for he would follow her into it, give a quick look around, then sweep everything in reach to the ground. During the night I often heard him busily sorting through the food boxes and the beer crates, whose clattering bottles provided him with endless entertainment.

About this time Jespah began to emerge as the accepted leader of the pride. One evening when Elsa and the cubs walked back to camp with us from the big rock, she and Jespah got in front of us while Gopa and Little Elsa stayed behind. This worried Jespah very much, and he rushed to and fro trying to marshal his pride, until finally his mother stood still and allowed us to pass her, thus reuniting the family. Afterward she rubbed our knees as though to thank us for having taken the hint.

On June 20, when the cubs were six months old, George celebrated the occasion by shooting a guinea fowl. Little Elsa took possession of it and disappeared into the bush. Her indignant brothers went after her but returned defeated and, tumbling down a sandy bank, landed on their mother. She was lying on her back, her four paws straight up in the air. She caught the two cubs and held their heads in her mouth until they struggled free and pinched her tail.

After a splendid game together, Elsa walked up to me sedately and embraced me as though to show that I was not to be left out in the cold. This apparently angered Jespah, for whenever I turned my back he began to stalk me. Each time I turned to face him, however, he stopped and looked most bewildered and uncertain. Then he seemed to find the solution: he would go off. He walked straight into the river and

made for the other bank. Elsa rushed after him. Borana tribesmen had recently been trespassing and poaching over there and, considering the area dangerous, I shouted, "No, no!" But my warning was without effect; Elsa and the others continued to follow Jespah. This left us in little doubt that they had all now accepted his leadership.

When they finally returned, Elsa dozed off with her head on my lap. This was too much for Jespah. He crept up and began to scratch my shins with his sharp claws. I could not move my legs because of the weight of Elsa's head, so I tried to stop him by stretching my hand slowly toward him. In a flash he bit it, making a wound at the base of my forefinger. Luckily I always carry a disinfectant powder and was thus able to treat it at once. All this happened within inches of Elsa's face, but she diplomatically ignored the incident and closed her eyes.

When we were alone together Elsa was as devoted as ever, but she normally took great care not to show too much affection for me in the presence of her cubs. Once when she visited us in camp, however, some experience had left her very nervous; she affectionately allowed me to use her as a pillow and also hugged me with her paws. Jespah apparently did not approve, for after his mother had left he crouched and then started to charge me. He did this three times and though he always swerved at the last moment, pretending to be more interested in elephant droppings, his flattened ears and angry snarls left me in no doubt about his jealousy. But, significantly, he started to attack only when his mother could not observe it. To placate him I gave him some tidbits and then tied an inner tube to a ten-foot-long rope which I jerked about.

By now we were beginning to worry about his relationship to us. We had done our best to respect the cubs' natural instincts and to permit their being real wild lions, but inevitably this had resulted in our having no control over them. Little Elsa and her timid brother were as shy as ever and never provoked a situation that required chastisement. But Jespah had a very different character, and I could not push his sharp, scratching claws back, saying, "No, no," as I had done when Elsa was a cub, to teach her to retract her claws when playing with us. On the other hand, I did not want to use a stick, for Elsa might resent it and cease to trust me. Our only hope seemed to lie in establishing a friendly relationship with Jespah, but for the moment his unpredictable reactions made a truce more possible than a real friendship.

Recently the crocodiles, which had scattered during the floods, had reassembled in the deep pools. This worried us because Elsa often took her meat down to the river, and several times after dark, when her growls had brought us to her with torches and a rifle, we found her defending her "kill" against a "croc." It invariably vanished as soon as we came on the scene, for however carefully we stalked these reptiles they almost always outwitted us. We had only their eyes to aim at in any case, as all the rest of their bodies was submerged. They have the most highly developed sense of impending danger of any wild animal I have ever known.

Elsa and the cubs were well aware that the crocs were not friendly and often watched the water attentively for any suspicious eddy or floating sticks. On the other hand they had moments of unconcern—and I was anxious about their safety. One afternoon I called to Elsa, who was on the far bank. She appeared at once and was preparing to swim across with the cubs, when suddenly they all froze. Then Elsa took the cubs higher up the river and indicated that they were to cross there, the water being very shallow at that point in the dry season. In spite of this they did not cross for an hour, nor did the cubs indulge in their usual splashing and ducking games. This was reassuring, for it showed their prudence, but it was characteristic of their variable reactions that next day when I called Elsa from the same place at the same time, they all swam across at once and without the slightest hesitation. Then I noticed that Elsa had a wound the size of a shilling in her tongue and a very deep gash across the center that was bleeding. Surprisingly, this did not prevent her from licking the cubs.

When it was getting dark we were all sitting near the river. Suddenly Elsa and the cubs looked at the water and stiffened, and three or four yards away I saw a big croc. I fetched my rifle and killed him, and afterward Elsa came and rubbed her head against my knee as though to thank me.

One night in mid-July Elsa arrived in camp long after dark with only two cubs. Jespah was missing. Much worried, I called his name over and over till Elsa decided to go look for him, taking the two cubs with her. For over an hour I heard her calling, the sound gradually receding into the distance. Then suddenly there were savage lion growls, accompanied by the terrified shrieks of baboons. We knew that a fierce lioness was lurking near, and I was sure Elsa was being attacked by this stranger. Miserably I awaited the outcome.

When Elsa finally returned she was covered with scratches, and the root of her right ear was bitten through, leaving a gap into which one could stick two fingers. This was much the worst injury she had ever suffered, and Little Elsa and Gopa sat near, looking frightened. I tried to disinfect Elsa's wounds, but she was far too irritable to let me near her, nor was she interested in food. She sat holding her head to one side, the blood dripping from her wound, while the cubs ate, then called them and waded across the river.

That morning Makedde, Nuru and I followed Elsa's spoor to a cave and were relieved to find the entire family there, including Jespah. All the cubs seemed very subdued. Elsa's wound was still bleeding profusely, and at intervals she shook her head to drain the cavity. That evening, when she and her family came by the camp to be fed, I put some medicinal tablets into her meat, hoping to prevent her wound from becoming septic.

Elsa also returned to camp the next evening. But that night two strange lions noisily cracked the bones of a goat we had laid out in front of George's tent. They spent a long time over their meal, then crossed the river with many grunts and whuffings in reply to the barking of baboons. We later found the spoor of a large lion and lioness, and Elsa kept away for days.

After much vain searching for her I became anxious, for her wound greatly handicapped her for hunting and also left her vulnerable to the poachers. When I saw vultures circling one evening, I feared the worst. But next morning all we found was more evidence of poachers—curing hides, ashes and charred animal bones.

Next day two men of the Game Patrol, sent out to deal with the poachers, reported seeing Elsa across the river. She was lying under a bush, and the cubs were asleep. The men said she saw them approach but did not move—which sounded odd unless she was so ill that she did not care. I went to this lie-up and called to her, and she emerged, walking slowly, her head bent low to one side. I was alarmed that she should

have settled in such an exposed place. Her ear had gone septic, was discharging pus and obviously gave her great pain; and when she shook her head, as she often did, it sounded as if her ear were full of liquid.

When George arrived from Isiolo—I had been in camp without him for three weeks—he decided to scare off the strange lioness that had attacked Elsa. She and her mate had now chased Elsa away completely. George and I spent two days covering the boundaries of Elsa's territory, partly on foot and partly by car. We did not find the belligerent strange lioness. And though we searched eight hours a day, we learned nothing of Elsa.

George left in the last week of July, and I continued the search. It was very hot and, after several hours of tracking, Makedde and I sat down to rest. My spirits were low. It was now over two weeks since Elsa's fight, and when I last saw her wound it had grown worse. So how could she hunt food or protect her cubs against the poachers?

"You have nothing but death in your mind," Makedde scolded angrily, after watching my deepening depression. "You think of death, you speak of death, and you behave as though there was no Mungo [God] who looks after everything. Can't you trust Him to look after Elsa?"

On the fifteenth night after her disappearance I had reason to remember this reprimand. I had just lighted the lamps, poured myself a drink and was sitting quietly and straining for any hopeful sound. Suddenly there was a swift flurry, and I was nearly knocked off my chair by Elsa's affectionate greeting. She looked thin but fit, and her wound was healing from the outside, though the center was still septic. She seemed in a great hurry, pounced on the meat I gave her, gorged herself on half a goat, then disappeared within half an hour.

She did not then bring in her cubs. But at dawn on August 1, I was waked up by their hungry meowing. I was relieved, but puzzled to see that there was not a single new scratch on her or the cubs, although they must have hunted regularly during all this time in order to live. I asked Makedde to follow Elsa's spoor and find out what she had been up to. He traced her to the limit of her territory and there, on some rocky outcrops, found not only her pug marks and those of the cubs, but also the spoor of at least one other lion, if not two. So it seemed probable that when Elsa was driven from her territory by the hostile lioness she had joined with a new male lion.

This solution had not occurred to us, for as Elsa was still suckling her cubs we had not expected her to be interested in a mate. It is generally believed that wild lionesses produce only every third year, because in the interval they are teaching the young of the last litter to hunt and become independent. But perhaps Elsa felt that since we were supplying unlimited food, it was enough for her simply to produce cubs. Obviously she could not know it, but we had no intention of running a lion canteen indefinitely.

The animals who lived near our camp got so used to us that a Garden of Eden atmosphere often prevailed there. A bushbuck ram, for example, came every day while we were at lunch to drink in the river opposite us, sometimes browsed within sight for an hour and remained unconcerned even when we talked or moved about. A waterbuck family, consisting of two males, three does and three youngsters, frequently allowed us to come quite close. And the baboons, who sometimes ran in troupes of fifty-odd, were our oldest friends. Indeed we had lived side by side for so long that we paid no attention to each other unless something unusual happened. Normally, no scene could be more peaceful. But violence and danger were always close.

About nine o'clock one dark night Elsa and the cubs appeared in front of my tent and began calling for their supper. I asked Makedde and the toto to help me drag in a half-eaten goat carcass Elsa had left near the river. Silently the three of us set out on the narrow path we had cut through the dense bush; Makedde, armed with a stick and a hurricane light in the lead, the toto close behind and I, carrying a bright pressure lamp, bringing up the rear.

We had walked but a few yards when there was a terrible crash and out went Makedde's lamp. Then my lamp was smashed, too, as a monstrous black mass hit me and knocked me over. The next thing I knew, Elsa was licking me. She seemed to realize that I was hurt and was most gentle and affectionate. As soon as I could collect myself I sat up and called to the boys. Makedde yelled that he was all right, but only a feeble groan came from the prostrate toto. Then, holding his head, he got up shakily, stammering, "Buffalo, buffalo!"

Makedde had suddenly jumped to one side and hit at a buffalo with his stick, the toto breathlessly informed me, and the next moment first he and then I had been knocked down. Luckily the toto had no worse injury than a bump on his head, caused by crashing into a fallen palm trunk, but my arms and thighs were bleeding and painfully bruised from the trampling I took. As for Makedde, I later found him in the kitchen, completely unhurt and having a splendid time recounting his single-handed combat with the buffalo.

I had no doubt as to the identity of our assailant. For several weeks past we had seen the spoor of a bull buffalo, leading to a nearby sandbank where he had a well-marked drinking place. He had never come out until after midnight before, though we had often heard his snortings and splashings in the early morning hours. This evening, however, he had come out early, had evidently been frightened by our moving lamps and had rushed up the nearest path to safety, only to find us blocking his way. What happened when Elsa and the buffalo met none of us will ever know. But she had obviously come to protect us from him.

The next afternoon Elsa took care to drag her "kill" a long way upstream, across the river and then up a bank so steep it was unlikely any beast would come after it. I wondered whether this unusual behavior was due to her having been as frightened by the buffalo as I had been.

One day after Elsa had fought yet another battle with her fierce lioness enemy, Nuru and I, after much searching, found her lying up with her cubs, far from home. Again she had suffered a bad mauling. She was deeply gashed, in great pain, and certainly in need of treatment. It took a lot of coaxing to get her to follow us, and we made our way back to camp slowly. When I thought we were nearly there I sent Nuru, who was acting as my gun bearer, ahead on an errand. After he had gone I found I had miscalculated and had lost myself in the bush. By then it was midday, and the lions stopped under every bush to pant in the shade.

I knew that the best thing to do was to find the nearest *lugga,* or stream bed, and follow it, for it must lead to the river, and the river would give me my bearings. Fairly soon I came upon a lugga and walked along between its steep banks; Elsa followed me, and the cubs scampered some distance behind her. At a bend I suddenly found myself standing face to face with a rhino. There was no question of "jumping nimbly aside and allowing the charging beast to pass," as

one is supposed to do in such encounters, so I turned and ran back along my tracks as fast as I could, with the beast puffing and snorting behind me.

At last I saw a little gap in the bank, and, before I knew I had done it, I was up the bank and running into the bush. At this moment the rhino must have seen Elsa, for it swerved abruptly and crashed up the opposite side. Luckily for me, Elsa ignored her habit of chasing any rhino she saw, and stood very still watching the pair of us.

For Elsa, the main peril of the bush came from another quarter. Predators might still eye her cubs, and lion feuds might embroil her, but her chief danger lay in poaching tribesmen. It was this fact which upset all our plans for Elsa and her family.

We wanted them to lead natural lives and had every intention of leaving them to look after themselves as soon as Elsa recovered from her savage fight with the lioness. But just as her ear wound had more or less healed, the Game Scouts antipoaching team brought in prisoners with news that changed all our plans. For an informer among the prisoners told George that the poachers had determined to kill Elsa with poisoned arrows as soon as we left the camp.

The dry season was on, and as the drought increased, so would the poachers' activities. Unless we fed Elsa it would be impossible for the antipoaching team, however efficient, to prevent Elsa from hunting further afield and risking an encounter with the tribesmen. Obviously, if we stayed on, the cubs' education in wild life would be delayed and they would probably get spoiled. But it was better to face this than risk a tragedy.

However long we supported her, Little Elsa remained truly wild, snarled if we came close and then sneaked away. Though much smaller than her brothers, she had a quiet and efficient way of getting what she wanted.

Gopa, I noticed, was becoming very jealous, not only of me but also of his brother. When Jespah played with their mother, Gopa would push his way between the two, and when Elsa came close to me, he crouched and snarled until she went over to him.

Jespah had lost his earlier truculence, was most friendly and had begun to imitate his mother in her relation to us. He often wanted to play with me, and sometimes would come and lie under my hand, evidently expecting to be petted. And though it was against my principles, I occasionally did pet him.

By now, both Jespah and Gopa as well as Elsa used George's tent as a sort of den, and he found it rather crowded at night. He preferred to sleep on a low hounds-field bed, and with Elsa, Jespah and Gopa around it I wondered whether there might not be trouble some night. They all behaved reasonably well, however, and whenever Jespah tried to play with George's toes, George's authoritative "No!" made him stop at once. The extent to which the lions felt at home was illustrated one night when Elsa rolled around and tipped over the bed, throwing George on top of Jespah. No commotion followed and Gopa, who was sleeping near George's head, did not even move.

At eight months Jespah had lost his baby fluff, and his coat was rather like a rabbit's. Now growing very fast, he was a grand little lion, but so insatiably curious and so full of life and fun as to be a problem. Elsa often helped me control him, either by adding a cuffing to my "no's" or by placing herself between the two of us. But I wondered how long it would be before my commands would fail to have any effect.

Once, in chasing after his brother and sister, Jespah tipped a large water bowl over on Elsa, giving her a drenching. She clouted him for his pains, then squashed him under her heavy, dripping body. It was a funny sight, and we laughed. But this tactlessness offended Elsa and, giving us a disapproving look, she walked off followed by her two more obedient cubs. Later she jumped on the roof of the Land-Rover, and I sought her out there to make friends again and apologize. The moon was full, and in its brilliant light Elsa's great eyes appeared nearly black, owing to her widely dilated pupils. They looked down at me reproachfully as though saying, "Tonight you spoiled my lesson."

The time had come for us to leave the lion cubs to live their natural lives. They had become a little too used to camp life. Certainly Jespah was now on quite intimate terms with us, although Gopa and Little Elsa still put up with us only because their mother insisted we were friends. It now seemed possible for us to leave the camp. Elsa had at last got the upper hand of the fierce lioness and was able to defend her territory. The poachers seemed to have left the district, and we hoped they would not return until the next drought, by which time new antipoaching measures might be able to deal with them. Besides, the cubs were now powerful young lions, quite able to hunt with their mother. When they were ten months old we had noticed signs of adolescence in both Jespah and Gopa. They had grown fine fluff around their faces and necks, and if they looked a bit unshaven their appearance was certainly very endearing.

We decided to space our absences, spending longer and longer periods away each time until finally we would not return to camp at all. On the first occasion we intended to be away for only six days, but because of heavy rains it was nine days before I could return. I came alone this time, made my way to the big rock and came upon Elsa trotting along with the cubs. Gopa and Little Elsa kept their distance, but Jespah was as delighted as Elsa to see me and struggled to get between us so as to receive his share of the welcome.

All were in excellent condition. Elsa had a few bites on her chin and neck, but nothing serious. Gopa had grown a much longer and darker mane than Jespah, whose coloring was light and tawny. In a year's time, I thought to myself, what a handsome pride they would make—two slender, graceful lionesses, accompanied by one blond and one dark lion.

A Postscript to Elsa's Story

After Joy Adamson had completed her book, *Living Free,* there were somber developments in the family of Elsa the lioness. Late in January 1961, George Adamson found Elsa ill under a bush.

"That night I slept beside Elsa in the bush to guard her against the attentions of wild lions and hyenas," Adamson wrote in the *East African Standard.* "Her cubs appeared and played around my bed, but Elsa would not tolerate them near her. In spite of her weakness she twice rubbed her face against mine with all her old friendliness. Late in the morning she was desperately ill, with labored and painful breathing. I stayed with her all day and from time to time tried to give her water in my cupped hands, but she seemed unable to swallow, though obviously she was thirsty.

"Finally, thinking the end was near, I roused my camp, and on an improvised stretcher four of my men and I carried her back to my tent. She appeared to settle down, and I lay beside her and was dozing off when suddenly she got up and quickly walked to the front of the tent and collapsed." A postmortem showed that Elsa was heavily infected with *Babesia,* a tick-borne parasite which attacks red blood cells.

After their mother's death, the three cubs began to maraud native herds of goats and cattle. The Adamsons paid heavy compensation for damages, but the natives tried to kill the cubs with poisoned arrows. Jespah, the leader of the three, had an arrow stuck in his hindquarters for a month, although he was not poisoned.

Finally George Adamson was told that unless he could trap the animals and place them in a game reserve, he would have to shoot them. Adamson chose to trap them. Three large crates were built with steel bars and trap doors, and food was put out every night, first near the crates and finally inside. The cubs were not nervous and often they fed and spent the night inside the crates. But the Adamsons did not spring the traps until the floods had subsided and the cubs could be moved at once through eight hundred miles of bush to Serengeti National Park, Tanzania. They were set free there in May 1961.

Cat with a
Telephone Number

by FRED SPARKS

IT'S A HUMILIATING confession for a bachelor to make, but whenever my phone rings the call most likely concerns not me but my cat, name of Stoop. We live, Stoop and I, in a New York apartment one flight up. The branch of an oak tree brushes the railing of our back terrace, providing a feline staircase that enables Stoop to live a double life—civilized and sedentary at home, completely uninhibited when he climbs down the tree and prowls the outside world.

I first met Stoop three years ago. I was walking home on a bitterly cold night when I saw a tangerine-red kitten sitting on a snowy brownstone stoop. As I approached, the creature tried to stand, wobbled, then fell down a step, half frozen. I wrapped the few ounces of shivering fur in my scarf and got an immediate purr of confidence. At home, Stoop (an obvious christening) responded immediately to an eyedropper-feeding of warm milk lightly laced with brandy. Within a week he was frisking around my place, and by spring, thanks to the spreading oak tree, he had discovered the exotic world of New York's sidewalks.

At last, I bought a light collar and had a tag inscribed:

THIS IS NOT A STRAY. IN
EMERGENCY PHONE FRED SPARKS
BU 8———.

Unlike full-time alley cats, who flee any-

thing on two legs, Stoop is trusting. As he wanders through the neighborhood, strangers stop to pet him. Attracted by the tag, dozens of them have phoned me. They seem under the impression that Stoop has run away or is lost. They sound disappointed when I assure them that he can find his own way home. A gentleman I had not seen in years called up. "Well, well, it *is* a small world. I stop to pet a cat and find you're back in town. Remember that twenty dollars you owe me?"

That wasn't the only time Stoop was expensive. One caller identified himself as the owner of a seafood restaurant down the block. He complained that cats had been raiding his kitchen through a basement window, filching crabs and lobsters. "The only one I could catch had this telephone number," he said. "Please give me your address. I'm going to send you a bill for his share." I obliged, convinced it was a joke. As I walked away from the phone something crunched under my shoe. A lobster claw.

By the time Stoop had been on the streets for six months, he was a combat veteran of the cement jungle. His nose was crisscrossed with scratches, and his ears were nicked with notches like a Western badman's belt. But in spite of the horrendous things that supposedly happen to small animals loose in the big city, he shows no evidence of ever having been mistreated. In fact, many of the phone calls come from friendly souls who want to be sure of doing the right thing. "I've got your nice cat with me in a phone booth," a man said recently. "Is he allowed to eat a fig?" Another wanted to know if

Stoop could safely handle lamb-chop bones.

Stoop certainly gets around. One morning he climbed into a cab parked down the street. I heard about it when an excited voice on the phone asked, "You-the-guy-widda-cat?" When I said I was, he rattled on, "Holy smoke! I'm a taxi driver and I thought I'd seen everything. But when I got in line at Grand Central Station, I find this cat sitting in the back seat. With a telephone number, yet!"

"Where is he now?" I asked.

"In a coin locker. Pick up the key at the starter's office and leave me the quarter. And say, Mister! How about a tip? Nobody —not even a cat—is supposed to ride free."

Stoop gets around locally, too. A call came late at night from an indignant female. "Your *cat*—he's under my bed!"

Trying to calm her down, I said, "How do you know that it's a he?"

"Because he's corrupting *my* cat, a *her*."

Curtly she gave me her name, Helen ——, and her address, a ground-floor apartment across the yard. When I went over to collect my housebreaking cat, I tried to apologize for his bad manners, but she slammed the door on both of us. Two nights later it happened again. This time I brought along a box of chocolates for Helen and a catnip mouse for her tortoise-shell pet. She found this amusing, and I found her really an attractive girl. We agreed to have dinner.

Stoop doesn't see Helen's cat any more. But I still see Helen. Now when the phone rings, I know that at least sometimes it's for me.

The World's Most Famous Talking Bird

by CARVETH WELLS

ONE NIGHT in 1939, when my wife, Zetta, and I were camped in the Malay Peninsula, the silence of the jungle around us was broken by a loud squawking. A marauding snake had climbed a tree and caught some sleeping bird. Next morning we found the scene of the tragedy. Black feathers were scattered at the base of a tall tree, and about thirty feet up a baby bird's head with wide-open mouth appeared from a hole in the trunk. Ali, one of our Malays, climbed up the tree and rescued the little orphan. He was an ugly fellow, all mouth and nearly naked except for a few black pinfeathers. Ali said, "It is a clever kind of bird—when it is older it will be able to talk." So we came into possession of Raffles.

When we brought him to this country the customs officer scanned our declaration and said, "What kind of bird is this?"

"He's our talking bird," Zetta answered.

The man frowned. "You can't bring in a parrot. They have diseases!"

"He isn't a parrot. He's a mynah bird."

It was a cold day, so Zetta was carrying him under her fur coat. She took him out and placed him on her finger. He ruffled his feathers, looked at the officer and said in a friendly, coaxing tone, "Hello, Joe!" Joe was the name of our cabin steward. Fortunately for us it was also the name of the customs officer. He was flabbergasted. "He knows my name! He's no parrot, he's a mind reader. Okay, you can bring him in!"

Mynahs, as common in Asia as blackbirds are in America, can imitate human speech perfectly. Unlike parrots, they reproduce the tone and inflection of their owners. They can simulate almost any sound.

Raffles was black, with shiny, iridescent feathers, except for two small white patches on his wings. His beak was bright orange. By the time he was three months old he was repeating "Hello, darling" with as much affection in his voice as Zetta had in hers. Whenever he saw Zetta preparing his food, he would say in a tone of keen anticipation, "Oh, boy!" It wasn't long before he was calling my wife Zetta and me Carveth. Since he imitated my wife's voice exactly, I often answered—only to find it was Raffles that had called.

Many persons scoff at the suggestion that mynahs can think. But if Raffles wanted a grape, he would say, "Have a grape!" If we offered him something else he would screech and repeat, "Have a grape!" When we turned on the water in the tub, Raffles would exclaim, "Have a bath!" If we turned on the faucet in the kitchen he said nothing. Raffles always said, "Hello! Hello!" when the telephone rang. Once when Zetta phoned me from outside our apartment, I let her speak to him over the telephone. Raffles listened intently, then called, "Zetta, Zetta!" and when she didn't appear he pecked the receiver angrily.

One day when Sarah Churchill was staying in our apartment in New York, a friend telephoned and asked for the man who was her husband at the time. "Tony is in California and I'm here in New York alone," Sarah said.

Just then Raffles, who was perched nearby, exclaimed in a seductive male voice, "Hello, darling!"

"I thought you said you were alone!" said the friend. "Who's your visitor?"

"I *am* alone," protested Sarah, "except for Raffles, and he's just a bird." The voice sounded so human that Sarah had to invite the man to come and see Raffles for himself.

Before Raffles was six months old he had learned to whistle "The Star-Spangled Banner" as far as "the twilight's last gleaming." Then he learned "You're in the Army Now," "Hail, Hail, the Gang's All Here" and "My Country 'Tis of Thee."

Fred Allen started Raffles on the road to fame when he engaged our bird as a guest on his radio program. The mynah put on a phenomenal performance, and fantastic offers

for Raffles' services poured in from all parts of the country. He was a guest at "Duffy's Tavern" and on the Lowell Thomas program. In Hollywood many film stars flocked to meet him. Walt Disney was so entranced that he gave a luncheon in the bird's honor. The hit that Raffles made was summed up as follows by *Time*: "Hollywood has found a sensational new comic of peerless proportions. He is an orange-beaked bird named Raffles, which has a positive genius for saying the wrong thing at the right time, in an Oxford accent."

Our mynah's greatest triumph was to be engaged as guest artist with the San Francisco Symphony Orchestra at the party held to celebrate that organization's thirty-third birthday. About twelve thousand persons jammed the immense Civic Auditorium when Zetta, with Raffles perched on her wrist, walked to the center of the huge stage. Never before had he seen such strange-looking objects as timpani, bass viols and horns. As he eyed these monsters suspiciously, Zetta and I wondered whether our pet would refuse to perform. We needn't have worried. For the next five minutes Raffles held the immense audience spellbound. And when he closed his performance by whistling the national anthem, the applause was deafening.

In 1943 we decided that Raffles must devote his entire time to working for Uncle Sam. He sold fifteen million dollars' worth of War Bonds and was awarded the Lavender Heart for entertaining the wounded in veterans' hospitals.

He had just finished his tenth performance in the wards of the Great Lakes Naval Hospital when a woman came up to Zetta, her eyes red with weeping. "My son is dying," she said. "He has heard Raffles on the radio many times. Yesterday when he learned that Raffles was coming to visit this hospital he said, 'Mother, the thing I want most in the world is to see that bird.' "

As we entered her son's room, my heart sank. Attached to the boy's nose was a rubber tube which coiled over the coverlet. Even mynahs that have never seen a snake have a horror of anything resembling one, and I expected Raffles to give a terrified screech and fly out of the room. The tube on a vacuum cleaner in our home was enough to send him off screaming in terror. But with the uncanny instinct this extraordinary little bird had for doing the right thing at the right moment, he flew straight to the bed. Alighting gently on the dying boy's arm, Raffles, in his most endearing tone of voice, exclaimed, "Hello, darling!" The boy stirred. Then Zetta said, "Star-Spangled Banner!" and Raffles whistled the song. The doctor turned away; the nurses wept. But the mother's face was transformed with joy as her son looked at Raffles and smiled his recognition. The boy died that night.

Little did we dream that Raffles, too, was soon to die. One day while performing at a veterans' hospital in New York, he caught cold. That night he started coughing and sneezing. By morning he could neither talk nor whistle, but in a wheezy whisper kept saying, "Poor Raffles! Poor Raffles!" We nursed him day and night for a week, but nothing that doctors and bird specialists did could help him.

Raffles was eight years old when he died. For a time after his death his body was exhibited in New York City's American Museum of Natural History as the world's most famous talking bird.

Leading
a Dog's Life

by ALBERT PAYSON TERHUNE

THERE IS a self-immolating hero streak in dogdom which is found in no other mammal except man. Man has the precepts and the shining examples of the ages to urge him toward heroism. Also a hope of reward or glory. The dog has none of these to impel him to stake his life for others. Yet more than once his instinctive heroism has made a dog sacrifice his life for the sake of his human gods.

A fox terrier awakened her master and his family one night by shaking them and shrieking in their ears when a fire assailed their home. Not until firemen carried the last of the three children safely to the street did she turn back into the blaze to rescue her own newborn puppies.

Many a dog, by the way, has been acclaimed a hero for merely giving the alarm when fire threatened. There is no more heroism in such an exploit than in the sneeze of a hay-fever patient. A dog's sensitive nostrils are tormented by smoke. It gives tongue, awakens the family and then gets much acclaim—merely for voicing its fright. But it is true heroism when a dog conquers its instinctive dread of fire to save human lives. Such a dog was Tige, who aroused his

farmer master when the house was burning. Man and wife and baby got out into the yard. There a neighbor wrapped the baby in a blanket and carried it next door. A relative missed the child and feared it might still be in its crib. She pointed to the flaming farmhouse and shrilled: "In there, Tige! Find Baby!" Unflinchingly, Tige plunged back into the fiery ruin, where he was burned to death. He knew the peril. But he understood the command, the supposed need; and he obeyed instantly.

In Oregon a marble shaft keeps bright the memory of another fire-hero dog—Shep, a big collie that belonged to A. R. Mansfield. Mansfield and his wife were working in the fields at some distance from the cabin where their baby daughter, Shirley, was asleep. Shep sniffed the air, then broke into wild barking. The Mansfields looked up to see their cabin ablaze. By the time their stumbling rush could carry them to the open doorway, a sheet of flame hurled them back. Mansfield called to the trembling dog: "Shep! *Get* her, Shep! Get *Shirley!*"

Through the flame sheet the collie cleaved his way. Part of the roof caved in behind

298

him, cutting off the doorway. Using his uncanny collie brain as well as his courage, Shep reached the crib. Thence he dragged the baby to the farthest window. Leaning in, Mansfield snatched the child from him. Shep's work was done. At last there was time to think of his own safety. Out through the window he leaped—his coat a mass of fatal fire. Henry Daniel, president of the Oregon Humane Society, said at Shep's grave: "His heroism is one of the outstanding cases in history."

Malakoff was a giant Newfoundland, watchdog for a Paris jeweler. The jeweler's apprentices hated the dog. Led by one Jacques, they coaxed him out to the end of a pier. There, Jacques tied a rope around the dog's neck, with a heavy stone at the other end, and shoved him into the Seine. As the dog fell, Jacques' ankle was caught in the rope and into the river he went. He did not know how to swim.

Malakoff came to the surface and struck out for shore, dragging the stone which had not been quite heavy enough to keep him under. Then he caught sight of the man who had tried to kill him. Jacques was sinking. Malakoff hurled his own weighted body forward and caught him by the collar. He could have reached shore easily enough, despite the stone. But he could not make any

progress through the whipsaw crosscurrents while he held up the added weight of Jacques. It does not seem to have occurred to the mighty dog to save himself by letting go of the man who had sought to drown him. Malakoff managed to keep the man's head above water until a passing scow rescued them both. Weepingly, Jacques told the whole story. Henceforth, Malakoff was the hero of Paris. When he died, almost every apprentice in the city followed him to his grave.

Sport was a big crossbreed. His master was André Minette, a woodsman who lived in a clearing near Sequin Falls, Canada. Minette and his wife had a baby son, Jean, whom Sport adored. Jean was in his perambulator in a patch of meadow close to the forest. Minette was on his way home from the woods, with Sport. Suddenly, the dog bounded toward Jean at express-train speed.

Minette saw then that three gaunt timber wolves were stealing toward the sleeping child. The man was too far away to be of aid. But Sport was not.

A lesser dog would have flung himself on the wolves, in an effort to guard the baby. But Sport knew that, in such a case, he would be killed, leaving Jean at the mercy of the merciless. He stopped in his onrush as the wolves wheeled about to face him. Then he danced away, in such a direction as to keep their backs to the baby. There was something infinitely insulting in his tactics. When the wolves were angry enough, Sport turned about, as if in craven terror, and ran, the wolves hot on his trail. By that time, Minette, axe in hand, reached the clearing.

Sport never came back. He laid down his splendid life for the child he loved. But he did not do it foolishly. He made certain first of Jean's safety. Then he paid the price, knowing he had won.

The Moose
Who Liked People

by CARL C. ANDERSEN

SOME YEARS AGO I was summoned one morning by my managing editor. "Andersen," he said, "you must find us a cow moose—and quickly." The only cow moose in Denmark had died. Twenty years earlier she and two magnificent bull moose had swum from Sweden to Denmark across the treacherous, powerful currents of the sound—an extraordinary feat. They were the first of their kind to appear in our forests in eight hundred years. Now it was feared that the line would die out. Hundreds of letters from our readers demanded that we find a new companion for the bulls.

To find a cow moose seemed impossible. Nevertheless, we were ultimately successful. Some years before, Torsten Kreuger, the Swedish newspaper publisher, had found a baby moose with a broken leg on his farm and had nursed her back to health. As a gesture of friendship he now gave her to Denmark. Svea, the moose, was escorted to our country by two solemn Swedes, Mr. Reen and Mr. Rasmussen, who had helped to raise her.

"Svea is not easy to handle," Mr. Rasmussen told the press. And Mr. Reen added darkly, "She likes people."

Svea was turned loose in the Gribskov woods. It was hoped that the bull moose would find her and that nature would take its course. But Svea had other ideas. One evening there was thumping at the door of Ranger Joergensen of the Royal Danish Forest Service. His daughter, Kirsten, opened the door—and screamed. The caller was a moose. The ranger came running, gun in hand. Moose can be extremely dangerous, can kill a man with one chopping blow of their forehooves. But Svea just stood there, hanging her head.

"What kind of animal *is* this?" growled Joergensen.

"Maybe it wants to be petted," said his daughter. And that was exactly what Svea wanted. She was lonely.

Timidly, Kirsten scratched the top of the huge head. Svea nudged the girl for more. It was the beginning of a friendship. Every morning Svea would come to the house at the edge of the forest and wait for Kirsten to appear. Like a dog, the tremendous animal would dash up to her and skid to a stop, nibble her shoulder gently and talk. Above all else, Svea liked conversation. She listened, her big melancholy eyes concen-

301

trated on the speaker. And she would reply with a deep grumbling in her throat that could express many sentiments.

One morning a breathless constable rushed into a meeting of the town council of Helsinge, in Gribskov Forest. "Mayor, mayor!" he shouted. "There's a moose in the streets! What shall I do?"

Svea had discovered Helsinge and liked it. She also liked children. At first they screamed and ran away, but gradually they came back to take another look at the great beast that seemed so friendly. Now, for such an appreciative audience, Svea was prancing and pirouetting up and down the main street. The council went to the scene in a body. The mayor waved his arms and shouted. Ranger Joergensen tried to push the animal off the road, but Svea braced her legs and would not move. At last the ranger's daughter was summoned. She spoke sharply, and Svea, after a contemptuous glance at the council, trotted slowly off toward the woods.

On her next visit to Helsinge, Svea discovered Mr. Rosendahl's pastry shop. Like a child, Svea pressed her huge muzzle against the window and stared at the pastries. The baker tried to disregard the eerie vision, then flung open the door and shouted, "Go away!" But Svea poked her head through

the doorway and looked around appealingly. The baker gave her some of his fresh bread —and that was his undoing. Every morning from then on, the moose was there when the bread came out of the ovens. Svea liked pastry, too, but since this was too expensive for a handout the animal devised a way of getting people to buy the sweets for her. She would cavort in front of the store until the usual crowd of children had gathered, then pick a victim and shove him gently inside. Svea always got her pastry.

Svea was fascinated by automobiles. She liked to stop them, investigate the occupants, have a chat. A friend of mine had one of these unnerving experiences. Coming around a bend in the road through the Gribskov Forest, he suddenly saw a huge animal, broadside, ahead of him. A deer would have been gone in a flash. Not Svea. The motorist jammed on his brakes barely in time. Svea looked down from her great height at the small open car. Slowly she ambled around to the driver's side and amiably prodded the terrified man with her muzzle. She sniffed at the back of the automobile and then with a last friendly poke sauntered away.

After a number of such incidents, it was decided to take a firm stand with Svea. She had been brought over from Sweden to produce a strain of Danish moose, not to amuse the children. So Svea was sent to a game reserve in northern Zealand where the bulls now ranged. Rangers who were watching her reported that she didn't seem to care for the bulls. But she was eating natural food and the rangers were sure that

she would eventually "become wild," as they put it. Then suddenly Svea disappeared.

A few mornings later Mr. Rosendahl saw the familiar face pressed against his shop-window. Svea munched her fresh bread and went off on her accustomed round of visits. The town council met in stormy session. "Svea," said one of the councilors, "must be made to realize that she is an animal. She must not be permitted to disrupt the orderly government of our town." An offer from the Copenhagen zoo was accepted.

Svea's arrival at the Randers Zoological Gardens was a performance in her grandest tradition. She was meek enough as she descended from her truck. For an hour or so she was content to inspect the big enclosure assigned to her. And then she gathered herself. A charge, a flying leap, and she had cleared the nine-foot moat. Once more Svea went for a walk. With regal dignity she poked into parked automobiles, sniffed at people, nuzzled children and before long discovered a pond in which she took a leisurely bath. Then she returned to the moat, leaped over it without effort and settled down with apparent satisfaction in her new home.

In 1952 Svea died of pneumonia. The newest medicines were powerless to save her. All Denmark mourned. A few days after her death my managing editor and I talked about moose once more. "Shall we try to find another one?" he asked.

"Another Svea?" I said. "That would be impossible."

"Then write an obituary," he said, "that does her justice."

303

The Wonderful
White Stallions
of Vienna

by FREDERIC SONDERN, JR.

FOR ALMOST every visitor to the charming old city of Vienna there is one spectacle which he must not miss: a performance in the venerable Spanish Riding School of the Hofburg, ancient palace of the Hapsburg emperors. Each Sunday, in a great white-walled riding hall, a masterpiece of baroque architecture, the world's most unusual horses produce a classic ballet that fascinates today's audiences as it once did royalty.

With apparent effortlessness, twenty snow-white Lipizzaner stallions—powerful yet exquisitely graceful—go through an intricate routine with the precision of a West Point review and the fluid motion of a line of Rockettes. For an hour and a half they march in formation, dance and prance to the rhythm of stately old Viennese melodies. Their magnificent necks arched, they pirouette like ballerinas, raise their forelegs in the elegant *levade* and soar above the tanbark in the flashing *capriole*. And all the while their riders sit ramrod-straight in the saddle, never moving a rein perceptibly.

At the head of the column of stately horses that pace sedately into the hall for the performance rides Colonel Hans Handler, commander of the Spanish Riding School (so called because the Lipizzaners originally were Spanish-bred offspring of Arab stock). Colonel Handler, formerly on the faculty of Theresianische Militaer Akademie, the Austrian military school, became commander in early 1965 when Colonel Alois Podhajsky retired. Colonel Podhajsky had been the commander for more than twenty years. Both Colonel Podhajsky and Colonel Handler are recognized by leading horsemen in Europe and the United States as great masters of the *haute école,* or "high school," of riding.

My introduction a few years ago to the famous Lipizzaner stable was unforgettable. I was greeted at the school by Colonel Podhajsky. The moment the colonel and I entered the long hall of stalls and the "children" heard his voice, the neighing and whinnying began, punctuated by sharp raps

of forehooves against stall doors. Twenty great white heads turned in our direction. Nuzzled by one of these heads, the colonel would present a lump of sugar from the leather bag he always carried on his inspection rounds. "These strange horses," he remarked, "require the kind of affection that humans do. If one of them is dissatisfied with me, he won't take the sugar and then I know that something's wrong."

The stranger at the colonel's side met the gentle but penetratingly inquisitive stare of huge, intelligent brown eyes that literally looked him up and down. A politely delicate sniff followed. There was either an approving nudge of the muzzle—with perhaps a startling lick from a long tongue—or an abrupt about-face to the trough. "They can be most arrogant," said the colonel with a smile.

They sometimes display an uncanny sense of propriety. Some years ago one of the horses, Pluto Theodorosta (their names are as imposing as themselves), captivated the Court of Saint James's. When the stallions were performing at the Horse Show in London, Queen Elizabeth fell in love with Pluto on the spot. A dedicated horsewoman, she insisted on riding him later. Although the Queen did not know the signals that the Lipizzaners follow, Pluto, to her great delight, took her without guidance through the gentler maneuvers which he himself knew so well.

To watch the stallions at their daily schooling is a moving lesson in what understanding humans and intelligent animals can do together. The riding hall is very quiet. It is a tradition of the school that commands are always muted. "Scolding, shouts or violence of any kind," said Podhajsky, "would damage the art that these creatures inherently have and the pleasure that they find in their artistry."

Horses are selected for the riding school with utmost care. Some twenty-five Lipizzaners are born each year at the school's stud farm in Piber, high in the beautiful hills of Styria, Austria. The stallions with special aptitude and the mares whose build and temperament seem to suit them as dams for the next generation are singled out. But they know no discipline except a halter until they are four years old. Lipizzaners mature slowly and then live to a remarkable old age, often into their thirties. The school believes it would be a mistake to hurry them, for they are all individualists. When they do start to work, the school wants them to really enjoy it.

Their training requires infinite patience. Schooling is limited to forty-five minutes a day; it is felt this is all that the mentality of even these extraordinary horses can take. They must never leave a lesson tired or disappointed.

After a young stallion, still dapple-gray (he is born very dark and gradually turns snow-white with full maturity), has learned the conventional walk, trot and gallop, he masters increasingly difficult maneuvers. First is the *passade,* an elegant high-stepping walk; the stationary trot of the *piaffe* comes next; then the circular *pirouette* and the sideways walks and trots used in the group's final quadrille.

This is known as the "school on the ground." The "school off the ground" calls for even more patience. In the *levade,* the horse bends back on his haunches, raises his forelegs and remains like a statue until ordered to return to four feet. In the *courbette,* he makes several jumps on his hind legs without touching the ground with his forelegs. In the *croupade,* he leaves the ground entirely with legs bent under him. And finally, in the fantastic *capriole*—mastered by only a few—he soars like a

306

Pegasus into the air with his hind legs out-thrust and his beautiful mane and long tail fluttering.

Many of the Lipizzaners' maneuvers are based on inherited traits. As colts, the Lipizzaners play games that are similar to the routines they finally learn to execute on command. The leaps, for example, come perfectly naturally. Many of the turns and steps are a legacy from the days when their forebears carried fighting knights and used swift circling or sidestepping movements to avoid an attack or to close in on an opponent.

The riders of the school are as carefully chosen and trained as the horses. Their education takes about five years. Each accepted apprentice-candidate faces two stern instructors: an experienced senior rider and an equally experienced horse. "The older men," said one school official, smiling, "teach the young horses. The older horses teach the young men." Frequently, a new apprentice thinks that the horse, since he obeys so easily, is simple to handle. The Lipizzaner, revealing a sardonic sense of humor, will wait until his pupil-rider becomes a bit careless, then rear up in a sudden *levade* and deposit the unsuspecting aspirant neatly on the tanbark.

Gradually, the apprentice learns the delicate system of communication between man and animal. To the trained Lipizzaner, the slightest movement of the reins or the least shift of weight by the rider is a signal. The clack of a tongue, a quiet *"nein, nein," "gut, gut"* or *"schön"* ("nice") is immediately understood. The rider wears spurs but uses them, as he does the traditional birch twig he carries, only to touch the sensitive stallion as a last resort.

The ceremony that opens every performance in the school often brings the audience to its feet. The big doors at one end of the hall swing open. With Colonel Handler at the head, the stallions pace sedately in. The magnificent white chargers move forward until they face the portrait of Charles VI of Austria-Hungary, which has hung at the end of the hall ever since it was completed in 1735. Slowly, in unison, while the horses stand like statues, the colonel and the riders behind him raise their cocked hats and extend them at arm's length in solemn salute to the monarch—who is depicted in armor, mounted on a Lipizzaner.

One of the very few others to ever be saluted in this manner was an American. In early 1945, U.S. bombs began to rain down on Vienna, a strategic link between Germany and Italy. Colonel Podhajsky wanted to get the priceless horses out of the city, but the Nazi authorities would not give permission. If the school was closed and all the horses removed, not only the Viennese but the whole of Austria would realize that the Nazis had irretrievably lost.

Podhajsky decided to try to smuggle riders and horses to safety. He persuaded a railroad official to allow him to hook a car loaded with stallions onto the back of a train leaving Vienna. Fortunately, Nazi officials were too busy to investigate. Later, the train to which the Lipizzaners' car was attached was strafed and bombed. "The horses," said the colonel, "were the calmest of us all. They were scared, but they had the discipline of their inflexible dignity."

It took them four days to reach the little village of St. Martin's, in upper Austria, less than two hundred miles from Vienna. There Podhajsky stabled his horses on a friend's estate. Their troubles were far from over, however. Fodder was scarce. Desperate refugees tried to steal the horses for food.

Salvation came suddenly. When elements of the U.S. Third Army moved into St. Martin's, an officer, recognizing the Lipizzaners and Podhajsky, sent word to General George S. Patton's headquarters. Both Patton and Podhajsky had ridden in the Olympic games; the general knew of the great riding master and responded at once. The colonel was to arrange a showing of the Lipizzaners for Under Secretary of War Robert Patterson and himself the next day.

While Patton and Patterson watched from an improvised stand, and rows of fascinated GIs sat on the grass, the horses, hungry and nervous as they were, put on a superb show. "They sensed," said Podhajsky, "that they were facing a crucial test." After the concluding, beautifully executed school quadrille, the colonel rode forward to face Patton, who stood at attention. Podhajsky's speech was short. "We ask your protection," he concluded. The iron-faced general nodded and there was a breathless silence.

"Magnificent," rasped Patton. "These horses will be wards of the U.S. Army until they can be returned to the new Austria." Podhajsky and his riders slowly raised their hats. The Lipizzaners stood at attention. No one there will ever forget the scene.

There is a sequel in what to the Austrians has become a patriotic saga. The Lipizzaner mares and foals were still a hundred miles away, at Hostoun, Czechoslovakia. The Russians were advancing fast toward Hostoun. It was a question of hours as to whether the East or the West would have the priceless horses. A message flashed to Patton from Colonel Charles H. Reed, commander of the Second Cavalry Group, whose Intelligence had discovered the location of the stud farm.

Patton's reaction was characteristic. "Get them," the general radioed. Reed sent a task force across the Czech border. The force avoided Nazi SS border patrols and found the horses. Many of the members of the rescue party happened to be Texans; they herded the Lipizzaners back into Austria with little trouble. The Russians complained bitterly when they discovered the horses were gone. Patton, when confronted with the criticism, is reported to have shrugged and said in his pithy fashion that the Lipizzaners were far more valuable, and much nicer, than most Russian generals.

Crip,
Come Home!

by RUTH THOMAS

WHEN CRIP first came to our hill in Arkansas and claimed the east yard as his nesting territory, he was like other brown thrashers. I knew him only by the aluminum band, 308978, that I had placed on his left leg. Three summers he and a faithful mate built their nests in a great tangle of climbing roses. The spring that Crip was four years old he lost this territory to a pair of strange thrashers. His old mate failed to return, and he finally settled in my north flower garden.

On June 9 he fluttered across our lawn, his right wing dragging, plainly broken. For the rest of the summer, still and fluffed, he waited in the old lilac bush by the gate for the grain and nutmeats that I scattered on the ground. He grew very gentle, and even as I stood close by, watching, he would begin to eat. And yet, I thought, what hope for a bird that cannot fly?

The summer ran out, and the wing healed in a crooked way, drooping from the shoulder. Crip became more active, went in long leaps across the lawn and often got into trees by springing to the lowest branches. In the middle of September—the wonder of it —he could fly! I had seen him glide down from a tree, landing with a topple to the right, but now he made short, level flights from tree to tree. Then came the day that

he lifted himself awkwardly from the ground.

When it was time to migrate Crip moved only from the north garden to the roses, and the thorny canes became his winter stronghold. Many times a day I took him food.

Another autumn came and again Crip stayed on his hill. Wrapped in a moody silence, he heard the geese going over and watched the warblers in the oaks. But by the next autumn he had grown so used to the stiff wing, so confident in his use of it, that one sunny October day he joined the bird travelers moving southward. He still could fly for less than a hundred yards. There would be open spaces to cross in his miles of travel through strange country and, night or day, enemies quick to pounce on a weary, crippled old brown thrasher. All that day I thought of him slipping from thicket to thicket, watching, always watching.

Winter in Arkansas is short. By March 1 the jonquils were in golden bloom, cardinals were whistling and the mockingbird sang and mimicked his bird neighbors. On March 14 a brown thrasher sang from the north garden, and I hurried out with binoculars. The bird high in the oak had two bands on the right leg—one, my own red celluloid identification band, the other, the metal government band. Last summer "Red" had owned as his territory the north lawn and garden. He and Crip established a dividing line, and seldom did either one trespass on the other's property.

The next afternoon I found Greta, the thrasher that had been Crip's mate for the last two seasons, in a banding trap in my garden. Red moved uneasily in the branches above us and as soon as she was released he flew to her side. They moved on down my border of shrubs, tossing the old brown leaves of winter, digging into the soft earth, and Red, in the way of a thrasher newly mated, whispered a song. Faithless Greta had not waited for Crip's return.

All the next day I watched. "Crip, come home! Take back your wife." Seven more days went by. "Crip, are you coming? Too late to have your wife. Red and Greta are building a nest in the big honeysuckle. But they also claim the territory of the roses.

They eat at your table and loiter in your thicket of thorns. Hurry, Crip!"

On the morning of March 26 Crip came home. At six that morning I went to the kitchen and put up the window shade. At the edge of the roses I saw a small whirlwind of old leaves. Two brown thrashers were in a furious fight, and I saw that one had a stiff right wing. Crip!

I thought Red was killing the old thrasher, and ran out. Our two Scotties rushed after me, and the thrashers separated, Red flying away, Crip streaking to the roses. So Crip would have back his territory, for with birds he who stays is the victor. He looked old, I saw (he would be eight that spring), his color was faded and his tail and the right wing were frayed at the edges.

Later that morning I realized that Crip had come home to grief and trouble. He and his old mate were on the lawn only two feet

apart, pretending to forage, while Red was a few yards to the north. Crip's feathers were puffed, he was on truculent guard. Red seemed uneasy and afraid. He was the first to fly up a tree, Greta followed, and then old Crip, lifting himself in his hard way, perched between them. Immediately Red and Greta flew to their garden, leaving Crip huddled in dejection.

Crip might have accepted the loss of his former mate if she had stayed in Red's territory. But Crip's home had been her home, and she continued her visits, keeping him in a state of alternate hope and bafflement. He whispered songs, carried twigs and leaves as symbols of his eagerness to be at nesting. Greta's nest in the garden was finished, Red was the mate that had helped her build it and the new bond was stronger than memories of Crip. Rebuffed, the old thrasher turned in fury on Red.

Scene followed scene. On the third day Crip seemed weary and confused; his occasional songs were thin and perfunctory, his manner toward Greta changed to timid doubt and the rushes at Red took more and more of his strength.

On the fourth day Crip was visibly drooping. In the afternoon both Red and Greta ate at the feeding table and then defiantly flew to the roses. Crip had ignored the two at the table, but no thrasher's pride could endure a neighbor male in the home sanctuary. With an obvious effort he leaped into the roses and chased Red a few yards toward the north garden. Then he fluttered to the ground and slumped against a tree. His eyes were closed, his wings sagged, all his feathers were curiously loosened. Was my thrasher dying? Red slipped back to the roses, and old Crip, fierce and pitiful, started up. It

was time to interfere, and I went out and drove Red and Greta away.

But next day Crip's luck changed. For one thing, I piled extravagant heaps of nut-meats on a shelf in the north garden so Red and Greta would have little reason for going into Crip's territory. Of far greater importance, a single female thrasher arrived. All the forenoon Crip sang the bold and beautiful songs of courtship from an oak on the south hillside. Somewhere below him was the thrasher that he was asking to be his mate. By afternoon he had called her to the roses, where I saw her sprawled, sleepy and basking, at the sunny edge of the tangle.

But the lady was not yet won. For three days, from dawn to twilight, Crip sang his courtship songs. Not even in winter had my nutmeats served him so well. Taking no time to forage for natural foods, he sailed down to the feeding table, ate hurriedly, then fluttered to the roses, leaped up through the canes, thence to the branches of the nearest oak and on to the topmost twigs. In his new joy, Crip regained his old energy and spirit. One day he caught Red under the roses and gave him a savage drubbing.

On the morning of April 2 Crip, old and dingy-brown, his right wing stiff, walked beside a mate of shining rufous-russet, small and trim, a maiden come to her first nesting. They dug in the grass together, tossed the wind-blown leaves, and twice Crip gave his lady a possessive peck. Her meek submission told me of her youth. Crip carried twigs to the roses, to begin the foundation of a nest. Even at his work he sang tender whispers of a song. Our old crippled thrasher had not only come back to us, he had won out in a battle as old as the world. For me, there could never be a more glorious spring.

Rolf, the Dog
That Found Things

by ROBERT LITTELL

D AY AFTER DAY, on the roads of Denmark's island of Fünen, one could see a small blue pickup truck with a big dark dog sitting beside the driver and looking at him as if listening to his instructions. Whenever the truck went by, the people of Fünen turned and stared, some in wonder, others in grateful recognition. For on its tailboard were lettered the words *Sporhunden Rolf* ("Rolf, the Tracking Dog") and a telephone number. This was actually the business card of a dog that was hired to find things people had lost. Between 1950 and 1962, Rolf and his owner, Svend Andersen, recovered some $700,000 worth of missing watches, jewelry, tools, currency, heirlooms, bonds, cows, geese, pigs and other dogs. Rolf's exquisitely sensitive nose found these things in dank bogs, on busy streets, floating on water, encased in ice, buried under manure.

Rolf was a German shepherd. His partner, a secondhand dealer in the town of Glamsbjerg, had an assistant tend his shop so he could be free to answer the six hundred to

seven hundred calls for help that he and Rolf got every year. Four out of five times, according to Andersen, they found what they were summoned to look for. Whenever the telephone rang in Andersen's house Rolf was instantly alert. If he heard Andersen mention one of the dozen objects they were most often asked to find, Rolf would dash to the truck, eager to be off to work. On the way Andersen would repeat over and over again the name of what they were going to look for. When they arrived, usually at some field or farmhouse, Rolf circled, backtracked and circled again until he picked up the faint, far scent (this is Andersen's explanation) of an object lying in a spot where it didn't belong, out of its proper place or context.

In 1954 Edvard Christensen, a Glamsbjerg businessman, lost his gold watch while hunting wild boar. It was nightfall before he appealed to Andersen, who, with a flashlight, set Rolf to quartering the ground in the 1600-acre forest. Three hours later Rolf had not only found the watch but had conscientiously brought in a dozen shells ejected from Christensen's gun. A visitor to a cattle show sneezed so hard that he lost a gold filling. Rolf found it, several yards from the place of the sneeze, in turf that had been trampled by hundreds of feet. A farmer lost one thousand crowns in bills and small change in one of his fields. Rolf recovered all but two cents' worth of it, including some copper coins no larger than a thumbtack.

Mogens Pedersen carelessly let his eleven-year-old daughter, Yutta, play with a fine

heirloom watch which belonged to her grandmother. When Yutta lost it in a straw rick, fifty children were turned loose to look for it. No luck. Next day the police came with a dog, later with another dog; both failed. Nine days after this, Rolf was sent for. Ignoring the rick, Rolf began to nose about in a root pit some distance away—where he found the watch in a matter of minutes. Someone had taken a forkful of straw from the rick and dumped it into the pit. Ole Eriksen lost his wallet while driving a hay kicker. But Rolf showed no interest in Erik-

sen's hay field. Obeying his nose, he ambled over to a farm two fields away, where he found the wallet impaled on a tooth of the hay kicker—which Eriksen's neighbor had borrowed from him.

Rolf often found things which the owners didn't know they'd lost. After a troop of Boy Scouts had spent a restless night in a hayloft, one of them missed his wallet. When a dozen boys failed to find it, Rolf was sent for. Besides the wallet he fished out of the hay a couple of harmonicas, four ball-point pens, two flashlights, the mouthpiece of a trumpet, a button off a tunic, a whistle and a shoe.

Once when Andersen reproved him sharply for failing to find a lost watch, Rolf went off sheepishly and returned a little later in triumph with a watch in his mouth—followed by an angry, half-naked man shouting: "I was getting dressed when this damned dog poked his head in the door and lifted my watch from the table!"

In 1956 I went to Glamsbjerg to make sure that Rolf's exploits were not just another fairy story by Hans Christian Andersen (no relation to Svend), who was born at Odense, only a few miles away. Svend Andersen and his wife, Valborg, were living in a one-story house with few comforts. He was a chunky, round-faced man and about fifty when I met him, with oddly oblique lids which gave his eyes a hooded expression. Over coffee and cakes we talked and watched Rolf. The dog's stare was mysterious, impersonal. He seemed incredibly alert, yet at the same time profoundly calm. The telephone rang, and then I heard Andersen saying, "A wallet? Five hundred crowns? I can't guarantee. . . ."

An hour later we were in a park near the city of Fredericia, tramping among the beech trees with Axel Jensen, an agent for agricultural machinery. Jensen had lost his wallet somewhere in these woods ten days before while picking anemones with his wife. Since then hundreds of people had gone walking here, and it had rained.

For half an hour Rolf ranged in wide, broken zigzags. Occasionally Andersen would call him back, or tell him to keep looking. No wallet. We drove to another part of the forest where anemones might tempt wallets to fall from pockets. Again Rolf ranged, nose to the boggy earth, while Andersen encouraged him from time to time. I don't know at what moment we began to notice that Rolf was padding about in narrower loops and that Andersen was now standing at the brink of a ditch, motionless, tense, as if giving orders that only Rolf could hear.

Suddenly Rolf began to paw the soft earth. He stopped, cast about and scratched again a few feet away. Then he changed his mind and began to dig farther to the right. All at once he trotted out of the bog, head proudly high, holding something dark in his mouth. It was the wallet. Jensen roared with surprise and joy.

Later, over a glass of beer, and after Jensen had paid Andersen for the job, I asked Andersen how a dog goes about finding a piece of leather five by seven inches in a third of a million square feet of sod and undergrowth trodden by hundreds of strollers. Andersen said he had known there was nothing in the first seventy-five acres because of Rolf's total lack of interest. "But in the swamp I could tell from the way he behaved that he had picked up a trail. The scent had reached him through the air from the spot where the wallet was dropped."

Andersen had picked Rolf from a litter sired by his father's all-Scandinavian prize-winner because Rolf had the biggest head and snuffled more eagerly along the ground than any of the other six pups. Rolf found his first watch, a neighbor's, when he was only five months old. After a year's careful training and amateur watch-and-wallet work he became a professional. To answer the calls that began to come in, Andersen had to buy a light truck. Then, to pay for the truck, he had to start charging fees. (They were never high—twenty to forty crowns, or about four to eight dollars, depending upon the object's value and the customer's finances.) What began as a hobby became a business, finally an all-absorbing passion.

During Rolf's lifetime nothing ever got lost in the Andersen's house. Coins, nails, buttons—the ever-watchful Rolf picked them all up without being told. To demonstrate this, Andersen put a spoon on the floor, called Rolf in from the next room and ordered him to lie down. We went on talking. But Rolf couldn't stand it. In a few minutes he got up, seized the spoon in his mouth and delivered it to his master. Sometimes Rolf's helpfulness struck Andersen as exaggerated. "If I stay too long with friends at a pub," he said when I saw him, "and Valborg starts out with Rolf to find me, I haven't got a chance."

What particularly interested one police expert, who was a judge at some official trials in which Rolf took part, was the "fantastic coöperation between dog and guide." Andersen's skill in keeping up Rolf's interest by quiet remarks seemed to him "like the conversation of two friends."

Between Andersen and Rolf there was a deep and subtle sympathy. But there was also something mysterious, beyond rational explanation. If Andersen was tired, Rolf was less efficient. Andersen believes his own concentration helped Rolf in a search. When Rolf failed on a job, Andersen would lie awake that night, going over and over the ground in his mind. Often he got out of bed and drove with Rolf to the scene of their failure, where they would go hunting again by flashlight. "The night is quiet," he would say, "and it is a good time to hunt a thing that is lost." More often than not, they found it.

"When we found something," said Andersen, "there was no feeling like it. I don't know who was happier, Rolf or me. Then I could relax—until the telephone rang again." And ring it did, right up until 1962 when Rolf died at the age of fifteen. "His death was worse for me than if he had been a person," Andersen says today. "My wife and I still visit his grave every week. And we're hoping his granddaughter—his son is dead —will pass on his heritage."

Petronella

by A. G. McRae

I STOOD in the dusty pound at Lydenburg, South Africa, and watched the unwanted donkeys being put up for sale. Most of the unfortunate animals were sold, and I didn't like the way their new owners took possession, thrashing their purchases before ever a task was set them and their willingness tested. One by one the little pilgrims were set on the dreary road that leads through labor and starvation to merciful death.

At last there was only one left, an old gray jenny with one eye blinded and one torn ear hanging loppily from its middle. She was covered with ticks, her knees were bent and her head hung down—a picture of dejection. A young native bid sixpence for her and laughed raucously. I was prospecting for gold at the time and almost down but not out, for I still had my tools and six shillings in cash. I had intended buying a bag of meal and supplementing my sugar and coffee supply. But now I knew that I must buy the aged jenny and sacrifice a precious cartridge as well. Between the eyes, and she'd never know what hit her.

I raised the bidding to a shilling and watched my extra coffee go down the drain. The other fellow bid one and three. I sent my sugar ration after the coffee and upped it threepence more. My opponent made a scornful remark and slouched off; the donkey was mine to release through the barrel of my old Smith and Wesson, as soon as we could get out of town. For no reason at all I named her Petronella. Getting her out of town wasn't going to be easy, by the look of her, so I dug into my pack for some salt, which is ambrosia to asses the world over. Her good ear pricked up as I held the dainty under her muzzle. Her nose wrinkled ecstatically as she crunched it, and she emitted those curious, death-rattlelike sounds which in the asinine etiquette indicate pleasure. With more salt on my palm, I led her away.

It is bad manners to carry a gun in town, so the old Smith and Wesson was in my pack. When we came to a sufficiently remote spot I transferred its holster to my belt. The action reminded Petronella of goodies and she edged nearer ingratiatingly. I gave her a little salt and then, for some quite inexplicable reason, I fastened my pack on her emaciated back. She pricked her good ear forward and started off up the mountain trail in front of me as a well-trained pack animal should. Gone was the air of dejection, and gone, too, the bent and trembling knee. In place of the sorry moke in the pound was a frail but determined old lady, loved and ready to get back to the sort of task

316

she understood. She brought a curious kind of dignity to her labor. I thought, "Well, if she gives me any trouble or looks like falling, I'll bump her off, but it's nice not having to carry the pack." Even then I knew I could no more shoot Petronella than fly.

She gave me trouble all right. The very first night she chewed my pack about, trying to get the salt inside. The next night, after we had made camp, she disappeared. I thought, "Good riddance," but then I started worrying in case she had broken a leg, or a snake had bitten her, so I spent half the night searching. When I finally gave up and returned, she was lying next to the ashes of my fire, chewing away at the pack once more. After that I stopped worrying, and in the year during which she and I fossicked around she often went off on her own for a few hours.

She invented a little game after she felt she knew me well enough to take liberties. Whenever we approached a spinney where the bush was thick, she would gallop ahead and hide in it. Having found the sort of cover she needed to fool me, she would stand dead still while I fumed and fretted, usually within a couple of yards of her hide-out. After half an hour of this kind of fun she would bray derisively, to show me where she had been all the time. Those were halcyon days, for our needs were small and the country supplied most of them. Long, hot days and clear, cool nights, rain sometimes, but always followed by the drying-out sun and wind. We knew thirst too, but never badly, for Petronella's infallible instinct always led us to a waterhole.

One day an old fellow turned up with a whole string of donkeys, and one of them was a jack. Petronella should have known better, at her age. But girls will be girls, and in due course the horrible truth became obvious—Petronella was about to become a mother. When her time was near, I had to go into Lydenburg on urgent business, and so I left her in charge of a boy I thought I could trust. I returned inside a week, late at night and during a terrific storm. I went to look for my boy to find out how Petronella fared. He had disappeared, and so had most of my kit. I stumbled around in the mud and rain, waiting for flashes of lightning to show me where the jenny was. And then I heard the jackals yip-yapping and snarling on a plateau above the spring.

I got there just too late, for the brutes had torn at the little body of the foal as it was born, and it died as I lifted it up. Petronella had fought them off for as long as she was able. She was in a terrible state, her muzzle ripped and her flank savaged. Carrying the dead foal, I led her back to the shack and bedded her down where I had light to see to dress her wounds. All next day she followed me about like a dog, and when I stopped she pressed her head against my thigh, her misery too much to bear alone. She would not eat or drink, and her one fear seemed to be that I would go away and leave her again. She died on the evening of the second day after my return, with her maimed ear pressed against my side and her poor, thin flank heaving less and less, until it finally went quite flat and was still.

I dug a deep hole where no gold would ever be found, and cheated the jackals by laying heavy rocks over her body and over the closed grave as well. I buried the child of her dotage with her. As I did so I remembered the black cross etched over her withers, the beam straight down her spine and the bar crucifix from side to side. Native servants in the Cape used to tell us, long ago, that the mark was imprinted on the hides of gray donkeys because once The Man rode such a donkey in triumphant humility before all mankind.

The Rooster
That Served
the Lord

by H. GORDON GREEN

LIKE MOST MEN whose faith is really profound, Father lived quietly with his religion. And as I look back now, I cannot help but marvel that he achieved so sure a belief in a Creator who was all good and always concerned, when his life had so much of struggle and heartbreak in it.

The soil of our farm in Ontario was heavy and sour, and there were only forty acres of it to sustain eight children. Father, one of a pioneer family of eleven, had had just three years of schooling, and it had taken him twenty years of hard labor and frugal saving to accumulate the down payment for the farm. Now the Great Depression was stalking the land. Yet through all that grim time I can never remember him voicing the slightest doubt of the essential goodness of the Master Plan. To him, the proofs of the Lord's goodness were everywhere. Not least of these was our friend Prunejuice, the Dark-Brown Leghorn.

It all started at the camp meeting held annually in a nearby woods by a nonsectar-

ian group known simply as "The Saints." Our family attended every summer. One morning it was announced that the treasury was dangerously low, and the evangelist that year—a colorful old glory thumper from Kentucky—treated us to a special sermon on stewardship. "Now see here, brethren!" he shouted. "It's a downright disgrace for us to be so hard up for money! The Lord is a good provider, isn't He? Then why are we scraping the bottom of the barrel? I'll tell you why! Because we are afraid to put our faith to work for us, that's why! Well, brethren, this morning we're going to change all that!"

Gradually he made his plan clear to us. Instead of taking up a collection, the ushers would pass among us with new dollar bills which he had induced the board to withdraw from the meeting's bank account. "This time," cried the evangelist with a dramatic shake of his jowls, "these here ushers are asking you to *take* money! There's seven hundred dollars in those collection baskets

319

right now—seven hundred dollars of the Lord's money. And we're asking you to take out what you figure would be a right share and invest it for the Lord. I'm not going to advise you how to invest it, because the Lord will tell you that when you get around to asking Him. All I'm asking is that, whatever you do, you do it with faith that the Lord will attend to His own. Then, when the next camp meeting rolls around, and it's time to pass these here baskets out to you again, we're going to ask you to just give the Lord back His own money."

I can still recall the look of bewilderment on the faces of the congregation. Here was a preacher full of the spirit and all that, but after all he *was* an American. And these Americans were sometimes more spectacular than sensible. Father had reservations, too. "Seems as though we're supposed to put God on trial," he whispered to Mother. But he took five one-dollar bills, the same as most of the others did.

"It's too late to do any planting with it," he said on the way home. "Looks to me as if it will have to buy some sort of livestock."

After some discussion, he and Mother decided that the five dollars should buy a setting of chicken eggs. The trouble was that Mother had chickens of her own—a lovely flock of White Wyandottes. "We'll have to buy a different kind," she said. "Else we won't be able to keep track of them handy."

Father had several reasons for choosing Dark-Brown Leghorns. One was that in those impractical days a farmer would often choose a particular breed for its beauty of feathering as much as for its earning power —and of all the fowl which ever strutted in the sun the Dark-Brown Leghorn is surely one of the most gorgeous. Another reason was that Dark-Brown Leghorns cost five dollars per setting of fifteen eggs; the other kinds were much cheaper. This meant that the Lord was getting the very best.

One of Mother's hens, carefully selected, was given the divine mission of hatching out the Lord's eggs. She was faithful to the end. But, for all her trouble, only three chicks broke out of their shells on the twenty-first day. This was bad luck; still worse was to come. Two of the chicks gave up the ghost that first day. The one remaining had now become so precious that Father took it away from the hen and gave it a box behind the kitchen stove. "Isn't it pretty?" one of my little sisters cried, hugging the chick to her cheek. "Just the color of prune juice!"

"Well, Prunejuice," Father said, "you're sure going to have to lay one awful lot of eggs between now and next camp-meeting time if you're going to pay the Lord back His five dollars!"

A few weeks later, however, when fluff gave way to feathers and a little scarlet comb began to bud, it became quite evident that this chicken would never lay *any* eggs. Prunejuice was going to become a rooster.

The affection that soon developed between this special young bird and the family was, of course, inevitable. Father kept him in a little box near the head of the bed with the lamp burning in it all night to warm him. It was the maintenance of that lamp which caused the first entry in Prunejuice's expense account: "Extra coal oil—ten cents," Father wrote on the back of the calendar. When Prunejuice no longer needed mothering, we tried leaving him in the henhouse with the other fowl. But he would have nothing to do with such ordinary creatures,

and every time the screen door was left open he would come into the kitchen. If someone tried to catch him, he would go upstairs. When he was two or three months old, he began to follow Father to his work in the fields. "Never saw a bird like him," Father would say to the neighbors. "Sometimes you'd swear he was part human."

But there came a day when Father wasn't quite so affectionate. Prunejuice was strutting around the back porch when one of the girls gave a saucer of milk to the cat. Immediately Prunejuice laid claim to it. There was a battle, in the middle of which the rooster suddenly rose in the air like a helicopter and descended into a half can of cream cooling in the water tank by the well. "I ought to drown you in it!" Father said as he pulled out the sputtering bird. He threw the cream to the pigs, and that night he chalked up the second entry in Prunejuice's account.

Two days later the cat and the rooster had another argument, and before it was over two panes of glass in our hotbed cover had been broken. Then, late in August, Prunejuice got a leg under a wheel of our Model T when Father was backing it out of the garage. The veterinarian had a good laugh that night when Father came in. "I've prescribed for goldfish and canaries," he said. "But, so help me Hannah, this is the first time I've ever been asked to splice a drumstick!"

Now Prunejuice was shut up in the duckpen back of the woodshed to recover. "I really don't know why we're keeping him," Father said to Mother one night. "He'll never amount to anything more than he does right now." We kept him nonetheless.

Then one blustery night there was a great commotion at the window of our parents' bedroom. Prunejuice, who had been carefully locked in the duckpen, was outside squawking as if a banshee were at his tail.

Father slid into his trousers, picked his shotgun off the wall and went outside. He was none too soon. The two boys who had unlatched the duckpen door were just leaving with two of our ducks in a bag. "We were hungry, mister!" the older of the pair begged.

Father emptied the sack of its terrified booty and studied the shivering lads closely. He recognized them both. "You're not working now?" he asked the older youth. "All right, I need a hired man to help in the bush. You report here tomorrow morning and cut wood with me, and we'll say no more about this. And you," he said to the younger one, "you're supposed to be in school these days, aren't you? Well, you just mind that I don't hear of you playing hooky if you don't want me to turn you in. Understand?"

The boys, sobbing with relief, disappeared into the night. And, bright and early next morning, our new man timidly declared himself ready for work. He stayed with us until the very last load of firewood came out of the woods that winter. "Come seeding time, I'd like to get that lad back," Father said when the boy finally left us. "Yes, sir, Prunejuice did us a mighty good turn that time! It's worth something to find a good hired man these days."

But how much was it worth? Now Prunejuice's account ran something like this:

Expenses

Camp-meeting money	$5.00
Coal oil	.10
Half can cream all shot	3.25
2 panes glass busted	1.20
Veterinarian—leg busted	1.00
Feed (approx.)	.32
	$10.87

. . .

To the Good

Two ducks saved	$3.50
One hired man found	???

"Of course, there's still the worth of his carcass to be figured in," Father said. "But, at a quarter a pound, say, for a five-pound bird, we're still on the minus side."

It wasn't time yet to strike the final balance, however. One bright morning in May a big Packard pulled into our lane. "You've got Dark-Brown Leghorns here, I believe," the driver said. "Henry Becker tells me he sent you a setting last year."

"We didn't have very good luck," Father explained. "We just raised one chick. A cock bird."

"Well, happens it's a cock bird I'm after. I've got two dozen hens that's getting mighty lonesome. Where is he?"

"That's him over by the well trying to pick a fight with that tomcat," Father said.

We boys caught Prunejuice and brought him to the man to examine. "He's got a crooked leg!" our visitor exclaimed.

"I was going to warn you about that," Father said. "I ran over him once."

The man in the Packard lit a cigar. "Well," he said, "I was hoping to find a bird I could take to the shows, too, and this one would only be good for breeding. Oh, I could offer you, say, fifteen dollars, if you're interested. . . ."

"Under the circumstances," Father said quietly, "I doubt if I could refuse." He ran a hard but loving hand through the magnificent mahogany sheen of the rooster's hackle, and then bent over to nuzzle him against his cheek. "Good-bye, Prunejuice!" he said.

And when Prunejuice was ours no more, we thought that even the tomcat seemed a little sad. "Anyhow," Father said, "it's nice knowing he's going to a good home. And he's squared his account now, too. Let's see —we're near eight dollars to the good, plus the first five. . . . I'll have thirteen dollars to put in when they pass that basket again."

But when camp-meeting time came round again, Father put in an extra five—just to make sure.

THE DOG
FROM
NO·MAN'S·LAND

Condensed from One Man and His Dog

by ANTHONY RICHARDSON

THE DEAFENING CRASH was followed almost at once by a long, grinding roar. The noise was terrifying, and the German shepherd puppy, reacting frantically, struggled to get on his feet. He fell over helplessly, uttering a tremulous cry. He was too weak from starvation to stand up.

The farmhouse which was his home lay in no-man's-land between the Maginot and Siegfried lines. A few days earlier—it was now February 12, 1940—great thunderblasts of artillery had toppled its walls, killed his mother and litter mates, and sent the farm family scurrying. The puppy had lain alone in the ruined kitchen ever since, cowering whenever the shelling recurred. But that last blast had not been gunfire. It was the crash of a low-flying reconnaissance plane, followed by an explosion of petrol and the roar of flames. A few minutes later two airmen from the French First Bomber-Reconnaissance Group, both lucky to be alive, spotted the ruins of the farmhouse. The pilot, Pierre Duval, had taken a bullet

through his calf, so it was Jan Bozdech, observer-gunner, who walked cautiously forward to investigate.

As he stepped inside past the sagging kitchen door, revolver in hand, Jan heard the sound of quick, excited breathing.

"Put up your hands and come out," he ordered, covering a suspicious-looking pile of rubble. There was no reply. With pounding heart, the airman finally came forward and peered over the debris.

"Well, I'll be damned," he said. Then he began to laugh.

Pierre hobbled in, trailing blood but still curious. "What is it?" he asked.

"I've captured a German," Jan replied. Reaching down, he brought up the tawny German shepherd puppy. Although the animal was quivering with fright, it bared its milk teeth, snarled defiantly and even nipped at his hand.

"Here now," Jan said, stroking the base of the dog's ears, "you've just been saved from execution. I almost shot you, you know."

325

Under this reassuring touch, the puppy relaxed in Jan's arms.

A ground fog had thus far protected the two downed airmen from German eyes. But this might lift at any time, and it would not be safe to try for the French lines until night. They settled down to wait. The wounded Pierre rested in a chair and closed his eyes. Jan dug out his chocolate ration and offered a lump to the dog. It sniffed the morsel, but did not eat until Jan melted a piece over a flame and rubbed the softened chocolate on his fingers. Once started, the puppy happily licked the airman's fingers clean again and again. Then it snuggled into his arms and slept contentedly.

Using one hand, Jan spread out a map on the floor and studied it. It showed a wood about a mile away. If they could make this, they should be in French territory. At six o'clock Jan shook Pierre awake. "It's dark," he said. "We'd better be getting on."

For a moment they studied the puppy, now sleeping peacefully on the floor. They couldn't take it along, for if it whimpered even once it might betray them. They left some of their rations beside a pan of water, and Jan propped the door sideways across the entrance so the puppy could not follow. Then they stole away. As they set off for the wood an exchange of gunfire broke out. They inched forward on hands and knees. Before they had moved thirty yards a magnesium flare sputtered almost overhead, brilliantly lighting the terrain, and the two men flattened themselves instinctively. As the flare died away, Jan heard the noise he had been dreading—the frantic yelping of a puppy who knew he was being abandoned.

The animal would have to be silenced. Jan felt for his knife, and motioning Pierre to lie still, crept back. As he neared the farmhouse, he heard the puppy hurling itself against the barrier he had braced across the entry. Two forelegs momentarily hung over the edge while the hind legs scrabbled desperately. Then the dog slipped back down again.

Jan peered over the barricade, straight into the puppy's imploring eyes. He turned away. It was unthinkable to kill a dog with a knife. He searched the ground for a heavy stick with which to stun the animal, but there was none. Thinking of Pierre lying injured in the darkness, he began to panic; he must hurry. Then he heard an anguished whimper from the other side of the door. "Oh, hell," he muttered, and the last shreds of his resolution snapped. Reaching down into the dark, he lifted the puppy and slipped it inside his flying jacket.

It took the two men almost seven torturous hours to reach the fringe of the protective wood. Pierre, weakened by his wound, was at the limit of his endurance, and even Jan collapsed, utterly spent. During all this ordeal the puppy hadn't made a sound. But now he began to whine uncontrollably. The noise roused Jan from near-sleep. "Be quiet," he muttered.

"Listen," Pierre said. "He hears something that we can't." Then, like a pistol shot in the dark silence, a twig snapped and half a dozen figures emerged from the trees. Jan sprang to his feet, holding the dog with one hand and reaching for his revolver with the other. But in the shifting moonlight he saw the uniforms of the French infantry. They'd made it to safety!

Using their rifles and a greatcoat to improvise a stretcher, two of the soldiers carried Pierre to the nearest blockhouse. Next day he was sent to the hospital. And Jan, gently clutching the puppy, was driven back to his squadron base at Saint-Dizier. Here he belonged to a particularly close band of seven Czech exiles. All seven had been members of the Czech air force before Hitler invaded their country. They then had escaped through Poland, joined the French Foreign Legion in Africa, and later had been seconded to the French air force. All had the same fighting spirit, all had the same determination to strike back against the Germans at any cost.

Perhaps it was their very homelessness which made them so susceptible to Jan's puppy. They loved him at once, immediately adopted him as a mascot and after some discussion named him Antis after the A.N.T. bombers they'd flown back in Czechoslovakia. As Joshka, a slight, curly-haired youth from Moravia, commented, "The name should be unique, short and typically personal for our dog."

"*My* dog," Jan corrected. But he assented to the name.

Every night Antis slept in the blockhouse at Jan's feet. As the weeks passed he flourished and grew and, being intelligent and lovingly instructed, he learned to shake hands with each of his friends. No one knew just how much he understood this symbol of unity, but in time the dog's loyalty would be tested to the utmost. Antis was to go through a great deal with these men.

France tasted defeat that spring when Hitler's panzer divisions drove south with demoralizing speed. The squadron fled from one threatened airfield to another until the day Paris fell. Then it was assembled for the last time. "Gentlemen," the adjutant announced solemnly, "the unit is disbanded. Now it is every man for himself. May God be with you!"

The seven Czechs held a council. "We came here to fight, not to run away," said Vlasta, the senior member of the group. "I suggest we stick together, try to get to England and carry on from there." There

was no dissent. Within fifteen minutes the seven had piled all their possessions on an ancient cart, and perching Antis atop the load, joined the stream of refugees fleeing southward. And because they were both determined and lucky, some two weeks later they found themselves in the small Mediterranean seaport of Sète. From there they made their way to the British naval base at Gibraltar.

Once the British had satisfied themselves about the Czech fliers' credentials, they assigned all seven to the Royal Air Force and ordered them to proceed on the trawler *Northman,* bound for Liverpool. They were finally going to England! There was, however, one small problem: No dogs were allowed on board. British regulations absolutely forbade it. A flying wedge of Czechs smuggled Antis up the gangplank in a raincoat and spirited him into the stokehold. Jan loyally remained with the dog, spreading a blanket on the grimy coal.

On the second day out, the *Northman*'s engines broke down, and all passengers were ordered to transfer to another vessel. Hurriedly the Czechs divided Jan's baggage among themselves so that there would be room to conceal Antis in his duffel bag. All went well until they reached the deck of the new ship, where Jan paused momentarily to shift the weight of the bag.

"Move along, please," the ship's interpreter remarked curtly, and at the sound of the strange voice the duffel bag wriggled perceptibly. As it did, Jan lost his grip on the cord enclosing its neck. Immediately Antis thrust his head through the opening and looked out—directly into the astonished eyes of the British officer of the watch. The seven Czechs all stood as if paralyzed.

"Hullo," said the officer with a grin, "a stowaway! Well, let the poor beggar out; you'll have him suffocating." He released the cord and Antis dropped to the spotless deck, shaking a cloud of coal dust around him like a satanic halo. "Now get him below and give him a bath before the captain sees what a bloody mess you've made of his deck," the officer said, turning away to check off another group of transferees. As they crowded aboard, Jan was pushed along in a daze, with Antis trotting at his heels. The rest of the trip was made in luxury—real bunks, clean laundry, washbowls in the cabins. Antis, given his freedom, regained his vitality and glossy coat.

As they approached Liverpool, however, the fliers received devastating news. All animals had to be quarantined in port for six months; animals whose owners could not pay the kennel fees would be destroyed. All the money the fliers had among them would not ransom Antis for more than three weeks. But resourceful men have coped with greater problems than this. And by now the Czechs were seasoned conspirators.

At two o'clock on the afternoon before debarkation all animals were rounded up. Minutes later Jan and an interpreter were summoned before the captain. "You've not handed over your dog," the captain said severely. "Where is he?"

"I don't know." Which, at that very moment, was technically true.

"You know this is a serious offense?" the captain inquired.

"I've done nothing, sir," Jan replied. "I just haven't seen the dog." They searched the ship, peering into corners and racks, cabins and hatches; they flung open lockers and lifted containers. No Antis. At five o'clock they gave up.

When the ship docked at Liverpool the next evening Jan and Vlasta wangled the assignment of overseeing the unloading of the detachment's baggage. After the last of it had been stacked in the cargo net, they carefully placed a large, oddly shaped duffel bag stenciled "Jan Bozdech" on top of the pile. Within the hour, the bags were stacked neatly on the platform at Liverpool Central Station, Jan's still on top of the heap. Three minutes before their train steamed in, a platoon of soldiers marched up, halted and ordered arms. A rifle butt struck the bag labeled Bozdech, and immediately there was a loud yelp of protest.

Immediately the military police converged on the pile. The Czech detachment, always eager to help, joined in the search, heaving the baggage about and passing Jan's bag from hand to hand under cover of the general confusion until it was well clear of the suspected area. Surreptitious yelps with an imperceptible Czechoslovakian accent also misled the pursuers. When the airmen's train arrived, the police gave up in disgust.

A quarter of an hour later the seven comrades were on their way to their first camp in the United Kingdom. The date was July 12, 1940.

For men who had been on active combat duty, going back to flying school was irksome. At Cosford, and then at the Duxford RAF station, the Czechs also spent many exasperating hours poring over a book called *Fundamentals of English*. This was an impossible language which was spelled one way and pronounced another, and they almost welcomed the sporadic German air attacks which disrupted their study routine.

Jan devoted his spare time to training Antis. He was no expert handler and treated the animal simply as though he were a fellow human being; Antis responded with the most devoted and intelligent obedience. He quickly mastered all the standard commands, learned to close doors when ordered, and unfailingly fetched Jan's gloves when his companion dressed to go out. While Jan was in class,

Antis stayed with the armorers. He developed an unusual ability to detect enemy aircraft, and was always minutes ahead of the base's high-frequency direction finders. The warning system worked only when the planes were flying high. When the Germans came in at tree-top level, it was of little use. But Antis, the armorers claimed, invariably alerted them in time to take cover.

Jan was skeptical, for he had always been in class at the start of the raids. But one night, when he was studying in his bunk, Antis suddenly woke up and trotted to the window, ears cocked. There was no sound except the hiss of rain, but the dog began to growl and his back bristled. He walked to the door and stood there pointedly.

"Don't be silly," Jan said. "There's nothing out in this weather, Antis. Go and lie down."

Antis whined persistently. Then, seeing that Jan had no intention of moving from the bunk, he flattened his ears reproachfully and lay down. Half an hour later Joshka looked in as he came off duty from Operations Room. "Thick out," he said. "I wouldn't have been up there tonight for anything. I'll bet the German who came over was lost."

"Tonight?" Jan asked. "I didn't hear anything."

"About half an hour ago," Joshka said. "Very high. We were plotting him just over fifteen miles away when he turned back."

"Well, I'll be damned," Jan said, and by way of apology reached down and rubbed Antis' ears. The canny dog had been right all the time.

That fall, when the Czechs were transferred to Speke Airfield, five miles from Liverpool, Antis' peculiar ability became very important. Liverpool was a major target, subject to massive bombardment. The dog's warnings were uncannily accurate, and

the men came to depend on him to alert them whenever the immediate area was threatened.

One night when Jan and Vlasta were returning from liberty in town, the dog began to whine just as they neared a massive archway beneath the Speke viaduct. Over Liverpool, the air was ribbed with searchlights and the horizon blinked with exploding bombs, but as yet there had been no warning whine from the siren.

"They must be headed this way," Jan said as the animal's whine grew more insistent. "Come on, let's hole up under the archway." Almost immediately they heard the approaching engines. The first bomb burst just as they flung themselves under the protection of the viaduct. Now explosion followed explosion; a girder fell, splitting the granite pavement and striking sparks; masonry toppled at either end of the arch. Where there had been a neat row of houses beside the viaduct, there was only rubble. A long silence ensued, and then suddenly someone began to scream.

"Come on," Vlasta yelled. "We've got to get them out." They ran into the street. A man with blood spurting from a mangled arm blundered into them.

"Save her!" he shouted. "She's under there. We were having a cup of tea . . ." His voice trailed off, and he sat on the curb, plucking at his sleeve and sobbing. A rescue worker thrust a pick into Jan's hands. Antis, standing by the shattered remains of a kitchen cupboard, his forepaws deep in broken china, began to bark. Jan looked closely and saw five fingers moving in the rubble. Digging quickly, he uncovered a dazed and bloody woman.

"Good dog," the rescue worker said. "Bring him over here, will you? There's bound to be others. Lord, what a shambles!"

Jan followed the man to a pile of smoking plaster and shattered furniture. "Seek!" he ordered. Halfway up the heap Antis stopped, sniffing. An RAF officer started to dig where Antis stood, and within a few minutes he had a man out who had been totally buried and was still unconscious.

"Nothing like a trained dog for this job," the rescue worker said.

"He's not trained," Vlasta snapped impatiently. "He's just a damned good dog."

They continued working until two in the morning. When the rescue-squad leader finally passed the word that the job was done, the dog's coat was matted, his paws were cut and bleeding from scrambling over the jagged wreckage.

"There's no more we can do here," Vlasta said. "Let's go back and have Antis tended to." But Antis was straining at his leash once more, dragging Jan toward a sagging brick wall.

"No more, boy," Jan said. "We've had enough—" A crash cut him short as the wall collapsed. Horrified, he felt the leash jerk out of his hand.

"Antis!" he shouted in the din. "Antis!" Vlasta flashed his light to where the wall had been. There was now only a head-high pile of brick and timbers. Instantly Jan was on his knees, flinging great chunks of plaster in every direction. Again he shouted, almost hysterically, "Antis!"

From somewhere behind the rubble came an answering bark. The men quickly broke through to a little room knee-deep in debris. A woman, sprawled on her back under a mass of plaster, was dead. But in the far corner Antis stood by a crib; the child in it was still alive.

The rescue-squad director was visibly moved. "You know, boy," he said to Antis, "we just couldn't have done the job without you."

By early January 1941, Jan, Stetka and Josef had completed their flying-school and flight training and, with Squadron No. 311 (Czech Squadron of Bomber Command), were posted to East Wretham for combat duty. The move reunited them with the other Czechs who had been training elsewhere, and gave them at long last a chance to get at the enemy. But it meant that Antis, for the first time, had to accustom himself to separations from Jan, for the night bombing missions which the squadron was soon flying often lasted from late evening until dawn.

For weeks Antis was moody and dispirited. Then he established rapport with the maintenance crew assigned to *Cecilia,* his master's plane, and seemed to adjust himself to the absences. The dog would accompany Jan to dispersal, see him aboard the big Wellington, then retire to the maintenance tent, which stood at the edge of the field. Once there, he would settle down for the night and not budge as long as the planes were out. But sometime before dawn he would suddenly rise and cock his ears, and the maintenance crew knew then that the squadron was returning. As soon as Antis discerned the particular pitch of *Cecilia's* propellers, he began to bound and prance excitedly—his war dance, the mechanics called it—and would trot out to watch the planes come in and to greet Jan. The ritual never varied.

One night in June, however, after Jan had flown more than ten missions, the mechanics noted a sharp departure from routine. Shortly after midnight Antis became unusually restive. "What's the matter with him?" one of the men asked. "Are we expecting visitors?"

"No," replied Adamek, the crew chief, "no Jerries about tonight." He spoke directly to the dog. "Antis, come here for a scratch—and calm down." But the dog ignored him and went to the tent flap. Suddenly he lifted his muzzle and let out a long, piercing howl. Then he lay down outside, not resting, but with his head up as if preparing for a long vigil.

At half past one the first returning Wellington blinked her identification lights and rumbled down the runway. She was followed at regular intervals by other planes until all but *Cecilia* were accounted for. Two hours passed; there was still no sign of Jan's aircraft. "No point hanging on here," one of the mechanics finally said. "She'd have run out of gas by now."

"We'll give it fifteen minutes more," Adamek said. When the time was up and the plane had not appeared, the crew decided to disperse for breakfast. "Come along, Antis," said Adamek. The dog would not move.

Just then the squadron's popular wing commander, Lieutenant Josef Ocelka, drove up to the tent. A long-time admirer of Antis, he had promised Jan that he would look after the dog if Jan ever failed to return from a mission. "Any news of *Cecilia,* sir?" one of the mechanics asked, while Adamek struggled with Antis.

"Not yet. Give him a shove, Corporal," Ocelka suggested.

"It's no good, sir," Adamek replied. "He won't move until Jan shows up. I know him."

"So do I, dammit," Ocelka said. "Let's go. Perhaps he'll change his mind when he gets hungry." After breakfast Adamek went back to the tent with a plate of liver. Antis ignored it, as he ignored the driving rain that had begun to fall. When Adamek saw that no amount of coaxing would move the dog, he spread a tarpaulin over him and left.

Late that afternoon Operations Room was informed that *Cecilia* had been hit by flak over the Dutch coast, but had managed to limp back to Coltishall Airfield with only one casualty: Air gunner Jan Bozdech was in Norwich Hospital undergoing treatment for a superficial head wound. The Czechs were elated at the good news. But no one could convey it to the dog.

All that night Antis stayed at his post. Next morning, at the time when the squadron customarily returned from raids, he rose and paced about. An hour after dawn, when no plane had appeared, he began to howl disconsolately. "He'll starve," Ocelka said, "and drive us crazy while he does. We've got to think of something."

It was the station chaplain, Padre Poucnly, who provided the solution. Less restricted by ordinary command channels than the other officers, he went straight to the heart of the matter by telephoning the medical authorities at Norwich. Sergeant Bozdech was not badly hurt, he suggested persuasively as he explained the situation. Would it be possible to run him out for a short trip in an ambulance, and then board the dog at the hospital for a few days? (A prolonged medical consultation followed.) Yes? It would be? Thank you so much.

And that was that. The ambulance arrived that afternoon, and the two inseparables rode back together to Norwich Hospital. There both of them were outrageously spoiled by the nurses until Jan recovered.

By the time Antis had waited out thirty of *Cecilia*'s missions, all the crew felt they knew his habits thoroughly. But one night shortly after the air-crew roll call, the dog disappeared. Although there was no trace of him anywhere, and it was unlike him to alter a long-established routine, no one was particularly concerned. Antis had long ago proved that he could take care of himself.

When the plane leveled off at eight thousand feet, Jan gave a last worried look at the Wretham airfield, now indistinguishable in the darkened English countryside. Then he put the dog out of his mind and concentrated on checking his guns.

"Navigator to wireless operator," the intercom crackled suddenly. "Can you hear me?" Engrossed in his own duties, Jan only half listened to the reply. But the navigator's next words jarred him to full attention.

"Am I going round the bend, or do you see what I see?" he asked. There was a flurry of incredulous profanity. Then, "He must have got into the emergency bed by the flarechute. Someone forgot to check it. Jan, open your turret door—we have a stowaway aboard."

Jan knew at once what had happened. He opened the hatch, and as nonchalantly as if it were an everyday occurrence, Antis crawled into the turret and settled down between his feet. "You villain!" Jan exclaimed. "We ought to drop you out with the bombs." But nothing could be done about it. The Wellington droned on, and Antis drifted off to sleep.

As they went over the target a dense curtain of flak rocked the aircraft, but the dog stayed calm as long as Jan appeared unmoved. In response Jan found himself forcing signs of encouragement despite the intensity of the barrage, and thus each drew strength from the other. Then in a few moments the danger had passed, and they were on their way home unscathed.

They had just disembarked when Ocelka drove up. Since it was against Air Ministry regulations to take an animal on missions, the men braced themselves for a sizzling tongue-lashing. Like many easy-going officers, Ocelka could be vitriolic when the occasion demanded. "How did you make out?" he asked coolly, casting a sidelong glance at Antis. The pilot, Jo Capka, described the run and the heavy fire they had encountered. The crew shuffled nervously as the recital came to a conclusion.

"Heavy fire, eh? What do you think of that?" Ocelka asked, looking Antis squarely in the eye. "Don't you think these poor boys need someone to hold their hands?"

Jan could stand it no longer. "I can explain, sir," he began, but Ocelka cut him off.

"What the eye doesn't see the heart doesn't grieve," he said curtly. "I've enough trouble on my hands with two-legged beasts without looking for any from four-legged ones. Now let's get back to Operations and make out the reports."

From then on Antis was accepted as a regular member of *Cecilia*'s complement. His unruffled behavior under fire was all the more welcome because the men were nearing the end of their standard tour of combat duty. This was always a time of increased tension for any air crew, for they all knew that more than one plane had gone down on its last trip. Unaware of their anxieties, Antis raced for the plane as if each mission were a pleasure trip, and inevitably something of his élan communicated itself to the crew. He began to amass quite a respectable combat record, and eventually sustained two wounds in the line of duty. The first occurred over Kiel, when a fragment of shrapnel creased his nose and lacerated his left ear, which acquired a permanent droop. The second ended his flying career.

During an attack on Hanover, just as *Cecilia* was turning homeward after releasing her bombs, a shell exploded directly beneath her, sending showers of fragments into the fuselage. The engines were unharmed, and no one reported being wounded; but when they reached East Wretham the undercarriage jammed and they had to belly in. Only as they were extricating themselves from the damaged aircraft did Jan discover that Antis had a three-inch shrapnel wound in his chest.

Jan rushed the dog to Station Sick Quarters, where he was stitched up and bandaged. Thereafter Antis was grounded and barred from the field. Much as the dog resented the restrictions, they were somewhat easier to bear because he did not know Jan was still flying. While *Cecilia* was being repaired the crew was assigned another plane, and since its propeller pitch was unfamiliar, Antis simply ignored it.

A short time later Jan completed his tour of forty-one missions (of which Antis had shared seven) and was relieved of further combat duty. He spent the remaining two years of the war first as an instructor, then in flying antisubmarine patrol. Antis reveled in their regular hours together, and when Jan was stationed in Scotland, reaped honor by winning a dog show. He also ran away for five days with a wild female in the Highlands, but later showed little interest in the responsibilities of fatherhood. The pups were left to run wild with their mother.

The first years of peace were blissfully happy ones for Jan. When he returned to his triumphantly liberated country, he was given a captaincy in the Czech air force and eventually assigned to the Ministry of National Defense in Prague. Both he and Antis became well-known to the public, for Jan wrote three books about service in the RAF. Almost every newspaper in Czechoslovakia carried tales of his war experiences with the dog.

When Jan married a golden-haired girl named Tatiana, Antis distinguished himself at the wedding by becoming entangled in the bridal veil. (He later made up for it by his steady devotion to Tatiana.) And when a son, Robert, was born to his idols in 1947, the baby became the dog's personal charge. At night he slept near the crib, alert on the instant if the child woke or cried. The dog would then rise, steal to the side of the big bed and thrust his cold nose against the mother's bare shoulder. And if this failed to waken her, he would drag the covers away. It was a wonderful time for all of them, but it was not to last.

On March 7, 1948, Jan Masaryk, minister of foreign affairs and godfather to little Robert, telephoned from Cernicky Palace. "Come round and see me," Masaryk said. "I have a present for your boy."

As he put down the telephone, Jan knew that this summons might bring his life crashing about his ears. He had seen Masaryk only the previous day, so why should this good friend ask to see him again at this moment? There could be but one reason, and Jan approached the Cernicky Palace with dread.

"You are high on the Communist blacklist, Jan," Masaryk told him. "The blow can fall any time now. You must keep this completely to yourself. Even Tatiana must not know. It is imperative for you to get out of Czechoslovakia."

This then was the "present" for little Robert. But even that ruse had been necessary, since every telephone was tapped. Acting through the Czech Communist Party, Soviet Russia was implacably taking over the country. As the cold war intensified, everyone who had had associations in the West became suspect, and for months Jan had been aware that his apartment had been under surveillance. His friends knew it and no longer dared visit him. The Defense Ministry was being packed with Communist informers, many of whom spoke Russian. Recently two strange officers had been installed in his own department—ostensibly learners, but unquestionably spies.

Three days after Masaryk's warning was issued, it was grimly underscored by the fact that Masaryk himself was dead. According to the Communists, he had "jumped" from a Foreign Office window.

Jan faced an agonizing dilemma. He could not leave his wife and son while there was any possibility of a life for them together. But if he were imprisoned, they would be in a far worse position than if he fled. It was hard to know what to do, and for weeks he vacillated. Then one morning General Prachoska of the Czech intelligence service summoned him, and the decision was taken out of his hands.

"Sit down, Bozdech," the general greeted him. "Major Marek, my aide, would like to ask you a few questions."

"You are the author of these?" Marek began curtly, handing Jan three books and a folder of press clippings.

Jan nodded.

"And there have been broadcasts, radio plays, all glorifying the British?"

"I served in the RAF," Jan explained. "My writing is only a record of my experiences, without political significance—"

"On the contrary," Marek interrupted. "This work is treasonable. If you continue writing, your attention will be directed to the Red air force only. That is an order." He paused. "And there is one other matter. You are a member of the Air Force Club?"

"Yes, sir," said Jan. The organization was often referred to as the English Club because of the high percentage of members who were ex-RAF officers.

"We know that all sorts of opinions are openly expressed in this establishment, and we are interested in them. To put it bluntly, Captain, we want you to listen to, and if necessary encourage, criticism of the present regime. You will then report to this department the names of any members whose remarks indicate that they are enemies of the state."

Jan was aghast. But as he began to protest, Marek brandished a blue document that had been lying on his desk. "I have here a police warrant for your arrest, dated Friday. You have three days to make up your mind."

Jan did not return home until late that night. Long after dark he walked the streets alone, desperately seeking some way out of the trap set for him. He would never spy on his friends; that much was sure. If he remained in his post and defied the Communists, imprisonment and death were almost certain. His course was plain. No option remained but to flee the country.

To his great surprise he woke the following morning with his mind refreshed and his nerves calm. Now that the long-dreaded blow had fallen and his intentions were resolved, his problems seemed almost preternaturally clarified. He set off for the office at the usual time.

Some fifty yards from the Ministry of National Defense, a passerby awkwardly blundered into him. "Excuse me, Brazda," Jan said in embarrassment, recognizing the man as a casual acquaintance, an instructor at the Sokol physical-training college.

"If you are in trouble," Brazda said in rapid undertones, "tonight at eight. The Café Pavlova Kavarna at Strahove. The password is, 'May I offer you a vodka?'" Then begging Jan's pardon for his clumsiness, Brazda went on his way. The machinery of the underground movement had begun to turn.

At eight that night, when he appeared at the Café Pavlova Kavarna, the machinery caught him up smoothly. A dapper little man led him to a small upstairs room where he was confronted by two other members of the underground, a student and an elderly man who had obviously once been a soldier. There were no introductions. The former military man, who was the leader of the group, wasted no time on formalities.

"Captain Bozdech," he said, "the dead-line for your arrest is Friday." Jan was surprised at the accuracy of their information. "That gives us only one day to get you out of the country. It is not much time. You must make your decision quickly. You understand the risks, of course. If you are caught attempting to cross the frontier, they shoot first and ask questions later. So you must go alone, and perhaps we can arrange for your family to follow later by a less dangerous route. Agreed?"

Jan's heart sank, but he nodded.

"Very well," the spokesman said. "Now, here are your instructions. Listen carefully." And for the next five minutes the three anonymous agents outlined down to the smallest detail what Jan would have to do the following day. Then with a warm bon voyage they dismissed him.

Tatiana was asleep when Jan returned home that night. Looking at her face, sweet in repose, he recalled Masaryk's warning, "Even Tatiana must not know." Of course Masaryk was right, Jan mused as he turned out the light. Both for her safety and little Robert's, it was best that he slip off this way. But next morning when he said good-bye to her, he found it almost impossible to keep his voice steady, and the closing of the door behind him was like a blow above the heart.

When he reached the office, he summoned his civilian clerk, Vesely. He had decided during the night that risky as it might be, he would have to make one change in the underground's careful plans. Antis would have to come with him. Otherwise, as Jan knew from long experience, the dog would stubbornly refuse to eat; and Jan simply could not condemn him to certain starvation. "Vesely," Jan said, "I've an appointment for Antis at the vet's at eleven o'clock. Would you go to my flat later and collect him? I'll give you my gloves so he'll follow you."

"Very good, sir," Vesely replied, elated at the chance to get away from the wretched office for a while.

Two hours later, when his unwitting accomplice returned with the dog, Jan knew that the time had come. The escape was now to begin. As he went out the door, he stopped for a moment casually. "I'll be back after lunch if anyone wants me," he said.

One of the Stalinist spies looked up from his paper work. "We'll hold the fort," he said sarcastically. "Take your time."

"Thanks," said Jan. "I will."

Following the underground's instructions, he took a tram to the Vaclavska Namesti and went into the busy public lavatory there. When he asked a prearranged question, the attendant at once handed him a parcel containing a change of clothing. He was to travel as a peasant with a knapsack full of butter to sell. The attendant kept Antis while Jan changed in one of the booths. Everything was complete, the sizes right—from the rough felt hat to the heavy boots. There were also a dozen packages of butter.

"You look a treat," the attendant muttered as Jan emerged from the booth and handed him a five-hundred-crown note along with the parcel (which now contained Jan's smart air-force uniform). "I hope you get a good price for your butter."

It was a hundred fifty yards to the Wilsonova Station. But no one took the least notice of him as he clumped through the tumult of traffic in his strange new boots, entered the station and bought a ticket. The train came in, and he and Antis climbed aboard. Six minutes later, still following instructions, he alighted at Smichov.

This was but the beginning of a long and circuitous course which eventually brought Jan to a certain farmstead where he spent the night. Next morning a taciturn driver concealed him, along with Antis, in the back of a two-ton van. After a long ride they stopped at a remote cottage in a heavily wooded area. "This is Anton's," the driver said. "I leave you here."

"Who is Anton?"

"A forester. He will guide you over the border. I know nothing else about him."

As the van drove away a tall, deeply tanned man stepped out of the cottage. "What can I do for you?" he asked evenly, his eyes on the dog.

As he had been told to do, Jan offered him a package of a certain brand of cigarettes. The man turned it over in his hand ruminatively. Finally he said, "Why have you brought the dog?"

"Wherever I go, he goes too," Jan said.

Anton's face darkened. "Wherever you go, he goes," he repeated. "My God, some of you people! Do you think this is a picnic outing? One bark from him and we're dead. You'll have to leave him behind."

"Then I'd better start back," Jan said.

"You'll have a warm welcome. They'll have raised the alarm by now."

Jan realized this was true, for it was now Friday. But about Antis his mind remained stubbornly set.

"So you really want to risk your neck for the dog, eh?" Anton said. "Well, we'll see what Stefan says. He'll be coming with us." He called into the cottage and in a moment a bearded, erect man emerged. Anton explained the situation to him, but the man said nothing, staring at Jan and Antis as if trying to recall something.

"Antis is trained," Jan said quickly. "He won't make a sound, and he may be able to help us."

"Antis," Stefan said. "That's it. I've read about you two and seen your picture in the papers. He can come along, as far as I'm concerned."

Anton shrugged, then smiled at Jan. "You'd have found it a long walk back to Prague," he said. "But I like your spirit. You'll do. Now wait here, both of you."

He went into the house and returned immediately with two revolvers. "I hope we don't have to use them," Anton said, "but the positions of the observation posts are always changing. You never know."

Squatting, he began to trace a map on the ground with a stick. "Here," he said, pointing, "is our first obstacle, a forest about two miles deep. It's infested with patrols. We come out of the forest here"—he indicated the spot—"then cross a small valley, which is also constantly patrolled. Then here is the West German frontier, and half a mile past it, the village of Kesselholst. Once we're there, we're safe. We'll leave immediately. I want to reach the far side of the forest in daylight. Then we'll hole up and make the last dash across the valley after dark."

A car carried them fifteen miles to the edge of the forest, and early that afternoon they plunged into the matted underbrush. Unavoidably they made a lot of noise, and as a precaution against being surprised by roving border patrols Jan sent Antis ahead with instructions to "seek." Twice the dog stopped, growling a low warning when no other sound was audible, and seconds later the men heard the faint, far-off sound of snapping twigs and hailing voices. They lay in the underbrush without stirring until the patrols passed, then moved cautiously on. It was almost sunset when they finally reached the far side of the wood. From its verge they carefully scanned the open valley that lay between them and Kesselholst. To their left was a narrow road and, paralleling it, a turbulent river. No patrols or strongholds were visible. As the evening light waned and the lights came on in the village, Anton murmured, "All right, let's go."

They had covered only a short distance when they heard movement nearby. Jan dropped to the ground beside his companions as four dim figures stole past them down the slope.

Without warning, two searchlights suddenly split the night, sweeping across the valley. Rocks, bushes and boulders seemed to leap out of the darkness as the lights passed, converging, separating, then pouncing simultaneously on their prey. Four men, scarcely fifty yards from Jan, were caught scrambling frantically for the trees. Before they reached them the machine guns of a strong point opened fire, and all four fell.

Two trucks then sped up the road, each carrying four men and a dog. As the men alighted to collect the bodies, one of the dogs began moving toward Jan and his companions. A low growl rose in Antis' throat. Jan pressed his hand around the animal's muzzle. One of the guards noticed the wandering guard dog. "Come here, you," he shouted. The dog trotted obediently back to his handler, and within a few minutes the trucks drove off.

"We're lucky to be alive," Anton whispered. "The way I intended to take is blocked by a new post, and if those four hadn't passed us, we'd have walked right into it. We'll have to double back and take another route across the river." They crept silently back to the wood and then spent a hellish hour struggling blindly through the close-set firs to the riverbank. As soon as Jan stepped into the water, holding Antis by the collar, the current began to undermine his footing.

"Link hands," Anton said.

Jan clamped Antis' jaws onto the tail of his coat, and the four of them, clinging tightly to one another, edged their way toward the center of the swift-flowing river. As the current swirled about their waists, Jan slipped on a loose stone, staggered and lost his grip on his companions' wrists. Immediately he was swept downstream, dragging Antis with him, until he struck a boulder and managed to grasp it. Recovering his balance, he saw that he had been carried into shallower water, and he waded the few yards to the far shore.

Antis was still with him, but there was no sign of Anton and Stefan. He dared not shout. Kneeling beside the dog, he ordered, "Seek! Go seek!" For several minutes there was no sound but the roar of the river. Jan wondered if he had been a fool to send the dog on such a hopeless errand—the current could carry a man fifty yards in a few moments. Then suddenly he felt a blow on the shoulder and as he reached for his gun a voice beside him began to curse violently. It was Anton.

"Sorry," he said. "I was crawling and bumped you with my head. Thank God for the dog. We'd never have got back together without him. Do you think he can manage to find Stefan?"

At an order from Jan, the dog again disappeared. It was some time before he returned, leading his exhausted quarry. "I was swept a long way downstream into a pool," Stefan explained. "But Antis found me. I think he saved my life."

After a moment's rest they pressed on, climbing toward a ridge that lay within a few hundred yards of the frontier. A dense fog shrouded the forest near its crest, and it became impossible to see a foot ahead. Antis ran from man to man, as a sheep dog handles his flock, guiding them and keeping them in touch with one another. But at the top of the rise Anton decided that it was useless to continue while the mist obscured all landmarks, and the four settled down to await the dawn. At first light they moved behind a giant boulder to plan their final dash across the border. Jan posted Antis atop the rock as lookout.

Since Anton had no idea what new posts they might encounter, they decided to cross the valley one at a time, and Anton broke a twig in lengths for lots to see who would go first. As he extended his hand, Antis growled and leaped from the top of the boulder. There was a clatter of stones, a stifled cry and savage snarling. Gun in hand, Jan ran around the rock. Antis was straddling a soldier who lay sprawled on his back, rifle useless beneath him. Anton sprang at the guard, his knife upraised.

"No!" Jan cried. Anton hesitated.

"Jan is right," Stefan said. "It would be murder."

"The swine deserves to die," Anton said, but he grudgingly got off the man's chest. Quickly they gagged him and lashed him

securely to a nearby tree, then ran down toward the valley.

At the edge of the wood they stopped abruptly. In the meadow ahead a single guard post, with telephone wires running from its roof, blocked their way. Helpless, they crouched in the brush for almost an hour, watching the hut. There was no sign of movement. "Try the dog," Anton whispered finally, and Jan sent Antis to "seek." Antis trotted out and stood sniffing beside the closed door. Then he barked. There was no response. "I think there was only one guard in there," Stefan said, "and now he's tied to a tree."

Jan was on his feet, shaking with excitement. "Let's go," he cried, and they sprang into the open field. Far off down the valley someone shouted, but the three men and the dog raced on, down the slope and across the

stream at its base. Far behind them they heard a telephone jangling in the hut in the meadow, and the sound of a distant whistle reached them.

"On! On!" Anton cried. Another open field lay before them and beyond, a wood. They ran for the sanctuary of the trees, and at last they knew that their feet were treading on German soil.

As soon as he had delivered his charges safely to the West German authorities, Anton bade them farewell. He would return to Czechoslovakia and risk his life again to keep the escape route open for other proscribed men. "Pray God we meet again in happier times," he said in parting. "I certainly proved wrong about the dog, didn't I? He was our salvation."

Within a week after the arrival in West Germany Jan received heartening news from his homeland. A Czech refugee who had known him in Prague brought word that Tatiana and Robert had suffered no reprisals and were living quietly with her parents. After he received this report, he was convinced that his decision to flee Czechoslovakia had been right. He applied for reenlistment in the RAF and was accepted.

On this trip to England, however, there was no squad of loyal Czechs to smuggle Antis past the inspectors, and Jan had no choice but to surrender him for the legal six-month quarantine. Now a familiar difficulty arose. Upon reenlistment Jan had reverted to the lowest rank in the service, and his entire salary would not cover the cost of the kennel fees. In desperation he applied for help to the People's Dispensary for Sick Animals in London, submitting a full report on the dog's history.

The clinic's response went far beyond Jan's expectations. Not only were the fees paid, but Antis' remarkable story was widely publicized. As a result, in March 1949, he was awarded an unprecedented tribute. He became the first non-British dog to receive the Dickin Medal, the Victoria Cross of the animal world. In a moving presentation speech Field Marshal Archibald Wavell, one of England's greatest soldiers, cited Antis' "outstanding courage, devotion to duty and lifesaving on several occasions while serving with the Royal Air Force.

"I am sure," the Field Marshal concluded, "that everyone will join with me in congratulating you on your award, Antis, and we wish you many years in which to wear it."

Actually there were to be few more years for him, but during that time he and Jan were closer than ever. Jan heard no more from his wife, son or parents, so Antis became his only family. As Antis' sight dimmed and his muzzle whitened with age, he could not bear even the slightest separation from his beloved master.

Each year, wherever they were posted, Jan performed an unvarying ritual on Christmas Eve. Beside a miniature Christmas tree, glittering with tinsel and artificial frost, he set out photographs of Tatiana, Robert and his parents, thus preserving at least one tangible link with home. On Christmas Eve of 1952 Jan finished his small arrangement and went to bed early. Sometime that night he awoke, conscious of a strange weight on his chest. Reaching out, he found that it was Antis, resting his head there. This was most unusual. Once the dog had retired for the night he could be depended on to stay on his blanket until morning. "What's the matter, Antis?" Jan asked. "Go back to bed now, old-timer."

Jan heard a tremulous sigh, then the scrabbling, uncertain sound of the dog's paws on the floor, then the sound of a falling body. Instantly Jan switched on the light. Antis was lying on his side, unable to rise.

Jan carried him to his bed and began to massage his legs, continuing the treatment at intervals all that night. By noon of the next day Antis managed to stand, but he was too weak to follow his master outside, and Jan stayed with him during the base's Christmas festivities. From his window he could see the lights in his mess and hear the sound of laughter and singing, and twice friends looked in to suggest that Antis might be left for a while. Jan thanked them, but stuck to his vigil.

He sat by the table with the Christmas tree on it and took up Tatiana's photograph. She looked radiant in her wedding dress, and he remembered how Antis had become entangled in her veil when they left the church. Now across at the mess they were playing "Silent Night," and Jan remembered Christmases at other posts. The room was full of the ghosts of old companions; and soon Antis would be with them.

It seemed to Jan that a hundred years had passed since the day—twelve years ago —when he found that small, frightened puppy in no-man's-land.

I'm a Cat Convert

by ALLEN RANKIN

WHEN OUR SMALL SON smuggled our first cat into the house, my wife and I, confirmed dog lovers, vented our misgivings by naming him Macavity after the cat of T. S. Eliot's rhyme:

Macavity, Macavity, there's no one
like Macavity,
For he's a fiend in feline shape, a
monster of depravity.

Immediately, Mac began to live up to his name with such villainous consistency that we were stunned into a kind of awe. Mac liked our living room better than the back alley he came from, and decided to claim it for his own. At the time, he was a fuzzy gray kitten no larger than a tennis ball. He was opposed in his ambitions by our dachshund, Joe, who must have looked to him as big as a locomotive, and by at least two people, who towered over him like Chimney Rock. Yet, being a cat, Mac knew how to handle us all. In two hours he charmed us with what looked like cute kitten play. He pretended to mistake the dog for his mother —a duplicity that so touched poor Joe that he allowed the little cat to sleep in his arms and even climb in and out of his mouth. By the time Joe realized he was abetting a

Brutus, it was too late. One day when Joe presented his quivering, curious nose as usual—*Pssztz! Slash!* Mac let him have it. Since then Mac has never given Joe—the friend and protector of his kittenhood—so much as a civil glance.

In a year Mac developed into one of the handsomest, most murderously efficient animals imaginable. He acquired the haughty swagger of a cavalier adventurer. His splendid getup matched his dandy's personality —vest and gloves of purest white with gray-and-black cloak striped and whorled like the ancient taffeta of Baghdad *attābi* (whence the name "tabby"). Along with his new magnificence came a disdain for his human "masters." Now he refused to be petted except at his own convenience. At other times, he drew himself up like an emperor whose robes had been besmirched by a group of sticky-fingered peasants.

"All right, we'll see who's boss around here," I threatened—and we did. Mac was boss. I found this out one cold night when Mac, having gone for a stroll, wanted to get back in the house. "Ah, ha!" I said, when I heard his "meow" at the door. "Now we'll make you say uncle! We'll just let you cool

341

off out there until you appreciate us more." Any good dog would have whined and begged at the door all night. Mac simply stalked away, obviously preferring to sleep in the garage rather than demean himself. Since then, we have reached an honest unilateral agreement with our cat: He does exactly what he wants to do and we do exactly what he wants us to do. This is about the same arrangement men have had with cats since before 300 B.C., when the Egyptians first "domesticated" certain small wildcats. Mac has made it plain that a cat does nothing that doesn't give *him* satisfaction. He is not, like a dog, "man's best friend," or anything so obsequious. He is his own best friend.

This selfish attitude came as a shock to me, spoiled by the slavish devotion of dogs. I tried to find some weakness in Mac, some flaw to throw up to him to deflate his monstrous ego. Didn't dogs do more tricks? So weren't they, as we'd always heard, smarter than cats? Carl Van Vechten, in his book *The Tiger in the House,* knocked this notion into a cocked hat. "Most professors," he reminds us, "judge an animal's intelligence by his susceptibility to discipline, by his comparative ability to become the willing slave of man. The cat is far too intelligent to be inveigled into any drudgery or mummery. He compels his human friend to accept him on his own terms." So it's not that Mac can't do tricks, but simply that he won't—at least not for such pauper's pay as a pat on the head. Let a cat face problems meaningful to a cat and he'll show ingenuity enough. Show and circus cats, for example, perform brilliantly—for high salaries of meat and fish.

I've finally had to face it: In any serious comparison with an alley cat, our dog, Joe, is the veriest boob, and so is any other dog. Mac bathes and keeps himself immaculately

clean (so mice can't whiff his presence, authorities say); Joe would be impossible to live with if these services weren't performed for him. Mac digs his own plumbing and squeamishly buries anything unpleasant, including certain meals he disapproves of. Joe lacks any such sense of delicacy.

The dog suffers also from a terrible disadvantage unknown to cats—a conscience! Surprise Joe stealing a nap on your bed or filching a snack from the table, and he tucks his tail guiltily, expecting a reprimand. After the rare nights when he dares sneak out on the town to follow his natural impulses, he comes cringing home looking as sheepish as a civic-club president caught on a bender. Mac, on the contrary, is joyously unafflicted by any stuffy guilt complexes. He comes and goes when and how he pleases. Plainly he considers the innumerable amours and fights he negotiates on the back fences his natural right and due. When he does finally come home, he looks at us with an evil but happy contempt as if to ask: "And how did you dull clods spend the evening?"

A patrician, the cat scorns labor. True, he has always been employed as a mouser. In rat-plagued San Francisco during the Gold Rush, a shipload of cats brought up to twenty dollars a head. But hunting is no labor for cats. They hunt for the sport of it. Still, any cat can take to the woods and hunt for a living when necessary. Their accomplishments don't stop here. From heights that would shatter a man, a cat can dive and land lightly on its feet. Cats can hear sounds far out of range of human ears—sensing vibrations as high as thirty thousand cycles per second. They can see in the dimmest light.

In pitch darkness they can feel their way with their sensitive antenna-like whiskers.

What do I get out of being a cat convert? The pleasure of humoring one of nature's noblemen and of watching a true artist in action. Mac brings to our suburban house and yard a touch of jungle grace and beauty. To see him merely lie down or get up is to watch a ballet the most sinuous dancer cannot imitate. With his staring owl's eyes and probing claws, Mac is eternally examining everything; he has a scientific curiosity, a thirst for knowledge we've been told is possessed only by Russian schoolchildren. He is a master showman. We never tire of his morning entrance. Someone cracks the back door just enough, and in he comes with a silken, pantherlike swoosh, tail held high like a banner, soft pads flying, mustaches smiling. That means he's ready for his breakfast and all the other good things of the day. On hearth or sofa, he relaxes with a completeness impossible to his neurotic betters. By the time his drowse-squinted lids finally slide down, we've been hypnotized into a sense of tranquillity and well-being.

These performances Mac gives only when he chooses. At other times he is off to pursue the private and wonderful things important to a cat: to smell some secret flower; to cavort with a whirling leaf; to drink his fill of sun on a window ledge; to duel to the death with a rival in black night; to dance some savage adagio with a new conquest. He goes off by himself to see things we don't see, hear things we don't hear, feel things we don't feel ... to live life, every treasured second of it, with the keen-whetted joy, the grace and dignity possible only to a cat.

The Terror
of the Deep

Condensed from Pearl Diver

by VICTOR BERGE, as told to Henry Wysham Lanier

I HAVE HAPPENED, during twenty years as a pearl diver, to wander over a vast expanse of the South Pacific. I've been down in countless places, drifted for miles along the bottom behind my lugger, and I've encountered many strange undersea creatures. I've learned a few things about sharks—I once fought for my life with a tiger shark that hunted me as a cat hunts a rat. Yet, among all the formidable monsters of a diver's world, it is the giant octopus that holds first place. He is the terror of the deep.

This terrible creature has eight long arm-feet, radiating out from around a hideous mouth. The beast that almost killed me had a body the size of a flour barrel and arms eighteen feet long. The strength of these arms is almost unnatural, and their swift flexible movements are precisely those of an active snake. When the creature climbs swiftly up over a cliff like a spider, or creeps under an overhanging reef, he is horribly, squirmingly, frighteningly alive. And then suddenly he'll stop and be as horribly dead. Lying in wait for his prey, he'll turn to any color to match his background—pink, red, purple, blue. I've even seen him break out with dark stripes.

Along the inside of each arm is a double row of suckers that can cling like a monstrous leech; and where these radiating lines of suckers meet around his voracious mouth there is another mesh of suction disks. Any prey forced by these loathsome muscular arms into that pit of adhesiveness is held fast in the very jaws of destruction. For just within his great gaping mouth is a big hooked beak, like an overgrown parrot's, that can tear to pieces any flesh that reaches this torture chamber. He digests with incredible swiftness—his belly seems like some devouring mechanism where fiery acids instantly dissolve the ingredients poured in.

Then his eyes! They are small, oval, slanting; intent with a terrifying expression of cold malignity toward all other life. Devilish is the only expression that describes his steady, evil glance.

With a powerful effort he can shoot himself backward like a rocket, fifty to a hundred feet, almost faster than the eye can follow. It is a tiger's spring, the fastest movement I have seen in the water world. His long arms trail back close to his body—he steers with them, I fancy—and the instant he reaches his mark those snaky arms whip out

344

and drag it down. In addition, he can squirt out a cloud of blue-black liquid, laying his own smoke screen while he darts in among the rocks and creeps out for an assault from an unexpected point. He is incredibly hard to kill. You can cut him in half, and the two pieces will apparently continue fighting.

During my first year as a pearl diver I had listened to plenty of awed tales of this monster of the water underworld. At nineteen, with a year of experience and no serious misadventures, my answer had always been, "Rubbish!" Then I got my lesson.

Coming down from Borneo to Macassar Strait, I noticed some promising-looking shell on the sea floor. I got into my diving suit and went down to explore. The water was fairly deep, about twenty fathoms. To one side of me there was an open space between masses of coral. I worked my way down into it and stooped to pick up a shell. At that instant I felt something touch me lightly on the left arm.

Instinct and underwater training saved my life. I grabbed the razor-sharp knife from my belt and slashed. By luck I severed two of the lassoing arms of the giant octopus that was gripping me; in another instant he would have had my arms pinioned helplessly. As I felt the blade cut through a mass of soft flesh, two more arms laid hold of me, one around each ankle. I felt a vicious jerk at my legs that almost upset me.

No description could paint the horror of that moment. It was murky in this place, but I could see a sort of shapeless mass and wavering, squirmy arms—even one severed stump. I had a swift picture of my companions above pulling up a severed, dangling lifeline and air hose; of a human being—myself—gripped close to the maw of this loathsome monster.

Meanwhile, I was fighting automatically. Each time I would bend to try to cut my ankles free, the creature would jerk me so violently that I seemed to be a little boy pulled about at will by a strong man. Helmet and breastplate banged against my head and chest with punishing force. I strained and fought with all my strength, trying to cut more of these fetters.

My mind, somewhere, was carefully weighing chances, attempting to decide whether I dared give the last signal a diver resorts to—four pulls, meaning, "Pull until the line breaks." I feared my air pipe and lifeline might have become tangled in some of the coral projections; should they be fouled, such a strain from above might cut them off or leave me hopelessly jammed into a crevice.

I maintained my footing with the greatest difficulty. I had to keep my helmet above my body—otherwise the air there gets into the body and legs of the suit and a man is finished. Through all this struggle I fought to right myself after every jerk at my ankles.

And it was as if the devilish brain in that voracious, pulpy creature understood all this perfectly. The instant my hand would stretch down with the big knife he'd give a terrific jerk, sometimes dragging me ten feet, jamming the heavy helmet against my jaws and skull, bruising me against the rough, crusted rock wall. All this in a pool now blackened and turbid with the ink the beast had squirted out.

After a while a slight current set through and carried off some of the thickest discoloration. When I got a glimpse of that disgusting mass of arms and squirming legs, and especially one look into those diabolical eyes, I stretched up to give the danger signal. Instantly the octopus yanked me a dozen feet, and I had all I could manage not to topple over.

Our hellish duel must have occupied ten to fifteen minutes—it was an eternity to me.

I began to realize I could not last much longer. The first severe knock with the helmet had cut and dazed me; the subsequent battering against the coral had worn down my strength. I knew I was going. Just before a wave of unconsciousness swept over me I threw up my arms, caught both lines, gave four frantic pulls. There was an instant when I had the sensation of being pulled in two. Then I knew nothing.

Up above, my Polynesian partner Ro had been tending me from the lugger's deck. He could see nothing down there, but his water sense told him something was wrong. All during that eventful quarter of an hour he had been waiting, taut, certain I was in trouble, yet fearing to destroy me if he acted before receiving some signal.

At my four jerks Ro pulled. Nothing budged. He shouted to a man at the pumps. This fellow ran across the heaving deck and lay to behind him. Still no give. In a frenzy he brought a third man, but all their strength could not stir whatever was holding me down below. It was then that Ro's quick thinking saved me from a horrible death. The boat was rising and falling on the swell. He took several turns around a stout stanchion, ordered the two men to strain up till my lifeline and air hose were taut just as the lugger was at the bottom of one of these surges. The ocean swell picked her up, and the full force of the lift came on my two tight lines.

My captor must have been caught while shifting those two arms by which he had been anchored to a solid support, for I shot suddenly up to within ten feet of the surface. At this moment I regained consciousness with a jerk.

I woke to the same dream of being pulled in two. Looking down I could see the sea demon's suckered arms still fast about my ankles; the loathsome mass of his body was suspended below, pulling with all its force. The instant I was close enough, the men got a stout line about my body and hauled me upward, while Ro slipped into the water, his big knife ready. In two sure slashes he had cut off those horrible arms.

They hauled me to the surface more dead than alive, with the pieces of suckered feelers still coiled about my legs. They got me on deck and took off the helmet. I looked as if I had been through the worst fight of my life—blood all over my face and neck, arms and legs torn by the suckers, bruised from head to foot by the banging about. I was pretty well all in.

Dimly I saw my three chums standing about in the bright sunlight with anxious faces. But they and the familiar lugger looked strange. If a dead man could come back to life he would feel as I did then.

The Crow
in Our Lives

Condensed from Home in the Country

by FREDERIC F. VAN de WATER

SILAS WAS A FLEDGLING, wistful little crow when he joined our household in the early summer. His eyes were china-blue, and the engaging bluntness of infancy still clung to beak and tail. He was frightened, too, and later it was a comfort to look back at the time when we filled him with dread. That period lasted forty-eight hours. For forty-eight hours, too, we were grateful to the man who cut down Silas' family tree and gave us the pick of the hatch. We wondered, afterward, whether it was native generosity or reprisal for some inadvertent offense of ours that inspired the gift.

At first we kept Silas in the garage, and when he yelped I stuffed bread and milk and chopped meat into his pink, diamond-shaped mouth. He was shy at first. But the rations were better than those he had shared in his nest, and for their sake he overlooked my very faint resemblance to his mother. He lost all fear of me in a single day. Into his infantile blue eyes crept a precocious and avaricious glitter. "How long," I could see him wonder, "has this been going on? The more racket I make, the more I get to eat. Maybe I've got something." Forthwith, he stopped cowering behind boxes when I en-

tered and instead met me at least halfway, with wings and mouth outspread.

No pup or kitten with millenniums of domesticity behind him could have oriented himself so rapidly. Within two days of his abduction from the nest Silas had become, in his own eyes, a human being—and a remarkable one at that. In a fortnight, his ego overflowed the confines of that impersonation. Mere equality was not enough. He promoted himself from fellow to critic. He never did anything worthwhile, but he told us all how everything should be done. We suffered his opinions on how the lawn should be mowed, the garden weeded, the corn planted. There were moments when he would abandon his critical pose and show us how things really should be done. He would demonstrate how to pick—and eat—raspberries.

He talked all day long and seven days a week. The words were crow but innumerable, and were uttered in a dozen different voices so that Silas, going full blast, sounded like a heated debate among a whole round table of sophisticates. He visibly admired his every utterance. If no one else would laugh at him, he gave his wit the tribute of his own eldritch merriment. Whenever there were

two or three human beings together outdoors Silas appeared among us to become the most active member of the party. His appearances, usually, were dramatic.

An elderly caller sat on our porch one day. He had bared his bald head to the August breeze when I heard a sound in the lilac bush and broke in upon his mild soliloquy. "If a crow—" I began hastily, but was not in time. Silas launched himself from the lilac, screeching like a witch. He planed down over the visitor's head, grazed his pate and zoomed with harsh merriment into the locust tree. It is nerve-shattering to be bombarded, without warning, by a crow. His victim came halfway up out of the chair, then collapsed.

Our lawn chairs have latticed seats. It was the joy of Silas to sneak on foot toward any stranger, preferably female, who lounged in one of these chairs and through the seat's interstices to drive upward a ribald and penetrating beak. Usually, after a scream and violent heave, our visitor glared at me. I know she felt that I had misspent many hours drilling an innocent bird in a bit of vulgar comedy.

Frequently the sufferer suggested that the crow should be punished, but she never told me how it could be done. It is hard to chastise a bird. There is no available place to spank. You could not appeal to Silas' higher nature. He had none. If you scolded him, he merely scolded back. When, driven beyond endurance, I would pick him up and shake him, he would scream and bite my hand. More than once I gripped him in a rage and flung him away, as one hurls a baseball. I think he rather enjoyed that, for he would let himself go to the zenith of my throw and then spread his wings to return, swearing and unrepentant, to my feet.

He coveted all our possessions. He feared but one—a looking glass. He would flee, screeching, at the sight of himself in a mirror. It was his passion to save for a rainy day. Silas hoarded. He also stole—anything not too big to haul away. Surplus food, defunct bugs, tinfoil, bright paper, pins, needles, thimbles were added to the fund. Sometimes they were hidden carefully at a distance. Often they were deposited in your shirt collar. He remembered always where each item was hidden. One day I saw, and heard, him following Harry, the hired man, through the garden. Silas walked in haste, and his voice was piercingly protestant. "I know what's the matter," his quarry explained. "He wants them 'tater bugs he stuck in the cuff of my overalls yesterday." Where-

upon Harry halted, and Silas withdrew his deposit and flew off with it.

Despite his caustic pose, our critic loved to be petted. Silas would sit, complacent, in my wife's lap, while she caressed him. If she stopped before he was bored, he would bite her. When he himself had become satiated and had flown away, the cadence of his chuckles was definitely caddish.

Edgar Allan Poe seems to have considered his housebroken and laconic raven a superlative affliction. But the record shows that Poe's bird merely sat, and uttered a comparatively inoffensive trisyllable. He did not spend his waking hours squalling and gibbering. He did not use opprobrious language to the stranger. The guest who might drop in to share Poe's misery did not have his own materially heightened by a black and raucous buccaneer who swooped down upon him to sample his ear, or to untie his shoelaces and bite him smartly on the ankle. Poe didn't know his own luck. He should have known Silas.

As summer waned, Silas' interest in our farm's affairs dwindled. I think he had grown a little tired of casting his pearls before us. Or perhaps among his own kind he had discovered associates who were awed by his sophistication. One day I saw him with two satellites in a butternut tree. I called, but he squawked a derisive reply. Since then we have not seen him. He may have gone south to winter in warmer climes. Wherever he is, we hope he enjoys himself. And we hope, too, that he stays.

If there are moments when we miss him, as one might miss an aching tooth that has been pulled, we stifle sentiment with the knowledge that Silas doesn't miss us at all. He deserted us simply because he wanted to. He never in his life did anything for any other reason.

A Horse for Wezie

Condensed from The Little Kingdom

by HUGHIE CALL

W E NAMED our little girl Louise, but she was never called anything but Wezie. She was born into a man's world on a ranch in the high sheep country of Montana—a bit of lagniappe given to Tom and me when our two sons were of school age and we thought our family complete. But it could never have been complete without her. She was the leaven in the loaf, the special ingredient that seasoned everyday life.

Wigwam Canyon, where the ranch house stands, stretches from sun to sun. A narrow, willow-lined stream courses through its length, westward into the valley. This sturdy, tow-headed little girl rushed through life like that sparkling mountain stream, finding in our ranch a little kingdom—a realm inhabited by her family, the men who worked for us and the animals she passionately loved.

From the time she could walk, a horse's back was as familiar to her as a chair. At first she rode with her father, Tom, on his big bay mare, perched between him and the saddle horn. By the time she was six, she was riding her own pony, Patches, a spunky pinto gelding, part Welsh, part Shetland, but mostly heart.

The two were inseparable. He'd wait out- side the gate for her every morning, pacing the fence, snorting and whinnying at the two retired sheep dogs that had the run of the yard. These tantrums amused everyone except Wezie. "He's just showing off," I tried to reassure her. "He'll calm down."

"No, Mother. Not as long as the dogs stay in the yard. He's afraid I'll like them best," she said, wise beyond her years.

There's no way of explaining the tie that existed between the little girl and the little horse. Perhaps it was their lively curiosity. Perhaps that trait of utter fearlessness both of them had. Long before we thought her old enough, they were jumping ditches and fences. One day I saw her try to jump a narrow place on Wigwam Creek. Patches stumbled and she sailed right over his head. The pony reared, so close to her body that my heart stood still. But he twisted clear, brought his hooves down at a safe distance and stood statue-still until she got to her feet. From that day on I worried no more.

Wezie never left Patches without a quick hug or a kiss on the white spot between his eyes, and he never failed to whinny when he saw her coming. The tie between them strengthened with the years.

351

Then Wezie was ten, and growing. She must have known that she'd soon be too tall to ride Patches. "Better trade in that overgrown jackrabbit for a real horse before your heels start draggin'!" a herder shouted one day as she rode past.

That night as I passed Wezie's room, I heard muffled sobbing. When I tiptoed in, she flung her arms around my neck. "Oh, Mother, the herder was right," she said. "But how can I tell Patches? He'll think I don't love him when I ride another horse." We talked until her sobs subsided.

Some weeks later she came to me. "If I have to have another horse," she said slowly, "I want a Mountain Lily."

Mountain Lilies are descendants of a long-dead Arabian stallion that escaped his owner and ranged with a herd of wild horses. Occasionally, when wild horses are rounded up to be shipped to the meat packers, a colt with something of the Arab stallion's proud look turns up in the herd.

More than a year passed before a ranch hand reported that a neighbor had a Mountain Lily, captured during the winter. Wezie went over, and when she returned she told Tom excitedly, "I've found my Lily, Daddy!

352

He's shiny black with a star on his forehead, and his name is Nig."

Tom finally agreed to buy him, and one day they set out to bring him home. A short time later I heard the pound of hoofbeats coming down the hill. From the window I saw a flash of blue overalls, flying blond hair and the radiant face of my child as she galloped past on her Mountain Lily.

Patches, munching grass along the creek, saw her too. He jerked up his head, flattened his ears, backed up a few steps and let out a shrill, outraged whinny. Then he whinnied again, and this time flung his head from side to side. Now he picked up his hooves and charged toward the barn, bent on mischief. Wezie barely had the black horse shut inside the corral before he reached it.

When she came in she mourned. "I should have put Patches in the barn so he couldn't see me on another horse."

Wezie tried taking Patches for long walks alone and talking to him. "He loves it, Mother," she would say upon her return. But nothing could assuage the little horse's grief and, whenever she rode off on Nig, the pony's squeals of outraged protest could be heard a mile away. Bucking and snorting, he tore around the corral like a wild thing.

Whenever the two horses were together, Patches never lost a chance to nip or lash out with his hooves at the larger horse. Eventually Nig began to retaliate. Patches, being smaller and fleeter, had the advantage in a running battle, but Nig had heavier hooves and stronger teeth. So, more and more that summer, Patches took to the hills to run with the unbroken string.

At first, Wezie was hurt by Patches' defection. Then she accepted it and grew closer to Nig. But I noticed that she never went out to give him a good-night pat as she had the pony. Nig took Patches' place in Wezie's life, but never in her heart.

Winter came early. A glaze iced over the snow, so the sheep couldn't paw through to grass. The constant blizzards made it impossible to haul hay to the camps, and the whole flock was herded to the home ranch. The mournful bleating of the sheep mingled with the wind that howled against the eaves. The bleakness was a terrible portent.

One night early in January, Wezie became violently ill. Friends brought their shovels and cleared the road so we could get her to a Butte hospital. There we learned that she had a rare virus infection which baffled the doctors. They could do nothing. Tom and I sat by her bed around the clock. But neither all our love nor all our prayers could save her. Wezie died three days later.

I don't know how I lived through the next few days. Tom was the strong one. My mind was a blank. Worst of all was coming home from the cemetery. We didn't talk. I'd been staring ahead blindly, dreading the first sight of the ranch, when Tom exclaimed, "Look!" and stopped the car.

We'd reached the gate, and there on the other side, heads close together, stood Wezie's two horses. Patches had been high in the mountains with the unbroken horses, Nig with the work and saddle horses in a pasture near the ranch. Fifteen miles apart. Yet some amazing instinct had brought them together; these two that could never meet without lashing and biting and furious neighing were standing quietly side by side.

Tom put his hand over mine. "They're not fighting anymore," he said in an odd choked voice.

I closed my eyes . . . saw a rapt young face . . . felt a rush of warmth, as if Wezie had touched my hand. And suddenly, wondrously, I knew that she was still a part of our lives and of the ranch she loved—the canyon, the creek, the mountains, the rushing winds, the very air we breathed.

My Date
with Graybeard

by ROBIN COLLINS

WHEN I WAS A BOY in Natal, South Africa, the farmers of the district organized a hunt each year in the Umzimkulu valley, using a hundred native beaters and their dogs. A variety of wildlife finds refuge in the valley—monkeys, baboons and an occasional leopard—but the creature most sought after is the wily gray bushbuck. With his speed and cunning, his ferocity when wounded or cornered, he is a quarry worthy of any hunter's gun.

There was one buck we called Graybeard, a magnificent old-timer who year after year survived the hunt. I was ten years old when I had my first glimpse of him, stepping proudly across a small clearing. His horns were long and sharp. His fur was a deep gray mottled with white. It was every hunter's desire to kill him, and from that day I could think of little else. I somehow felt that my initiation into manhood would consist of claiming Graybeard for my own.

My father had insisted that I wait until I was fourteen before I could go hunting, so I spent the next three years in a fever of anxiety, fearful that some other hunter would shoot my buck. But Graybeard survived. Once he followed silently behind a younger buck and, as it fell under a blast of shot, he jumped the clearing before the hunter could reload. Once he used a pair of legally protected does to shield him past the line of fire.

The third year the hunters chose their gun stations between the cliffs and the river so cunningly that it seemed as if no game could slip through. After the native beaters dispersed into the bush I heard their excited cries as they sighted Graybeard. I was perched on the cliffs, and from my vantage point I watched him run from their dogs straight toward the concealed hunters. I clenched my fists as I waited for the shot which would rob me of him. Then suddenly he turned, scattered the pursuing dogs and made straight for the line of beaters, who hurled their spears and knobbed throwing-sticks at him. Just when I feared he had been struck down, I heard the yelping dogs pursuing him into the bush behind the beaters, and I realized that he had broken through to safety.

That evening the farmers could talk of nothing except how Graybeard had escaped into the bush for another year. I smiled, for next year I would be old enough to take my place in the line of guns.

All through that year I cherished one bright vision—the picture of myself, a skinny boy of fourteen, standing astride the magnificent creature. When my father offered me my first shotgun I rejected the light 20-gauge which would have suited my frail build and chose instead a heavy 12-gauge so that I could have a weapon worthy of Graybeard. On the day of the hunt I wanted to rush straight to the valley at dawn, but my father forced me to eat breakfast. "Graybeard will still be there," he said pushing me down in my chair.

In the gray light of early morning we congregated in the valley. The beaters were dispatched to the top end and we hunters drew lots for positions. The best positions were close to the cliffs, because bushbucks tend to climb in their effort to escape the pursuing dogs. To my bitter disappointment I drew a position down near the river. Then I heard my father, who had drawn a good stand, say, "I'll change with my boy. I'd like him to have a good place for his first hunt." As he walked past me he patted my shoulder. "See that you get the old one," he whispered with a smile.

I scrambled up the steep slope, determined to outdistance the others and find the best possible place of concealment. I selected an outcrop of broken boulders, well screened by bush, which gave me a line of fire across a small clearing. For a long while there was no sound. Then came the shouts of the beaters, the sound of sticks beaten against trees and the yelping of dogs.

First came a doe, blundering past me in panic-stricken flight, then a young buck. I let him pass. Graybeard might be following, and I was determined not to betray my position. But there was no further movement, and I wondered if Graybeard had crossed lower down. Then a trembling of the brush caught my eye. Not ten yards from me, Graybeard stepped to the edge of the trees, silently inspecting the clearing. I had only to lower the muzzle slightly to cover him. The ambition of my youthful life was at the point of achievement. Graybeard stood motionless before me. I had only to pull the trigger to bring him down.

Yet something made me hold my fire. The buck had turned his head now, and his great ears twitched to catch the baying of the dogs. His moist nose trembled, and his eyes, softly luminous, alert without being fearful, seemed to stare right at me. There was pride and dignity in every line of his body, and I knew suddenly that I could not destroy him. For several breathless moments he remained where he was, and then a vagary of the breeze carried my man-smell to him. In two huge leaps he crossed the clearing and was gone. I stayed where I was, silent and enraptured.

When the drive was over, my father came up the slope. I unloaded my gun and pushed the shells back into the loops on my belt. My father's quick eye took in the details of the stand I had occupied and the full belt of cartridges. "No luck?" he asked.

I shook my head.

"That's funny," he said. "The boys sighted Graybeard coming in this direction, and none of the other guns saw him."

I looked down at the ground. My reticence must have aroused his suspicions, for he walked across the clearing and paused beside the deep imprints the buck had made in the moist earth as he jumped. I walked away, unable to face the condemnation which I imagined on my father's face.

As we drove home, the thought of old Graybeard gathering his does together for another year of safety gave me a thrill of pleasure. But my father's silence had put a constraint upon us. Finally he asked, "What happened, son?"

Shyly, stumblingly, I tried to tell him. I described Graybeard as I had seen him—majestic and fearless. I tried to explain why, when the moment had come to fire, I knew I could not buy the hunter's badge at the price of so much splendor.

My father was silent for a moment and then he said slowly, "You've learned something today, son—something that many men live a lifetime without knowing." He put an arm around my shoulders. "You've learned compassion," he said softly.

A Dog
Named Shep

by PAUL FRIGGENS

FORT BENTON is a picturesque prairie town nestled in the bluffs of the looping Missouri River in north-central Montana. There, one day in August 1936, a funeral car bearing the body of a sheepherder arrived at the Great Northern depot. Only one mourner was at hand to see the sheepherder off on his last journey: Behind the funeral car trotted a big, shaggy, crossbred collie. As the casket was lifted onto the train the dog whined pathetically and attempted to follow. "Sorry, old fellow," said the station agent. "This is one time you can't go with him."

The train puffed away, and the sheep dog stood looking disconsolately after it. Then he lay down beside the tracks. That night he burrowed under the station platform to await his master's return.

The big sheep dog was to maintain an unbroken watch for his master for five and a half long years! And at the end of that time his passing would produce some thoroughly remarkable consequences.

In the beginning, the dog's vigil was routine. Rain or shine, he trotted out to meet Fort Benton's four trains a day. He eyed the passengers as they alighted, sniffed at the baggage-car doors, mutely questioned each passerby. Then he would stand wistfully, watching the train until it disappeared from sight. *Someday* his master would come back.

Station employes soon found that the collie answered to the name Shep. But in general he remained aloof, as if reluctant to be distracted from his patient watching. Not until after dusk would he eat the meat scraps that station agent Tony Schanche left by his burrow. Later, in the black of night, he would trot lonesomely over a three-quarter-mile trail to drink from the river. But even dogs can stand utter loneliness only so long. One night during a lightning storm, section foreman Pat McSweeney found Shep crouching at his door. He succeeded in coaxing him inside. When the bitter Montana winter came, Pat fixed him warm quarters in the freight house, but first the big Irishman had to stretch out on the pad with Shep to provide reassurance.

Months passed, and news of Shep's vigil traveled beyond Fort Benton. Newspapers picked up the story, and mail began pouring in for Shep. Dozens of dog lovers sent him cash gifts. These the railroad returned. One Christmas a woman in England mailed Shep a bone-and-suet cake. Pet fanciers from

Florida to California offered to give him a home. Sheepmen in several states made good offers for the trained shepherd. When Shep was featured in Ripley's "Believe It or Not," an avalanche of mail came to Fort Benton, plus tourists who wanted to see the dog whose loyalty had become a legend.

All this attention affected Shep little. His purpose in life remained unchanged: His master would show up someday, and he, Shep, would be there to meet him. But there came a day when Shep could no longer bound out of his quarters and trot along the tracks. Instead, he padded slowly, and his hearing and sight commenced to fail. On occasion, when sub-zero weather stiffened his aging legs, he would limp to the trains. January 12, 1942, was such a day. Shep started down the track to meet the 10:17. He stood between the rails, waiting. As the train approached, bystanders expected him to jump to safety. He jumped—but a second too late. . . . Shep's long vigil was over.

Trainmen selected a grave site for the big sheep dog—at the top of a bluff overlooking the depot. Station agent Schanche fashioned a casket, and members of Boy Scout Troop 47 volunteered to be pallbearers. Schools were dismissed that day, and townspeople, together with farmers and ranchers from miles around, attended Shep's funeral, held appropriately at the station. The Reverend Ralph Underwood of the First Christian Church delivered George Graham Vest's well-known "Eulogy on the Dog": "The one absolutely unselfish friend that man can have in this selfish world, the one that never deserts him, the one that never proves ungrateful or treacherous, is his dog." Then, as Boy Scout bugler Kenneth Vinion sounded taps on the wintry air, Shep's casket was lowered into the earth and the service ended.

But Shep's story was far from ended. After Shep's burial, Fort Benton citizens erected a profile monument of him atop a bluff. Below it they lettered the name "Shep" in whitewashed boulders. Trainmen installed a spotlight to illuminate the monument at night, and as streamliners sped through the Montana hamlet, conductors, stewards and porters would recite to curious passengers the story of the dog's long devotion to his master.

Eventually, conductor Ed Shields wrote Shep's story in a booklet which trainmen sold. Before long, the booklet netted two hundred dollars, and Shields cast about for a worthwhile way to spend it. He found it: at the Montana School for the Deaf and Blind at Great Falls. It was Christmas 1946 when conductor Shields dropped by the school with his "gift from Shep" and inquired what the hundred children there needed most. "Something that says, 'We love you,' " said Glenn I. Harris, superintendent at the time. "Toys, candy, skates—luxuries the legislature can't buy for us."

So Shep played Santa Claus that year, and a little blind girl cuddled a doll, crying, "She's *mine*," and there was ice skating on a pond behind the school, and there were toys and special treats for every child.

"Shep gave us the best Christmas we've ever had," Glenn Harris told the Great Northern conductor.

In the years since that memorable Christmas, Shep's story has inspired a host of other contributions: some $55,000 to date, plus substantial bequests in wills. Through the gifts—which are put into the "Shep Fund" —the school has been able to embark on a year-round program of extra care, a whole new therapy of love and security for its deaf and blind. Take Tina, a teen-ager who had spells of depression and severe headaches. After a doctor had pronounced the child to be in sound health, Harris called in her housemother. "You know what ails a thirteen-year-old girl—something medicine can't cure," he said. "Here's five dollars to take Tina downtown, and for heaven's sake spend it foolishly!" So Shep bought new bobby sox, jewelry and a dresser set, and before long Tina found herself feeling better. Eventually she went on to sweep the sewing and dressmaking contests at the state fair.

When I visited the Great Falls school a few years ago, a sharp-looking deaf youngster came up to me to show off his new Shep-bought shoes. Afterward, Harris confided, "Pete broke thirteen windows his first day in school here." He went on: "Quite often, institutional children are destructive, but it's hard to believe what these gifts have done for our boys and girls. We estimate that the Shep Fund saves us probably three thousand dollars a year in breakage."

The Shep Fund is also bringing these children exciting adventure: trips to the state capitol at Helena; weekends at some of Montana's famous dude ranches; camp-outs in Yellowstone National Park.

Ordinarily, fewer than 10 percent of the graduates of state schools for the deaf are able to enter college. According to percentage of population, Montana would normally send one student per year to Gallaudet College for the deaf in Washington, D.C. Yet, in recent years 25 to 40 percent of the Montana graduating class has qualified. As a result of this achievement, a larger share of outside gifts is being channeled into college scholarships.

As I walked down the hall to leave, Glenn Harris proudly pointed out photos of the many honor graduates. "There's a potential in every boy and girl here today," he told me. "But first we must unlock their hearts." Shep's big heart has helped the school to do just that.

A Runt
of a Horse

by FREDERIC LOOMIS, M.D.

MY WIFE AND I were in Oregon some years ago for the annual Pendleton Round-up when we first met Frank and Katie Frazier. We visited them many times after that, and in their home we learned much of the big and little things that spun the remarkable fabric of their long life together: their pioneering struggles in early Oregon, their single-minded devotion to each other—they never had children—and finally their one great love.

Here is the story of that love, for a little runt of a horse, as Frank and Katie told it to me.

"Poker Nash called me one day," said Frank, "and asked if I wanted to buy a horse. I told him I didn't want one of his because it probably didn't have any teeth. He said, 'All right, you old fool,' and hung up. So of course I called right back to see what it was all about. Well, he'd seen a colt he was all het up about, and he'd seen me racing against the Doc's trotting horses, and I always got beat. He didn't like the Doc too well. Maybe that was it.

"Well, I wrote to a friend who knew horses to go see this colt, and next day I got a wire to send six hundred dollars, so I did. In a few days I received the bill of sale for Chehalis.

"Like a fool, I went blabbing around town that I'd got me a real Kentucky two-year-old—and then along he came in a boxcar and I almost died. He was the littlest, puniest thing I ever saw. I led him up the back streets so the boys wouldn't see him.

"But the minute Katie saw that poor little potbellied horse she began to talk baby talk to him, and damn if he didn't nuzzle her neck as if she had brought him up on a bottle. She didn't know if he was any good or not, and didn't care. She kept saying, 'I just love that horse,' and at the crack of dawn she was out talking to him again.

"I bought an old high-wheel sulky and took the little runt out on the dirt road. I hit him one lick with the whip, and I pretty near had the seat of my pants taken off. That little devil went like a bat out of hell. When I got home Katie thought I'd gone nuts.

"At first I didn't show him off much, pulled him down when anyone was around; and then one day Doc came along the road with his bay trotter and called out, 'Hey, Frank, is that the beautiful new *horse* I been hearing about—or is it a kangaroo?'

"Chehalis must have heard him, too. I spoke once, and in a split second we was hightailing after him. We caught up so fast I was afraid we'd step on him. I yelled, 'Git out of the way, you old coot, and let the kangaroo go by.' Doc looked around with his eyes bugging out and lit into his horse with the whip, and that's all I saw when we passed him. I knew that I had a real racer, and that he knew racing was to beat the other horse. Sometimes a horse never learns that.

"We trained Chehalis all summer and I drove him always. That was Katie's idea. She said if he never knew the feel of any other hands I could talk to him and tell him what to do. After his exercise Katie'd be waiting, and he'd hunt around for the piece of sugar that she had carried out for him.

One day she put the sugar in her pocket and tucked a handkerchief on top of it, not thinking, and that horse took the handkerchief out of her pocket and stood there holding it. Looked silly to me, but Katie thought it was wonderful and she did it every day.

"When I figured he was ready I took him down to Sacramento. There were sixteen horses in his race, and that little black horse flashed by 'em all so fast they looked like they was tied. So we made a tour, Katie and Chehalis and I, around the western tracks, and he won twelve out of thirteen races. The papers were filled with stories about the little black Oregon wonder that 'floated through the air.'

"Well, the next spring at our first meet, in Montana, Chehalis won his race easy, so I slowed him down a little at the wire—and then the head judge announced we came in third! The crowd nearly mobbed the judge's stand, and a Texan, a big man in the racing game, bounced up the stairs and threatened to kill the judge. But it was too late to change the decision. I was so disgusted I was ready to quit.

"But the Texan says, 'Listen to me, son, you won't quit if you've got any guts. You got a fine little horse. Mebbe if you were to train him over a little longer distance . . .' and then he talked to us very earnestly about an idea that might mean something wonderful.

"Right away Katie and I began making new plans that took our breath away. We kept Chehalis in shape for the mile races, but every morning I began to train him over a two-mile stretch. And along toward the end of the season we went down to the big fair at Salem, Oregon. But we couldn't get a race—wasn't a horse there fast enough to give Chehalis any competition. My little horse was a great drawing card, and the judges wanted the crowd to see him in action. Of course the early morning 'clockers' had seen us going that two-mile stretch. So the judges asked me if I was figuring on breaking the two-mile pacing record—4:24¼. Told me if I could, they'd give me five hundred dollars and another hundred for each second we took off. We took them up. It seemed like the little horse was ready."

"Yes, and you were ready, too," Katie interjected. "You should have seen him—he had a light-blue satin jacket, a navy-blue cap with a long visor, white linen pants, all shining new. He and the little black-velvet horse certainly made a picture.

"I sat in the judge's stand and I thought I'd die of waiting. Didn't anyone think he'd make the world's record—he was so little— except maybe Frank and me, and maybe Chehalis himself. Then away they went and I just held my breath. I heard the judges say, 'thirty seconds at the first quarter . . . too fast, going to get tired . . . 1:04 at the half . . . 1:35 third quarter.' And they came down the stretch on the first mile, the little horse going steady as a machine.

"My heart almost choked me when the judges yelled, '2:09 for the mile—can't keep it up!' And then they almost screamed, 'My God, see that hoss go!' and pretty soon they began to cheer just like they weren't judges at all. Frank and Chehalis came tearing down the stretch—Frank didn't even have his whip out, but I could see him saying, 'Boy, Boy, Boy'—that's all.

"And then they flashed by, and the judges began to dance around and they kept yelling, '4:19¼!' That was the fastest two miles ever paced against time in the world. Frank and Chehalis had taken five seconds off the record. The crowd howled when Frank came back with the little horse, jaunty as you please. They hung a great wreath of red roses around Chehalis' neck, and I began to cry. My, it was wonderful!" Katie's voice choked with emotion.

Then she whispered: "And that wasn't all. Going to the hotel Frank had a great big package under his arm with a red string around it. The moment we got in our room he tore the package open and there was the wreath of roses they'd put around Chehalis' neck at the track. Frank dropped it around my shoulders, and it reached the floor. Then he said, 'Katie, *you* did it—you loved that little horse so much he just had to win—and now he's a world champion!' "

Then Frank spoke. "Well, after that we had to hit the Grand Circuit. Those harness races still seem more wonderful to me than the running races of today—the wheels of the sulkies flashing in the sun and the society crowd all dressed up in Prince Alberts for the men and wonderful lace dresses with big bustles under them for the women, and those dinky parasols.

"Near the end of the season Katie took sick in Buffalo. She talked me into going on to Boston without her. I left orders with a florist to send her yellow roses every odd day of the month with a card saying, 'With love from Chehalis,' and every even day red roses 'With love from Frank.'

"We kept on winning, but half the fun was gone out of it. Every time I went to the stall, Chehalis would look around as much as to say, 'Where's Katie?' And then one day there was a letter from Katie's doctor telling me I must move her to southern California for the winter. Said it might mean losing her if I didn't.

"I sat down and tried to think. I was no millionaire, and I'd been offered five thousand dollars for Chehalis—and Katie was sick. I knew she wouldn't ever agree to sell him if I asked her, so I wrote her that I'd already sold him. I told her I was going to race him Saturday for the last time and then I'd come and take her home.

"There wasn't a letter from her on Saturday and I thought she must be sicker. I pretty near decided not to race. Then I thought of all the money that had been bet on Chehalis and knew I couldn't be a quitter. I was going to sell him after the race.

"So I got up in the sulky and we walked past the grandstand. The crowd cheered Chehalis, they always liked the little black tike, and I looked up to touch my cap to them—and by God, there was Katie! I saw first the dinky striped parasol I had bought her in Chicago, and then her face. She was pale as death, but smiling.

"She waved her hand. A minute before I hadn't cared, but now! I kept saying to Chehalis, 'Katie's here, boy, Katie's here,' and maybe he understood.

"We got caught in a pocket at the start, but the little horse fought his way out—and at the last eighth he came up from behind and began to fly. I'd seen him go but never like that. There were three horses ahead. He passed the third and he passed the second and when we came down the last hundred yards I thought the stands would go crazy. There was a roar like Niagara, with thousands of people on their feet, and papers and handkerchiefs and hats waving—and then we were across. We won by a head.

"I looked up in the box and Katie wasn't there! I dashed up to the stands and there she was, lying in a faint in the middle of a circle of people. The excitement had been too much for her.

"That night in the hotel the man who wanted to buy Chehalis came up to me and said, 'Frank, seventy-two hundred dollars cash.' I thought of Katie's white face and answered, 'Chehalis is yours, mister.'

"Next morning Katie felt strong enough to go down to the stables and, honest to God, that horse smiled at her. He whinnied like he used to do back home, and nuzzled her, and she began to cry. He reached across the bar of his stall and picked her handkerchief out of the pocket of her dress the way he used to, and the last we saw of him he was standing there watching us, holding that handkerchief in his mouth, a white blur against his shiny black coat."

"That was more than forty years ago," Katie said. "I'm a one-man woman and Chehalis was a one-man horse. He never won a race after Frank gave him up—not one single race—and he died of a broken heart."

She ran across the room to Frank and nestled in his arms, her head on his shoulder. He held her tenderly, patting her cheek. And then—I couldn't see anything clearly anymore, but in my mind I saw a vision of Frank, dapper in blue satin jacket and white trousers; of the little black Chehalis flying down the track before cheering thousands to make a world's record; and of the last sight of the horse as he stood that day in Boston, a bit of white fluff in his mouth, looking vainly after them as they walked away, their only great sorrow and their only other love.

RING OF
BRIGHT WATER

Condensed from the book

by GAVIN MAXWELL

MANY PEOPLE find a special attachment for a dog whose companionship has bridged widely different phases in their lives. My dog Jonnie and his forebears had spanned my boyhood, maturity and the war years. I have never had another dog since Jonnie, and I have never wanted one. But after his death, my home seemed a little lifeless, for I was living at the time in an isolated cottage, Camusfeàrna, on the wild Scottish coast across the sound from the Isle of Skye.

I began to review in my mind various animals that might keep me company. Having in my childhood kept pets ranging from hedgehogs to herons, I was familiar with a considerable list of creatures, but after a while I realized that none of them would meet my present requirements.

Early in 1956 I traveled with Wilfred Thesiger, the Near East expert, to spend two months among the little-known Marsh Arabs of southern Iraq. By then it had crossed my mind that I might like to keep an otter, and that Camusfeàrna, ringed by water, would be a suitable spot for this experiment. I mentioned this to Thesiger and he replied that I had better get one in the Tigris marshes before I came home, for they were

as common as mosquitoes and were often tamed by the Arabs.

We spent the better part of those months squatting cross-legged in the bottom of a *tarada,* or war canoe, traveling in a leisurely, timeless way between the scattered reed-built villages of the great delta marsh; and toward the end of our journey I did acquire an otter cub. At Basra, where we had gone to collect our mail, we found that Thesiger's had arrived but that mine had not, so I arranged to join him later. Two days before we were to meet, I came into my bedroom in the Consulate General to find two Arabs squatting on the floor. Beside them lay a sack that squirmed from time to time. They handed me a note from Thesiger: "Here is your otter. You may want to take it direct to London—I'm sure it would be a handful in the tarada."

With the opening of that sack began a phase of my life that in the essential sense has not yet ended, and may not end before I do. It is a thralldom to otters, an otter fixation, that I have found to be shared by most people who have ever owned one.

The creature that emerged, not greatly disconcerted, onto the floor of the bedroom did not resemble anything so much as a very small dragon. From head to tail he was coated with symmetrical pointed scales of mud, between whose tips was visible a soft velvet fur like that of a chocolate-brown mole. It was not for another month that I contrived to remove the last of his camouflage and see him in his true colors. Yet even on that first day I recognized that he was an otter of a species that I had never seen, resembling only a curious otter skin that I had bought in one of the marsh villages. I called him Mijbil, after a sheik with whom we had been staying.

For the first twenty-four hours Mijbil was aloof and indifferent, choosing to sleep on the floor as far from my bed as possible, and to accept food and water as though they were things that had appeared before him without human assistance. Food presented a problem, but Robert Angorly, a British-educated Iraqi friend, brought me every day half a dozen small reddish fish from the Tigris. These Mijbil consumed with gusto, holding them upright between his forepaws, tail end uppermost, and eating them like a stick of hard candy, always with five crunches of the left-hand side of the jaw alternating with five crunches of the right.

Mijbil and I enjoyed the Consul General's long-suffering hospitality for a fortnight. The second night Mij came onto my bed in the small hours and remained asleep in the crook of my knees until morning, and during that day he began to take a much too keen interest in his surroundings. I fashioned a collar, or rather a body belt, for his head was no wider than his neck, and took him on a leash to the bathroom, where for half an hour he went wild with joy in the water, plunging and rolling in it, shooting up and down the length of the bath underwater, and making enough slosh and splash for a hippo. This, I was to learn, is a characteristic of otters; every drop of water must be, so to speak, extended; a bowl must at once be overturned, or, if it will not overturn, be sat in and sploshed in until it overflows. To otters, water must be kept on the move and made to do things; when static it is as wasted and provoking as a buried talent.

Two days later Mijbil escaped from my bedroom as I entered it, and by the time I had caught up with him he was in the bathroom fumbling at the chromium taps with his paws. I watched, amazed by this exhibition of intelligence; in less than a minute he had turned the tap enough to produce a dribble of water, and, after a moment or two of distraction at his success, achieved the full flow. (He had, in fact, been fortunate to turn the tap the right way; on subsequent occasions he would as often as not screw it up still tighter, chittering with irritation at its failure to coöperate.)

The Consulate General had an enclosed tennis court in which I exercised Mijbil. Here I established after a few days that he would follow me without a lead and come to me when I called his name. By the end of a week he had accepted his dependence on me; with this security established he began to display the principal otter characteristic of perpetual play. Very few species of animal habitually play after they are adult, but otters are one of the exceptions to this rule, and in the wild state their play does not even require a partner. They will play alone for hours with any convenient floating object in the water, and at Camusfeàrna all the otters' "holts," or dens, contain a profusion of small shells and round stones that can only have been carried in for toys.

Mij would spend hours shuffling a rubber ball around the room like a soccer player, using all four feet to dribble the ball, and he could also throw it, with a powerful flick of the neck, to a surprising height and distance.

These games he would play either by himself or with me, but the really steady play of an otter, born of a sense of well-being and a full stomach, seems to be when it lies on its back and juggles small objects between its paws. This it does with the concentrated absorption and dexterity of a conjurer perfecting a trick. Marbles became Mij's favorite toys for this pastime, and he would lie on his back rolling two or more of them up and down his wide, flat belly without ever dropping one to the floor, or, with forepaws upstretched, rolling them between his palms.

Even during that first fortnight in Basra I learned a lot of Mij's language, a language largely shared by other species of otter. The sounds are widely different in range. The simplest is the call note: a short, anxious, penetrating, though not loud, mixture between a whistle and a chirp. There is also a query, used at closer quarters. Miji would enter a room, for instance, and ask whether there was anyone in it by the word "Hah?" uttered in a loud, harsh whisper. If he saw preparations being made to take him out or to the bath, he would stand at the door making a musical bubbling sound. But it was the chirp, ranging from a single querulous note to a continuous flow of chitter, that was Mij's main means of communication. He had one other note: a high caterwaul, a sort of screaming wail, that meant unequivocally that he was very angry and if provoked further would bite.

An otter's jaws are enormously powerful. Their teeth can crunch into instant pulp fish heads that seem as hard as stone. Like a puppy that nibbles one's hands, they seem to find the use of their mouths the most natural outlet for expression. I appreciate what efforts my otters have made to be gentle, but their playful nips are gauged to the sensitivity of an otter's, rather than a human's, skin. Mij used to look hurt and surprised when scolded for what must have seemed to him the most meticulous gentleness, and although he learned to be soft-mouthed with me he remained all his life somewhat hail-fellow-well-bit with strangers.

The days passed peacefully at Basra, but I dreaded the prospect of transporting Mij to England. Finally I booked a Trans World flight to Paris, with a doubtful Air France booking the same evening to London, where at that time I had a flat.

Trans World insisted that Mij should be packed into a box not more than eighteen inches square, and that this box must be carried on the floor at my feet. Since Mij's body was at that time perhaps a little over a foot long and his tail another foot, the designing of this box and its construction by native craftsmen caused me many anxious hours. Zinc-lined, it was delivered on the afternoon before my departure, and to my inexperienced eye it appeared as nearly ideal as could be contrived.

The flight was at 9:15 p.m. I put Mij into the box an hour before we left, so that he would become accustomed to it. I then left for a hurried meal. When I returned, barely in time to reach the airport for the flight, I was confronted with an appalling spectacle. There was complete silence from inside the box, but around its air holes and the hinged lid blood had trickled and dried in patches on the white wood.

I whipped off the padlock and tore open the lid, and Mij, exhausted and blood-spattered, whimpered and tried to climb up my leg. He had torn the zinc lining to shreds, scratching his mouth, nose and paws, and had left it jutting in spiky ribbons all around the inside of the box. When I had removed the last of the zinc, it was just ten minutes until flight time, and the airport was five miles distant. It was hard to bring myself to put the miserable Mij back into that box, which now represented to him a torture chamber, but I forced myself to do it. Then began a journey the like of which I hope I shall never know again.

I sat in the back of the car with the box beside me as the Arab driver tore through the streets of Basra like a ricocheting bullet. Donkeys reared, bicycles swerved wildly; out in the suburbs goats stampeded and poultry found unguessed powers of flight. Mij cried unceasingly in the box, and both of us were hurled to and fro and up and down like drinks in a cocktail shaker. Exactly as we drew up to a screeching stop before the airport entrance I heard a splintering sound from the box beside me, and saw Mij's nose force up the lid. He had summoned all the strength in his small body and torn one of the hinges clean out of the wood.

As I was rushed through the customs by infuriated officials I was trying to hold down the lid of the box with one hand, and with the other, using a screwdriver purloined from the chauffeur, to force back the screws into the splintered wood. I knew that it could be no more than a temporary measure, and my imagination boggled at the thought of the next twenty-four hours.

It was perhaps my only stroke of fortune that the seat booked for me was at the extreme front of the airplane, so that I had a bulkhead before me instead of another seat. The other passengers stared curiously as I struggled up the gangway with a horrifyingly vocal box, and I had a moment of real dismay when I saw my immediate neighbor was to be an American woman in early middle age. She would, I thought, have little tolerance for a draggled and dirty otter cub. Then the engines roared and we were taxiing out to take off; whatever was to happen now, there could be no escape, for the next stop was Cairo.

I had brought a briefcase full of old newspapers and a parcel of fish, and with these scant resources I prepared myself to withstand a siege. I arranged newspapers to cover all the floor around my feet, rang for the air hostess and asked her to keep the fish in a cool place. I have retained the most profound admiration for that air hostess; she was the very queen of her kind. The events of the last half hour had shaken my equilibrium, and I was not too coherent, but she took it all in her graceful sheer-nylon stride and received the ill-wrapped fish as though I were royalty depositing a jewel with her for safekeeping. Then she turned and spoke with the woman on my left. Would I not prefer, she then inquired, to have my pet on my knee? My neighbor had no objection. I could have kissed her hand in gratitude. But, not knowing otters, I was quite unprepared for what followed.

I unlocked the padlock and opened the lid, and Mij was out like a flash. He dodged my fumbling hands with an eel-like wriggle and disappeared. As I tried to get into the aisle I could follow his progress by a wave of disturbance among the passengers, not unlike that caused by the passage of a fox through a chicken yard. There were squawks, shrieks and a flapping of coats, and halfway down the fuselage a woman stood up on her seat screaming, "A rat! A rat!"

By now I was in the aisle myself, and, catching sight of Mij's tail disappearing beneath the legs of a portly white-turbaned Indian, I tried a flying tackle, landing flat on my face. I missed Mij's tail, but found myself grasping the sandaled foot of the Indian's female companion; furthermore my face was inexplicably covered with curry. I staggered up babbling inarticulate apology, and the Indian gave me a long, silent, utterly expressionless stare. I was, however, glad to observe that something, possibly the curry, had won over my fellow passengers, and that they were regarding me now as a harmless clown rather than as a dangerous lunatic. The air hostess stepped into the breach once more.

"Perhaps," she said with the most charming smile, "it would be better if I find the animal and bring it to you." She would probably have said the same had Mij been an escaped rogue elephant. I explained that Mij might bite a stranger, but she did not think so. I returned to my seat.

I was craning my neck back over the seat trying to follow the hunt when suddenly I heard at my feet a chitter of recognition, and Mij bounded onto my knee and began to nuzzle my face and neck. In all the strange world of the airplane I was the only familiar thing to be found, and in that first spontaneous return was sown the seed of the absolute trust that he accorded me for the rest of his life.

For a few hours he slept in my lap, and whenever he appeared restless I rang for fish and water, for otters are extremely bad at doing nothing. They cannot, as a dog does, lie still and awake; they are either asleep or entirely absorbed in some activity. If there is no acceptable toy, or if they are in a mood of frustration, they will, apparently with the utmost good humor, set about laying the land waste. There is, I am convinced, something positively provoking to an otter about order and tidiness in any form, and the greater the state of confusion that they can create about them the more contented they feel. This is due in part to intense inquisitiveness. An otter must find out everything and have a hand in everything; most of all he must know what lies inside any container or beyond any obstruction, and to help him he has an uncanny mechanical sense of how to get things open.

We had been flying for perhaps five hours when one of these moods descended upon Mijbil. It opened comparatively innocuously, with an assault upon the newspapers spread carefully around my feet, and in a minute or two the place looked like a street upon which royalty has been given a ticker-tape welcome. Then he turned his attention to his traveling box, which was filled with fine wood shavings. First he put his head and shoulders in and began to throw these out backward at enormous speed; then he got in bodily and lay on his back, using all four feet in a pedaling motion to hoist out the remainder. I was doing my best to cope with the litter, but it was like a ship's pumps working against a leak too great for them, and I was hopelessly behind in the race when he turned his attention to my neighbor's canvas travel bag on the floor beside him. The zipper gave him pause for no more than seconds; he yanked it back and was in headfirst, throwing out magazines, handkerchiefs, gloves, bottles of pills. By the grace of God my neighbor was sleeping profoundly; I managed, unobserved, to haul Mij out by the tail and cram the things back somehow. I hoped that she might leave the plane at Cairo before the outrage was discovered, and to my infinite relief she did so.

I think it was at Cairo that I realized what a complex creature I had acquired. I left the plane last, and during the forty minutes that we were grounded he was no more trouble than a Pekingese dog. I put the lead on him and exercised him around the edge of the airfield; there were jets landing and taking off with an appalling din all around us, but he gave no sign of noticing them, and when I went into the refreshment room for a drink he sat down at my feet as if this were the only life to which he was accustomed.

My troubles really began at Paris, an interminable time later. Mij had slept from time to time, but it was by now more than thirty-six hours since I had even dozed. I had to change airports, and there was no alternative to putting him back into his box. However, the box was now useless, with one hinge dangling.

When the plane was half an hour from Paris I explained my predicament to the air hostess. She went forward and returned after a few minutes saying that one of the crew would nail down the box and rope it for me. She warned me at the same time that under Air France's regulations the box from Paris on would have to travel in the freight compartment.

Mij was sleeping on his back inside my jacket, and I had to steel myself to betray his trust and listen to his pathetic cries as he was nailed up in what had become to me suddenly reminiscent of a coffin. There is a little-understood factor that is responsible for the deaths of many wild animals in shipment; it is generally known as "travel shock," and I was afraid it might kill Mijbil inside that box. We disembarked in torrential rain, and after an hour's wait at Orly Airport, during which Mij's cries gave place to a terrifying silence, I and three other London-bound passengers were hustled into an airplane. I had clung to the unwieldy box all this time, but now Mij disappeared into the darkness of a luggage compartment.

When we arrived at Amsterdam instead of London, Air France was profusely apologetic. There was no flight to London for a further fifty-five minutes. No one seemed to have a very clear idea of what had happened to any of the luggage belonging to the London-bound passengers, but a helpful official suggested that it might still be in Paris.

I went to the Air France office and let the tattered shreds of my self-control fly to the winds. At my elbow an American businessman was threatening legal action. When the shindy was at its height another official arrived and said calmly that our luggage was now aboard a British European Airways plane due for take-off in seven minutes, and would we kindly take our seats.

Muttering, "I'm going to cast my personal eyes on that baggage," my American companion spoke for all of us waifs. So we cast our personal eyes on the freight, and there was Mij's box, silent in a corner.

It was the small hours of the morning when we reached London Airport. As there are fortunately no quarantine regulations for otters, the box and all my luggage were soon loaded onto a car and we were on the last lap of our journey. What meant still more to me was that from the box there now came a faint inquiring chitter.

Mijbil had in fact displayed a characteristic shared, I believe, by many animals: an apparent step on the way to travel-shock death, but in fact a powerful buffer against it. Many animals seem to be able to go into a deep sleep, a coma almost, as a voluntary act; it is an escape mechanism that comes into operation when the animal's inventiveness in the face of adversity has failed to help. It is almost a norm of animals kept in cramped quarters in zoos and in pet stores. I came to recognize it later in Mij when he traveled in cars, a thing he hated; after a few minutes of frenzy he would curl himself into a tight ball and banish entirely the distasteful world about him.

He was wide awake once more by the time we reached my door, and when it closed behind me I felt a moment of deep satisfaction, almost of triumph. I opened the box, and Mijbil clambered into my arms to greet me with a frenzy of affection that I felt I had hardly merited.

In London I lived in one large room with a sleeping gallery, and a section at the back containing kitchen, bathroom and storage room. These unconventional premises held certain advantages for an otter, for the storage room opening from the bathroom provided quarters in which he might be left for short periods with all his essential requirements. But just how short those periods would be—a maximum of four or five hours —had never struck me until Mij had become the center point around which my life revolved. Otters reared by human beings demand human company and affection; without these they quickly become unhappy.

Exhausted as he was that first night, Mij had not been out of his box five minutes before he set out with terrifying enthusiasm to explore his new quarters. I had gone to the kitchen to find fish for him, expected by prearrangement with my charlady, but I had hardly got there before I heard the first crash of breaking china in the room behind me. The fish and the bath solved the problem temporarily, for when he had eaten he went wild with joy in the water and romped ecstatically for a full half hour. But it was clear that my crowded and vulnerable flat would require considerable alteration if it was to remain a home for both of us. Meanwhile sleep seemed long overdue, and I saw only one solution; I laid a sleeping bag on the sofa and anchored Mij to the sofa leg by his lead.

I have never been able to make up my mind whether certain aspects of otter behavior merely chance to resemble that of human beings, or whether there is actual mimicry of the human foster parent. Mij, anyway, seemed to regard me closely as I composed myself on my back with a cushion under my head; then, with a confiding air of knowing exactly what to do, he clambered up beside me and worked his body down into the sleeping bag until he lay flat on his back inside it with his head on the cushion beside mine and his forepaws in the air. In this position, such as a child devises for its teddy bear, Mij heaved an enormous sigh and was instantly asleep.

Mij and I remained in London for nearly a month, while, as my landlord put it, the flat came to look like a cross between a monkey cage and a warehouse. In the storage room Mij had a tattered armchair of his own and an electric heater; a wire gate was fitted to the stairs; the telephone was enclosed in a box (whose fastening he early learned to undo) and the wiring in plywood tunnels that gave the place the appearance of a powerhouse.

All these precautions were necessary if Miji were occasionally to be excluded from the studio itself. But if he thought that he had been excluded for too long, especially from visitors whose acquaintance he wished to make, he would set about laying waste with extraordinary invention. More usually, however, he would play for hours at a time with what soon became an established selection of toys: marbles, Ping-Pong balls, rubber fruit and a terrapin shell I had brought back from his native marshes. With a Ping-Pong ball he invented a game of his own. I had a damaged suitcase the lid of which, when closed, sloped from one end to the other. Mij discovered that if he placed the ball on the high end it would run down the length of the suitcase. He would dash around to the other end to ambush its arrival as it reached the drop to the floor, grab it and trot off with it to the high end once more.

These games were adequate for perhaps half of the time he spent indoors and awake, but several times a day he needed a prolonged romp with a human playmate. Tunneling under the carpet and affecting to believe himself invisible, he would shoot out with a squeak of triumph if a foot passed within range. Or he would dive inside the loose cover of the sofa and play tiger from behind it. Or he would simply lay siege to me as a puppy does, bouncing around in a frenzy of excited chirps and launching a series of tip-and-run raids.

I soon found an infallible way to distract his attention if he became too excitable. I would take the terrapin shell, wrap it in a towel and tightly knot the loose ends. He came to know these preparations and would wait absolutely motionless until I handed him the bundle; then he would straddle it with his forearms, sink his teeth in the knots, and begin to hump and shuffle around the room in a deceptively aimless-seeming manner. Deceptive, because no matter how complex the knots he would have them all undone in five or ten minutes. At the end of this performance he liked, and seemed to expect, applause, and he would then bring the towel and the shell to be tied up again.

Outside, I exercised him on a leash and, like a dog, he soon showed preference for certain corners at which dogs of all sorts had left stimulating messages; messages that were, perhaps, the more fascinating for being, as it were, in a foreign language. I was afraid to allow him to meet any dog nose to nose, and for his part he seemed largely indifferent to them.

Mij quickly developed certain compulsive habits on our walks, akin, clearly, to the rituals of children who on their way to and from school must avoid stepping on a crack or pass to the outside of every second lamppost. There was more than one street in which Mij would use one sidewalk only, refusing with dug-in toes to be led to the other side. On his way home, but never on his way out, he would tug me toward a low wall along the front of a school, jump up on it and gallop the full length of its thirty yards, to the hopeless distraction of both pupils and staff within.

Many of his actions, indeed, appeared ritual. I think that few people who keep wild creatures realize the enormous security value of routine in keeping an animal contented. Every living creature exists by a routine of some kind, and the small rituals of that routine are the landmarks, the boundaries of its security.

It was about this time that Mij delivered his first serious, intentional bite. He fed now mainly upon eels, which I had learned to be the staple food of many species of otter and which I gave him in the bath. On this occasion Mij elected to bring an eel out and eat it in the studio. To this, though he was sodden with water and the eel very slimy, there seemed no alternative, for it is folly to try to take away from a wild animal its natural prey; but when after a few mouthfuls he decided to carry it upstairs, I determined to call a halt, visualizing a soaking, eel-slimed bed.

I put on three pairs of gloves, the outermost being a pair of heavily padded flying gauntlets. I caught up with him halfway up the stairway; he laid down the eel, put a paw on it and hummed at me, a high, continuous hum that could break out into a wail. I talked quietly to him, telling him that he couldn't possibly hurt me and that I was going to take the eel back to the bathroom. The humming became much louder. I bent down and put my heavily gloved hand upon the eel. He screamed at me; then, as I began to lift it, he bit. His teeth passed through the three layers of glove and met in the middle of my hand with an audible crunch. He let go almost in the same instant and rolled on his back squirming with apology. I still held the eel; I carried it back to the bath, where he refused to pay any further attention to it, fussing over me and nuzzling me with little squeals of solicitude.

There were two bones broken in my hand,

and for a week it was the size of a boxing glove, very painful, and an acute embarrassment to me with those who from the first had been skeptical of Mij.

As may be imagined, Mij caused no small stir in his walks through London. It was not strange that the average Londoner should not recognize an otter. Otters belong to a comparatively small group of animals called mustelines, which includes the badger, weasel, skunk, mongoose and mink, among others. Now, in the London streets, I faced a barrage of conjecture that hit on practically everything from a baby seal to a squirrel. "Is that a walrus, mister?" reduced me to helpless laughter outside Harrod's, and "a hippo" made my day outside Cruft's Dog Show. A beaver, a bear cub, a newt, a leopard—one, apparently, that had changed his spots—even, with some dim recollection of schoolroom science, a "brontosaur"; Mij was anything but an otter.

But the question for which I awarded the highest score—a question hinting that someone had blundered when Mij was formed—came from a Herculean laborer engaged, mightily and alone, in digging a hole in the street. I was still far from him when he laid down his pick, put his hands on his hips and stared, an outraged, affronted stare, as though to say that he was not one upon whom to play jokes. I came abreast of him; he spat, glared and then growled, "'Ere, mister—*what is that supposed to be?*"

His question reminded me of my own ignorance; I did not, in fact, know what Mij was supposed to be. I knew, certainly, that he was an otter; but, judging from the zoological literature I had read, he must be one of a species which, if known to the scientific world, was at least not known to live in the marshes of Iraq.

I telephoned the Natural History department of the British Museum, and the same afternoon Mr. Robert Hayman arrived at my flat to examine Mij. There is in the serious zoological world a dead-panness, an unwillingness for committal, that must rival that of consulting physicians. Hayman was too competent not to know that he was looking at an unfamiliar animal, but he did not betray this. He took such measurements as Mij would permit, examined him closely, peered at his teeth and left.

In due course, Mij's new race was proclaimed. Hayman summoned me to the museum to see the cabinets of otter skins from all over Asia. Various subspecies similar to Mij ranged over most of eastern Asia, but none had been recorded west of India, and none had Mijbil's chocolate color.

There are very few people, and even fewer amateur zoologists, who stumble upon a sizable mammal previously unknown to science; the few who had given their own names to species—Steller's eider, Sharpe's crow, Grant's gazelle and so on—had been surrounded for me as a child with an aura of romance; they were creators, partaking a little of the deity. So, when Hayman suggested that the new otter should bear my name, something small and shrill from my nursery days shouted inside me that I could become one of my own early gods. So Mij and all his race became *Lutrogale perspicillata maxwelli*. There was now a Maxwell's otter.

In early May I felt I could wait no longer to see Mij playing under the Camusfeàrna waterfall. I went by way of Monreith, my family home in the south of Scotland, where Mij could taste a guarded liberty before his emancipation to total freedom.

Traveling with otters is a very expensive business. There was no question of again confining Mij to a box; he therefore traveled with me in a first-class sleeper, a form of transport he enjoyed hugely. He soon decided that in the washbasin lay the greatest pleasure potential; he curled up in it, his form fitting its contours as an apple fits a dumpling, and his paws began increasingly feverish experiments with the tap. It was, however, of a type new to him, operating by downward pressure, and not a drop could he draw from it for a full five minutes; at last, trying to lever himself into an upright position, he put his full weight on the tap handle and suddenly found himself, literally, in his element.

Later that evening an incident bade fair to bring the whole train to a stop. We were roaring up through the Midlands in summer dusk and I was looking out the window, for it had not occurred to me that Mij could, in that confined space, get into any serious mischief. It had not crossed my mind that by standing on the piled luggage he could reach the emergency-stop cord. This, however, was precisely what he had done, and when my eye lighted on him he had it firmly between his teeth while exploring with his busy paws the tunnel into which its ends disappeared from sight.

As I started toward him he removed his fingers from the recess and braced them against the wall for the tug. I caught him around the shoulders, but he retained his grip, and as I pulled him I saw the cord bulge ominously outward; I changed my tactics and pushed him toward it, but he merely braced his arms afresh. Suddenly inspiration came to me. Mij was extremely ticklish, particularly over the ribs. I began to tickle him feverishly, and at once his jaws relaxed into the foolish grin he reserved for such occasions and he began to squirm. Later he tried several times to reach the cord again, but I had redisposed the suitcases.

It was in unfamiliar surroundings such as these that Mij appeared most often to copy my actions. Although at home he slept in-

side my bed with his head at my feet, that night he arranged himself as he had on the first night at my flat, on his back with his head on the pillow and his arms outside the bedclothes. He was still there when the attendant brought my tea in the morning. He stared at Mij, and said, "Was it tea for one, or two, sir?"

During his stay at Monreith, Mij's character began to establish itself. In the big loch by the house, and then in the sea, he demonstrated not only his astonishing swimming powers but his willingness to reject freedom in favor of human company. He wore a harness to which a leash could be attached in emergency, but its function was as much to proclaim his domesticity to human aggressors as one of restraint.

This time of getting to know a wild animal on terms of mutual esteem was wholly fascinating to me, and our long daily walks were a source of perpetual delight. It remained difficult to lure him from some enticing piece of open water, but he was otherwise no more trouble than a dog and infinitely more interesting to watch. His hunting powers were still undeveloped, but in the streams he would sometimes catch frogs, which he skinned with a dexterity seemingly born of long practice. I had rightly guessed that his early life in an Arab household would have produced an enlightened attitude toward poultry—for no Arab would tolerate a predator among his scrawny chickens— and in fact I found that Mij would follow me through a crowded and cackling farmyard without a glance to right or left.

Even in the open countryside he retained his passion for playthings, and would carry with him for miles some object that had caught his fancy: a fallen rhododendron blossom, an empty cartridge case, or, on one occasion, a woman's comb set with artificial brilliants. This he found at the side of the drive as we set off one day, and he carried it for three hours, laying it down on the bank when he took to water and returning for it as soon as he emerged.

Following daily the routes for which Mij expressed preference, I found myself led into the world in which the otters of my own countryside lived, a watery world of deep-cut streams between high, rooty banks; of unguessed alleys and tunnels in reed beds by a loch's edge; of islands tangled with fallen trees among whose roots were earthy excavations and a whisper of the wind in the willows. Now that I had become conscious of otters, I saw all around me the signs of their presence: a smoothed bank of steep mud that they had used for tobogganing; a hollowed-out tree stump formed into a dry sleeping place. Yet in none of these traces did Mij take the slightest interest, perhaps because he did not recognize in them the products of his own kind.

During all the time that I had him he killed, so far as I know, only one warm-blooded animal, and then he did not eat it. On this occasion he was swimming in a reedy loch when he caught a moor hen a few days old, a little black golliwogg of a creature half the size of a day-old chick. He had a habit of tucking his treasures under one arm when swimming—for an otter swimming underwater uses its forelimbs very little—and here he placed the chick while he went on. It must have drowned during the first minute or so, and when at length he brought it ashore he appeared disappointed by this unwarranted fragility; he nuzzled it and chittered at it in a pettish way, then finally left it where it lay and went in search of something more coöperative.

We arrived at Camusfeàrna in early June, soon after the beginning of a long spell of Mediterranean weather that seemed to go on and on through timeless hours of sunshine and stillness. When I think of early summer at Camusfeàrna a single enduring image comes through the multitude that jostle before my mind's eye—wild roses against a clear blue sea. They are a deep, intense pink that is almost a red, and one sees them at Camusfeàrna against the direct background of the ocean, free from the green stain of summer.

Into this bright, watery landscape Mij moved and took possession with delight; he seemed so absolute a part of his surroundings that I wondered how they could ever have seemed to me complete before his arrival. At the beginning, while I was still cautious, his daily life followed something of a routine; but, as the weeks went on, this relaxed into total freedom, at the center point of which the house remained the den to which Mij returned when he was tired. He would wake with bizarre punctuality at exactly twenty past eight in the morning, come up to the pillow and nuzzle my face and neck with small squeaks of pleasure and affection. If I did not rouse myself very soon he would set about getting me out of bed with the slightly impatient efficiency of a nurse dealing with a difficult child. He began by going under the bedclothes and moving rapidly around the bed with a high-hunching, caterpillarlike motion that gradually untucked the bedclothes from beneath the mattress. When everything had been loosened to his satisfaction he would flow off the bed onto the floor—except when running on dry land, the only appropriate word for an otter's movement is flowing; they pour themselves, as it were, in the direction of their objective—take the bedclothes between his teeth, and, with a series of violent tugs, yank them down beside him.

Eventually I would be left uncovered on

the undersheet, clutching the pillows rebelliously. But they, too, had to go; and it was here that he demonstrated the extraordinary strength concealed in his small body. He would work his way under them and execute a series of mighty hunches of his arched back, each of them lifting my head and shoulders clear of the bed, and at some point in the procedure he invariably contrived to dislodge the pillows while I was still in mid-air, much as a practical joker will remove a chair upon which someone is about to sit. Then I had to dress, while Mij looked on with an all-that-shouldn't-really-have-been-necessary-you-know sort of expression.

Mij's next objective was the eel box, which I kept in the burn. Having breakfasted, he would tour the three-quarter circle formed by the burn and the sea; shooting like an underwater arrow after trout where the burn runs deep between the trees; tobogganing down the sand slope; diving through the waves on the beach and catching dabs; then, lured in with difficulty from starting on a second lap, home to ecstatic squirming among his towels.

This preamble to the day, when Mij had a full stomach and I had not, became longer and longer, and after the first fortnight I took, not without misgiving, to going back indoors myself as soon as he had been fed. At first he would return after an hour or so, and when he had dried himself he would creep up under the loose cover of the sofa and form a hump at the center of the seat. But as time went on he stayed longer about the burn, and I would not begin to worry until he had been gone for half the day.

There were quantities of black cattle at Camusfeàrna that year, and Mij seemed to detect in them an affinity to the water buffaloes of his native marshes, for he would dance around them with excited chitterings until they stampeded. Thus massed they were too formidable for him, so he finally devised a means of cattle baiting at which he became a master. With extreme stealth he would advance flat on his belly toward the rear end of some heifer whose black-tufted tail hung invitingly within his reach; then, as one who makes an impatient tug at a bell rope, he would grab the tuft between his teeth and give one tremendous jerk upon it, leaping backward exactly in time to dodge the lashing hooves. At first I viewed this sport with the gravest alarm, but Mij was able to gauge the distance to an inch, and never a hoof so much as grazed him. As a useful by-product of his impish sense of humor, the cattle tended to keep farther from the house, thus reducing the Augean litter of dung at my door.

I was writing a book that summer, and often I would lie sunbathing and writing in the grass by the burn while Mij quartered the stream's bed. Every now and again, with delighted squeaks, he would bound up the bank to deposit a skinload of water indiscriminately upon myself and my manuscript, sometimes adding insult to injury by confiscating my pen as he departed.

In the sea Mij discovered his true, breathtaking aquabatic powers. He would swim beside me as I rowed in the dinghy, and in the glass-clear waters of Camusfeàrna bay, where the white shell sand alternates with sea tangle and outcrops of rock, I could watch him as he dived down, down, down, fathom after fathom, to explore the gaudy sea forests with their flowered shell glades and mysterious shadowed caverns. He was able, as are all otters and seals, to walk on the bottom without buoyancy, for an otter swims habitually underwater and does not dive with full lungs, depending for oxygen, one presumes, upon a special adaptation of the venous system. I once timed Mij below the surface at almost six minutes, and I had the impression that he was in no way taxing his powers. Normally he would return to the surface every minute or so, breaking it for only a second, with a forward diving roll like that of a porpoise. Swimming at the surface, he was neither very fast nor graceful, using a laboring dog paddle in amazing contrast to his smooth darting grace below. For hours he would keep pace with the boat, appearing now on this side, now on that, sometimes mischievously seizing an oar with both arms and dragging on it, and from time to time bouncing inboard with a flurry of water, momentarily recalled to his mission of wetting people.

Mij caught a number of fish on his daily outings, and as his skill and speed grew, their size and variety increased. In the burn he learned to feel under stones for eels, reaching in with one paw and averted head; and I in turn learned to turn over larger stones for him, so that after a time he would stand in front of some boulder too heavy for him to move and chitter at me to come and lift it for him. Often, as I did this, an eel would streak out from it into deeper water and he would fire himself after it like a brown torpedo beneath the surface.

Near the edge of the tide he would search out the perfectly camouflaged flounders until they shot off with a wake of rising sand grains like smoke from an express train. Farther out in the bay he would kill an occasional sea trout; these he ate treading water as he did so, while I thought wistfully of the Chinese who employ trained otters to fish for them. Mij, I thought, with all his camaraderie, would never offer me a fish. But I was wrong. One day he emerged from

the sea onto the rock ledge where I was standing and slapped down in front of me a flounder a foot across. I took it that he had brought this for congratulation, for he would often bring his choicer catches for inspection before consuming them, so I said something encouraging and began to walk on. He hurried after me, slammed it down again with a wet smack at my feet, and sat there looking up and chittering at me.

I was in no hurry to take the gesture at its face value, having once, to my cost, deprived Mij of his prey. But when he redoubled his invitation, I reached down cautiously for the fish. Mij watched me with approval while I picked it up and began a mime of eating it; then he plunged off the rock into the sea.

Watching Mij in the rough equinoctial seas, I was at first sick with apprehension, then awed and fascinated, for his powers seemed little less than miraculous. During the first gale we had, I tried to keep him to rock pools and sheltered corners, but one day his pursuit of some prey took him to the seaward side of a high reef at the very tide's edge. As the long undertow sucked outward he was in no more than an inch or two of marbled water with the rock at his back, crunching the small fish he had caught; then, some forty yards to seaward of him, I saw a great snarling comber piling up higher and higher, surging in fifteen feet tall and as yet unbreaking. I yelled to Mij as the wave towered darkly toward him, but he paid no heed to me. It curled over and broke just before it reached him; all those tons of water just smashed down and obliterated him, enveloping the whole rock behind in a booming tumult of sea. Somewhere under it I visualized Mij's smashed body swirling around the foot of the black rock. But as the sea drew back in a long hissing undertow I saw, incredulously, that nothing had changed;

there was Mij still lying in the shallow marbled water, still eating his fish.

He rejoiced in the waves. He would hurl himself straight as an arrow right into the great roaring gray wall of an oncoming breaker and go clean through it as if it had neither weight nor momentum. He would swim far out to sea through wave after wave until the black dot of his head was lost among the distant white manes. More than once I thought that some wild urge to seek new lands had seized him, that he would go on swimming west into the Sea of the Hebrides and I would not see him again.

As the weeks went by, his absences did grow longer, and I spent many anxious hours searching for him. When I had drawn a blank at the falls and at all his favorite pools in the burn or among the rock ledges by the sea, I would begin to worry and to roam more widely, calling his name. His answering note of recognition was so like the call of a small bird that inhabits the trees by the waterside that my heart would leap a hundred times before I was certain I had heard him, and then my relief was so unbounded that I would allow him to dry himself on me without protest.

The first time that I found him in distress was in the strange, beautiful, but inhospitable world of the dark gorge above the waterfall. Here, in summer, when the water is low, one may pick one's way precariously along the rock at the stream's edge, the almost sheer but wooded sides rising a hundred feet at either hand. It is always twilight; the sunlight comes down thin and diffused by a stipple of oak and birch leaves far overhead. Here and there a fallen tree trunk spans the cool, moist gorge, its surface worn smooth by the wildcats' feet. There are foxes' and badgers' and wildcats' dens in the treacherous, near-vertical walls of the ravine; and the buzzards and hooded crows nest every year in the branches that lean out over the dark water.

I have never been at ease in this gorge, but it became Mij's special haunt, and one from which it was almost impossible to extract him, for the clamor of the water almost drowned the calling human voice. On this occasion there was more water in the burn than is usual in summer, and I was wet to the waist after the first few yards of the burn's bed. I called and called, but my voice was lost, and the mocking little birds answered me with Mij's own note of greeting. At length one of these birds called so insistently as to germinate in me a seed of doubt, but the sound came from far above me and I had been looking for Mij in the burn. Then I saw him, high up on the cliff, occupying so small a ledge that he could not even turn to make his way back, and with a fifty-foot drop below him. He was looking at me and yelling his head off.

I had to make a long detour to get above him with a rope, and then I found that the trees at the cliff top were all rotten. The stump I made the rope fast to grew in soft peat and gave out an ominous squelching sound when I tugged on it. I went down that rock with the rope knotted around my waist and the feeling that Mij would probably survive somehow, but that I should most certainly die.

He tried to stand on his hind legs when he saw me coming down above him, and more than once I thought he had gone. I had put the loop of his leash through the rope at my waist, and I clipped the other end to his harness as soon as my arm could reach him, but the harnesses, with their constant immersion, never lasted long, and I trusted this one about as much as I trusted the stump to which my rope was tied. I went up the rope with Mij dangling and bumping at my side like a cow being loaded onto a ship

by crane, and in my mind's eye were two jostling, urgent images—the slow, sucking emergence of the tree roots which held me, and the gradual parting of the rivets that held Mij's harness together. It was one of the nastiest five minutes of my life; when I reached the top the roots of the stump were indeed showing—it took just one tug with all my strength to pull them clean out.

Another time of anxiety and search stands out in my mind, for it was the first time Mij was away for a whole night. I had left him in the early morning eating his eels by the burn, and I began to be uneasy when he had not returned by midafternoon. I had been working hard at my book; time had passed unheeded, and it was a shock to realize that I had been writing for some six hours. I went out and called for Mij down the burn and along the beach, then went again to the gorge above the falls. But there was no trace of him anywhere.

I left the burn and went out to the nearer islands. It was low tide, and on the sand I found otter footprints leading toward the lighthouse island, but I could not be certain that they were Mij's. All that evening I searched and called, and when dusk came and he still did not return I began to despair, for by sundown he was always asleep in front of the fire.

By eleven o'clock it was blowing up a gale from the south, and a heavy sea began to pile up; enough, I thought, for him to lose his bearings if he were trying to make his way homeward. I put a light in each window, left the doors open and dozed fitfully in front of the fire. With the first faint paling of dawn, I went out to get the boat, for by now I had somehow convinced myself that Mij was on the lighthouse island. My little cockleshell was in difficulties from the moment I launched her. I had a beam sea to cross before I could reach the lee of the islands, and she was taking a slosh of water all the way.

After half an hour I was both wet and scared. The bigger islands gave some shelter from the wind, but in the passages between them the sea was foaming white and wicked-looking over the many rocks and reefs; if I took a moment to bail I would have been swept onto those black teeth. To complete my discomfort, I met a killer whale. He broke the surface no more than twenty yards to the north of me, a big bull whose saber fin seemed to tower a man's height out of the water; and, probably by chance, he turned straight for me. I swung and rowed for the nearest island as though man were a killer's only prey. A hundred yards from the island I grounded on a reef, and slithered and floundered in thigh-deep water until I had lifted the flat keel clear; the killer, possibly intent upon his own business and with no thought for me, cruised around a stone's throw away while I managed to struggle to the shore.

The lighthouse island, when I eventually reached it, was a jungle of summer briers that gripped my clothing with octopus arms. I felt like a dream walker who never moves, and my calling voice was swept away northward on gusts of cold, wet wind. I got back to the house at nine in the morning, with a deadweight boat more than half full of water and a sick emptiness in mind and body. By now part of me was sure that Mij too had met the killer, and that he was at this moment half digested in the whale's belly.

All that day I wandered and called, and at about five in the evening I began to remove the remaining evidence of Mij's past existence. I had taken from beneath the kitchen table his drinking bowl and carried it to the scullery, when I thought I heard his voice behind me. The impression was strong enough for me to set down the bowl

and hurry back into the kitchen. There on the kitchen floor was a large, wet footprint. I looked at it. I thought, I am tired and overwrought; and I went down on my hands and knees to inspect it. It was certainly wet, and it smelled of otter. I was still on all fours when from the doorway behind me I heard an unmistakable "Hah?" Then Mij was all over me. I had been reassuring myself and him for some minutes before I realized that his harness was burst apart, and that for a day or more he must have been caught, like Absalom, struggling, desperate, waiting for a rescue that never came.

I am aware that this scene of reunion, and the hours that for me had preceded it, must appear to many a reader overly sentimental. There is, however, an obligation of honesty upon a writer. I knew by that time that Mij meant more to me than most human beings of my acquaintance, and I was not ashamed of it. Perhaps I knew Mij trusted me more utterly than did any of my own kind, and so supplied a need that we are slow to admit.

When I missed Mij I would go first to the waterfall, for there he would spend long hours alone, chasing the one big trout that lived in the pool below the falls, catching eels or playing with some floating object that had been washed down. Sometimes he would set out from the house carrying a Ping-Pong ball, purposeful and self-engrossed, and he would still be at the waterfall with it an hour later, pulling it underwater and letting it shoot up again, rearing up and pouncing on it, playing his own form of water polo. Once, I remember, I went to look for him there and at first could not find him. Then my attention was caught by something red in the black water at the edge of the foam, and I saw that Mij was floating on his back, apparently fast asleep, with a bunch of scarlet rowanberries clasped to his chest with one arm.

One day, by a dry-stone wall that runs between the waterfall and the house, I saw a figure approaching me whom I recognized as the literary editor of an English magazine, the *New Statesman*. I exchanged greetings with her over the wall, and as we began to talk Mij climbed onto the wall beside me and watched.

Now Mij had a vice that I have not yet mentioned; a vice that I had been unable to cure, partly because I did not understand its motivation. To put it bluntly, he bit the lobes of people's ears—not in anger, but simply because he liked doing so. He just nipped through them like an efficient ear piercer and apparently felt the better for it. I had had both ears pierced early in my association with Mij, but it was now so long since he had met strangers that I had forgotten his deplorable proclivity. My visitor leaned an arm on the wall as she talked, with her head a mere foot from Mij's, and Mij reached out, without comment, and sharply pierced the lobe of her left ear with surgical precision.

It was her finest hour. I had seen many lobes pierced by Mij, and I was a connoisseur of reaction to the situation, ranging from the faint shriek to the ominous flushed silence. I thought I knew them all, but I was wrong. Not by the smallest interruption in her flow of speech did she betray that she had perceived the incident; only her eyes, as she continued her sentence, assumed an expression of unbelieving outrage entirely at variance with her words.

I returned to London with Mij in the autumn, and with his usual good humor he adjusted himself quickly. In the station hotel he lay beside my chair while I had tea, and when a waitress brought him a saucer of milk he lapped it as delicately as any drawing-room cat. He entered his first-class sleeper as one long used to travel, and at the studio flat next day seemed pleased to be among his old surroundings. He settled quickly into his earlier routines, and even went shopping with me.

One local shop devoted to oddities allowed him to make his own selection. He had a passion for rubber toys, especially those that squeaked or rattled. I was hesitating one day between a chocolate éclair that whistled and an India-rubber mackerel that wheezed when the clerk said, "Why not let him make his own choice, sir?" and placed both on the floor. Mij plumped for the éclair, to the clerk's surprise, and thereafter Mij chose his own toys and himself bore them home in triumph.

In November I had to be away from London for three days, and this was Mij's first and only imprisonment away from people and surroundings that he knew. I arranged for him to be boarded at the zoo sanatorium in Regent's Park and took him there in a taxi. Once inside the zoo he plodded sturdily ahead at the end of his leash; only when he passed the aviaries containing the great birds of prey did he cower and tug the other way —a memory, perhaps, of his native marshes where eagles must be the otter's only natural enemy. I left him in a grim cage with only my sheepskin coat for company, and when the door was closed on him his wails went to my heart. I could hear him long after I had closed the gate of the sanatorium yard.

The evening of the next day I telephoned from the north to inquire if he had settled down. Too much, I was told; in fact he had insulated himself in the same deep coma into which he had sunk in his box on the air journey. He had refused all food, and after digging at the iron and cement that enclosed him until his feet bled, he had curled up in my sheepskin coat and refused to be roused. I was advised to come back for him as soon as possible.

I rushed back to the zoo at once. I could not at first even see Mij in his cage. There were a lot of dead fish lying about untouched; the sheepskin jacket was huddled in the middle of them, and there was no movement anywhere. I went in through the steel-barred door and putting my hand into the jacket I felt him warm and breathing, as far into the armhole as he could push himself. Only when I touched his face did he begin to awaken, with a slow, dazed air as if he were emerging from a trance. Then suddenly he was out and leaping in a frenzy of joy, clambering over me and inside my coat, and rushing around and around that barren cage until he threw himself down panting in front of me.

In those two days he had taken on the sour odor of stale urine and dejection and indignity that is the hallmark of the captive who has lost his self-respect; his usually sweet-smelling fur stank like an ill-kept ferret's. I never repeated the experiment.

He paid one more visit to the zoo, but this time not as a captive. I had long wanted to have a clear, eye-level view of his performance underwater, and the zoo aquarium allowed me to set up a large glass tank I had hired for the day. I asked an artist, Michael Ayrton, to come and make drawings of Mij, and provided a number of goldfish for Mij to catch. He set about their destruction with a display of virtuosity for which even my long hours of watching him from above had left me unprepared. As with his toys, he was not content to possess only one fish at a time; having captured one, he would tuck it under an arm and swoop, sometimes "looping the loop" as he did so, upon another—at one moment he had fish under both arms and a third in his mouth.

His speed was bewildering, his grace breathtaking. He was mercurial, sinuous, wonderful. I thought of a ballet dancer, of a bird or an airplane in aerobatics, but in these I was comparing him to lesser grandeurs; he was an otter in his own element, and he was the most beautiful thing in nature that I had ever seen.

What little there remains to tell of his story I shall write quickly, for anyone who has shared some of my pleasure in Mij's life must share, too, a little of my unhappiness at his death.

I had arranged to go to Camusfeàrna to spend the spring and summer in his company, and there to write a book about him. I was to leave London early in April, but I needed a fortnight's freedom from his incessant demands upon my time, and I arranged that he should precede me to Scotland in the charge of a friend. I packed his "suitcase," a wicker basket whose contents seemed to become more and more elaborate —spare harnesses, leads, cod-liver oil, toys partially disintegrated but long favored; and I traveled with him in a hired car from my flat to Euston Station. It was a big Humber, with a broad ledge between the top of the back seat and the rear window. Here, I recall with a vividness that is still painful, he sprawled upon his back and rolled my fountain pen to and fro between his forepaws or held it clasped with one of them against his broad, glossy belly.

At the station he tugged purposefully at the leash all the way to the sleeper, where he made straight for the washbasin and accommodated his plastic body to the curves. His left hand reached up and fumbled with the tap. That was the last I ever saw of him.

During the next ten days I received letters telling of Mij's delight in his renewed freedom, of fish he had caught; of how he would come in dog-tired and curl up before the fire; of anxious hours of absence; of how it had been decided he would be safer without his harness, which, despite the care that had gone into its design, might catch upon some underwater snag and drown him.

On April 16 I was packing to leave for Camusfeàrna when I received a telephone call from the estate agent of the property to which Camusfeàrna belonged. It was rumored, he told me, that an otter had been killed at a village north of Camusfeàrna. And Mij was missing. However, the otter that had been killed was said to have been so mangy and scabby that the killer had not thought it worthwhile to preserve the skin.

I arrived at the village the following afternoon. I had heard conflicting tales at the station, on the launch, at the village pier. Some said that a very wild otter had been killed, but that Mij was already safely returned, others that he had been seen in a village miles to the south of Camusfeàrna. I did not believe them. I knew that Mij was dead, but I was driven by a compulsive desire to know by whom and how he had been killed.

A roadman called Big Angus, I was told, had been driving his truck past the church when he had seen an otter on the road where it bordered the sea and had killed it. I waited in the village to see him. Big Angus came at last. Yes, he had killed an otter yesterday; but the skin was half bald, and he had not kept it. He was soft-spoken and ingenuous.

"How did you kill him?" I asked. "With a stick?" "No, sir," he said, "I had a pickax in the back of the truck." Yes, he thought that a wild otter would wait in the road while he went to fetch the instrument of its death. He stuck to his story. "I threw the carcass in the river," he said, "and I don't remember where." He had been well briefed and well rehearsed, as I learned later, for he had gone in a panic to seek advice. Brave murderer; for his lies and deceit I could have killed him then as instinctively as he had killed Mij. Instead, I pleaded with him to tell me. I tried to make him understand what it would be like for me to remain at Camusfeàrna waiting day after day for the return that I did not believe possible. He did not give way an inch.

I learned later, from someone else with more humanity.

"I felt I couldn't sit by and see you deceived," he said. "It's just not a decent action in a man, and that's the truth. I saw the body on the truck when it stopped in the village, and there wasn't a hair out of place on the whole skin. If he didn't know before that it was yours, he knew then because I told him."

I got the story little by little. Mij had been wandering widely for some days past, though he had always returned at night. Earlier that day he had been recognized near the village where he was killed. A man who saw an otter in his hen run had fetched his gun before he was struck by the otter's indifference to the chickens and made the right deduction. Mij had been on his way home when he had met Big Angus, and he had never been taught to fear or distrust any human being. I hope he was killed quickly, but I wish he had had one chance to use his teeth on his killer.

He had been with me for one year and one day.

I missed Mij desperately, so much that it was a year before I could bring myself to go to Camusfeàrna again. He had filled that landscape so completely, had made so much his own the ring of bright water I loved, that it seemed, after he had gone from it, hollow and insufficient. In London, I moved to

Chelsea, partly because I found the elaboration of otterproofing devices in my old premises too constant a reminder of my failure to keep Mij alive.

It was early spring when I made up my mind to go back to Camusfeàrna. There, dimly at first, then clear and undisguised, came the thought that the place was incomplete without an otter, that Mij must have a successor; that, in fact, there must always be an otter at Camusfeàrna for as long as I occupied the house.

Having made up my mind, I began a systematic examination of all the holts I knew up and down the coast. One of the islands in the bay is called Otter Island, and on it is a tumbled cairn of boulders forming a system of low caves much used by otters. One year there had been a litter of cubs there, but now, although several of the inner chambers had been lined with fresh bedding, there was no sign of young. Nor was there in the other holts I visited.

Still, I did not despair of acquiring a cub locally, for otters have no breeding season, and cubs have been found in every month of the year. But as a second string I wrote to my Iraqi friend, Robert Angorly, to ask if he would try to find another of Mij's species for me.

The Marsh Arabs soon brought him a succession of cubs, three of which were *Lutrogale perspicillata maxwelli,* but each died within a few days. The next cub lived, and I arranged for it to be flown to London on July 15. On Monday, the fourteenth of July, revolution swept Iraq, and of my friend Angorly, who never took much interest in politics, there has been no word since.

In the autumn I made another attempt to acquire an otter, but by now with diminishing hope. A friend arranged to import two Indian otters through a London dealer; he was to keep one and I the other. They were described as young and tame, one a male, one a female.

They were due to arrive at London Airport at about one o'clock in the morning, and such was our anxiety for their welfare that we were there to meet them. There was, however, no trace of them, and, reflecting that they were safely consigned to a dealer to whom they represented hard cash, we returned to bed. Hours later we found them at the dealer's, the crate still unopened; the two occupants were feeble, shivering, soaked in their own excrement, almost too weak to stand. They died early next day, mine in the zoo hospital, my friend's in his wife's lap; she had sat up all night trying to coax the pathetic little creature back to life.

I returned to Camusfeàrna in the spring of 1959, and I had been there for no more than a week when there occurred the strangest episode in the saga of my efforts to replace Mijbil, a coincidence so extravagant that had it been unwitnessed I should hesitate to record it.

On April 19 I motored to the railhead village to meet a guest and had lunch in the large glossy hotel that caters to the transatlantic tourist trade. Now, in the spring, it was comparatively empty; and, falling into conversation with the hall porter, I found that we had many acquaintances in common. While I waited for the train we exchanged stories and memories.

I met my guest at the station, and we returned to the hotel for a drink before setting off for Camusfeàrna. We were sitting in the lounge when suddenly the hall porter came running over to us. "Mr. Maxwell!" he called. "Come quick and tell me what's this strange beast outside!"

I have an open mind on the subject of extrasensory perception in general. I have had one or two curious experiences, but none quite as strange as the overwhelming and instant certainty that I felt then of what I was going to see outside the door.

Four people were walking past the hotel. At their heels lolloped a large, sleek otter, with a silvery-colored head and a snow-white throat and chest. I had a feeling of unreality, of struggling in a dream. I rushed up to the party and began to jabber, probably quite incoherently, about Mijbil, and about my frustrated efforts to find a successor. I must have been talking a great deal, because what they were saying in reply took a long time to sink in, and when it did the sense of dreaming increased.

"Got her in West Africa . . . only eight months old . . . brought her up myself with a bottle. In six weeks we've got to go back. . . . She can't travel. . . . Pitiful state when we got here from Lagos . . . so it looked like a zoo for her—everyone admires her, but when it comes to owning her, they shy off.

. . . Poor Edal, it was breaking my heart. . . ."

We were sitting on the steps of the hotel by this time, and the otter was nuzzling at the nape of my neck—that well-remembered touch of hard whiskers and soft face fur.

By the time I had taken in what her owners were saying, the party had dwindled by two. It transpired that the only reason her owners had been in the village was to drop two hitchhikers. And the only reason I was there was to meet my guest, and the only reason we had met at all was that two hours earlier I had made the acquaintance of the hall porter. If he had not called me they would have passed by the hotel and gone home, and I should have gone back to Camusfeàrna.

Ten days later Edal became mine, and there was once more an otter at Camusfeàrna, playing in the burn and sleeping before the hearth.

A Fish Named Ulysses

Condensed from The Living Sea

by JACQUES-YVES COUSTEAU with James Dugan

OUR UNDERSEA EXPLORATION had taken us to the Indian Ocean, and one day we dropped *Calypso*'s anchor in crystal-clear water just off Assumption, a tiny scimitar-shaped atoll near the equator. I passed the word that we would stay three or four hours and have a look around.

Jean Delmas, a member of our research team, was the first to dive. He went head-down through the looking glass into the most enormous vistas he had ever scanned in the underwater world. The sea was transparent for two hundred feet in every direction. He had never seen corals so rich, or fish so plentiful and so fearless. They came in multitudes, wearing every color imaginable. He stumbled back on deck under his heavy gear and said, "Let's stay here for a while. This is the place to make friends with fish."

Before I could reply, Luis Marden returned with the second relay of divers, and he was just as enthusiastic. "It is incredible down there," he said. "When I tried to take close-up photographs of the fish, they came too near to stay in focus. When I backed off, they came with me."

Then two more divers went down—veteran, objective men, Frédéric Dumas and Albert Falco—and came out babbling. I couldn't get a sober report from either of them. I hefted an aqualung onto my back. Underwater, while I still had a hand on the ladder, I was enslaved by Assumption Reef myself. I climbed back and said we would stay as long as our fresh water lasted.

The structure of the island was classic. A shallow fringing reef, sparkling with sunshine and dancing color, extended perhaps three hundred feet from the white beach. It dropped off rather abruptly in a chaos of standing coral and grottoes to about two hundred feet, where a gray sedimental plain faded away into the ocean. Every foot of the slope was laden with coral unsurpassed in richness and beauty. Along the bank, mixing in friendly anarchy, were most of the species of fish we had met in a thousand different places and a quantity of new ones we had never seen before—as well as some that no one had ever seen. One incredible little fish sported a body pattern of perfect red and white squares—literally a swimming checkerboard. Among the animals there prevailed a spirit of mutual interest, almost as though the struggle for life were suspended.

We stayed forty days, and none of us lost

our enthusiasm for Assumption Reef. One of the reasons was a remarkable fish Luis Marden encountered—a sixty-pound grouper with a brownish coat and a pale, marbled pattern that changed from time to time. The huge fish strolled up to Marden, and he prepared to take its portrait. The grouper nudged the flashbulb bag with its nose. Luis backed away to get proper focus. The fish followed. By a series of retreats, Marden finally shot it in focus and swam away to find other fish. The grouper tagged along, nuzzling the photographer and his glittering gadgets. As Luis lined up another subject, the big fish interposed itself in the camera field. The diver dodged and made his shot. When Marden told us about his new acquaintance, we went down into the grouper's territory with a canvas bag full of chopped meat. The big fish came to us without hesitation. When we released some food in the water, the grouper's cavernous mouth opened. Like a flock of birds entering a tunnel, the meat scraps vanished. When we experimented cautiously with hand feeding, the big fish plucked meat off our fingertips harmlessly. We named the clever beast Ulysses.

Ulysses became our inseparable friend. He followed us everywhere, sometimes brushing against our rubber fins. When, after deep dives, we decompressed thirty feet down on a weighted and measured cable, Ulysses relieved our boredom by horsing around with us until we went up the ladder. Afterward he would hang around just under the surface, like a boy sadly watching his playmates being called in to supper. Ulysses quickly got on to our diving schedule and would be found early in the morning waiting under the ladder for the day's first sortie. He would go bounding down with us for a round of clumsy mischief and meals from the canvas bag. In a good mood Ulysses would let any of us pat him and scratch his head. Once Dumas, partially concealing the meat bag in his hand, turned in a slow, three-step tempo. Following the bait around, Ulysses joined the dance. When Dumas spun the other way, the fish followed right on the beat. It was done so lightly and rhythmically that we were able to film it as a waltz.

But Ulysses had a temper, too. Sometimes he bungled into camera setups, and we would have to shove him away. Then he would flounce off, "slamming the door" behind him. (His first tail stroke was so powerful that it made an audible boom.) He also grew angry with us when we forgot to bring the meat bag. He would hang thirty feet off, keeping that distance whether we went toward him or away from him.

One morning, as Delmas opened the canvas meat sack to feed Ulysses, the big grouper made a rapid dash, tore the sack from Delmas' hand and swallowed it whole. Then he marched brazenly away, well aware that there was no more food forthcoming. The next morning there was no Ulysses under the ladder. In the afternoon we spread out to look for him. We found him lying on the sand in front of his den, a deep crevice in the coral hardly big enough to contain him, but with the security of two entrances. The lair was thirty feet down, opening on a terrace of white sand.

But Ulysses was not enjoying his terrace this day. His gills were pulsing at an unreasonable rate. He had no interest in us. The following morning he was still in bed. On the third day, we found the fish flat on his side, seemingly critically ill. I consulted our ship's surgeon, Dr. Denis Martin-Laval, who said Ulysses was in danger of a fatal intestinal obstruction. Martin-Laval was confronted with his most unusual case. Since he could not bring the fish to his surgery, he prepared to operate in the patient's bedroom. He gathered anesthetics, knives, surgical clips, and catgut and needle to suture the opening after he had removed the bag from Ulysses' tortured interior. The surgeon briefed three divers to act as his assistants. It was sundown before the preparations were completed. We went to sleep hoping that Ulysses could last through the night. At first light, a reconnaissance team plunged. Ulysses was gone from his veranda. Several divers roamed about, looking for him. One felt somebody pulling at his back harness. It was Ulysses, announcing that everything was okay. He was gay and hungry. He had managed to eliminate the meat sack.

We experimented with feeding other denizens of the reef, and they all responded heartily. Watching us feed them put Ulysses in a towering rage. He would crash into the sack, bite our fins, tug on our bathing trunks and whip his big tail to scatter the smaller fish. We wanted to film a golden host of yellow snappers following a manfish across the reef, but Ulysses kept breaking it up. Finally we assembled our antishark cage and dropped it to the bottom. Ulysses supervised the placing of the cage and the opening of the door. Delmas waved his feeding arm toward the opening, and after the grouper swam in, the door clanked shut behind him.

Delmas decided that Ulysses should have a special treat while he was in jail. That day we had killed a twenty-pound barracuda. We took it down to the cage and poked its head through the bars. Without hesitation Ulysses gulped in half the barracuda's body, which was as long as he was, leaving the tail end sticking out from his jaws. Ulysses seemed to regard this as nothing out of the ordinary and remained for hours with the barracuda protruding from his mouth. When we left for the night, about a third of the barracuda was still visible. In the morning it was gone.

Ulysses was caged for three days while we filmed the feeding of the others. When we opened the jail door, he watched with interest but made no move to depart. Accustomed to the abundant food we provided him in the cage, he preferred to stay there. When we pushed him through the door, Ulysses swam off in a sulk, at a very slow pace. He was fat and out of shape.

After five weeks at the reef, we ran low on food. I asked Delmas to go down and spear a grouper. I accompanied him, and so did Ulysses. It was like hunting with a retriever dog. Delmas selected a black grouper and triggered his spear gun. As though synchronized with the flight of the spear, Ulysses hit the fish at practically the same instant. The fish's tail and the four-foot harpoon protruded from Ulysses' mouth. Delmas placed his foot against our friend's head and heaved hard to extract the spear. This gave Ulysses more room to accommodate the catch, and he swallowed it all except the tip of the tail.

The time had come to continue our cruise. "Let's take Ulysses with us," Delmas suggested. The idea was met with enthusiasm, but I had to oppose the notion. In France, Ulysses would face life imprisonment in an aquarium, or he would have to be liberated in the Mediterranean. He was probably not adapted for colder water. Moreover, he was so friendly that the first spearman he met would have an easy kill. We dived for the last time and waved good-bye to him.

Later, after Ulysses had become a movie star in our film, *The Silent World,* a boat sailing around the world made a special call at Assumption Bay and sent divers down to look for him. They reported, "Ulysses is doing fine. He was easy to recognize. He swam up immediately to the divers." Perhaps we shall go back someday and find Ulysses again. He is a fish worth going halfway around the world to see.

All-Too-Human Chumley

Condensed from The Overloaded Ark

by GERALD M. DURRELL

I FIRST MET CHUMLEY in West Africa while on an expedition to capture wild animals for British zoos. He had been the pet of a district officer, and I had agreed—sight unseen—to deliver him to the London Zoo. But I got a rude shock the day Chumley arrived at our camp. Having visualized a small, young chimpanzee, I was shaken to discover that he was full-grown—a veteran of eight or nine years, with huge arms and a massive, hairy chest that measured at least twice the size of mine. His head was nearly bald, and bad tooth growth gave his face a weird, pugilistic look. But even though not handsome, he certainly had personality.

He rode into our camp in a small van, seated sedately in a huge crate, and when its doors were opened, stepped out with all the self-confidence of a film star. Surveying the surroundings, he turned to me and held out a soft, pink-palmed hand with that bored expression one often sees on the faces of professional handshakers. Around his neck was a chain whose length, some fifteen feet, extended back into the crate. This would have been a sign of subjugation with an animal of less aplomb. Chumley wore it with the superb air of a Lord Mayor. After

shaking my hand, he gathered the chain carefully into loops and walked into our hut as if he owned it.

Chumley seated himself in a chair and looked hopefully at me. It was obvious that he expected some sort of refreshment after

his tiring journey. I called to the cook to make tea, for which I had been told Chumley had a great liking. I sat down and was about to light a cigarette when a long, hairy arm stretched across the table and Chumley grunted. Wondering what he would do, I handed him the cigarette. To my astonishment he put it carefully in the corner of his mouth. So I handed him the matches, thinking *that* would fool him. He opened the box, took out a match, struck it, lit his cigarette and tossed the box on the table. Then, crossing his legs, he lay back in his chair, inhaling thankfully and blowing clouds of smoke out through his nose.

When the tea was ready, I filled a huge tin mug and added three tablespoons of sugar. "Ooooooooo, umph!" Chumley said approvingly, and carefully accepted the mug from me with both hands. Then, with lower lip extended, he tested the tea to see if it was too hot. It was, so he blew on it until it was right, then drank it down. Then he held out his mug for a refill.

Chumley's crate was placed where he could have a good view of everything that went on around the hut, and he often shouted comments to me as we worked. That first day I chained him to a stump near his crate. I had scarcely returned to the hut when a frightful upheaval took place among our monkeys, which were tethered nearby. I dashed out just in time to see a rock the size of a cabbage land in their midst—missing them, fortunately. Chumley, it seemed, was engaging in bowling practice. Seizing a stick, I raced down upon him, shouting and at the same time wondering what would happen if I dealt out punishment to an animal with twice my strength. To my surprise, Chumley lay on the ground, covered his face and head with his long arms and screamed at the top of his voice. I flicked him twice with the flimsy stick,

saying, "You are a very wicked animal."

"Whooooooooo," he replied, glancing up at me shyly. As I continued to scold, he squatted, rolled up my trouser leg and began to search my calf—for insect life.

That night when I carried Chumley's food to him, he greeted me with loud "hoo hoos" of delight and jogged up and down. Before he touched his dinner, however, he seized one of my hands. With some trepidation I waited as he carefully put one of my fingers between his great teeth and very gently bit it. Then I understood: in the chimpanzee world, to place a finger between another ape's teeth is both a greeting and a sign of trust.

I, in turn, soon ceased to look upon Chumley as an animal. He had so many habits which made him seem almost human, and his small, deep-set eyes looked at one with so much intelligence—and often with a glitter of ironic laughter. It amused him to examine the contents of my pockets, and only once did he refuse to give back everything—in this case, my handkerchief. He held it behind his back and passed it from hand to hand as I tried to get it. Finally he popped it into his mouth with an air of settling the matter. But I knew he would think he could get away with anything if I let him keep it, so for half an hour I kept after him until, reluctantly, he surrendered the sodden thing to me. After that I had simply to hold out my hand, and he would give me whatever I asked for without fuss.

Chumley's manners were exceptional. Given a bottle of lemonade and a glass, he would pour himself a drink with all the care of a barman mixing a cocktail. And he never grabbed his food and started guzzling, as the monkeys did. After first giving me a greeting and thanking me with a series of his most expressive "hoo hoos," he would eat delicately and slowly. His only breach of manners came at the end of a meal, when he would hurl his empty mug and plate as far as he could.

The time finally came to move on to another camp, and when the lorry arrived to load our collection, Chumley hooted and danced with excitement. He realized he was in for one of his favorite sports—a ride— and he beat a wild tattoo on his crate so that we should not overlook him. When his crate was hoisted aboard, he grinned with pleasure. We had not gone far when the staff started to sing. Chumley joined in with a prolonged and melodious hooting.

When we arrived at our new camp there was, as always, chaos at first. And before a suitable water supply could be established, Chumley made it quite clear that he was thirsty. To appease him I gave him a bottle of beer, which he accepted with gleeful lip-smacking. The lower the level fell in the bottle the more Chumley showed off, and the larger grew the crowd of natives that gathered around him. Soon he was covered with beer froth and enjoying himself hugely; he danced a curious side-shuffle, he clapped his hands, he turned somersaults. It took Chumley several hours to sober up, and it took three policemen to disperse the crowd.

Not long afterward the London Zoo's official collector arrived in Cameroun and with great regret I handed Chumley over to be transported to England. Four months later I visited Chumley in his large, straw-filled room at Regent's Park, where he had become immensely popular with the staff. I did not expect him to recognize me, for when he had last seen me I had been clad in tropical kit and sported a beard. But recognize me he did! He whirled happily around his room, then came rushing over to give me his old greeting—a gentle bite on the finger. I gave him sugar, and then we smoked a cigarette together while he removed my shoes and socks—an old habit— and examined my legs. Then he took his cigarette butt and carefully snubbed it out in a spot well away from the straw. When the time came to go, he shook hands with me.

I never saw Chumley again. His deformed teeth started troubling him, and he was moved to the zoo's sanatorium for treatment. Bored, apparently, by the sudden quiet, he twice broke out and sallied forth across Regent's Park.

The first time he found a bus conveniently at hand and, loving to ride, swung aboard, causing much horror among the occupants. In the excitement he even forgot himself so far as to bite someone. Leaving the bus, he walked down the road, made a pass at a woman with a pram (who nearly fainted), and was wandering about to see what else he could do to liven up life for London when a member of the zoo staff arrived.

Because of this and a second escape Chumley was sentenced to death. From being a fine animal, he had suddenly become an untrustworthy monster. I, however, shall always remember Chumley as a mischievous, courtly old man who for some reason had disguised himself as a chimpanzee.

Tigers in the Kitchen

Condensed from My Zoo Family

by HELEN MARTINI

THE POLLTAKER stood in the kitchen doorway, popping questions while I prepared a pie. "Your husband's occupation?"

"Keeper at the Bronx Zoo," I said proudly.

"Children?"

"Three," I replied. "Dacca, Rajpur and Raniganj."

There was a short pause. "Unusual names," he said.

At that moment, as though on cue, the three tiger cubs streaked into the kitchen. Detecting the stranger, they broke off their romp to stare wide-eyed—with sound effects intended to scare him witless.

"I was just leaving," said the polltaker, and he did, quick. I often wonder what he told his wife that night.

It doesn't occur to me to think of myself as an unusual woman who raises tigers in an apartment. I know only that I've had the thrilling opportunity of being a foster mother to some of the most delightful, lovable "babies" ever born in captivity.

It started when my husband, then an apprentice zookeeper, appeared at home one evening with MacArthur, a two-day-old lion cub whose mother had abandoned him. "I've told the curator you'd be glad to take care of him," Fred said.

I hadn't the slightest idea how to cope with a lion cub. "Just do what you would do for a human baby," Fred suggested. He handed the bedraggled cub to me gently. Suddenly MacArthur opened his mouth and went through all the motions of a grown lion delivering a mighty roar. What came out was a tiny husky cry. I laid him in a roasting pan and weighed him on my kitchen scales. Exactly three pounds.

Presently my kitchen was filled with nursing bottles and baby blankets. For a crib I lined a cardboard carton with bath towels, placing it in a corner away from drafts. Then our problems began: MacArthur stubbornly refused the bottle.

We tried every trick we could think of, with no luck. Suddenly an idea struck me. I got off the floor and sank into Fred's easy chair, with a pillow on my lap. When the cub was eased down into its softness, he immediately relaxed and took the bottle nipple, instinctively pushing alternately with his forepaws against my hand, just as he would to control the flow of milk from his mother. In a few minutes, MacArthur con-

393

tained three ounces of warm milk and was asleep in his box. I was ruefully nursing the first of the many scratches which I have since come to wear proudly—the badges of my success as a zoo mother.

When MacArthur returned to the zoo after two months, I found myself hoping that another big cat would turn prima donna and provide me with another dependent. Sure enough, a few weeks later I got my wish. And doubly—for this time Fred brought home a pair of tiger cubs.

Tigers rarely reproduce in captivity, and I knew I had been entrusted with a job of dramatic importance. Fred confirmed it. "Do your best, Helen. They're all holding their breath at the zoo."

With that he hurried back to work, leaving me to start the feeding. The new cubs took eagerly to the bottle. I felt so optimistic that I opened the atlas to the map of India and started looking for names suitable for tigers. Just then Fred burst in the door with a third tiger cub, emaciated, cold and deathly still.

"He's in a bad way," Fred mourned. Gathering the cub in my arms, I wrapped him in an electric heating pad, then struggled for six hours to get some warm milk down his throat. Shortly after dawn I heard a faint cry and felt the little tiger's front paws pushing against my hand. We'd made it!

My three tigers proved to be remarkably different in temperament. Raniganj would bite, scratch and squall unless he could have his way; Rajpur, fat and lazy, was perfectly agreeable in all matters; Dacca was a bright, mischievous female who tolerated no nonsense from her roughhousing brothers.

Fred built a playpen for them, but they spent their energy trying to climb out or crying to be picked up. I stood it as long as I could, then turned them loose in the kitchen. And from that point on, I got little

housework done. If I went into the living room and closed the French doors behind me, the cubs would line up behind the glass panel and cry piteously. When I went back into the kitchen, they would purr and climb into my arms.

It was fascinating to watch them rehearse their jungle strategy. With their little ears down they would stalk me when my back was turned. If I looked, it spoiled their game. When one of them gained his objective—my ankle, usually—he'd nuzzle it, purr and roll over in sheer delight. As their stalking skills sharpened, two of them would divert my attention while the third stalked from the rear.

When word got out about the tigers, they immediately became celebrities. Newspaper photographers haunted our apartment. It may have been all this publicity that made our elderly landlady decide, at long last, that her standing rule against animals in the house had been stretched beyond letter and spirit. The tigers, she announced, had to go.

I couldn't bear the thought of dumping them, "motherless," into the Lion House, and the curator agreed to let me stay with them there until they became acclimated.

The cubs promptly made themselves at home in their new cage. I set up a little tiger pantry behind the cage, with an electric hot plate to heat their milk. Hundreds of spectators gathered to see the famous brood,

and they watched with delight while the cubs played their favorite tug-of-war game with a scatter rug from our apartment.

That evening, when the zoo had closed, the tigers sensed that I was going to leave them. Raniganj climbed into my lap and refused to be put down; Dacca and Rajpur got firm holds on my ankles. Seeing this, Fred grinned. "Why don't we have supper here? I'll go out and get some food."

As Fred left, I relaxed and settled back happily. Suddenly I realized that, more than anything else, I wanted to stay here and help Fred. But *could* I be a zookeeper, a woman in no-woman's-land?

Next day, wandering around the Lion House, I found a storage room that just suited my plans. Then and there I resolved to ask the curator for it and tell him that I wanted a permanent job. I knew I was asking for the moon.

When I explained how easily I could fix up the storeroom, however, the curator smiled. He kept watching the cubs, who seemed to put on a special show for him. "We'll see," he said.

A week went by. Then I saw men carrying crates out of the storeroom; by night it was cleared. Nobody had told me formally the room was mine, but I knew and immediately plunged in to make it look as much like a real nursery as possible. I painted the ceiling pink, the walls a soft blue. For a final touch, I hung up my cubs' baby pictures—and we opened for business. I had become head of the Bronx Zoo nursery, the first of its kind in the world.

I was destined to raise orangutans, gorillas and dozens of other animals in that blue-and-pink room. Of them all, the most memorable, I think, was a black leopard cub christened Bagheera, from Rudyard Kipling's *Jungle Book*.

The little black leopard was a new challenge. Experts had warned me that this cat is a born killer, no matter how well he is treated as a cub. My little spitfire lashed out at me when I offered him the bottle, leaving my hands bleeding and sore. I didn't want to wear gloves because they canceled my sense of touch. For days we battled over the nursing bottle. Finally, after two weeks, he accepted the bottle willingly.

They say the problem child wins the mother's heart. I don't believe any animal ever captured my heart as did this troublesome black ball of fur with the lovely blue eyes. He was cautious but not unfriendly with

strangers, and if someone dropped in to see me, Bagheera would crouch at my feet, his tiny body bristling with protectiveness.

At nine months Bagheera was almost fully grown, and we led him around on a chain leash. He loved to travel in the car, stretched out on the shelf beneath the rear window, gazing keenly around him. Other drivers, stopping beside us at a red light, would stare.

"Is that really . . .?" they'd ask.

"It sure is," I'd reply.

They'd shake their heads and drive on, still not believing it.

We frequently brought Bagheera home at night with us (by this time we had bought our landlady's house). He liked to leap to the top edge of the living-room door and balance there with legs hanging down on either side, watching me get dinner.

One evening, I took the newspaper from our mailbox and put it in Bagheera's mouth. He carried it upstairs as proudly as any spaniel. We repeated the performance for six days, but on the seventh there was no newspaper delivery. That evening Bagheera waited by the mailbox, refusing to budge until I fished a scrap of paper from my purse. Always after that I had to have a piece of paper handy on the day when there was no newspaper.

Babies do grow up, however, and eventually I had to agree with zoo authorities that I'd better keep some steel wire between me and my beloved cats. It was a precaution I have always observed—except for a single unforgettable time. On coming to work one morning I noticed that the nursery cages were empty. Assuming the tigers were on exhibit, I entered the nursery cage and was busily scrubbing the floor when I heard the familiar purr of a tiger.

Turning my head, I looked into the mischievous face of Dacca, now two years old. It was the first time I'd been in a cage with her since she was ten months old.

If I had any doubts about what was going to happen next, Dacca dissolved them with her charm. She was delighted to see me. She began to nuzzle and lick me as she used to do, only now her tongue felt like a coarse file on my skin. After this introductory greeting, she rolled over and over in ecstasy. I slipped quietly out of the cage.

I'm convinced that, if any of my "children" ever hurts me, it won't be from intention but because they don't understand they've outgrown me. The key to success in taming wild animals, according to all my years' experience, is to get them as soon after birth as possible, and treat them even more gently than a human baby. Working with animals is startlingly like working with people. They make me laugh, cry, sigh and worry—but it's endlessly fascinating.

Hero in
Shining Feathers

by ELLA A. DUNCAN

WHEN THE DOORBELL RANG, that Easter morning, our two-year-old Susie found a duckling nestled in a basket on the front step. It was just a round, yellow ball of fluff with two black, shiny beads for eyes and a curious ebony bill that went poking about constantly into everything. Susie was ecstatic when the duckling scrambled from his basket and waddled at her heels about the room.

For him, there was no one else in the world but Susie. When she walked he followed; when she ran he rolled over and over like an animated yellow tumbleweed, trying to keep up with her. Susie named the duck "Waddles," and together that summer, in the high-fenced backyard, they found a complete world of magic. To Ann, the maid, and to me, it was amazing. The two chased butterflies, built castles in the sandbox, played hide-and-go-seek among the shrubs.

Waddles grew to be larger than most ducks, and was a strong, handsome fellow two years later when Baby Carol came. After silently studying the new red mite, Waddles suddenly beat his great wings against his sides, let out a trumpeting honk and sat down purposely beside the bassinet. With that wild, foreign cry Waddles was proclaiming to the world that he was at last an adult, that on his shoulders had descended the grave responsibility of guard for a new, helpless being. John finally had to pick him up and carry him—protesting and hissing—outside.

As the weeks passed, it finally seeped through Waddles' small duck brain that the only time his guarding act was necessary was when Baby Carol was put in the backyard for her sunbath. When that time drew near, he was always waiting. In a restrained frenzy of excitement he would settle beneath the carriage, every inch of his big body at strained attention.

I had reason to give thanks for Waddles as an aid to child rearing. It was impossible to teach Susie and her friends to close the back gate; but with Waddles around, neither man nor beast could enter that gate.

Then a plague of rabies broke out among the dogs of the town. And one Saturday morning when Baby Carol was in the backyard with Waddles on guard beneath the carriage, a friend phoned. "I just saw a dog turn into your driveway, and if I know a mad dog, that one is!" Prickles of fright broke out along my spine. Then I thought,